'A gruesome s... ...rogance, blood and cruelty, cunning ...d stupidity ... [Robert Hutchinson] tells the story of these princelings ... has created a delightful and instructive book'
Literary Review

...ll the while [Hutchinson] entertains us with fascinating close-ups of ...tlandish Tudor behaviour' *Daily Mail*

...obert Hutchinson is making a corner for himself in popular, well-...arched histories of the 16th century. The narrative is compelling and ...ible ... It is a riveting story, splendidly told' *Daily Telegraph*

...tchinson] writes with vigour and enthusiasm ... there are some ...did set-pieces (the account of Flodden, for instance, is riveting)'
BBC History Magazine

...tchinson is a lively biographer and brings the period vividly to life. ...e has a keen sense of its sights and smells as well as the less immediate ...k of fear, betrayal and unbearable pain ... This book gives a balanced ...view of the choices and compromises, the moral subtleties and the ...sical horrors of the age' *The Tablet*

ELIZABETH'S SPYMASTER

...bert Hutchinson's lucid and learned volume gives us a vivid portrait of ...singham ... an excellent book' *Independent on Sunday*

...ccessible, authoritative account ... The author is very good at evoking ...atmosphere of suspicion and paranoia during Elizabeth's reign ... ...es Elizabethan statecraft immediate and entertaining'
Book Magazine

...tchinson neatly combines his expert knowledge with an impressive ...rative suspense and a mordant sense of humour ... a darkly informative ...' *Waterstone's Books Quarterly*

...ccably researched ... the author has constructed what almost ...nts to a thriller in this gripping narrative which raises issues still ...nsely relevant to our own troubled times' *Good Book Guide*

Robert Hutchinson is a fellow of the Society of Antiquaries in London and an expert on the Reformation in England. He is a tutor in church archaeology for the University of Sussex Centre for Community Engagement, and the consultant on church monuments to the Diocese of Chichester Advisory Committee. He was a contributing author to *The Archaeology of the Reformation* and has written numerous papers on ecclesiology and church monuments. His acclaimed account of intrigues and conspiracies at the court of Elizabeth's father, *The Last Days of Henry VIII*, was published in 2004 by Weidenfeld & Nicolson. His works have been translated into eight languages. He was appointed OBE in the 200 New Year's Honours.

HOUSE OF TREASON

The Rise and Fall of a Tudor Dynasty

◆

ROBERT HUTCHINSON

PHOENIX

A PHOENIX PAPERBACK

First published in Great Britain in 2009
by Weidenfeld & Nicolson
This paperback edition published in 2009
by Phoenix,
an imprint of Orion Books Ltd,
Orion House, 5 Upper St Martin's Lane,
London, WC2H 9EA

An Hachette UK company

1 3 5 7 9 10 8 6 4 2

A CIP catalogue record for this book
is available from the British Library.

ISBN 978-0-7538-2690-4

Typeset by Input Data Services Ltd,
Bridgwater, Somerset

Printed and bound in the UK by
CPI Mackays, Chatham ME5 8TD

The Orion Publishing Group's policy is to use papers
that are natural, renewable and recyclable products and
made from wood grown in sustainable forests. The logging
and manufacturing processes are expected to conform to
the environmental regulations of the country of origin.

www.orionbooks.co.uk

For my Father

CONTENTS

◆

LIST OF ILLUSTRATIONS

◆

1 Henry VII by unknown 16th century artist (Photograph © Society of Antiquaries of London)

2 John Howard, 1st Duke of Norfolk by English School, 16th century (His Grace The Duke of Norfolk, Arundel Castle/The Bridgeman Art Library)

3 Thomas Howard, 2nd Duke of Norfolk by English School, 16th century (His Grace The Duke of Norfolk, Arundel Castle/The Bridgeman Art Library)

4 Henry VIII by unknown artist, late 1530s (Photograph © Society of Antiquaries of London)

5 Thomas Howard, 3rd Duke of Norfolk by Holbein, Hans the Younger (His Grace The Duke of Norfolk, Arundel Castle/The Bridgeman Art Library)

6 Anne Boleyn by unknown artist, c. 1533–1536 (National Portrait Gallery, London)

7 Henry Fitzroy (Mary Evans Picture Library)

8 Henry Howard, Earl of Surrey (From the collection at Parham House and Gardens, West Sussex)

9 Catherine Howard by follower of Holbein, 16th century (Hever Castle, Kent)

10 Tomb of 3rd Duke and wife at Framlingham (Reproduced by permission of English Heritage. NMR)

11 Thomas Howard, 4th Duke of Norfolk by unknown artist, 1565 (National Portrait Gallery, London)

12 Letter to William Dix from 4th Duke (His Grace The Duke of Norfolk, Arundel Castle/The Bridgeman Art Library)

13 Philip Howard, Earl of Arundel, by George Gower (His

AUTHOR'S NOTE

The Howard family were the wealthiest and most powerful aristocrats in Tudor England. They were the very last of the 'overmighty' nobles to survive from the Middle Ages and they reigned, with pride and egotism, over huge areas of England.

Up to the 1570s, the Dukes of Norfolk styled themselves 'right high and mighty princes' and lived in grand palaces and mansions in East Anglia and London. They were among the last to operate the hated medieval feudal system and their stewards regularly fined their bondmen for permission to move home, or for their daughters to marry.

The sixteenth-century Howards were cursed by a haughty arrogance that spawned contempt for those 'newly arrived' men of low birth, who increasingly supplanted the old noble families in Tudor politics and outwitted their attempts to win greater power and wealth.

Their overweening pride was breathtaking. The fourth Duke boasted that his income 'was not much less than those of the kingdom of Scotland ...' and that when he was in his tennis court in his palace at Norwich, 'he thought himself equal with some kings'.

The Howards had loyally served Tudor monarchs at the forefront of English military and naval exploits, but they were not content with the fame and fortune that battlefield glory brought them. Intrigue and conspiracy ran in their veins like their very lifeblood, but over successive generations they paid dearly for their fatal ambition and the crass stupidity that sometimes dogged their attempts to creep ever closer to the Tudor throne.

This book describes the human drama and tensions of a turbulent century in the history of the Howards, and of England.

Two Dukes of Norfolk were condemned as traitors and spent lonely years in the Tower of London. Another was beheaded. An heir to the dukedom was executed on trumped-up charges and one more died piteously in prison – and is now a saint because of his suffering for his Catholic faith. Two nieces who married Henry VIII were beheaded. Other family members were frequently incarcerated on suspicion of infidelity to the throne. As far as the Tudor monarchy was concerned, the Howards were a house of treason.

ACKNOWLEDGEMENTS

This book could not have been written without the willing help and support of my dear wife, Sally, who has journeyed with me through the endless and convoluted twists and turns of the dramatic history of the sixteenth-century Howards.

Much of the material for this book has been drawn from contemporary sources — it is illuminating and edifying to read an individual's original words, even though some have had to be modernised for the sake of clarity.

A great number of friends and colleagues have kindly given invaluable support and help in tracking down documents and rare books for the source material. In particular, I would like to thank Robin Harcourt Williams, Librarian and Archivist to the Marquis of Salisbury at Hatfield House; John Martin Robinson and his team of archivists of Sara Rodger, Heather Warne and Margaret Richards, for all their kindness during my time studying the archives at Arundel Castle, and the Duke of Norfolk for his kind permission to quote from these documents. Diana Spelman, whom I was very fortunate to find, was an assiduous and talented researcher, performing Herculean tasks in quickly tracking down documents in the Norfolk Record Office to answer my increasingly obtuse questions. I am also grateful to Bill Monaghan, archives assistant there, for earlier kindly copying a prodigious quantity of documents for me.

My thanks also go to Bernard Nurse, the former Librarian, and Adrian James, Assistant Librarian, at the Society of Antiquaries of London; Kay Walters and her team at the incomparable library at the Athenæum in London; the ever-willing and helpful staff at the National Archives at Kew and in the Manuscripts, Rare-Books and Humanities departments of the British Library at Euston, and also those at a number of record offices throughout England.

I am also grateful to Ian Drury and latterly Alan Samson and Lucinda McNeile of Weidenfeld & Nicolson for all their encouragement and assistance; Richard Collins, my editor; Alison Waggitt for the index; and, finally, Marcel Hoad and his team at Fowlers for their invaluable support in so many ways.

To all these kind people, I would like to pass on my grateful thanks. I must point out, however, that any errors or omissions are entirely my own responsibility.

Robert Hutchinson
West Sussex
January 2009

PROLOGUE

◆

'Jack of Norfolk, be not too bold – for Dicken thy master is bought and sold'

Anonymous warning to Sir John Howard, first Duke of Norfolk, before the Battle of Bosworth, 22 August 1485[1]

Henry Tudor, the twenty-eight-year-old Earl of Richmond,[2] landed at Milford Haven, on the South Wales coast, on 7 August 1485, in a desperately foolhardy attempt to seize the throne of England. He had spent the last fourteen years in dreary exile under the protection of Francis II, Duke of Brittany, after fleeing England in 1471, following the defeat of the Lancastrian cause at the battles of Barnet and Tewkesbury – seemingly the last bloody carnage of the cruelly internecine Wars of the Roses.

His dubious, certainly tenuous, claim to be the true and lawful King of England was based solely on the descent of his mother, the formidable and scheming Margaret Beaufort, from John of Gaunt, the third surviving son of Edward III. When the Yorkist monarch Edward IV died suddenly in 1483,[3] his two young legitimate sons mysteriously vanished and the English crown fell into the grasping, grateful hands of his brother, Richard, Duke of Gloucester. Here, then, was an opportunity for Henry to capture what he saw was his by birthright and he had sailed for England with another invasion fleet, timed to support a rebellion by Henry Stafford, second Duke of Buckingham.[4] But this insurrection was quickly suppressed and violent storms scattered Tudor's ships, forcing him to return to France with his would-be regal tail firmly between his legs.

Undaunted, the ambitious but militarily inexperienced Welshman embarked again at Honfleur on 1 August 1485, with just

3,000 French mercenaries and a handful of loyal English followers. However, warships, under the command of the Lord Admiral of England, Sir John Howard, first Duke of Norfolk, were guarding the English Channel and their patrols forced the Tudor flotilla further west before it could safely make landfall. It was a recklessly small army of uncertain loyalty that finally splashed ashore in Pembrokeshire, but the aspiring king hoped that his forces would soon be augmented by the disaffected flocking to his triumphant standard in their thousands. It was not to be: as he marched through Wales and on to Shrewsbury, only a few hundred Welshmen joined his colours. The remainder of the population, with dark memories of thirty-two years of brutal, bloody civil war, merely watched sullenly the column of soldiers trudge by.

There was a further worrying and frustrating factor that raised nagging doubts in Henry Tudor's mind. His stepfather, Thomas, Lord Stanley, Constable of England,[5] had not yet declared his support for the Tudor cause, his inaction doubtless influenced by the harsh fact that Richard III prudently held hostage his twenty-five-year-old eldest son, Sir George Stanley, Lord Strange,[6] to guarantee his loyalty. The odds on Tudor's rash gamble for the throne seemed to lengthen as each summer day passed.

The royalist army was being rapidly mobilised and the experienced old soldier Norfolk had brought 1,000 well-armed men wearing the Howard livery to join the various contingents mustering at Leicester on 16 August.[7] Ominously, some now warned the duke not to fight with Richard, but he characteristically brushed aside such arrant disloyalty. The king's forces moved on to camp on the summit and slopes of the two hundred foot (91.4 m.) high Ambion Hill, two miles (3 km.) south of Market Bosworth, Leicestershire, on the evening of Sunday 21 August, as Richard, another seasoned campaigner, attempted to block Henry Tudor's road south to London and power.

By early the next morning, his battle plans had been finalised. In front of the king's 8,000-strong army was his vanguard – a wedge-shaped formation of 1,200 archers, protected by two hundred heavily armoured horsemen. This was led by Norfolk, who was to fight that sunny day alongside his forty-two-year-old son, Thomas, Earl of Surrey, himself a veteran of many battles, who had been severely wounded at Barnet fourteen years earlier.[8] Mustered behind them was the main royalist force of 1,000 infantry armed with spears and halberds, surrounded by a further 2,000 pikemen, their long weapons used to ward off cavalry attacks. A reserve of 3,600 foot and horse, commanded by Sir Henry Percy, fourth Earl of Northumberland,[9] formed the rearguard.

There remained the threat of the still uncommitted Stanleys and their tactically important forces which had now arrived in the vicinity. Lord Stanley had earlier pleaded sickness as a rather vapid excuse for not rallying to the royal standard. Tired of his obvious prevarication, Richard sent his pursuivant, or messenger, to Stanley, commanding him to take his place immediately in the royal battle lines. If he still disobeyed, the king swore a terrible oath that 'by Christ's passion, he would strike off his son's head before he dined'. Stanley boldly shrugged off the ultimatum, retorting that he had 'more sons yet alive'.[10] Richard's advisers, Norfolk among them, convinced him not to execute young Stanley until the outcome of the day's slaughter had been decided.

Time was slipping away and the monarch's traditional speech to steel the hearts of the royal troops had to be delivered. The king promised them: 'One thing I assure you – that in so just and good a cause and so notable a quarrel, you shall find me this day rather dead carrion[11] upon the cold ground, than a free prisoner on a carpet in a lady's chamber. I will triumph by victory, or suffer death for immortal fame.' He expected his soldiers to be 'true men against traitors ... true inheritors against usurpers; the scourges of God against tyrants'. Finally, Richard ordered: 'Display my banner with good courage, march forth like strong and robust champions ...The battle is at hand and victory approaches.'[12]

These were brave words from a doomed king.

By now it was first light and no breakfast had been prepared when the leading echelons of Henry Tudor's 5,000-strong army were seen advancing east along a narrow country road (now called Fenn Lane) towards the royal forces perched high on Ambion Hill.[13] This was an unpleasant surprise; there was no time for the priests accompanying Richard's army to say Mass and there were frantic preparations for combat, as every man got ready to fight for his cause – and his life:

> Lord, how hastily the soldiers buckled their helmets; how quickly the archers bent their bows and brushed the feathers [of their arrows] and how readily the bill men shook their bills[14] and proved their staves, ready to approach and join when the terrible trumpet should sound the bloody blast to victory or death.[15]

As they scrambled to their places in the battle lines, even the most stolid and unimaginative of soldiers must have wondered if he would live to see another sunrise. The bulk of Tudor's troops, commanded by John de Vere, thirteenth Earl of Oxford,[16] kept the marshland of Redemore Heath on their right to protect their flank as they advanced at a moderate pace, with the rays of the rising sun glinting on the armour of their foes high above them on Ambion Hill.

Norfolk's battalion attacked as their enemy cleared the marsh. He was supported by the main body of the royalist army – their war cries and the clank of their armour drowned out by the sharp cracks of Richard's 140 light guns and bombards opening fire on the serried ranks of the insurgents below. Norfolk's men ran down the steep slope, splashed through two streams and arrived on level ground. Then the archers in the front ranks let fly their first volley of deadly arrows. Oxford's bowmen replied and both armies clashed in furious hand-to-hand fighting. After the first shock, Oxford pulled back to rally his men and to close ranks around his standards. He also must have been anxiously awaiting an intervention by the 2,000 troops of Henry Tudor's so-far neutral stepfather, Lord Stanley, and his brother, Sir William, who were mounted up and impassively watching from Crown Hill and atop a spur of land at Dadlington, one mile (1.6 km.) south of the fighting.

As that unnatural lull fell across the battlefield, destiny confronted the king.

From the lower slopes of Ambion Hill, he had seen the body-guard of 1,000 horsemen surrounding Henry Tudor on the western edge of the marsh, just behind the right flank of Oxford's panting troops.

Richard decided on an audacious, do-or-die charge to secure his crown once and for all. Calling together his squires and personal household – including his friends Sir Robert Percy and Francis, ninth Baron Lovell – he led a helter-skelter charge of 120 cavalry to force his way through the protective phalanx and to slay Henry in chivalrous, single combat. The hopelessly small force galloped down the hill, the royal standard, borne by Sir Percival Thirlwall, desperately trying to catch up with the king riding far out in front.

He nearly made it.

The shock of the assault, from behind Norfolk's left flank, punched through the packed ranks of standing Tudor horsemen. Richard swiftly killed Sir William Brandon who was carrying Henry Tudor's standard bearing the red dragon of Wales. He then fought Sir John Cheyne, 'a man of great force and strength', and knocked him clean off his horse. By now clearly battle-crazed, and scenting the heady, sweet smell of victory, Richard hacked his way 'by dint of sword' towards Henry Tudor, who reportedly '[with]stood his violence and kept him at the sword's point'.[17]

It was then that Sir William Stanley finally showed his hand.

If he ever nursed any doubts – he was already branded a traitor by Richard – he now chose to back Henry Tudor. He led his horsemen in a thundering charge along the eastern edge of the marsh, and wheeled right up Ambion Hill, cutting off both Norfolk's troops and Richard from any chance of reinforcement or rescue by Percy's now undecided and timorous reserve. Seeing the Stanleys' commitment to battle, Oxford renewed his attack and the fighting inevitably became more confused as opponents feverishly hacked at each other in a desperate mêlée, sometimes fatally tripping over the dead and wounded already littering the ground. Norfolk realised with horror that he and his troops were isolated and that he must cut his way to safety before he was completely overrun from front and rear.

Norfolk was distantly related to Oxford – his first cousin, Elizabeth Howard, was the earl's mother.[18] Not only did they have kinship, but they also enjoyed close ties of friendship – such is the dreadful tragedy of divisive civil war. Almost simultaneously in the tumult of combat, both captains recognised each other's identifying heraldic device – Oxford's rayed star embroidered on his standard and Norfolk's silver lion blazoned on his shield. Any memories of their happy times together instantly evaporated in the heat and sweat of battle.

Norfolk must have been desperately weary by this stage of the struggle. He was aged about sixty-three, more than twenty years older than his enemy. But the adrenalin of battle – the ruthless imperative to kill or be killed – enabled him to conquer his exhaustion and continue the fight. Like Oxford, he levelled his heavy fluted lance, and they both charged, almost a ton of horse and man hurling themselves at their adversary. Each weapon splintered with a crack on the other's armour, and the riders swayed back with the force of the blows.

This was no gallant joust with blunted lances in a festive, courtly tournament and there were no obsequious heralds present to award points in deciding the heroic victor. In the parlance of the day, both noblemen were fighting *à outrance* – to the bitter end.

Discarding their shattered lances, they drew swords and manoeuvred their warhorses closer in for the kill. Norfolk wounded Oxford, who had lost his shield in the charge, with a sweeping, cutting blow, the blade sliding off his helmet and slicing into his left arm. Almost at once, he lost his visor, as Oxford slashed across his bascinet, leaving his face exposed. The coded rationality of chivalry suddenly doused the fury of battle: Oxford refused to continue combat – shouting, above the din, that he now enjoyed an unfair advantage over Norfolk.[19]

Fate decided that this was no time for debate, or valiant niceties.

An arrow – was it a stray or deliberately aimed? – struck Norfolk in the face and pierced his brain. He slowly toppled out of his saddle, falling dead beneath the feet of his enemy's charger.[20]

His son, the Earl of Surrey, fighting close by, saw his father's death and swore immediate and bloody vengeance.

He spurred his horse towards the nearest group of enemy soldiers on the Tudor right wing, but was soon surrounded and fighting furiously for his life – 'Howard single, with an army fights'.[21] Two royalist knights, Sir Richard Clarendon and Sir William Conyers, tried to rescue him but were cut to pieces by Sir John Savage (a nephew of Lord Stanley) and his retainers. Surrey, now badly wounded, exchanged blow for blow with the grizzled veteran knight Gilbert Talbot who urged him to yield, but he refused to accept any quarter and fought on doggedly, even though unhorsed.

A foot soldier tried to capture him, but Surrey swung his sword high and severed the man's arm in one final blow.

Weak from loss of blood, he sank to his knees on the ground and surrendered himself to Talbot, begging him to kill him then and there, as he feared an ignominious and lonely death that night from some cut-throat looter searching for spoil among the dead and wounded on the battlefield. Talbot spared him and had him carried off the field to safety.[22]

No such mercy was shown to King Richard III.

Despite being cut off from his troops and impossibly out-numbered, he refused to flee for his life. The king must have been enraged to look east to see Northumberland's reserve still occupying the top of Ambion Hill,[23] having taken no part in the battle and probably never intending to. Hence his anguished and angry cries of 'Treason! Treason!' His last stand was probably in a bog on the edge of Redemore Heath. Surrounded, he was finally felled by a Welsh halberdier,[24] killed 'fighting manfully in the thickest press of his enemies'.[25] His body was stripped and taken stark naked to Leicester, trussed to a horse 'like a hog or a calf, the head and arms hanging on the one side ... and the legs on the other ... all sprinkled with mire and blood'.[26] It was taken to the town's Greyfriars church 'and lay like a miserable spectacle ... and [after two days] buried' without pomp or funeral rite in an unmarked grave in the choir of the church.[27]

Richard had reigned for just two years, two months and one day. Like so many other defeated foes in history, he has been vilified to this day.[28]

Norfolk's corpse was treated with greater respect – no doubt due to Oxford's intercession, after he finished mopping up the last stubborn vestiges of royalist resistance at Bosworth. It was taken via Northampton and Cambridge to the Cluniac abbey of Our

Lady at Thetford, in Norfolk, and there given decent Christian burial one week after the battle[29] among the tombs of the earlier Mowbray Dukes of Norfolk.[30] The chronicler Richard Grafton wrote that Norfolk

> regarded more his oath, his honour, and his promise made to King Richard, like a gentleman and a faithful subject to his prince, absented not himself from his master. But as he faithfully lived under him, so he manfully died with him to his great fame and laud.[31]

An exultant Henry Tudor was crowned with the circlet of gold worn on Richard III's helmet by Sir William Stanley, with the words: 'Sir, here I make you king of England.' Lord Stanley was reunited with his son, safe and well. Victory had been achieved against a numerically superior and battle-hardened army. The road to London and a glittering coronation as King Henry VII now lay open before him. He knelt in the bloody grass and gave 'almighty God his hearty thanks ... beseeching His goodness to send him grace to advance and defend the Catholic faith and to maintain peace and concord amongst his subjects and people'.[32]

About 1,000 of Richard's soldiers were killed in the two hours of fighting, compared with three hundred in Henry Tudor's army. Prisoners vastly outnumbered the dead, among them Northumberland, who quickly changed sides,[33] and the badly wounded Surrey, who was committed to the Tower of London.

Henry Tudor was duly crowned in Westminster Abbey on 30 October and wasted little time in wreaking retribution on the nobles who had fought for Richard. Both the dead Norfolk and his son were among those attainted for treason on 7 November[34] and their estates confiscated by the impecunious crown. Many Howard properties were shared out among the new king's cronies to reward their loyalty while he was in exile.[35] Oxford, now appointed Great Chamberlain, received one of the plums – the castle, lordship and manor of Framlingham and other properties in Suffolk and Bedfordshire, once owned by Norfolk.[36]

Surrey, now recovering from his wounds, was stripped of all titles and degraded from the Order of the Garter.[37] But amid the

Howards' adversity there was some kindness. His wife Elizabeth told John Paston on 3 October that she had found Oxford a 'singular, very good and kind lord to my lord and me ... for him I dreaded most and yet in him I found the best'.[38] At the beginning of December, she was in London staying modestly at St Katherine's hospital,[39] near the Tower, while she anxiously awaited news of her husband's fate. Sir John Radcliff, Steward of Henry VII's household, had tried to seize their manor at Ashwell Thorpe in Norfolk but was thwarted, as it was part of her own inheritance. Even so, he dismissed many of her servants, leaving her to maintain her household of four children with just three or four retainers.[40]

As he sat drearily in his room in the Tower – he was allowed £8 a month for his board and three servants, costing 3s 6d a week – he must have reflected bitterly on the complete downfall of his family, coming so soon after the triumph of his father being created first Duke of Norfolk.

Its proud line could be traced back to the reign of Edward I in the thirteenth century, to the tiny village of East Winch, six miles (9.7 km.) north-west of King's Lynn in windswept north Norfolk. This was the birthplace of Sir William Howard, the founder of the dynasty, who became Chief Justice of the Common Pleas in 1297 and died in 1308.[41] By loyal and accomplished military and naval service, coupled with a number of judicious marriages with rich heiresses, the Howards rapidly clambered up the greasy pole of aristocratic status throughout the next two centuries. In about 1420, Sir Robert Howard married Lady Margaret Mowbray, elder daughter of Thomas Mowbray, Duke of Norfolk, Earl Marshal of England and the great-great-grandson of Edward I. Their son, John Howard, was born around 1422 and had fought on the Yorkist side in the second Battle of St Albans, Hertfordshire, on 17 February 1461, and at Towton, North Yorkshire, on Palm Sunday, 29 March, the same year.[42] Edward IV ennobled him as Lord Howard some time in the late 1460s.

The death of the last of the Mowbray line, the young Lady Anne, only daughter of the fourth and last Mowbray Duke of Norfolk in 1481, left Howard, as her cousin, the senior co-heir to their extensive estates throughout England. But his very substantial inheritance had been blocked by her precocious marriage to Edward IV's younger son, Richard, Duke of York. No doubt, it was a cause of some celebration to Lord Howard when Richard, Duke of Gloucester, bastardised York and his elder brother, Edward V,[43] and they both mysteriously disappeared after entering the Tower of London. He certainly had no interest in them living. No surprise, then, that Howard enthusiastically supported Gloucester and he was handsomely repaid by being created first (Howard) Duke of Norfolk and Earl Marshal of England on 28 June 1483, a week after Richard had grabbed the throne. His first duty was to officiate at Richard III's coronation and, less than a month later, he was appointed Lord Admiral of England, Ireland and Aquitaine.

But he had picked the wrong side and paid the ultimate price on Bosworth field.

His son languished for three and a half years in the Tower. Its Lieutenant offered to arrange an escape for him in 1487, during an abortive rebellion by John de la Pole, Earl of Lincoln, but he wisely declined the use of 'the key to go out at his pleasure'[44] and this may have begun to convince Henry VII of his loyalty.

Thomas Howard stepped out of the gloom of the Tower into the bright new light of the Tudor age. He was firmly to bind his family's fortunes to those of the Tudor dynasty but over the next century, the raw ambition and unashamed lust for power of his descendants would imprison many of them within the walls of that grim fortress alongside the River Thames. Another would suffer appallingly for his religious faith.

Some never came out alive.

PART I

BACK FROM THE BRINK

I

REBUILDING THE DYNASTY

———◆———

'Sir, he was my crowned king. Let the authority of Parliament set the crown on that stake and I will fight for it. As I fought then for him, I will fight for you, when you are established by the same authority'

Thomas Howard, Earl of Surrey, to King Henry VII, 1485[1]

Thomas Howard, Earl of Surrey, was already middle aged when he saw his father die amid the din and slaughter of Bosworth. After recuperating from the serious wounds he suffered at the Battle of Barnet on Easter Sunday 1471, the following year, like many Howards before and after, he had married a carefully selected wealthy heiress. Elizabeth was the daughter of the minor Norfolk magnate Sir Frederick Tylney and the widow of Sir Humphrey Bourchier, a comrade-in-arms who had been slain during that same battle. She brought him twelve prosperous manors in East Anglia, as well as five surviving children,[2] one of whom was destined to play a momentous role in shaping the monarchy in sixteenth-century England: Thomas junior, born in 1473, was the uncle of two of Henry VIII's queens and, arguably, the principal political survivor of the bloody tumult of three Tudor reigns.

After the disaster of Bosworth and his imprisonment in the Tower, Howard was released in early 1489 by Henry VII, and the attainder for treason against him was reversed on 3 March that year by Parliament – although most of the lands he had lost were cannily withheld until he could demonstrate fully his loyalty to the crown.[3] In May, however, he celebrated his restoration to the title of Earl of Surrey.

He became the archetypal Tudor nobleman who maintained full allegiance to whoever sat on the throne, whatever policies they pursued. If God was in His heaven, and the king ruled with a firm but fair hand, the Howards were perfectly content. This deeply held fidelity to the crown – also destined to become his son's watchword – was born out of the family's intense desire to preserve social order and cohesion in the realm. The Howards were Tudor aristocratic anachronisms, with an inbred conservatism which led them to worship devoutly at the altars of hierarchy, autocracy, status and power. Over the next three generations, they kept one foot firmly grounded in the old confident and arrogant attitudes and beliefs of fifteenth-century noble England, despite the storm of change that raged all around them and which, several times, nearly brought them down.

Henry VII had no such luxury of certainty in the scheme of things. His claim to the crown was at best slender and secured only by right of conquest at Bosworth. He adroitly married Elizabeth of York, the eldest daughter of King Edward IV, on 18 January 1486 in an attempt to implant political unity into a still divided realm but was always apprehensive about the insecurity of the Tudor grip on regal power. A spate of rebellions (and a dangerous pretender to the throne) justified fully his fears. Later, these were to return again and again to haunt his descendants who wore the crown of England. A king's prime duty is to prolong his dynasty and, in this, Henry was in an almost indecent haste. Almost nine months to the day after the wedding, his lineage was safeguarded by the birth of a prince, at Winchester, christened Arthur. A second son, Henry, was born at Greenwich Palace on 28 June 1491.

Surrey began his long, careful journey back to power and status with an appointment as Chief Justice in Eyre North of the Trent in 1489. The following year, rioting and disorder broke out in Yorkshire after the king's imposition of new taxes and Surrey, at the head of a small royalist force, swiftly and efficiently quashed any opposition. As a grim public demonstration of his effectiveness in this police action, he summarily strung up the ringleaders at York. The main protagonist – the 'firebrand' John à Chambre – was executed 'in great state' as 'a traitor paramount' on specially constructed gallows high up on a stage, with fellow malcontents hung on 'the lower story round about him'.[4] Surrey was rewarded for his efforts on 20 May 1490 when Henry VII made him Vice-Warden of the East and Middle Marches on the borders of Scotland, as the operational deputy to the infant Prince Arthur who nominally held the top job.[5] He was granted power to negotiate with the Scottish king James IV over any breaches of a fragile Anglo-Scottish truce and to investigate 'all persons who have *covin* [treacherous dealings] with the enemy and [to] punish them'. Within two days, he published a proclamation warning the 'great numbers of Scots [who have been] applying themselves to idleness and begging [and have] over-run the realm' to immediately return home 'under pain of punishment'.[6]

He continued in the north as the king's lieutenant, administering law and order,[7] collecting taxes, suppressing dissent – such as further riots in the spring of 1492 at Acworth, near Pontefract, Yorkshire, over tax[8] – and handling the sometimes Byzantine diplomatic relations across the Scottish border. His first two sons, Thomas and Edward, the latter born in 1476, were educated as pages in Henry's household but they were, to all intents, being held hostage to guarantee his good behaviour as the king's viceroy in the north.

Surrey was increasingly regarded as Henry VII's best soldier and he was soon to prove his military mettle. In 1497, with a force of Yorkshire levies, he relieved a five-day Scottish siege of Norham Castle[9] which controlled a strategic ford over the River Tweed in Northumberland. Then he launched a retaliatory punitive expedition into the Scottish border country which destroyed Ayton Castle in Berwickshire before the onset of 'extraordinarily foul and stormy' weather drove him back into England.[10] Thomas and Edward accompanied him on the raid, both of whom he knighted at Ayton on 30 September. Surrey later concluded a new truce and began negotiations for the marriage of Henry's daughter, Margaret, to James IV of Scotland.

His wife Elizabeth died on 4 April that year at their newly built mansion at Lambeth, across the Thames from Westminster, but he did not wait long to find a second spouse. On 8 November, Surrey swiftly married Elizabeth's cousin, Agnes Tylney, the daughter of Hugh Tylney of Skirbeck and Boston in Lincolnshire,[11] in the chapel of the castle of Sheriff Hutton, near York.[12] She was to become a long-lived and formidable matriarch of the Howard clan, bearing him six surviving children. Through his brood of five living sons and six daughters from two wives, Surrey was to build marital unions with most of the prominent noble families in England. For example, his daughter Muriel[13] married John Grey, second Viscount Lisle, some time before June 1503.[14] Before he died on 9 September 1504, aged twenty-four, substantial properties in Somerset, Berkshire and Gloucestershire had been settled upon her.[15] Around May 1506, she took as her second husband Thomas Knyvett, one of the brash cronies who now surrounded young Prince Henry at Greenwich.

Surrey returned to court in 1499 and, two years later, became an influential member of Henry VII's Privy Council, joining a group of courtiers 'of singular shrewdness'. On 16 June 1501, he was appointed Lord Treasurer of England, a post the Howards were to make their own suzerain for the next four decades.[16] He thus became the third in importance of the king's ministers. Richard Fox, Bishop of Winchester, had been Lord Privy Seal since Henry's accession – so loyal, it was said, that he was willing to sacrifice his own father's life to save that of his sovereign. And William Warham, Bishop of London, was appointed Lord Chancellor and Archbishop of Canterbury in 1504. Under Surrey's careful management, royal revenues grew from £52,000 a year to £142,000 by the end of the reign in 1509.[17]

The earl benefited by the slow but sure recovery of some of his lost lands and property in East Anglia, his wealth augmented by gifts from a now grateful but ailing monarch.[18] Among a considerable parcel of manors acquired in 1507 was that of the former Mowbray possession of Kenninghall, a small village midway between Thetford and Norwich, where his son Thomas constructed a substantial palace of seventy rooms.[19] By 1506, Surrey had built up property holdings with an annual net income of £1,200, or well over £500,000 at 2009 cash equivalents.[20]

He was involved in negotiations concerning the marriage of the Spanish princess Catherine of Aragon to Prince Arthur on 14 November 1501 and was in charge of arrangements for Arthur's funeral after his premature death on 2 April 1502. The following year, he escorted Henry VII's fourteen-year-old daughter Margaret to Scotland for her marriage to James IV, and had the honour of giving away the bride, dressed in a gown of cloth of gold, in the chapel of Holyrood House, Edinburgh, on 8 August.[21]

Surrey was appointed one of the executors of the king's will, and, a few days before his death from chronic pulmonary tuberculosis[22] on 21 April 1509 at Richmond Palace, Henry VII suffered a rare attack of conscience. He restored all Surrey's lands, lost him by attainder twenty-four years before, as a mark of appreciation for his loyal service.[23] It was a crowning moment for the royal servant: after the defeat at Bosworth and the black despair of his incarceration in the Tower, all his hopes and dreams of the intervening years had at last been fulfilled.

Henry VIII was proclaimed king three days later. Surrey served as Earl Marshal at the coronation of the eighteen-year-old and, on 10 July the following year, was appointed to the position for life at a fee of £20 a year, triumphantly reclaiming the position once held by his father.[24] A month after the coronation, his second son Edward was appointed Royal Standard Bearer with an annual pension of £40. Surrey had high hopes of becoming the new king's chief minister, but was thwarted by an ambitious young cleric introduced to court by Bishop Fox, who was now climbing high in Henry VIII's estimation. Thomas Wolsey, the son of a prosperous Ipswich butcher, had been appointed royal almoner when Henry ascended to the throne and by 1511 his position at court was becoming unassailable.

Wolsey quickly flexed his political muscles. Surrey and Fox had signed an Anglo-French treaty in 1510, but the new minister was marching very much in time with the king's ambition for military adventures, and was intent on war with France. Surrey opposed this on diplomatic and fiscal grounds, but to his chagrin discovered that his second son Edward had 'marvellously' angered and incited the king over the Scots, France's traditional ally, 'by whose wanton means, his grace spends much money and is more disposed to war than peace'.[25]

During June 1511, Henry received complaints about the Scottish privateer Andrew Barton who was preying on English merchant vessels at the eastern end of the English Channel. Although there is little surviving evidence of the incident, the king apparently ordered the two Howard sons, Edward and his elder brother Thomas, 'in all haste' to capture Barton and his two ships, the *Lyon* and the *Jenett of Purwyn*. Richard Grafton, the chronicler, recorded that the Howards' ships were stationed in the Downs, off the east coast of Kent, on 2 August, when they

> perceived Andrew was making towards Scotland and so fast the lord [Thomas] Howard chased him that he overtook him and there was a sore battle. The Englishmen were fierce and the Scots defended themselves manfully ... Howard and his men, by clean strength, entered the main deck and the Scots fought on the hatches ... Andrew was taken and [was] so sore wounded that he died there and the remnant of the Scots were taken, with their ship called the *Lyon*.[26]

Edward Howard, meanwhile, intercepted the Scottish barque[27] *Jenett* and boarded her, 'slew many' and captured the surviving crew. Both vessels were brought as prizes to Blackwall on the River Thames and the Scottish prisoners transferred to the Archbishop of York's palace in London, before being repatriated.[28]

James IV, the Scottish king, was furious. He protested volubly about the Howards' 'outrage', fruitlessly demanded the return of the ships and sought the arrest and prosecution of the Howards for Barton's murder and for breaching the peace. Henry condescendingly pointed out that justice had merely been done to a 'crafty pirate' and thief.[29]

Surrey, meanwhile, was growing ever more anxious about the prospect of hostilities on two fronts with France and Scotland. He sought an interview with the king to dissuade him from embarking on war, but was received by Henry with 'such manner and countenance ... upon him that on the morrow, he departed home again'.[30] He obtained the king's leave of absence from court in September 1511 and retired in a huff to his estates in Suffolk and Norfolk to nurse his anger at being outmanoeuvred by Wolsey.

Sir Edward was appointed a vice-admiral on 7 April 1512, charged with maintaining control of the English Channel between the French port of Brest and the Thames Estuary. Over the next few months, his warships seized more than sixty vessels and imposed naval domination over the entire Channel. In response, the French began mobilising their own fleet and Howard, driven by his sovereign's lust for martial glory, set out to destroy it.

In the first week of August, Howard sailed from Portsmouth in his flagship, the newly built *Mary Rose*, leading a twenty-five-strong fleet, which included the mighty *Regent*, commanded by his brother-in-law, Sir Thomas Knyvett. Their objective was Brest, which was sheltering the thirty-nine ships of the French fleet. These enemy vessels left port on 10 August and had just cleared its approaches when the English vanguard attacked. In brutal fighting, *Regent* was shackled with chains to the French carrack[31] *Marie la Cordelière* and Knyvett boarded the larger enemy ship, ignoring the storm of arrows from her decks. As the French fought frantically to repel boarders, their vessel caught fire and the blaze spread rapidly across to the sails and rigging of the *Regent*. Very soon, it, too, was engulfed by flames. One desperate French gunner, deep in the bowels of the carrack, set fire to its powder magazine, choosing death rather than suffering the dishonour of his ship being captured.

Howard, coming up with the main body of his fleet, arrived to see both ships disappear in a series of catastrophic explosions, which hurled burning debris high into the air before falling back into the sea like a terrible deluge of fire. Inevitably, there were no survivors from either crew. Knyvett was dead, and so were all 700 of his men from the *Regent*,[32] together with 1,200 enemy sailors.

Bad news in war is never welcome. Henry had lost one of his closest confidants, but he managed to control his grief publicly. In London, Wolsey informed Fox of the loss of the *Regent*:

At the reverence of God, keep these tidings secret to yourself for there is no living man knows the same here but only the king and I.

Your lordship knows right well that it is expedient for a while to keep the same secret. To see how the king takes the matter and behaves himself, you would marvel ... [at] his wise and constant manner. I have not, on my faith, seen the like.

Howard had also lost a close friend and brother-in-law. He swore to make the French pay dearly, in blood and fire, for Knyvett's death. Wolsey added:

Sir Edward has made his vow to God that he would never look the king in the face until he had revenged the death of [this] noble and valiant knight.[33]

Knyvett's widow, Muriel, swore another kind of oath which, in its way, was as awesome as her brother's. When news of her husband's death reached her at their home at Buckenham, south-east of Norwich, on 12 August, she at once declared that she had made 'tryst with him in Heaven that day five months'. Her will was written on 13 October and she died, just as she had prophesied, on 12 January 1513. Muriel had pined to death, aged twenty-six, leaving two daughters and four sons by Knyvett.

Sir Edward was one of the many members of the house of Howard who attended her funeral, his craving for vengeance still burning as fiercely as ever. On 19 March, he was appointed Lord High Admiral of England, Ireland and Aquitaine, in succession to John de Vere, thirteenth Earl of Oxford, who had died nine days earlier. On Easter Sunday, 27 March 1513, he again departed Portsmouth with his fleet and headed back to Brest. So hellbent was he on revenge that he sailed without any supply ships.

The enemy fleet remained in the port's roadstead, blockaded by the English waiting impatiently for battle offshore. French reinforcements, in the shape of six shallow-draught, oar-propelled galleys, arrived in mid-April under the command of the Chevalier Gaston Prégent de Bidoux, immediately nicknamed 'Prior John' by the English. He put into Conquet, fifteen miles (25 km.) west of Brest, his vessels protected by powerful shore artillery batteries. Howard could not deploy his warships in the shallows, so he decided to pick off the French vessels by using fifteen rowing barges, or crayers.[34] The admiral quit his ship for one such boat, commanded by a Spaniard called Carroz, or Charran,[35] and crewed by sixteen English sailors. His plan was that the others would follow, but as the boat was lustily rowed through a hail of·arrows and gunfire towards 'Prior John's' galley, Howard found that he was alone. Undaunted, he clambered aboard and tried to capture the enemy ship.

Edward Etchingham, captain of *Germyn*, graphically described his commander's death to Wolsey on 5 May: 'The news ... be so dolorous that [hardly] can I write them for sorrow':

> On St Mark's day [25 April], the Admiral appointed four captains and himself ... to win the French galleys with the help of boats, the water being too shallow for ships.
>
> The galleys were protected on both sides by bulwarks planted so thick with guns and crossbows that the quarrels[36] and the gun-stones came together as thick as hailstones.
>
> For all this, my lord would needs board the galley himself for there [was] no man [to] counsel him the contrary.
>
> When my Lord Admiral leapt into the French galley, and all for fear of the ordnance that was shot from the galleys and from the land ... they left their admiral in the hands of his enemies.

Howard scrambled up over the bows into the forecastle of the French admiral's galley, together with the Spaniard and his small party of English sailors. They hitched their boat's cable to the capstan of the French ship, but it was either cut by the enemy or somehow let slip, and the boat was swept away on the tide, leaving them marooned on the enemy deck.

> There was a mariner wounded in eighteen places, who by adventure, [was] recovered [by the French] galley's boat. ... He saw my lord admiral thrust against the rails of the galley with morris pikes.[37] Charran's boy tells a like tale, for when his master and the admiral had entered, Charran sent him for his hand gun ... and he saw my lord admiral waving his hands and crying ... 'Come aboard again! Come aboard again!'
>
> When my lord saw they could not, he took his whistle from about his neck, wrapped it together, and threw it in the sea.

Later, under a flag of truce, 'Prior John' acknowledged that 'there was one that leapt into my galley with a gilt target [shield] upon his arm, [who] I cast overboard with moorish pikes and the mariner that I have prisoner, told me that same man was your admiral'.

Howard, encumbered by his armour, sank quickly beneath the waves and drowned. He was thirty-six. Etchingham ended his despatch:

> The great ships lay without doing anymore, for they knew not perfectly where my Lord Admiral was. Sir, when the whole army knew that my Lord Admiral was either taken or slain, I [swear] there never was men more full of sorrow than all were.
>
> There was never a noble man so ill lost as he was that was so full of courage and had so many virtues and that ruled so great an army as well as he did and kept so great order and true justice.[38]

Three days later, Howard's body was recovered from the sea by the French, disembowelled and embalmed, and buried nearby. Prégent wanted to keep Howard's heart but his whistle was sent jubilantly as a trophy of war to the French queen, Anne of Brittany, and his armour to Princess Claude.[39]

Sir Edward Howard died a swashbuckling hero, more corsair than naval commander. Admirals have no place in war in boarding ships with a handful of men to fight against overwhelming odds, cut off from any hope of reinforcement, or indeed escape. Their role is strategic or fighting tactical or strategic battles – not engaging in single-handed combat against lower-rank enemy sailors. His death was unnecessary, avoidable, and the result of crass, if not blind, stupidity on his part. Nonetheless, his 'death or glory' end, his relentless drive to destroy the enemy, warmed the heart of many a patriotic Englishman and saddened others. The symbolism of hurling his silver whistle – the badge of an admiral – into the sea, moments before he died, is the stuff of legend, if not a Hollywood epic.

Howard had married Alice Lovell, sister and sole heir of Henry, Lord Morley, in 1505, but the couple had no children.[40] He did, however, have two underage illegitimate sons. His will, written the previous January, made provision for them:

Whereas I have two bastards, I give the king's grace the choice of them, beseeching [him] ... to be [a] good lord to them and that when he comes of age, he may be his servant.

Him that the king's grace chooses, I bequeath him my barque called *Genett*[41] with all apparel and artillery and £50 to begin his stock with.

The other bastard I bequeath to my special trusty friend Charles Brandon [first Duke of Suffolk from 1514], praying him to be [a] good master to him. Because he has no ship, I bequeath to him one hundred marks [£66] to set him forward into the world.[42]

He left Henry's wife, Queen Catherine of Aragon, his 'St Thomas's Cup' – a superb silver-gilt and ivory 'grace' or loving cup – engraved with three inscriptions in Latin and English: 'Drink thy wine with joy'; the more sententious: 'Be sober'; and finally: 'Fear God'.[43] The pious Catherine would have thoroughly approved of the legacy. He also instructed that his local abbey, the Trinitarian priory at Ingham, Norfolk, should 'find a secular priest, to be called "Howard's Priest" and a friar, likewise named'. Brandon was left 'my rope of bowed nobles that I hang my great whistle by, containing three hundred angels',[44] and the king, his admiral's whistle.[45] Both were disappointed in their bequests, as these now lay in enemy hands.

Howard's brother Thomas was appointed Lord High Admiral in his place, providing him with his first opportunity to emerge from the shadow cast by the noisy bravura and derring-do of his younger sibling. Safe at home in Plymouth harbour and aboard *Mary Rose*, he sought to placate Henry's anger at the loss of admiral and ship:

As to the actual feats of all such noblemen and gentlemen as were pr[esent when] my brother, the admiral, was drowned (whom Jesu pardon), I assure your [highness so] far ... as I can ... anyway understand, they handled themselves as ... men did to obtain their master's pleasure.

It was the most dangerous enterprise [I have] ever heard of and the most manly handled.[46]

He would punish two men who 'did their part very ill the day my brother was lost ... Cooke, the queen's servant in a row[ing] boat, and Freeman, my brother's servant'.

But Thomas, Lord Howard, soon fell foul of Henry's over-arching need to make his mark on European politics through leading his army in a 'fire and sword' invasion of France. Although Howard needed to revictual his ships, his prime task was to engender a new spirit of élan among his dispirited, demoralised crews who were deserting their ships in shoals. He complained to Wolsey that his sailors would 'rather end up in purgatory than return to battle'.[47]

Despite these morale problems, the new admiral was ordered to take his ships from Plymouth to Southampton to escort a force led by Arthur Plantagenet, Viscount Lisle,[48] in a feint attack on Brest. The king and his main army, meanwhile, crossed the Channel further east to attack Louis XII of France. Howard's pleas that the wind was against him did not wash with an impatient Henry. Bishop Fox, in Southampton, told Wolsey on 19 May:

> The lord admiral ... with their whole army and their victuallers lie so far within the haven of Plymouth that they cannot come out of it without a north-west wind and the wind has been south-west continually three days past.[49]

All too conscious that he was making a hash of his first command, Howard galloped to London to explain his problems in person to his master. But both Henry and Wolsey refused to see him. How he must have suffered and squirmed in the face of these snubs! However, he cadged and wheedled fresh supplies and paid, out of his own purse, to transport the victuals down to Southampton. Eventually, he managed to escort the diversionary force across to Brittany and hastened northwards to the main theatre of war. He was soon sent home.[50]

Henry, fearful that James IV of Scotland would invade while he and his army were campaigning in France, appointed Surrey to guard England's northern marches. The ageing Earl of Surrey was the obvious choice for the job, given his years of experience in the region, but the old campaigner was less than happy at the mission, preferring to win his glory instead on a French battlefield. When Henry embarked at Dover in June, he took Surrey's hand, and told him: 'My lord, I trust not the Scots, therefore I pray you not be negligent.' An order is an order, and the earl replied:

> I shall do my duty and your grace shall find me diligent and to fulfil your will shall be my gladness.[51]

He said of the Scottish king:

> Sorry may I see him ere I die, that is the cause of my abiding behind. If ever he and I meet, I shall do that in me ... to make him as sorry [as] I can[52]

and he marched north on 22 July, gathering troops en route. He imposed strict discipline on his troops, issuing orders forbidding the playing of dice or cards by common soldiers, but allowing noblemen and captains 'to play at their pleasures within their own tents'.[53]

The king's instincts proved entirely correct.

On 11 August 1513, the Scottish herald Sir William Cumyng of Inverallochy, Lyon King of Arms, arrived at Henry's camp outside the French town of Thérouanne in the Pas-de-Calais and delivered a bleak ultimatum from his master, James IV. The 'Auld Alliance' between France and Scotland was alive and well. James demanded that the English monarch

> desist from further invasion and utter destruction of our brother and cousin, the Most Christian King [Louis XII], to whom ... we are bounden and obliged for mutual defence, the one of the other, like as you and your confederates be obliged for mutual invasions and actual war; certifying you we will take part in defence of our brother ...
>
> And we will do what thing we trust may cause you to desist from pursuit of him.[54]

Predictably, Henry lost his temper and shouted at the herald: 'I am the very holder of Scotland – he holds it of me by homage.'

The Scots were already prepared for war, with ample French military assistance, and their 35,000-strong army crossed the River

Tweed at Coldstream eleven days later, on 22 August. They attacked Norham Castle and James's newly acquired heavy bronze guns smashed the walls of the gatehouse. This artillery bombardment was followed by:

> three great assaults, three days together, and the captain [John Anislow] valiantly defended ... But he spent vainly so much of his ordnance, bows and arrows and other munitions that at last he lacked ... and so [on] the sixth day, [the shortages] compelled him to yield simply to the king's [James] mercy.
> This castle was thought impregnable ...[55]

The Scottish host marched eight miles (13 km.) further south and occupied a five hundred foot (152.4 m.) high, three-peaked hill called Flodden Edge, in Northumberland, erecting earth ramparts and digging trenches to defend their camp on its crest.

Surrey had reached Pontefract, Yorkshire, on his progress north and heard of the Scottish invasion on 25 August. Despite his age – he was now seventy – he hastened on towards Newcastle, sometimes travelling by carriage, as he was troubled with rheumatism or arthritis. The next day,

> was the foulest day and night that could be, and the ways so deep ... that his guide was almost drowned before him, yet he never ceased, but kept on his journey to give example to them that should follow.

His eldest son Thomas, Lord Howard, was bringing a contingent of 928 veteran soldiers and sailors up by ship: 'All that night the wind blew courageously, whereof the earl doubted least that ... his son ... should perish that night on the sea.'[56] Surrey heard Mass in Durham Cathedral and asked its prior to allow him to take into battle a local relic, St Cuthbert's banner. His request was an act of heavy symbolism: the banner had been carried at the Battle of Northallerton, Yorkshire, on 22 August 1138, during the first major engagement between the English and Scots since the Norman Conquest. That day, the Scots' king David I's invading army was routed in just two hours by the outnumbered English militias. By bringing Cuthbert's banner, Surrey planned to inspire his men by that famous victory, known as the Battle of the Standard.

Before there was any fighting in 1513, Surrey had to discover the Scots' strength and tactical intentions. He sent Thomas Hawley, Rouge Croix herald, with a trumpeter to James with two letters, one written in his own hand, and the other from his son, Lord Howard, who had now arrived safely. Surrey told the Scottish king that he

> unnaturally, against all reason and conscience, [had] entered and invaded his brother's realm of England and done great hurt ... in casting down castles, towers and houses, burning, spoiling and destroying of the same and cruelly murdering the [king's] subjects.
>
> Wherefore the said earl will be ready to try the rightfulness of the matter with the king in battle by Friday next coming at the farthest.

Time was running out for the English general. Surrey needed to destroy the Scots before his army melted away. Food supplies were dangerously low and for two days his troops had quaffed no beer, only 'water and could scarce get any other sustenance for money'.[57]

His son's letter was more provocative and more personal. It boasted that, during his voyage north, 'he had sought the Scottish navy, then being at sea, but he could not meet with them, because they were fled to France, by the coast of Ireland'. James had

> many times [sought Howard] to make redress for Andrew Barton, a pirate of the sea ... he was now come in his own person to be in the vanguard of the field to justify the death of [Barton] against him and all his people.

Howard pledged that neither he nor his soldiers would take any Scottish nobleman prisoner, 'but they should die if they come in his [reach], unless it was the king's own person, for he trusted to no other courtesy at the hands of the Scots'. This fighting talk was deliberately designed to antagonise James IV and force him into battle: if he retreated, he would be dishonoured as a coward.[58] The English commanders were not alone in disparaging their foes: among the Scots, Lord Patrick Lindsay dismissed Surrey as 'an auld crooked earl lying in a chariot' – a snide, sniping reference to his arthritis.

Rouge Croix returned with James's agreement to wait for battle until noon on Friday 9 September. All the bonhomie and boisterous goodwill of the wedding of his queen, Margaret Tudor, a decade before had vanished. The Scottish king contemptuously dismissed Surrey's letter as being unseemly for an earl to challenge a prince.[59] The herald also brought disturbing intelligence – that the Scottish army was positioned

> on a high mountain called Flodden on the edge of Cheviot, where was but one narrow field for any man to ascend up the hill ... to him and at the foot of the hill lay all his ordnance.
>
> On the one side of his army was a great marsh, encompassed with the hills of Cheviot, so he lay too strong to be approached on any side ... except that the Englishmen would have temerariously run on his ordnance.[60]

The Scots had chosen a formidable position and would quit it at their peril to fight on level ground. They clearly hoped to force Surrey to launch a suicidal uphill assault upon them, in the face of overwhelming artillery fire.

But the earl was too wily a general to sacrifice his hungry army on those steep slopes. On 8 September, just after noon, the 23,000 men of the English army struck camp at Milfield, south-west of Flodden Edge, and began a long march behind and around the Scottish flank. Their unexpected manoeuvre threw the Scottish commanders into confusion: were the English now invading Scotland? Were they going to attack them from the rear? Was their road back home now cut off? By the next day, James had to countermarch his forces north across Branxton Moor to deny the English the heights behind him. Surrey had lured the Scots out of their fortress-like prepared positions and neutralised their enormous tactical advantage.

James deployed his troops on the forward slope of Branxton Hill in four densely packed formations or 'battles', positioned two hundred feet (61 m.) apart, their movement hidden by dense clouds of acrid white smoke from burning piles of stinking, soiled bedding

straw. His army had substantially shrunk through desertion over
the previous few days, and he probably mustered 29,000 men for
the fight.

Lord Thomas Howard, riding ahead of the English vanguard,
suddenly saw his enemy, like black forests of pikes, as the smoke
cleared, not 440 yards (0.4 km.) away: 'The Lord Admiral was
confronted by the four great battles of the Scots, all on foot,
with long spears like moorish pikes, which [warlike] Scots bent
[lowered] them forward' ready to charge.

It must have been a dreadful shock. Howard snatched the med-
allion bearing the *Agnus Dei* – the Lamb of God – from around
his neck and sent it off by mounted messenger to his father, urging
him 'in all haste to join battle', while he hurriedly formed up his
men out of sight, in the boggy Pallinsburn valley.

The English forces ran up and deployed themselves into five
battles, each commanded by Surrey, Lord Howard, Sir Edmund
Howard (the thirty-five-year-old third son of the earl), Sir Edward
Stanley and Thomas, Lord Dacre.

The Battle of Flodden[61] opened shortly after four o'clock with
an hour-long exchange of artillery fire in pouring rain and high
winds. The heavy Scottish siege guns fired downhill but their
gunners found it difficult to depress the barrels sufficiently to bring
effective fire on the English. Their cannon balls either ploughed
into the soft earth, or flew overhead, doing little damage to Surrey's
troops, drawn up in 'dead' ground in the valley. For their part,
the English, armed with lighter cannon, fired more rapidly and
bounced their two-pound (0.91 kg.) stone shots at their targets.
They first fired at the Scottish artillery, and, after neutralising their
threat by killing their gunners, switched their aim to the enemy's
massed battles of roughly 9,000 men apiece, causing terrible
carnage as the shots scythed through the ranks.[62] As the Scots
pikemen fell like ninepins, James ordered his host to attack down
the slope. He dismounted from his horse, was handed a pike, and
went to the front of his own square of pikemen and led them on
towards the English lines.

As the Scots, their pikes levelled, reached three hundred paces
down the hill, they came within range of the English archers,

armed with the much-feared longbow that had created such deadly havoc among their ancestors in Anglo-Scottish battles down the centuries. That day, however, the weapon proved ineffective: the drenching rain had soaked the bowstrings, reducing the pull of the bow, and the strong winds disrupted the volleys. The Scots were also well armoured and the front ranks carried *pavises*, or tall wooden shields, for protection, so few were initially killed by arrow.

The 8,000-strong Scottish vanguard was made up of Gordon clansmen, armed with axes and mighty two-handed claymore swords, led by Alexander Gordon, third Earl of Huntly, and a deep phalanx of pikemen from the Borders, commanded by Alexander, third Lord Home. The nimble Gordons cleaved their way through the front ranks of Edmund Howard's division on the right of the English line, leaving gaps where the pikemen, by weight of numbers, crumpled resistance.

Edmund Howard and his captains tried to rally their 3,000 troops, but many fled, panic-stricken, abandoning their leaders to their fate. As the Scots skewered many an English soldier on the end of their sixteen-foot (4.88 m.) pikes, the nobles were left isolated in penny packets of resistance, fighting for their lives. Howard's personal standard-bearer was cut into pieces and his banner lost. Two of his servants were killed. He was beaten to the ground three times before Dacre swept across with Surrey's reserve of 2,000 border reiver cavalry and drove off the Scots, some of whom had become distracted by the lure of booty from the English baggage train. Edmund Howard still had to cut his way through to the refuge of his elder brother's 5,000-strong vanguard, on his left, on the ridge called Piper's Hill. This was now battling, beneath St Cuthbert's banner, with a thick mass of pikemen, led by the Earls of Errol, Crawford and Montrose.

The Scots had copied their tactics from the fearsome German *Landsknecht* mercenaries, who relied on collective discipline, large numbers, momentum and the length of their pikes, to roll over their foes. At Flodden, the charge by the three Scottish earls' 6,000 men was disrupted by a small stream called the Sandyford – scarcely wider than 'a man's foot over'. After clearing this, they had to clamber up the slope to reach Lord Howard's men less than one hundred yards (91 m.) away, considerably slowing their pace and breaking up their tight formation. Though the English recoiled, they absorbed their weakened charge and held their line. In the dense mêlée, the Scots pikes were instantly transformed from lethal weapons into unwieldy encumbrances, and were pushed aside by the English infantry, keen to come to close quarters to stab and hack with their shorter bills. The pikes were thrown down, swords drawn and axes pulled out of the Scots' belts for close combat.

Minutes later, further to the left, James's division clashed with Surrey's 5,000-strong rearguard, fighting under Henry VIII's royal standard of the red dragon, just west of the village of Branxton. The weight of their charge pushed the English back two hundred yards (182 m.), near to where today's monument to the battle now stands.

> The battle was cruel and none spared other and the king himself fought valiantly. O what a noble and triumphant courage was this for a king to fight in a battle as a mean soldier

wrote one contemporary chronicler.[63] James, who fought to within a spear's length of the Earl of Surrey, directing the battle from his carriage in the English rear, suffered five sword thrusts and an arrow wound but still managed to kill five English with his pike, before it shattered. He threw away the stump and with his sword slew five more. But then, surrounded by men-at-arms jabbing and slashing at him with their poleaxes, he was cut down.

A terrible blood lust now gripped the English.

Some of the Scottish nobles in the front ranks, hemmed in by the press of men behind, begged for their lives to be spared in return for a ransom.

> Many ... Scottish prisoners could and might have been taken but they were so [vengeful] and cruel in their fighting that when the Englishmen had the better of them, they would not save them, though it were that diverse Scots offered great sums of money for their lives.[64]

After three hours of fierce fighting, the low-born men in the rear of the Scottish phalanxes instinctively sensed the battle was going against them. One by one, then group by group, they began to melt away as terror and sudden cowardice, like an epidemic, swept through the ranks.

The Scots' division on the right, 6,000 lightly armed High-landers under the Earls of Lennox and Argyle, prepared to enter the fray to support their king's attack. But they were ambushed by Surrey's fifth battle, under Sir Edward Stanley, who had clambered up the steep north-east slope of Branxton Hill unobserved. A volley of arrows and a charge by Stanley's bill men routed them and they, too, panicked and fled the field.

As the Scots streamed away, Surrey was uncertain whether victory was truly within his grasp.

Before nightfall, he ordered his scouts to discover whether any of his enemies had rallied and if he faced another battle the next morning. The Scots were gone, many fleeing headlong back into their homeland across the Tweed at Coldstream. But some English scavengers looted the Scottish camp on Flodden Edge and found plentiful supplies of mutton, beef, cheese, and – praise be! – ale and wine. There were also four thousand feather beds.

As the English army remained under arms that night, amidst the groans of the wounded and dying, Surrey knighted forty of his gentlemen, including his younger son, Edmund.

Lord Howard returned to the army's camp and sent a short note announcing the victory to Catherine of Aragon, the Queen Regent in Henry VIII's absence in France.

The next morning, a small force of eight hundred mounted Scots tried to snatch back the seventeen captured cannon but were seen off by a volley from the English artillery.[65]

Dawn revealed the true extent of the slaughter.

The area at the bottom of Branxton Field was packed with thousands of Scottish dead, and their blood had tainted the Sandyford stream, itself choked with bodies, many stripped naked by night looters. The Scots army had lost around 12,000 men – just under half the host that had begun the battle. Among their dead was the king himself, his bastard son Alexander Stewart, Archbishop of St Andrews and Chancellor of Scotland, a bishop, two abbots, nine earls and fourteen barons. The Scottish aristocracy had been decimated: almost every noble family had lost a father, husband or son.[66] Estimates of the number of English dead ranged between 500 and 1,500.

James's body was found later that morning recognised by Dacre among the heaps of mangled corpses. The king had suffered 'diverse deadly wounds and especially one with an arrow and another [caused] by a bill, as appeared when he was naked'.[67] His sword, dagger and turquoise ring were removed and kept by the Howards.[68] The corpse was carried off to Berwick, where it was embalmed and encased in lead. It was then taken to the Carthusian monastery at Sheen, near Richmond in Surrey, where it lay unburied for many years.[69] A bloodied piece of the king's tabard (his coat bearing his arms) was sent to the queen as a trophy of war.[70]

On 16 September, a warlike Catherine of Aragon wrote to Henry reporting Howard's claim of 'the great victory that our Lord has sent your subjects in your absence'. She had sent on

> the piece of the King of Scots' coat which John Glyn now brings. In this your grace shall see how I keep my promise, sending you, for your banners, a king's coat.
>
> I thought to send himself to you, but our Englishmen's hearts would not suffer it. It should have been better for him to have been in peace than have this reward.
>
> All that God sends is for the best.
>
> Surrey wishes to know your grace's pleasure as to the burying of the king of Scots' body.

Catherine also sent a slip of paper found in a dead Scotsman's purse which contained details of 'the instigation used by France to induce James [IV] to go to war with England'.[71] The king, she added piously, if not a trifle pompously, 'must not forget to thank God' for the victory.

Henry's campaign in France was not nearly so spectacular. Thérouanne had fallen a week after an English victory at the so-called Battle of the Spurs on 16 August, which was more a skirmish than a full-scale engagement. The king, now encamped at Tournai and awaiting its formal surrender, triumphantly sent the news of

Flodden to Maximilian Sforza, Duke of Milan, his irrepressible swagger all too apparent:

> The king of Scots himself, with a great army invaded our realm of England and first took a little old town, belonging to the Bishop of Durham, already nearly in ruins and practically unfortified and on that account almost deserted.
>
> He then advanced four miles into our realm. There the noble lord, the Earl of Surrey, to whom we had committed the charge of repelling the Scots ... met with them in a battle which was long and fiercely contested ... With the Almighty ... aiding the better cause, our forces emerged victorious and killed a great number of the enemy and many of their nobles and put the rest to flight.

In a postscript, Henry added: 'Since these were written, we have received certain news that the King of Scots himself was killed ... so he has paid a heavier penalty for his treachery than we would have wished.'[72] He celebrated the victory with a *feu de joie*, a rippling salvo of 1,000 cannon, declaring: 'I will sing him a soul knell with the sound of my guns.'

In Rome there was initial news of a catastrophic English defeat, with Surrey a prisoner with fifteen other lords, and 30,000 Englishmen dead. In war, first reports are frequently wrong and this was no exception. Cardinal Christopher Bainbridge, Henry's ambassador to Rome, recounted gleefully how the 'French and Scots [in the city] were sought greatly but when the king's letter came all their joy was turned to shame'.[73]

Surrey received his just reward on Candlemas Day, 1 February 1514, at Lambeth Palace, when the earl, resplendent in crimson robes, was 'honourably restored unto his right name of Duke of Norfolk'.[74] Sir Thomas Wriothesley, Garter King of Arms, presented him with the engrossed patent of the dukedom and an augmentation to his coat of arms, an escutcheon bearing the lion of Scotland pierced through the mouth with an arrow, to mark his victory at Flodden.[75] A grateful king presented him with forty manors spread across Berkshire, Derbyshire, Hertfordshire, Kent, Nottinghamshire, Oxfordshire, Shropshire, Staffordshire, Warwickshire and Wiltshire, together with an annual pension of £40.

His eldest son Thomas was created Earl of Surrey in his place and also granted an annuity of £12 for life and sixteen manors and two castles, yielding a handsome annual income of £333 6s 8d.[76]

At the end of that September, and with peace declared, the second Duke of Norfolk escorted Henry's young sister Mary to France for her marriage to the elderly and sickening Louis XII. The journey was a chapter of unfortunate accidents. The newly ennobled Surrey, as Lord Admiral, had to shepherd the wedding party across the English Channel, but bad weather kept them at sea for four days of sickness and misery. The princess's ship became separated and finally it ran aground on a sandbank outside Boulogne, forcing her to be rowed ashore through the surf. She was less than pleased at the danger and the insult to her dignity.

Her marriage took place on 9 October, and, almost immediately, Norfolk was involved in a row over the dismissal of her English servants (who had been selected by Wolsey) and their French replacements. A fuming Mary wrote to her brother: 'I marvel much that my lord of Norfolk would at all times so lightly grant everything at their requests here ... Would [to] God, my lord of York [Wolsey] had come with me in the room of Norfolk, for then I am sure I should have been left much more at my heart['s ease] than I am now.'[77] There was only one saving grace for the princess. The marriage only lasted eighty-three days before her husband died (reportedly through overexertion on the marital bed, unwise for a man of his years and poor health) and she was free later to marry secretly her true love, Sir Charles Brandon.

Norfolk had gradually been edged out of the king's inner councils by Wolsey and it must have been a tedious duty for him to escort him during the ceremony in Westminster Abbey on 18 November 1515 in which he received his cardinal's hat, awarded by Pope Leo X two months earlier. Worse was to come: on Christmas Eve, Henry appointed Wolsey his Lord Chancellor.

It would be left to his son, Thomas, to neutralise the threat posed by the Cardinal.

2

GUARDIANS OF ENGLAND

◆

'A man of the greatest wisdom, reliability and loyalty'
The historian Polydore Vergil's description of
Thomas, second Duke of Norfolk[1]

It began, as many such riots begin, with a small, trifling incident –
merely a row over the purchase of two birds for an Englishman's
simple dinner. But this was a spark that set alight a powder keg of
resentment, hatred and violence in the narrow, filthy and stinking
streets and lanes of London.

Add rampant xenophobia, envy and the pain of declining wages
all together and you have a heady recipe for civil disorder. The
chronicler Richard Grafton described how, by 1517, French,
Genoese and other foreign merchants had flocked to London,
attracted by the rich pickings offered by Henry VIII's free-
spending and glittering court. 'The multitude of strangers was so
great . . . that the poor English artificers could scarce get any living.
Most of all, the strangers were so proud that they disdained,
mocked and oppressed the Englishmen,' he reported.

In early April that year, a carpenter called Williamson bought
two stock doves[2] at a stall in London's Eastcheap. As he paid with
a few coins from the purse at his belt, a passing Frenchman
snatched the birds out of his hand and told him that they were too
grand a dish for such a low-born tradesman. Despite his angry
protests, the Frenchman insisted the birds would make a perfect
meal for his master, the French ambassador Pierre de la Guiche,[3]
and carried them off – but not before he had called Williamson a
'knave'.[4] Diplomatic complaints followed about the carpenter's
manners and he ended up in prison, with the envoy declaring 'by
the Body of God, that the English knave should lose his life, for

no Englishman should deny what a Frenchman required'.

Meantime, another Frenchman was banished from the realm for killing a man and had a cross branded on his right hand to identify him as a malefactor. As one of the city constables led him away, they were jostled and shoved by the Frenchman's friends who taunted the officer: 'Sir, is this cross the price to kill an Englishman?' Another shouted: 'On that price, we would all be banished, by the Mass!'

Rumours spread of more incidents involving foreigners, which fanned the smouldering fires of resentment burning in Londoners' hearts. John Lincoln, a broker,[5] who was 'sore grudged' by the foreigners' behaviour, consulted a Dr Beal (alias Bell), a monk from the Augustinian priory and hospital of St Mary Spitalfields,[6] just outside the city walls, and told him: 'You were born in London and see the oppression by the strangers and the great misery of your own native country. Exhort the citizens to [unite] against these strangers, ravagers and destroyers ...'

Easter sermons at the priory were renowned throughout the city and were delivered from an outdoor pulpit, or preaching cross, within an enclosure near its churchyard. Immediately opposite was a small, two-storey building in which the Lord Mayor and aldermen of London gathered to hear the pious words.[7] On the Tuesday after Easter, Beal mounted the pulpit and urged his congregation:

> Take compassion over the poor people, your neighbours, and also of the great hurts, losses and hindrances ... [and] the extreme poverty [of] all the king's subjects that inhabit this city .
> The aliens and strangers eat the bread from the poor fatherless children and take the living from the artificers and the [business] from all merchants, whereby poverty is much increased [and now] every man bewails the misery of another, for craftsmen are brought to beggary and merchants to need ...[8]

As the monk warmed to his theme, his voice became edged with righteous anger:

> This land was given to Englishmen. As birds defend their nest,

so ought Englishmen cherish and defend themselves and hurt and grieve [the] aliens for the common good.

He turned to his text for that day – *pugna pro patria* ('Fight for your country')[9] – and emphasised that under God's law this was wholly legitimate. Beal then 'subtly moved the people to rebel against the foreigners and break the king's peace'.

The following Sunday, in the king's gallery at Greenwich Palace, the courtier Sir Thomas Palmer was chatting to some Lombardy merchants, among them Francis de Bard, who was enjoying considerable notoriety for successfully enticing and seducing an Englishman's wife and, what's more, stealing his plate. Laughing coarsely, the Lombards boasted that now 'if they had the mayor's wife, they would keep her'. Some English merchants were within earshot and the crude jests piqued them. One angry mercer, William Bolt, stalked over to the group and snarled: 'Well, you whore's son Lombards, you [may] rejoice and laugh, [but] by the Mass, we will one day [have you], come when it will.'[10]

Tempers were up and it was time for vengeance on the streets.

A few days later, on 28 April, foreigners were attacked in the city by apprentices and other young men – 'some were struck, some buffeted and some thrown into the canal' – but the Lord Mayor, John Rest, quickly arrested some of the ringleaders and threw them into prison.

He hoped he had contained the unrest, but this was merely the harbinger of worse violence to come.

Dark rumours quickly spread across London that the whole city would rise up as one on May Day and that all aliens found within the walls would be cruelly slaughtered. Word of the uprising reached Cardinal Thomas Wolsey, the Lord Chancellor, and he ordered the city authorities on 1 May to ban people from the streets from nine o'clock in the evening until seven the next morning and to increase patrols by the watch.

That night, as Alderman John Moody was hurrying home, he found apprentices playing the game of 'Bucklers'[11] – a mock fight with wooden swords and shields – in Eastcheap, watched by 'a great company of young men'. It was after the new curfew, although admittedly word of its imposition 'was scarce known'. He ordered the crowd of youths to disperse immediately but when one young man impertinently questioned his instruction, the alderman caught his arm and told him menacingly: 'You will know.' With that, he started to march him off to the nearest jail.

But his companions quickly tore him away and they shouted out a rallying cry: "'Prentices and clubs ... 'prentices and clubs!'

It must have been a pre-arranged signal for commotion. Instantly, the doors of houses along Eastcheap opened and angry young men poured out, armed with wooden cudgels. The alderman ran to save his municipally corpulent carcase and the disturbance rapidly spread west throughout the city:

> More people arose out of every quarter and out came serving men, watermen ... and by eleven of the clock, there were in Cheap[side] six or seven hundred.
>
> Out of [St] Paul's [Cathedral] churchyard came three hundred and so of all places they gathered and broke [open] the counters [prisons] and took out the prisoners.
>
> The mayor and sheriffs were there present and made proclamation in the king's name – but nothing was obeyed.
>
> The people of St. Martin's [le Grand] threw stones and bats [wooden sticks] and hurt many honest persons that were persuading the riotous people to cease and they bade them hold their hands, but still they threw out bricks and hot water.
>
> Then all the misruled persons ran to the doors and windows of St. Martin's [le Grand church] and spoiled all they found [there] and cast it into the streets and left few houses unspoiled.[12]

The mob ran back eastwards, headlong into Cornhill and Leadenhall streets, and broke into the house of a French merchant called Meutas, who was particularly loathed by the Londoners. If the rioters had found him 'in their fury, they would have struck off his head' but they had to be content with murdering his servants. Houses were set alight and watermen raided foreigners' homes at Whitechapel and threw their boots and shoes into the Thames. Sir Thomas Parr galloped through the violent, noisy streets, west out of the city, to Wolsey's home at York Place in Westminster, to warn him that the commotion was getting out of hand. The Lord Chancellor summoned help from the nobles living around the capital and prudently fortified his home, drafting in extra troops and artillery. Sir Richard Cholmley, the Lieutenant of the Tower of London, in 'a frantic fury', opened fire on the city with several guns on his ramparts. Little damage was done but at least the thunder of the salvoes made him feel better.

The disorder continued until about three in the morning when most rioters returned home, happy with their night's work. As they broke up into smaller parties, the apprentices were picked off by the city's watch and detained. More than three hundred were arrested and marched off to the Tower, to Newgate and other prisons. Two hours later, reinforcements arrived in London, led by the experienced generals Thomas Howard, Earl of Surrey, and George Talbot, fourth Earl of Shrewsbury and Lord Steward of the royal household, who had speedily mustered what forces they could gather in order to suppress the revolt. The apprentices[13] 'scattered by sudden fright, just like sheep at the sight of the wolf' under the hooves of Surrey's heavily armed horsemen.

Lincoln and Beal were immediately arrested. Soon after, the second Duke of Norfolk arrived with 1,300 armed retainers from East Anglia, which he rapidly deployed at strategic street corners throughout the capital, ready to quash any fresh outbreak of civil disobedience. His soldiers, ingrained with the countryman's traditional disdain for 'townies', spoke 'many opprobrious words to the citizens, which grieved them sore'. Many in that now nervous city were convinced that Norfolk had nurtured a deep grudge against its inhabitants since one of his chaplains was murdered in Cheapside the previous year. Then he had angrily declared: 'I pray God I may have the citizens in my danger [at my mercy].' They feared his pitiless reprisal for their night of sweet revenge upon the foreigners in what was now being called the 'Evil May Day' riots.

Norfolk issued strict proclamations that 'no women should come together to babble and talk, but that all men should keep their wives in their houses'. Was this bizarre edict an indication of the duke's opinion on the cause of the riots?

Then he moved on to inflict legal retribution for the mayhem. Three hundred of the captured rioters were arraigned before an oyer and terminer trial on 4 May at the Guildhall, presided over by Norfolk, his son, and Rest, the Lord Mayor.[14] Another 224 followed them on indictment. The prisoners were herded through the hushed streets to the court, tied together by ropes, between files of halberdiers:

Some men, some lads, some children [aged only] thirteen. There was a great mourning of fathers and friends for their children and kinsfolk. Among the prisoners were many not of the city; some were priests and some husbandmen and labourers and they were all arraigned for treason.[15]

Common law treason was a convenient, ill-defined crime in England which could involve many types of offences, grave or minor, but woven into most cases was the common thread of displeasing the monarch. The principle upon which the law rested was allegiance to the crown, due from every subject of fourteen years and above.

Henry VIII, who could never stomach any kind of opposition, believed the apprentices had damaged the amity he enjoyed with his fellow Christian princes and therefore, according to the king, they were traitors.

The next day, the court found thirteen guilty and ordered them to be publicly hanged, drawn and quartered – the barbaric method of execution reserved for those condemned for high treason, whereby the victim was hanged until half dead, cut down from the gallows, then castrated, his vital organs ripped from the still living body and burned before his eyes. Finally, the corpse was beheaded and chopped into four quarters by the axe-wielding headsman. Such places of execution must have resembled a gory butcher's shop.

Twenty-two gallows were erected in the London streets where the offences were committed: at Aldgate, Whitechapel, Grace-church Street,[16] Leadenhall and in front of the city's prisons at Newgate, St Martin le Grand, Aldersgate and Bishopsgate. The prisoners were brought out and executed in the most rigorous manner, in the presence of the Lord Edmund Howard, son to the Duke of Norfolk, and knight marshal, who showed no mercy but extreme cruelty to the poor young[sters] in their execution.

And likewise, the Duke's servants spoke many opprobrious words, some bade: 'hang' some bade: 'draw' and some bade: 'set the city on fire' but all was suffered.[17]

The severed heads and body quarters were prominently displayed to deter future transgressors against the king's peace.

Two days later, on 7 May, Lincoln, two brothers called Bets, another man Shirwin, and 'diverse others' were also sentenced to death. Lincoln pleaded 'not guilty' and defiantly told his judges:

My lords, I meant well. If you knew the mischief that is issued in this realm by strangers, you would remedy it. Many times I have complained and then I was called a busy[body]. Now our Lord have mercy on me.[18]

The condemned men were tied to sheep hurdles and dragged and bumped through the foul mire of the streets to the Standard in Cheapside, a water conduit then frequently used as a place of punishment for serious offenders. As the hangman's noose was roughly looped over one prisoner's neck, a horseman galloped up and halted further executions. He carried a message from Henry to reprieve the malefactors but he was too late to save Lincoln, who had been the first to die. The crowd, packed into the narrow street, down from the Eleanor Cross, cried out: 'God Save the King', as, of course, they were intended to do, as a result of Henry's populist gesture.

On 11 May, the king returned to Greenwich Palace from Richmond where he had been safely ensconced during the riots. Vengeance soured his heart but Queen Catherine pleaded with him to show mercy to the remaining prisoners. Others, including Norfolk and some of the London aldermen, also urged compassion, but he sternly told the city fathers:

Truly, you have highly displeased and offended us and you ought to [be]wail and be sorry for the same. And where you say that you, the substantial persons were not consenting to the [riots], it appears to the contrary. For you never moved to let [hinder] them nor stirred once to fight with them ...

At this time, we will grant to you neither our favour nor goodwill, nor to the offenders mercy.[19]

Three days later the king came to Westminster Hall, attended by Wolsey, Norfolk, Surrey and many other nobles. What followed was a carefully timed and orchestrated demonstration of the generosity of the royal prerogative. The mayor and aldermen had been kept waiting, dressed in the finery of their best livery, since nine that morning. At the upper end of the twelfth-century hall had been suspended a gold cloth of estate and the walls were hung with rich tapestries. Against this magnificent backdrop stood the grim-faced king, who commanded that the surviving prisoners should be brought into his presence. The royal guards, pushing and shoving, lined up the wretches in rows to face their sovereign and their fate:

Then came in the poor [youngsters] and old false knaves, bound in ropes all along, one after the other in their shirts, and every one a halter about his neck, to the number of four hundred men and eleven women.

The Cardinal sore laid to the mayor and aldermen and commons, their negligence and to the prisoners he declared that they deserved death for their offence.

Then all the prisoners cried: 'Mercy, gracious lord, mercy!'[20]

Wolsey, Norfolk and the other nobles then knelt before Henry and humbly pleaded for the lives of the Londoners. No doubt after a suitable, agonising wait, the king nodded his peremptory assent.

Instantly, and not unnaturally, all the prisoners shouted for joy and threw their halters up high towards the hall's magnificent timbered roof.[21] It was all pure theatre and, of course, cost Henry nothing.

The gallows were taken down in the city and 'many a good prayer [was] said for the king and the citizens took more heed to their servants' – which is only what any reasonable monarch would expect of them.

Aside from all these alarums and excursions, the Howards were still determinedly seeking to fulfil all their political and dynastic ambitions. Wolsey had by now eclipsed Norfolk's position and influence at court – deeply to his chagrin – but the family's power base, created by their mounting wealth and considerable military and diplomatic skills, remained very much intact. In June 1520, when Henry and Wolsey took more than 5,000 followers across to France for the sumptuous extravaganza with the new French king Francis I, on the Field of Cloth of Gold, Norfolk was left behind in England as a safe pair of hands to govern as the appointed 'Guardian' of the realm.

One dark, ominous cloud on the family's horizon, however, was the lack of a living son for Surrey, the heir to the dukedom and the proud future hope of the clan. After suffering so much during those long years in the Tower, could the second duke's cherished dreams of his family holding sway in England, yielding place to none, fade and die?

His eldest son Thomas had been betrothed to Lady Anne Plantagenet, third daughter of Edward IV and his queen Elizabeth Woodville in 1484, when she was aged nine.[22] After his father's release from imprisonment and his loyal service in the north, Henry VII was graciously moved to grant permission for the wedding to go ahead. It was a signal mark of royal favour towards the Howards: Anne was sister to his wife, Elizabeth of York, and one of her closest attendants at court. On 4 February 1495, the couple were married at Greenwich, with the queen settling a £120 annuity on the twenty-year-old bride.[23] Thomas had become the brother-in-law to the king, and uncle to his royal children.

The couple lived most of their time either at the Howards' home at Lambeth, built by the second duke, or at one or other of their properties in Suffolk. The union, which seems to have been happy, but marred by the wife's sickness in later years, produced at least four children. All died young, including two sons, Henry and Thomas, the latter born two years after their wedding but who died in August 1508.[24]

Anne's tuberculosis finally claimed her on 12 November 1511 at the age of thirty-six and she was buried in the Cluniac abbey at Thetford, Norfolk, already planned as a mausoleum for the Howard family. The widower, now desperate for a surviving heir, searched among the giggling daughters of the noble families of England in a quest for a new bedmate.

It was a pivotal moment in history for the House of Howard. His brother, the admiral, Sir Edward, had no legitimate child. England was at war with France and conflict also loomed again with Scotland. The Howards would always be in the forefront of any fighting and there was a palpable danger that one or more could be killed without continuing the family's precious blood line.

Thomas Howard soon found just what he was looking for. The feisty and self-willed Lady Elizabeth Stafford was one of the pretty, nubile daughters of Sir Edward Stafford, third Duke of Buckingham and Lord High Constable of England, who had the lengthy and proud pedigree, coupled with the requisite wealth and status, to match any and all of Howard's marital aspirations. Buckingham also expediently shared the Howards' opposition to the omnipresent influence of Wolsey at court.

However, there was a real barrier to the match. After two years of courtship, Elizabeth was deeply in love with Ralph Neville, later to become the fourth Earl of Westmorland, and was looking forward to marrying him at Christmas 1512. Howard, however, was not a man whose oily attentions could be easily denied by simple love or another's betrothal. At Easter that year he visited Buckingham and made his romantic intentions very plain. Neither of the duke's other two daughters would suit him; he *must* and *would* have the fifteen-year-old Elizabeth. The age gap between them yawned alarmingly: her bridegroom would be five years older than her father.

In the sixteenth century, noble alliances were always far more imperative than any young girl's starry-eyed yearnings and Buckingham happily approved this loveless and ill-fated match. The miserable Neville was forced to content himself with her second sister, Catherine, whom he married some time before June 1520, in Abergavenny, Monmouthshire.[25]

Buckingham produced a generous dowry for Elizabeth, totalling 2,000 marks (the equivalent of £558,110 in modern money), and Howard, in turn, settled a jointure on her of 500 marks, or £139,530 in today's terms.[26]

In the years that followed, Howard was to come bitterly to regret his haste in choosing his second wife. They married early in 1513 and in the long, sour and poisoned years that followed, Elizabeth would frequently reflect, with aggrieved rage, on how she had been cheated by Howard and denied a happy and loving life with Neville.

She gave birth to the Howards' first child – happily a son, christened Henry – in late 1513, probably at Tendring Hall at Stoke-by-Nayland in Suffolk. Henceforth, Elizabeth spent much of her time listlessly in and around court while her husband sat in the talking shop of Parliament. After his creation as Earl of Surrey, true to his arrogant character and with an all-consuming pride in his status, on 15 February 1514 he claimed precedence, as the eldest son of a duke, over all earls, both inside and outside the House of Lords.[27] However, two days later it was ruled that although Surrey had precedence outside Parliament, he would be seated in the House of Lords next to last among the earls.

Surrey joined the king's Council some time in 1515 but his membership was cut short the following year when Wolsey had him kicked out, with other nobles, for breaking the laws on keeping liveried retainers.[28] Was this because of a possibly apocryphal incident between the minister and the earl in which Surrey angrily drew his dagger and attacked Wolsey during an argument in council?[29]

The earl was, meanwhile, finding life with his new wife far from peaceful. What cannot have endeared the Howard family to Elizabeth – and, doubtless, was a source of furious, accusing letters between husband and wife – was the cruel destruction of her father, who had suffered strained relations with, if not open hostility from, his son-in-law.

Wolsey cunningly appointed Surrey as Lord Deputy of Ireland, based in Dublin, on 10 March 1520 to remove him from the court while the jaws of his subtle trap snapped shut on Buckingham, who had done little to hide his unvarnished contempt for the self-made and ambitious minister.[30] He once emptied the basin of water he was holding for Henry VIII over Wolsey's feet as the Cardinal was washing his hands in it.[31] Like the Howards, he was scornful of the young men now surrounding Henry at court and complained that the king would 'give his fees, offices and rewards rather to boys than to noblemen'.[32] Moreover, Buckingham's claims of royal descent made him an ever-present latent but dangerous threat to the Tudor throne,[33] and his opposition to a new alliance with France was a tiresome political obstacle. For his part, Henry had grown jealous of the former royal favourite's huge land holdings, and now thoroughly mistrusted his loyalty.

In October 1520, Buckingham told his chancellor Robert Gilbert that he had been such a sinner, he was sure that he lacked grace. While he may have hoped for forgiveness from his Maker, he was to receive no mercy from Henry.

Wolsey's poisonous gossip against the duke quickly bore fruit: on 8 April 1521, Buckingham was summoned to London from his estates in Thornbury in Gloucestershire and was arrested by Sir Henry Marnay, the captain of the guard, with one hundred halberdiers, at Hay Wharf at the end of his journey by barge down the Thames. He was quickly committed to the Tower.

The charges against him were patently trumped up.

Henry wanted to fire a warning shot across the overwhelming pride and majesty of his nobles, so cynically he appointed the second Duke of Norfolk as Lord High Steward to preside over Buckingham's trial. The duke was truly aghast at this unwanted role: despite the bitter enmity between his son and his father-in-law, he fully endorsed Buckingham's views on many political issues and enjoyed a friendship that stretched back almost three decades. As was the norm in Henry VIII's reign, the outcome of the trial, on 13 May before Norfolk and seventeen peers in Westminster Hall, was decided long before Buckingham was ever called into court, accused of high treason.[34]

The charges, covering the period 1511–20, alleged that he had listened to prophecies forecasting both the king's imminent death and his own succession to the throne of England. Not wishing to leave anything to the hand of Fate, he had also planned to assassinate Henry by stabbing him with his dagger as he knelt before him. When the indictment was read, Buckingham snapped: 'It is false and untrue and [was] conspired and forged to bring me to my death.' Norfolk told him:

> The king our sovereign has commanded that you shall have his laws ministered with favour and right to you. Wherefore, if you have anything to say, you shall be heard.[35]

He must have known he spoke with a lie on his lips.

Wolsey had lined up Buckingham's chancellor, Gilbert,[36] his chaplain, John Delacourt, and his sacked surveyor, Charles Knyvett, as witnesses against their master. But the duke's downfall was caused by his spiritual adviser, Matthew Hopkins, a monk from the Carthusian priory at Hinton, Somerset, and vicar of the conventual church there, who was famous locally for his cryptic prophecies. He was the source of the damaging, fateful talk of a Stafford *coup d'état*[37] against the crown. Under strict instructions, Norfolk refused permission for the prisoner to cross-examine any of the witnesses ranged against him. Frustrated, Buckingham lashed out like a wounded animal against his enemies. 'Of all men', he said, 'Surrey hated him the most and had hurt him most to the king's majesty.'

Inevitably, despite his angry, blustering protestations of innocence, he was found guilty.[38] Beginning with the Duke of Suffolk, each of his peers was asked by Norfolk: 'What say you of Sir Edward, Duke of Buckingham, touching these high treasons?' Each one placed his right hand on his breast and answered: 'I say that he is guilty.' Seventeen times Norfolk scribbled, in his cramped handwriting, each peer's verdict on a small piece of parchment: *Dicit quod est culpabilis* – 'Found guilty and is culpable.'

Buckingham was brought to the bar to hear sentence. For long, agonising moments, Norfolk sat silent, chafing and sweating profusely. He recovered himself, bowed to the court, and stared hard at the prisoner. There was another long pause. Then he declared: 'Sir Edward, you have heard how you are indicted of high treason. You pleaded not guilty, putting yourself to the judgement of your peers, [who] have found you guilty.' Norfolk suddenly burst into a torrent of uncontrollable tears and it was some time before he could compose himself to pronounce falteringly the dreadful, final words of the sentence of death for a traitor.[39]

On the following Friday morning, 17 May, between eleven and noon, Buckingham was escorted out of the Tower by the Sheriffs of London, Sir John Skevington and John Kyme, and led to the public scaffold on Tower Hill. Three blows of the axe were necessary to sever his head from his body. He was forty-three years old and had followed his father's example in being executed for high treason. Six poor friars, shouldering a rough wooden coffin, picked up the corpse and carried it to the church of Austin Friars for its burial.

As befits all traitors, Buckingham was attainted and his goods and lands confiscated by the crown under Act of Parliament dated 31 July 1523.[40] Norfolk received his due reward for services rendered to the crown with the grant of a number of manors from the duke's forfeitures. He clearly enjoyed no sense of irony.

Thomas, Earl of Surrey, had been with his wife and family in Dublin, suffering from intermittent and distressing bouts of dysentery. Elizabeth had earlier provided him with more children. First came Mary, delivered in 1519 in one of their East Anglian homes; Charles, who died in infancy; and finally Thomas junior – the all-important spare heir – who was born around 1520, when the marriage was already looking shaky because of Surrey's rows with Buckingham. There was also a fifth child, who must have died very young.[41] Surrey was finally recalled to London at the end of 1521 after eighteen months of fruitless, frustrating service in Ireland, trying to separate the warring Irish power blocs.[42]

There was, however, no respite in his demanding service to the crown. Following his command of a punitive raid through northern France, launched from Calais in the autumn of 1522, he was made Warden-General of the Scottish Marches. Then, on 26 February 1523, he became Lieutenant General of the English army against Scotland, and this post took the Surreys north, away from the comforts of their estates, with more lengthy periods apart.[43]

The poet John Skelton[44] dedicated his lengthy and rather self-congratulatory poem *A Goodly Garland or Chaplet of Laurel*, completed at the end of 1523, to the Countess of Surrey who was then living at the castle of Sheriff Hutton while her husband campaigned on the Scottish borders.[45] Skelton was always welcome at Sheriff Hutton, possibly because of his cheeky and pointed criticism of Wolsey after 1518,[46] although he happily wrote in praise of Surrey – 'our strong captain' – in a poem specially commissioned by the Cardinal.[47] In the *Garland* poem, he describes how an allegorical figure named 'Occupation' led him up a winding stair into the presence of the countess, who was sitting in splendour surrounded by ten of the ladies of her household:

> She brought me to a goodly chamber of estate
> Where the noble Countess of Surrey in a chair
> Sat honourably, to whom did repair
> A bevy of ladies with all reverence
> 'Sit down, fair ladies and do your diligence
> Come forth gentleman, I pray you,' she said.
> 'I have contrived for you a goodly work
> And who can work best now shall be assigned
> A crown of laurel with leaves light and dark
> I have devised for Skelton my clerk
> For to his service I have such regard
> That of a bounty we will him reward.'

Her attendants included several whose names indicate their Norfolk origins, the daughters of local gentry firmly hitched to the Howards' noble coat-tails. The others were kith and kin – Lady Elizabeth, one of the daughters of the second Duke of Norfolk by his second wife, Agnes Tylney,[48] and Lady Anne Dacre, step-daughter of the same duke by his first wife, Elizabeth Tylney, the widow of Sir Humphrey Bourchier.[49] Another figure in this cosy domestic scene, set among the richly woven tapestries and carpets, was the 'little lady' Mirriel, or Muriel, possibly another daughter of the countess, who does not appear in the complex Howard genealogy[50] but may be her lost fifth child and named after Surrey's sister.

Life for the Countess of Surrey was later to become far less comfortable, however.

Norfolk remained bruised and shaken by the cruelty and injustice of Buckingham's trial. He was now an old man[51] and had become weary of the intrigues and conspiracies surrounding his vibrant young monarch. He decided, after so many vicissitudes in a lifetime of service to so many kings, that it was time to retire gracefully from the hubbub of life at court. On 4 December 1522, he resigned as Lord High Treasurer in favour of his son, and gave up all other duties save that of Earl Marshal. The last time he met Henry was early the following year, 'when he had a short and apparently affectionate conversation' with the king.[52] After attending the opening of Parliament in May 1523, Norfolk retreated to the rural calm of his castle at Framlingham in Suffolk for the last months of his eventful life. A visit to the Surreys' home at nearby Tendring Hall is recorded on 5 and 6 August. The earl was, predictably, away in the north, but Elizabeth served up a tasty meal of mutton, beef, chicken, rabbits, partridge and venison pasties for her visitor.[53]

Norfolk died at Framlingham on 21 May 1524, aged eighty-one, and the dukedom passed immediately to the Earl of Surrey, who, at fifty-one, became the third Duke of Norfolk[54] and one of the richest men in the realm, with an annual income of more than £4,000, or nearly £2 million at 2009 prices.

The funeral spectacular that followed befitted a nobleman who saw himself as a prince – indeed, his will, signed on 31 May 1520, employed the royal plural throughout: '*We, Thomas, Duke of Norfolk ...*'[55] Even in death – that great leveller – the Howard preoccupation with rank, status and prestige had to be properly and lavishly observed. The new duke was away on the king's business, again commanding English troops on the Scottish borders, so his half-brother, Lord William Howard, was appointed his deputy as chief mourner for the lengthy obsequies, planned in detail by the duke before his death. The public rooms at Framlingham Castle were heavily draped with black cloth and his coffin lay in state for a month before the altar of the chapel there 'which his grace kept prince-like for he had great pleasure in the service of God'.[56] Every day, three solemn Masses were said, attended by nineteen mourners kneeling about the wooden hearse,[57] which was festooned with candles and heraldic shields and badges. During the stillness of the night, the corpse was watched over by twelve gentlemen, twelve yeomen, two gentlemen ushers and two yeoman ushers from the Howard household.

On 22 June, the second Duke of Norfolk began his last journey to the Cluniac abbey at Thetford for burial in a new vault already prepared by him there. Although the monastic house was only twenty-four miles (38.6 km.) away from Framlingham, the procession was so huge and progress so slow that it had to stop at Diss and was there met by Richard Nykke, the Bishop of Norwich, dressed in his full pontifical vestments, to escort the coffin into the choir of the church for its rest overnight.

It was an astonishing spectacle and a funeral worthy of a king. Crowds in their thousands must have lined the hot, dusty roads of Norfolk and Suffolk as the cortège passed slowly by, the silence broken only by the chants of the accompanying friars and the priests who left their churches en route to offer up prayers for the departed – and the steady clip-clopping of more than five hundred horses.

Six gentlemen attended the chariot carrying the coffin, followed by four hundred hooded men carrying torches. The bier supporting the coffin was surmounted by one hundred wax effigies of heraldic beasts and 'weepers' – little figures with rosaries and other objects of reverence. The Howard household included Norfolk's chamberlain, carrying his staff of office and the master of his horse, leading a 'sumpter horse'[58] draped with a glittering cloth of gold, blazoned with heraldry. There were another five hundred black-clad mourners, riding behind two by two, lords, ladies, knights and gentry, in order of carefully considered precedence. Among the hobbledehoy that followed were representatives of the apprentices of London, who were there in grateful remembrance of Norfolk's efforts to persuade the king to show mercy after the riots of seven years before.

The third Duke of Norfolk joined the funeral party at Diss, taking back the role of chief mourner from his half-brother, and the next day the winding procession plodded on to Thetford, where the coffin, covered by a 'cloth of majesty', was laid on a catafalque within a hearse, bedecked with eight bannerols and one hundred pencils (small heraldic pennants), together with seven hundred flickering candles.

Beginning at five o'clock the next morning, two Masses were heard, culminating in a high requiem, sung by Nicholas West, Bishop of Ely, which included the dramatic entry into the nave of the church of a mounted knight, wearing the duke's own armour, his visor closed to hide his features, escorted by Thomas Hawley, Carlisle Herald, who as Rouge Croix had served at Flodden.[59] The armoured man carried a battleaxe in his right hand, with the blade head down to symbolise the death of its owner. Dismounting at the screen before the choir, the knight presented it to the bishop who reverently laid the weapon, with the duke's heraldic achievements, on the high altar.[60]

The hour-long funeral sermon that followed was preached by Dr Matthew Mackerell, the abbot of Barling Abbey in Lincolnshire, who took his text from the Book of Revelation, chapter five, verse five: 'Behold the lion of the tribe of Judah has triumphed ...'

His was no tedious or bland homily. The abbot's fearsome, ferocious words sparked immediate apprehension in the hearts and minds of the congregation and many mourners fled the abbey church in terror, leaving him standing alone with the corpse.[61]

Order restored, six gentlemen carried the coffin from the hearse in the choir and lowered it into the vault before the high altar, as the bishop intoned the stark words of the burial service. The officers of the duke's houschold snapped their staves of office and threw the halves into his grave. Carlisle Herald stepped forward, and with his voice rising, clear and ringing to the roof vaulting above, declared:

Of your charity, pray for the soul of the right noble and mighty prince Thomas Duke of Norfolk, Marshal of England and late Treasurer of the same; Counsellor to the King, our Sovereign Lord, Knight Companion of the Garter.

Then followed a 'magnificent entertainment' involving the feeding of nearly 1,900 mourners. Generous alms were distributed to the eagerly waiting poor. In all, the funeral had cost a staggering £1,300, or £540,000 in today's monetary values.

Thomas Howard was the first Duke of Norfolk to be laid in the new dynastic vault at Thetford Abbey. He was also the last.

As the mourners left the church, no one could guess that his bones would not lie there peacefully for very long.[62]

PART 2

THE STRUGGLE FOR POWER

3
THE KING'S 'GREAT MATTER'
———◆———

'By the Mass, Master More, it is perilous striving
with princes . . .'

**Thomas Howard, third Duke of Norfolk,
to Sir Thomas More**[1]

On 9 October 1529 all the angry frustration and bitterness that
poisoned Henry VIII's heart after the continual failure to annul
his marriage to Catherine of Aragon finally burst out. Cardinal
Thomas Wolsey, proud prince of the Church and Lord Chancellor
of England, was accused by a Bill of Indictment for Praemunire of
the treasonable offence of serving a foreign dignitary, in this case,
Pope Clement VII.

Although the Bill was entered in the Court of King's Bench in
Westminster Hall by the Attorney General, Sir Christopher Hales,
the grubby fingerprints of Wolsey's greatest enemies, the third
Duke Norfolk and Charles Brandon, now Duke of Suffolk, were
all over the criminal indictment.[2]

He was accused of treason, but the Cardinal's true felony was
his own abject failure: the broken promise to give the king what
he wanted. And what an obsessed Henry desired most in the entire
world was for Norfolk's niece, the vivacious and assertive Anne
Boleyn, to be his loving wife – and the mother of strong, healthy
male heirs to the crown of Tudor England.

The king's living nightmare was the lack of sons from his present
marriage to Catherine of Aragon, aunt to the Imperial Emperor,
Charles V of Spain, and the pious widow of his elder brother
Arthur, who had died at Ludlow on 2 April 1502, another victim
of tuberculosis, at the age of fifteen, supposedly without con-
summating the match with the Spanish princess. Their marriage

was duly annulled by a dispensation of Pope Julius II in 1503, but the diplomatic imperatives of a union between the ruling houses of Spain and England remained: Catherine was therefore betrothed to the younger brother on 25 June that year. She declared that she had come to Henry, now crowned king, on their wedding night, on 11 June 1509, a 'virgin and an immaculate woman'.

Since then a succession of children had been born to the royal couple, but of the boys only Henry, Prince of Wales, survived his birth at Richmond Palace in 1511 and, tragically, he died seven weeks later. Hopes rose when a healthy daughter, Mary, was born at Greenwich on 18 February 1516, and the king declared cheerfully to the Venetian ambassador, Ludovico Falieri: 'We are both young; if it was a daughter this time, by the grace of God the sons will follow.' But his optimism remained unfulfilled. Catherine was six years older than Henry, and by now physically worn out by her many pregnancies.[3] In desperation, the king even solemnly promised God that he would crusade against the infidel Turks, in return for a male heir being born in wedlock. But as the years passed and Catherine, now growing stout, approached the menopause, any chance of safeguarding the uncertain Tudor dynasty with a set of lusty boys looked increasingly slender.

What redoubled the king's disappointment was his success in siring a bastard son with Bessie Blount, the willowy teenage daughter of a Shropshire knight and a maid of honour – the title seems oddly inappropriate – to Catherine of Aragon. The child, conceived when the queen was approaching her confinement (her pregnancies frequently triggered a bout of promiscuity by Henry), was born in June 1519. For decency's sake, Bessie was brought to childbed far away from the court, at the Augustinian priory of St Lawrence, at Blackmore, near Ingatestone, Essex.[4]

Such discretion was not to the euphoric king's taste, who may have felt his manhood and virility should be publicly vindicated, but he fully made up for this six years later. On 18 June 1525, Henry ennobled the child at a bizarre ceremony in Bridewell Palace on the western edge of the city of London. Henry, surrounded by Wolsey, Norfolk, Suffolk and other nobles, sat resplendent on a richly gilded throne as the little boy was tenderly ushered into the royal presence by his ladies-in-waiting. He proudly created him Earl of Nottingham, and moments later, Duke of Richmond and Somerset – significantly, the title once held by his father, Henry VII, with lands worth £4,845 a year. Offices of state were later showered upon the innocent, tousled head of the youngster by his proud father. The lad, declared Henry, 'is my worldly jewel'.

His open flaunting of his bastard son must have wounded Catherine dreadfully, but relations between king and queen improved briefly in the autumn of that year. Courtiers noted that they read a book together and seemed very friendly in their conversations, hardly a panacea for the improvement of marital relations. This was probably the last time Henry slept with his wife.[5]

From early in 1522 he had taken another mistress, Mary Boleyn, elder daughter of the third Duke of Norfolk's sister, Lady Elizabeth, and her ambitious husband, Thomas Boleyn, a soldier and diplomat. He was created Viscount Rochford in June 1525, as a reward for Mary's liberal bedtime favours.[6] But this discreet affair was merely another of Henry's petty dalliances and the notion of finding another wife to provide the all-important Prince of Wales gripped his mind. Some said it was Wolsey who suggested an annulment to Henry on the unsure biblical grounds of Leviticus, chapter twenty, verse twenty-one: 'If a man shall take his brother's wife, it is an unclean thing: he hath uncovered his brother's nakedness; they shall be childless.' The Cardinal, however, claimed he had pleaded with Henry not to discard his wife. Kneeling humbly before the king 'in his Privy Chamber ... the space of an hour or two, [Wolsey tried] to persuade him from his will and appetite; but I could never bring to pass to dissuade him,' he said unhappily afterwards.[7]

As Sir Thomas More, always ready with a pithy comment, told Thomas Cromwell, Henry's up-and-coming apparatchik, eight years later: 'If you follow my poor advice you shall in your counsel [to] his grace, ever tell him what he ought to do, but never what he is able to do ... For if a lion knew his own strength, [it would be] hard for any man to rule him.'

First Wolsey and then More would suffer the dire consequences of failing to do just that.

Henry fell ardently, passionately, hopelessly in love with Mary Boleyn's younger sister, the twenty-six-year-old black-haired Anne, probably in 1526. To modern tastes, she would not be considered a great beauty: short, rather than tall, with a sallow, if not swarthy complexion, a wide mouth and a long neck. Her black eyes, however, were compelling, if not electrifying.[8] She had returned from a period spent in Paris in 1522 and joined Henry's court, where her father was at the time Treasurer of the Royal Household. In March that year she took part in one of those spectacular masques so beloved of the king. This one was staged by Wolsey on Shrove Tuesday in March 1522, in honour of some visiting imperial ambassadors. Mary Boleyn, playing 'Kindness', and Anne, as 'Perseverance', were among eight fair maidens imprisoned in the triple-towered 'Château Vert' by the children of the Chapel Royal, disguised as 'Danger, Disdain, Jealousy, Malevolence' and the like. Despite a storm of dates, oranges and 'other fruits made for pleasure' being hurled vigorously in defence of the mock castle, the girls were chivalrously freed by a group of gallant knights, including Henry, performing the prophetic role of 'Ardent Desire'.[9]

Wolsey now became wary of Norfolk's machinations at court. While on a diplomatic mission to France during the summer of 1527, the Cardinal asked one of his allies, Sir William Fitzwilliam, now Treasurer of the Household, to discover who Henry was keeping company with during Wolsey's prolonged absence abroad. Worryingly, he was informed that the king 'usually supped in his privy chamber with ... the Dukes of Norfolk and Suffolk, the Marquis of Exeter and the Lord of Rochford'.[10] All were far from being his friends. Wolsey hurried back to London in September, writing to Henry from Compiègne that he was continuing his journey 'towards your highness with such diligence, as my old and [cracked] body may endure for there was never lover more desirous of the sight of his lady, than I am of your most noble and royal person'.[11]

Behind his sly sycophancy beat a heart of steel. On his return, he arranged for Norfolk's immediate departure to East Anglia to oversee a series of menial administrative tasks – among them the examination of grain production and North Sea trade – and ensured that the third duke's pleas to return to court were always refused. Even when Norfolk fell ill in early 1528, he was denied access to his London doctors.[12]

Probably based on what her sister told her of her lover's character and proclivities, Anne adamantly refused to become Henry's mistress and played a clever psychological game with the king's emotions. She quickly realised that the way to capturing Henry's heart was simple: the more unattainable she became, the more he wanted her. How much, in her feminine guile, she was counselled by her family, particularly her uncle Norfolk, must remain a matter of conjecture. He and Boleyn were greedy for the preferment, power and property that would be granted by a happy, contented sovereign to the Howard clan and its allies. However, both made a show of righteous disapproval over the relationship, if only for the sake of appearances.

The king's desire for Anne drove him to pen a series of love letters in French – a measure of how much he had fallen for her, as he made no secret of finding writing, in normal circumstances, 'somewhat tedious and painful'.

> My mistress and friend: I and my heart put ourselves in your hands, begging you to recommend us to your favour, and not to let absence lessen your affection to us ... Seeing I cannot be present in person with you, I send you the nearest thing to that ... my picture set in [a] bracelet ... wishing myself in their place, when it shall please you.[13]

When Anne adamantly refused to answer his notes, or come to court, Henry became quite distraught:

> I send you this letter begging you to give an account of the state you are in. That you may more frequently remember me, I send you by this bearer a buck killed late last night by my hand, hoping, when you eat of it, you will think of the hunter.[14]

Then desperate:

> I have been told you have quite given up the intention of coming

to court, either with your mother, or otherwise. If so, I cannot wonder sufficiently – for I have committed no offence against you and it is very little return for the great love I bear you to deny me the presence of the woman I esteem most of all in all the world.

If you love me as I hope you do, our separation should be painful to you.

I trust your absence is not wilful on your part, for if so, I can but lament my ill fortune and by degrees abate my great folly.[15]

Pathetic, lovesick Henry! In another billet-doux he complained that the short time since parting from her seemed like 'a whole fortnight', and that his letter was shorter than usual 'because of pain in my head'. He ended his cloying missive: 'Wishing myself specially an evening in my sweetheart's arms, whose pretty dubbys [breasts] I trust shortly to cusse [kiss].'[16]

In the late summer of 1527, the king, urged on by Norfolk and the Boleyns, decided that decisive action to end his unwanted marriage was now essential. Ignoring Wolsey's advice, he sent the experienced diplomat William Knight to Rome to achieve three very secret objectives. Firstly, he was to seek papal annulment of the marriage to Catherine and, secondly, absolution of the king's mortal sin (according to Leviticus) in living with her as husband and wife for eighteen years. The third objective was both controversial and damning: Henry was implicitly admitting his adultery and his desire to marry his mistress. In this there was an ironic obstacle. Knight had to acquire papal dispensation for the king to marry Anne Boleyn – 'a woman related to himself in the first degree of affinity', as the sister of his former bedmate in illicit wedlock, Mary. No wonder the contents of the letter that Knight was to deliver to Clement VII were kept confidential 'which no man doth know but they . . . will never disclose it to any man living for any craft the Cardinal or any other can find'.[17]

After much diplomatic activity, the desperately prevaricating Vatican could only limply propose a legatine commission to examine the validity of Henry's current marriage. It was all too frustrating.

Henry's chief minister was tasked to gather evidence to support the king's case for an annulment. Wolsey despatched officials to test the fading and feeble memory of the eighty-year-old Bishop of Winchester, Richard Fox, on whether Catherine and Arthur's marriage had ever been consummated – or if, indeed, Henry had been coerced by his father into wedding his brother's widow. Another group badgered more ageing veterans of Henry VII's court. Agnes, the Dowager Duchess of Norfolk, widow of the second duke, was closely questioned at Thetford Priory, and Mary, the wife of Henry Bourchier, second Earl of Essex, at Stansted, Essex. They both produced depositions about the intimate secrets of Catherine's first marital bed.[18]

The Cardinal promised to deliver an annulment on a golden plate to his master but Vatican officialdom continued to grind exceeding slow. Eventually, the legatine court met in the great hall of the Dominican monastery at Blackfriars in London, presided over by Wolsey and the gouty Cardinal Lorenzo Campeggio. Beginning on 31 May 1529, Henry's lawyers triumphantly produced reams of prurient evidence that Arthur had 'carnal conversation' with his blushing bride, but a shamed and humiliated Catherine, in a *coup de théâtre*, closely attended by four supportive bishops, eloquently appealed for her case to be heard by a higher jurisdiction.

Some weeks later, the case, still unresolved, was referred to Rome and the labyrinthine bureaucracy of the *Curia*. An incredulous Henry heard Campeggio's announcement of an adjournment on 23 July from the gallery above, and left the precincts for the nearby Bridewell Palace, his face black with anger. Suffolk, down in the hall, slammed his fist on a table and cried out: 'By the Mass! Now I see that the old saying is true! It was never merry in England while we had cardinals amongst us!'

Norfolk and Suffolk, both jealous of Wolsey's power and wealth, now sought ways and means to topple him. His failure to fulfil his pledge of success to Henry provided them with a weapon with which to cut him down. His departure from the corridors of power would also allow them to achieve another of their objectives: the reform of England's huge clerical estate.[19]

For a few weeks more, the Lord Chancellor continued to shuffle moodily through his piles of paper at the centre of Henry's government, as significantly, perhaps, the king enjoyed himself killing deer with Norfolk and Suffolk in the fresh air of Oxfordshire.

But Eustace Chapuys, the new Spanish ambassador in London,[20] perceptively reported at the end of August that the Cardinal's power was ebbing. And there were more straws of disaster for the minister blowing in the wind: foreign envoys were being denied access to him and increasing volumes of state business were now decided by Norfolk, Suffolk, and Rochford, Anne Boleyn's father.[21] At the end of August, Henry's new secretary Stephen Gardiner – formerly the Cardinal's own assistant – wrote to him, refusing to allow him to wait upon the king at Woodstock, and instructing him to put down on paper the issues he wanted to discuss.[22] Just over two weeks after this rebuff, Wolsey managed to arrive at court, which had moved on to Grafton in Northamptonshire, bringing with him his brother papal legate, the duplicitous Campeggio, who wished to offer up a formal farewell to the king on his departure for Rome. It was a poor pretext for a visit: when Campeggio limped in, he must have felt as welcome as the sweating sickness itself in Henry's presence chamber. The minister talked vigorously with his monarch for several hours before being peremptorily dismissed to spend the night at nearby Easton Neston, while his enemies busied themselves 'stirring the coals' of conspiracy at court.

The following day, the malice against Wolsey was palpable. Henry left Grafton with Anne Boleyn on a hunting trip she had hastily planned and, before riding off, roughly told the two cardinals there was no time for further talk.

He also instructed them to leave.[23]

Wolsey was a broken man, his face devoid of animation.[24] Back in London, he told the French ambassador Jean du Bellay that 'he did not desire ... power [and that] he was ready to give up everything, [down] to his shirt, and live in a hermitage, if the king would not keep him in his displeasure'.[25] But it was too late for any grand gestures, or uncharacteristic humility.

On 17 October, Henry, now ensconced at Windsor Castle, sent

an exultant Norfolk and Suffolk to Wolsey's opulent London home, York Place, to insist on his immediate surrender of the Great Seal of England, held by him as Lord Chancellor. The Cardinal refused, having demanded to see their warrant. They had come without it and, despite their angry blustering, they were forced to return empty-handed to Windsor to fetch the royal authorisation. This only postponed the denouement of the drama. The two dukes were back the next day with the correct paperwork and told Wolsey he had to retire to his manor at Esher, in Surrey. His goods, huge wealth and possessions were confiscated by the crown.

He finally handed over the Seal to the triumphant dukes at six o'clock in the evening in the gallery of his house[26] and later departed by boat down the Thames into exile, smarting from 'the sharp sword of the king's [displeasure] that had so penetrated his heart'. The French ambassador suspected a greater conspiracy: that 'these lords intend, after he is dead or ruined, to impeach the state of the church and take all their goods'.

In the days following Wolsey's downfall, there was inevitably much speculation about who would replace him as the king's minister. But, shrewdly, Henry was in no hurry to create another great panjandrum. Du Bellay reported on 22 October that Norfolk had been appointed President of the king's Council, with Suffolk deputising for him in his absence. 'It is not yet known who [will] have the [Great] Seal. I expect that priests will never have it again and that in Parliament, they will have terrible alarms,' he added.[27]

The successful conspirators in the Cardinal's disgrace then turned on each other. Norfolk, always jealous of another's status and influence, objected strongly to the proposed appointment of Suffolk as Lord Chancellor, and, three days later, after much indecorous haggling, a reluctant Sir Thomas More finally agreed to take on this unwanted, onerous and perilous duty. The Great Seal was delivered to him by the king in his chamber at Greenwich Palace and the next day, 26 October, he took the oath of fidelity in Westminster Hall. Norfolk and Suffolk escorted him to his seat in the Court of Chancery and by 'special command' of the king, Norfolk declared:

openly, in the presence of them all, how much all England was beholden to Sir Thomas More for all his good service and how worthy he was to have the highest rank in the realm and how dearly his Grace loved and trusted him.

He added that, for all this, he personally had 'great cause to rejoice'.[28]

Small wonder that Norfolk was happy. His comments had a double meaning. His presence there, and his public anointment of the new Lord Chancellor, were a clear signal that the old aristocracy had won back their power and clout in England. Indeed, in the days to come, Norfolk worked diligently to ensure that happened, building a caucus of 'old money' nobles around him to exercise authority on behalf of the crown. Even responsibility for the custody and education of the king's bastard, Henry Fitzroy, was transferred from Wolsey to Norfolk.

The duke, in his new role, received Chapuys with 'great distinction', and laughingly told him: 'How glad the Emperor [Charles V] will be to hear of the fall of the Cardinal and his loss of office!' The ambassador reported Norfolk 'highly pleased' with himself as he politely repeated his family's long-standing goodwill towards the Spanish crown:

No one lamented the great disagreements [with Spain] more than himself [but] that all the evil and misunderstanding ought to be attributed to those who formerly directed the king's counsels, acting by their own will and authority, with which the king himself was often dissatisfied.[29]

Henry, however, still had not got his annulment nor Anne Boleyn's hand in marriage – and she was becoming impatient. She suddenly turned on Norfolk, complaining that she was 'wasting her time and youth to no purpose' and he frequently suffered the unpleasant effects of the full force of his niece's fractious, petulant temper. Later, walking and talking with More in the new Lord Chancellor's Thames-side garden at Chelsea, Norfolk warned him, in his 'rough but friendly manner', of the great personal dangers posed by Henry's love for Anne Boleyn:

By the Mass, Master More, it is perilous striving with princes. And therefore, I would wish you somewhat to incline to the king's pleasure. For, by God's body, Master More, *indignato principis mors est* – 'the anger of the prince means death'.

More was totally unmoved by the advice. He told Norfolk:

Is that all my lord? Then in good faith, the difference between your grace and me is but this: that I shall die today and you tomorrow.[30]

These simple words offended the prickly duke and he stalked off, angry that his worldly-wise counsel had been so casually ignored. But More felt confident and relaxed: after all, did he not have Henry's personal pledge over the divorce: that he would 'never, with that matter, molest his [More's] conscience'?

Among the many casualties of Wolsey's downfall was Thomas Cromwell, his ambitious legal adviser. After talking with his stricken master at Esher, he rode hastily to London, to seek a seat in the new House of Commons, due to be sworn in two days later. In times of trouble, any politician calls in favours owed to him and he sent his servant Ralph Sadler to talk to Sir John Gage, Vice-Chamberlain of the Household, and an ally of Norfolk's. After much discussion, the duke graciously let it be known that he had spoken with the king 'and that his highness was very well contented that [Cromwell] should become a burgess [in Parliament and] should order [himself] according to such instructions as the Duke of Norfolk shall give you from the king'. Cromwell thus became Member of Parliament for Taunton.[31]

So Cromwell rescued his career from the ruin of Wolsey's downfall and lived to fight another day – and all at Norfolk's instigation. In the decade that followed, the duke would many times rue that cold night when he unwittingly rescued from the gutter of Tudor political life the man who was to become another powerful enemy.

Norfolk was, meanwhile, busy preparing the *coup de grâce* against his fallen enemy; a Bill of Attainder, with forty-six clauses, was down for debate as the first item of business at the opening session of Parliament. For him, settling old scores was always a joy. The Bill, nicknamed the Book of Articles because of its huge bulk, employed virulent language against Wolsey, including the outlandish allegation that he had attempted to infect the king with syphilis.[32] It was passed by the Lords on 1 December and immediately sent down to the Commons for their approval. Here, Norfolk had overreached himself. The Attainder was attacked over its intemperate wording – Cromwell himself argued against it 'discreetly ... with such witty persuasions and deep reasons'[33] – and it was quickly dropped, probably by royal command, before Parliament was prorogued on 17 December. Though the duke failed finally to destroy the Cardinal, at least he had thoroughly blackened his name.

So the problem of Wolsey's fate remained undecided. Henry clearly still harboured some sympathy for the broken old man and sent four of his physicians to nurse him through an acute attack of dropsy.[34] Norfolk thoroughly mistrusted his sovereign's compassion for his fallen minister and was painfully aware that, amid the shifting, uncertain loyalties of Henry's court, if the Cardinal ever managed to claw his way back to power he, Norfolk, would be the first to end up in the Tower. He therefore devised a plan to neutralise the threat still posed by Wolsey. Simply put, it was 'out of sight, out of mind', and after Wolsey's earlier banishments of Norfolk it had the sweet taste of apposite revenge. The prelate should now return to his benefice, ideally as far away as possible from London and the court, and live out his days quietly as a pious churchman. Wolsey had collected a number of clerical hats – Archbishop of York, and Bishop of Winchester, for example – and Norfolk believed that York, 175 miles (282 km.) north of the capital, would fit the bill admirably.

Wolsey grasped that proximity to the king might still bring reinstatement and salvation. When Cromwell informed him of the plan, he replied cheerfully: 'Well then Thomas, we will go to Winchester' – signalling his intention to take up residence at his rich bishopric in Hampshire, not far from London. He failed to realise he was speaking to a man who temporarily owed much to Norfolk and, anyway, was only interested in advancing his own fortunes. Cromwell hastened to the duke to pass on Wolsey's decision.

Norfolk often presented a mask of affability to the outside world. He was short and wiry, with a hooked, aquiline nose, inherited from his father, dominating his fleshy features. Beneath his cordial exterior and those hooded eyes lurked a violent temper, a cold brutality and a callous, single-minded determination. Now his friendly façade was swiftly stripped away and he answered Cromwell candidly:

> I think that the Cardinal ... makes no haste to go northward. Tell him, if he go not away shortly but shall tarry, I shall tear him with my teeth.
>
> I would advise him to prepare himself as quickly as he can, or else he shall be sent forward.[35]

Wolsey duly left for the north on 5 April 1530, and entered, for the first time, the Church province he had ruled as an absentee metropolitan since August 1514. He arrived at his decayed palace at Southwell, Nottinghamshire, on the 28th, whingeing about being 'wrapped in misery and need on every side' before moving on to Cawood Castle, twelve miles (19 km.) from York,[36] at the end of September. There he regained his refined taste for the trappings and splendours of ecclesiastical life and despatched a letter to Henry, seeking the rich 'mitre and pall[37] which he had formerly used ... in celebrating the divine office'. When he read the note, the king was astonished at Wolsey's 'brazen insolence' adding: 'Is there still arrogance in this fellow, who is so obviously ruined?'[38]

Cromwell tempered the king's reaction when he told his former master that Henry was 'very sorry that you are in such necessity ... The Duke of Norfolk promises you his best aid, but he wills you for the present to be content and not much to molest the king (concerning payment of your debts) for, as he supposes, the time is not right for it.' These were saccharic words and Cromwell knew it full well.[39]

Wolsey wrote to Norfolk on 30 October, in a disingenuous attempt to reassure his brooding enemy that he did not wish to be restored as Lord Chancellor and would be happy to spend the rest of his life in York. He sent Thomas Arundell, a gentleman of his privy chamber, to deliver the letter to the duke, then staying at Hampton Court. After reading it, Norfolk walked in the park, mulling over its empty promises, and then brusquely told the messenger that 'no man should make him believe that'. Arundell reported: 'The more I spoke to the contrary, the more out of frame I found him.'

The duke and his niece were yet more determined to tear down the Cardinal once and for all and Norfolk posted agents to watch the movements of the household at Cawood and to intercept the communications, in cipher, of his Venetian physician, Dr Augustine de Augustinis. One of the reasons for his angry rejection of Wolsey's blandishments was his knowledge of three secret messages sent by the Cardinal 'whereby it appears that [he] desires as much authority as ever [he] did'.[40] Furthermore, he disclosed to Chapuys that Wolsey had attempted, by different agents, to undermine Norfolk's position at court and they had told him all about it.[41]

Wolsey was arrested for treason as he sat down to dinner at Cawood on Friday 4 November. Augustine was also detained, tied backwards to a horse like all such felons, and led to London. After spending an uncomfortable night in the Tower of London to concentrate his mind, Augustine was quietly removed to Norfolk's town house in Broken Wharf, on the south side of Upper Thames Street,[42] and there gently interrogated, while being 'treated like a prince'. The Italian sang like a canary and his disclosures delighted his inquisitors. Wolsey, he chirruped, had asked Pope Clement to excommunicate the king and shut all the parish churches in the realm, unless Anne Boleyn was exiled from court and Catherine reinstated as queen. Moreover, he said, the Cardinal prayed that such an interdict would spawn a widespread popular uprising, when he could snatch back the levers of power in England.[43]

After hearing that Augustine had fallen into Norfolk's hands, Chapuys, the Spanish envoy, was worried that his own dealings in the murky business could be compromised by the doctor's disclosures. As he reported the latest developments, he tried to reassure himself:

I think the physician must have declared he had no intelligence with me. Otherwise the duke, who is a bad dissembler, would have said something about it. ... Were the physician to say all that has passed between us, he could not do anything but impugn me.[44]

Augustine provided the final proof of Wolsey's treason, or so Norfolk claimed. The Cardinal, being brought back to London by easy stages because of his poor health, died on 29 November 1530 at the Augustinian abbey of St Mary's, in Leicester, probably from dysentery, although there were some who believed 'he killed himself with purgatives'.[45] He was aged about sixty.

Norfolk delightedly claimed Wolsey's fleshy scalp as his own trophy. Anne's brother, George, specially commissioned a hastily written masque, charmingly entitled *On the Cardinal's Going into Hell*, that was performed at Greenwich Palace, to the gratification and merriment of the Howard and Boleyn clan.

Twelve days after Wolsey's death, his physician signed a recognisance pledging payment of £100 to the king to 'keep secret from any man all such matter as is mentioned in a book written with his own hand, concerning the late Cardinal of York and presented by him to my lord of Norfolk, President of the Council ...'.[46]

Although the threat posed by Wolsey had been extinguished, the secrets of his downfall had to be protected.

In June 1530, a huge and much redrafted document, signed with the seals of two archbishops, four bishops, twenty-five abbots, two dukes and forty other peers, appealed to the Pope to produce a speedy decision on the king's marriage to Queen Catherine. It was all to no avail: Rome had no real understanding of the serious ramifications of the issue, nor the need for its urgent resolution.

Catherine was in despair. 'God knows what I suffer from these people; enough to kill ten men, much more a shattered woman who has done no harm,' she wrote miserably to her nephew, Charles V, in mid-October 1531.

For the love of God, procure a final sentence from his Holiness as soon as possible.

The utmost diligence is required.

May God forgive him [the Pope] for the many delays which
he has granted and which alone are the cause of my extremity!
I am the king's lawful wife and while I live, I will say no
other.

The Pope's tardiness makes many on my side waver and those
who would say the truth, dare not.[47]

Norfolk, also weary of the whole business, lugubriously confided
to Chapuys that he would be prepared to sacrifice the greater part
of his wealth, if God was 'pleased to take to himself' both Catherine
and Anne 'for the king would never enjoy peace of mind till he
had made another marriage, for the relief of his conscience and the
tranquillity of the realm, which could only be secured' by a lawful
male heir to the throne.[48]

Wishing both ladies dead through some kind of divine thun-
derbolt was hardly a practical or plausible solution. A papal nuncio
visiting England, anxious to discover why the Pope was so unpopular, was amazed and intimidated by Norfolk and Suffolk's curt
declaration that they cared nothing for popes 'in England − not
even if St Peter came to life again. The king was [now] emperor
and pope in his own dominions.'[49]

Henry now moved to sever, irrevocably, his links with Rome
and to take the first steps towards independence of the Church
in England, through a series of legal measures steered through
Parliament by Cromwell.[50] An able champion of the annulment
arrived in the shape of Thomas Cranmer, who, although only
an archdeacon, was nominated as Archbishop of Canterbury in
succession to William Warham who had died in August 1532. His
loyalties to the cause of the 'Great Matter' were unimpeachable:
he had been private chaplain to Anne Boleyn's father, now elevated
to the Earldom of Wiltshire and Ormonde.

Henry's love for Anne remained wholly undiminished and he
was determined to demonstrate it. On 1 September 1532, she
enjoyed her first public mark of favour when she was raised to the
peerage in her own right as Marchioness of Pembroke, with a
generous annuity of £1,000 a year. He then took her on to a
glittering meeting with Francis I of France in Boulogne and Calais,

accompanied by a 2,000-strong English entourage, when she proudly wore a dazzling display of jewellery confiscated from Catherine of Aragon.

It was then, or shortly afterwards, that she allowed Henry into her bed for the first time.

About the middle of January 1533, Anne found that she was pregnant and a proud and expectant Henry swiftly, secretly and bigamously married her on the 25th in a chamber above the Holbein Gate in his new Palace of Westminster. Norfolk was not present at the ceremony.

Cranmer was a fervent supporter of the royal divorce being decided under English jurisdiction and now, naively, if not appeasively, Clement VII in Rome approved Henry's choice of him as Primate of England. The Pope issued the necessary nine bulls on 21–22 February, allowing Cranmer's consecration as Archbishop of Canterbury to take place on 30 March at St Stephen's Chapel, Westminster. So that there could be no doubt as to the reality of religious authority in England, Henry informed Cranmer that the primacy and its authority existed 'only by the sufferances of us and our progenitors' and 'you are, under us, by God's calling and ours, the most principal minister of our spiritual jurisdiction within this our realm'.[51]

The archbishop could waste little time, as Anne's condition was becoming every day more obvious and royal scandal was looming. An ecclesiastical court was established at Dunstable, Bedfordshire, close to where Queen Catherine had been exiled, to dissolve her marriage with Henry. It came as no surprise when she refused to appear before the tribunal, presided over by Cranmer. At ten o'clock on the morning of 23 May 1533, the Primate declared the matrimony 'to be against the laws of God' and 'therefore divorced the king's highness from the noble lady Catherine'.[52] Henry was free to marry again under the law, although in truth, of course, he had already jumped the gun.

Anne was crowned by Cranmer in Westminster Abbey on Whit Sunday, 1 June 1533, in a spectacular ceremony that was estimated to have cost Henry a staggering 100,000 gold ducats out of his own purse – plus another 200,000 sycophantically supplied by the

City of London,[53] equating to £55 million at current values.[54] This was a high price for love.

Norfolk had petitioned for the hereditary office of Earl Marshal to be returned to him six weeks before. It had been held by the second duke, but granted to the royal favourite Suffolk in 1524, which had been a source of rancour ever since.[55] The king belatedly agreed on 28 May, but, ironically, Norfolk was forced to hand over the Earl Marshal's responsibility for Anne's coronation to his half-brother William, as he was going to France to represent Henry at a meeting between Francis I and Pope Clement VII. The duke arrived in Lyons to accompany the French king to Nice for the discussions, but unexpected news arrived from Rome that so shocked him that he nearly fainted when he heard it.

On 11 July, Clement, in a secret consistory court hearing, had condemned both Henry's separation from Catherine and his marriage with Anne. The Pope set a deadline of September for Henry to take back his former wife, under pain of excommunication.[56] Norfolk despatched his nephew George Boleyn, now Viscount Rochford, to ride pell-mell to England with the news and to seek further instructions. As a result, Norfolk was summoned urgently back to court, and he rode almost five hundred miles in just eight days,[57] a remarkable achievement for a sixty-year-old man.

But all the duke's agitation and distress was a waste of energy. In the event, the sentence of excommunication was postponed for two more months and never promulgated.

The king easily shrugged off the papal condemnation, buoyed up, as he was, by the prospect that Anne would preserve the Tudor dynasty by presenting him with a lawful male successor. Physicians and astrologers had been consulted and their reassuring predictions gave him every hope that his problem would at last be resolved.

Anne was safely delivered of a fair daughter between three and four o'clock in the afternoon of Sunday 7 September 1533 in her opulently furnished room at Greenwich Palace. Norfolk hurried to London for the birth and the smile must have been quickly wiped off his face when he was told the news.

Henry presented a brave face to destiny's hard dealing, although the sex of the child was clearly a stunning shock. It was, moreover, hailed triumphantly as a sign of divine displeasure on the marriage by the many supporters of the discarded queen.[58] The baby was christened Elizabeth by Cranmer in the Church of the Friars Observant, just outside Greenwich Palace, the following Wednesday.

The Howards and Boleyns put on a plucky show. The old Dowager Duchess of Norfolk, wearing a mantle of purple velvet, with a train trimmed with ermine, was one of Elizabeth's two godmothers[59] who carried the infant to the font, its swaddling clothes set with pearls and gems. They walked beneath a canopy, borne by Anne's brother, George, Norfolk's half-brothers, William and Thomas, and Lord Hussey. Norfolk, carrying his white wand of office as Earl Marshal, was at his step-grandmother's right-hand side.[60] As was then the custom, neither parent attended the christening.

Chapuys, the Spanish ambassador, was keen to help the discarded Catherine and her daughter Mary, whom Henry planned to declare illegitimate. In late February 1534, he valiantly sought permission to address Parliament on their plight, even though he knew it was a forlorn hope. Henry prevaricated by asking the envoy to meet Norfolk and Cromwell to discuss his planned statement. When he arrived at Norfolk's town house, he found that Cromwell was absent due to a 'slight indisposition which kept him indoors'. No doubt, a diplomatic illness. After hearing Chapuys's arguments, Norfolk shrugged off the ambassador's comments

> by referring me to the people who, he said, understood affairs of that sort better than he. [Then] he asked me point blank what sort of statements I proposed making in Parliament. My answer was that, beyond the true and simple narrative of what had passed in the matter of the divorce, I would utter nothing that was not honest and reasonable ...

Inevitably, Norfolk told him his chances of success were minimal and assured him that he always favoured his master, the Emperor Charles V, rather than the French. The following Tuesday, Chapuys went to court but was intercepted, before he could see the king, by a breathless Norfolk, fresh from attending Henry. 'For God's sake, Monsieur,' he panted,

> I beg and entreat you on this day to use all your discretion and prudence and so moderate your language that you may not fall into trouble or inconvenience.
>
> You are about to enter matters so odious and unpleasing that not all the sugar or sauces in the world would render them palatable.
>
> That is why I again pray and entreat you, for God's sake, to be careful and guarded in your speech . . .

The duke repeated this last sentence, parrot-like, 'at least six times'. Plainly, he had just suffered the sharp edge of the king's tongue and he dropped a broad hint to the ambassador that the issue of Catherine could only be satisfactorily settled by her death. Norfolk scurried off, after being summoned back to the royal presence, and after half an hour Chapuys was allowed to see the king.

Henry was polite but uncompromising. The ambassador could not be ignorant of the fact that he was legitimately married to Anne Boleyn and that his former marriage had been judicially annulled. His first wife, still living, could not be called 'Queen' – or hold property allotted to her by her first marriage.[61] Nor could Princess Mary be called his legitimate daughter – and, even if she was, 'her disobedience to his commands would have been sufficient reason for disinheriting her'. Mary 'was in good health, well-lodged and nobody,' said Henry firmly, 'had any right to interfere in his domestic arrangements, for he could dispose of his daughter as he pleased'.

Chapuys realised 'there was no means of obtaining what I had come for' and, fearing that persistence might spark one of the king's notoriously violent tantrums, bowed humbly and backed out of the chamber.[62]

Queen Anne remained deeply unpopular among her subjects, just as Catherine achieved almost saint-like status. The Lancashire parson James Harrison declared: 'I will [have] none for queen but Queen Catherine! Who the devil made Nan Boleyn, that whore, queen?'[63] The Colchester monk Dan John Frances affirmed in January 1534 that when Henry had met Francis I in Boulogne, 'the Queen's grace followed his arse as the dog follows his master's arse'.[64] It was high time to nip such traitorous sentiments in the bud. Cromwell's Act of Succession, rapidly enacted in March 1534,[65] demanded personal commitment to the breach with Rome, from anyone in the realm aged fourteen and above. An oath drawn up by Norfolk and Suffolk sought both a declaration of sacred belief that the marriage between Henry and Anne was lawful and total allegiance to Princess Elizabeth and any other children of the union, as rightful successors to the throne of England.

It was now treason for anyone to oppose the succession and misprision[66] to speak against it.

It was also now treason, under Cromwell's new Treasons Act, to wish malicious harm to the king and queen or their heirs, to deprive them of their dignity or title, or claim that 'the king our sovereign lord is a heretic, schismatic, tyrant, infidel or usurper'.[67]

On 13 April 1534, senior members of the clergy, including John Fisher, Bishop of Rochester, who had opposed the annulment, were summoned to Cranmer's palace at Lambeth, across from Westminster on the south bank of the Thames, to take the Oath of Succession. Sir Thomas More, who had resigned as Lord Chancellor on 16 May 1532 over the breach with Rome, was also ordered to attend. He was happy, he declared, to swear the oath, but he refused to sign anything that contained the preamble to the Act, which laid out Henry's supremacy of the Church.

After months of imprisonment, Fisher, aged and infirm, was despatched to the executioner's block on 22 June 1535, his journey to the scaffold hastened by an inopportune decision by the new Pope Paul III to create him a cardinal. Then it became Sir Thomas More's turn to face Henry's harsh justice: the king's promises to him of immunity over the issue of the marriage proved utterly worthless.

Condemned to perpetual imprisonment in the Tower for misprision, More was too popular a figure to be allowed to avoid the oath. As Cromwell pointedly reminded him: 'You are not discharged of your obedience and allegiance to the king.' He replied that his 'poor body was at the king's pleasure and he wished that his death would do him good'.[68]

He duly came up for trial at Westminster Hall on 1 July and was condemned after perjured evidence against him by one of Cromwell's henchmen, the Solicitor-General Sir Richard Riche. The jury took just fifteen minutes to find him guilty as charged. More then dropped all pretence of guarding his tongue, and attacked the king's usurpation of supremacy. 'For the seven years I have studied the matter, I have not read any approved order of the Church that a temporal lord could, or ought, to be head of the spirituality.'

Sir Thomas Audley, the Lord Chancellor, was amazed: 'What! You wish to be considered wiser, or of better conscience, than all the bishops and nobles of this realm?' he demanded.

Norfolk, one of his judges, angrily snapped out that his old friend's malice was now patently clear. More retorted:

Noble sir, not any malice or obstinacy causes me to say this but the just necessity of the cause constrains me for the discharge of my conscience and satisfaction of my soul. I know well that the reason why you have condemned me is because I have never been willing to consent to the king's second marriage. But I hope in the divine goodness and mercy that as St Paul and St Stephen (which he persecuted) are now friends in Paradise, so we, though differing in this world, shall be united in perfect harmony in the other.

I pray God to protect the king and give him good counsel.[69]

More was executed with one blow of the axe at Tower Hill at around nine o'clock on the morning of 6 July 1535.

Meanwhile, despite all the blood shed for the sake of the marriage, all was not well with Henry and his new queen, who no longer lived up to her motto 'The Most Happy'.

In January 1535, Chapuys reported court gossip about Anne's peevish temper. Henry Percy, sixth Earl of Northumberland, her former love, talked freely of her arrogance and malice, saying that lately she had used 'such shameful words to the Duke of Norfolk as one would not address to a dog, so that he was compelled to quit the royal chamber. In his indignation . . . he uttered reproaches against [her] of which the least was to call her *la grande putain* [the great whore].'⁷⁰ Norfolk sulkily departed for the peace of Kenninghall, complaining to Chapuys that he was no longer held in any kind of esteem at court. The queen also lashed out at her former ally Cromwell and threatened to have him beheaded. By year end, when her pet dog Purkoy died after a fall, 'nobody dared tell her grace of it'.⁷¹

She even turned against her elder sister. In 1534, Mary had secretly married her second husband, Sir William Stafford,⁷² a soldier serving in the Calais garrison, but her obvious pregnancy revealed the relationship. Anne imperiously dismissed her from court and she was never again to be received there.

The origin of all this regal sound and fury was Anne's mounting worries over Catherine and Princess Mary remaining alive and the latent threat they posed her – coupled with her own persistent failure to produce a male heir. Chapuys

> feared that the king is getting so inured to cruelty [that] he will use it towards the Queen [Catherine] and the Princess at least in secret. To which, the concubine [Anne] will urge him with all her power, who has lately blamed the . . . king, saying it was a shame to him and all the realm they were not punished as traitresses, according to the statutes.
>
> The . . . concubine is now more haughty than ever and ventures to tell the king that he is more bound to her than man can be to woman, for she extricated him from a state of sin.⁷³

Dr Pedro Ortiz, the imperial ambassador in Rome, heard of Anne's hatred for her nineteen-year-old stepdaughter Princess Mary: 'She is my death and I am hers, so I will take care that she will not laugh at me after my death,'⁷⁴ he reported her as saying.

Further strains between Henry and Anne over her lack of a healthy son followed her miscarriage in July 1534. She was desperate to become pregnant again and was unwise enough to speak slightingly of her husband's lacklustre performance in bed, where, she whispered, he had shown neither skill nor virility. The queen also had 'suborned a person to say that he had [received] a revelation from God that she could not conceive while the two ladies [Catherine and Mary] were alive'.[75]

Henry's eye was also roving. Anne wrathfully demanded the dismissal of the modest, charming and fragile twenty-five-year-old Jane Seymour from court, and had behaved so violently that the king walked out on his queen, 'complaining of her importunacy and vexatiousness'.[76]

By the end of 1535, she may have lost her pet dog but things suddenly looked brighter. Anne was pregnant again, and, a few weeks later, on 7 January 1536, Catherine died, probably of cancer of the heart, at Kimbolton Castle, her lonely home in Huntingdonshire.[77]

News of the death delighted the queen. Showing 'great joy', Anne gave the messenger a handsome present. Her father, the Earl of Wiltshire, dryly commented that it was a pity Princess Mary 'did not keep company with her [mother]' and Henry dressed in celebratory yellow 'from top to toe, except for the white feather he had in his bonnet'.[78] But Chapuys whispered that Anne, in the privacy of her chamber later, 'cried and lamented, fearing she herself might be brought to the same end'.

Her fears were entirely justified – and not long in being fulfilled.

A few weeks later, on 26 January, Henry met with a terrible accident in the royal tilting yard at Greenwich Palace. 'The king, mounted on a great horse to run at the lists, both fell so heavily that everyone thought it a miracle he was not killed, but he sustained no injury,' reported an eyewitness.[79] In reality, the accident was far more serious: the heavy charger rolled over on to Henry, crushing him, and afterwards, he lay 'for two hours without speech' probably because of severe concussion.

Five days later, Anne miscarried a heavy male foetus, aged about three and a half months, after Norfolk had insensitively blurted out news of Henry's accident. The shock, she claimed, caused the loss of her son.[80]

The king had little sympathy for her plight. He now wanted rid of this fractious, haughty and overbearing tartar who had failed in her promise to give him his heirs. Chapuys happily seized on second-hand court gossip that Henry had apparently told a courtier in great secrecy and as a confession that he had been seduced and forced into this second marriage by means of sortileges [sorcery or witchcraft] and charms and that owing to that, he would hold it as nullified.

God, he said, had well shown his displeasure at it by denying him male children.

He therefore considered he could take a third wife which, he said, he wished much to do.[81]

Thomas Cromwell was just the man to arrange it for him and together with Norfolk, led a commission established to find fault in both the queen's character and behaviour.

Anne was arrested at Greenwich on 2 May and taken to the Tower of London, accused of adultery with five of Henry's courtiers, as well as plotting Henry's death. One was her brother, George, Viscount Rochford, charged with committing incest with the queen. Norfolk led her interrogation and, after all the recent slights he had suffered at her hands, clearly enjoyed the experience. During the questioning, he regretfully shook his head three or four times, pursed his fleshy lips and tut-tutted in mock despair as he considered her chances of survival.[82]

Anne was tried in the king's hall of the White Tower, within the fortress, on 15 May. Two thousand prurient spectators crowded in to hear the salacious details of her love life. Cromwell's key witness was Lady Jane Rochford, wife of the queen's brother, who discreetly wrote down on a slip of paper Anne's unwise words about Henry's inadequate performance between the sheets: 'Que le Roy n'estait habile en cas de soi copuler avec femme, et qu'il n'avait ni vertu ni puissance' – 'The King was not skilful when copulating with a woman and he had not virtue or power.' The damning paper was silently passed among the twenty-six peers sitting in judgement and each decided that if the queen could not have a child by the king, she would have looked elsewhere to father her child and pass it off as heir to the throne. Norfolk, with crocodile tears streaming down his face, sentenced his niece to death:

Because you have offended our sovereign, the king's grace, in committing treason against his person and here attainted of the same, the law of the realm is this: that you shall be burnt here within the Tower of London on the Green, else to have your head smitten off, as the king's pleasure shall be further known.[83]

It was all very neat and tidy. Two days later, the five courtiers and Rochford were executed and Cranmer declared that Princess Elizabeth was illegitimate. Anne's turn came on 19 May. Henry had decided she should be beheaded in the French manner, and a French executioner was brought over from St Omer, in the Pale of Calais, to perform the deed, with a two-handed Flemish sword.

He earned his fee of £24 well. One stroke swept her head off as she knelt on the scaffold, watched by Norfolk, the king's illegitimate son, Richmond, and a crowd of 1,000 people.

On 20 May, Jane Seymour was brought to Westminster and ten days later she became Henry's third wife in another secret ceremony, this time in the Queen's Closet in the palace there.

After Cromwell's cleverly engineered fall of Anne Boleyn, Norfolk's influence waned as a new breed of competent and ambitious courtiers, many of them evangelicals, made their mark at court. He tried hard to redress the balance by adopting the traditional tactic of the Howards – marriage. He had earlier sought to arrange one between Princess Mary and his heir, Henry Howard, Earl of Surrey, at the end of 1529. But the king was having none of it, and in April 1532 Norfolk agreed to a union for his son with the de Veres, the Earls of Oxford. Frances, the daughter of the fifteenth earl, married Surrey formally in the spring of the following year, although they did not live together until 1535 because of their tender age. At Anne Boleyn's urging, Norfolk had also achieved his aim of marrying close to the Tudor line on 26 November 1533, when his daughter Mary wed Henry Fitzroy, Duke of Richmond, the king's illegitimate son, now aged fourteen. They were also too young to cohabit, and the marriage was never consummated.[84]

His children, Henry and Mary, were later to threaten everything Norfolk strived for – and, indeed, his life.

4

A WOMAN SCORNED

———◆———

I know ... my husband's crafty ways of old. He has made me
many times promises ... never [fulfilled]

**Elizabeth Howard, Duchess of Norfolk,
to Thomas Cromwell, Lord Privy Seal[1]**

The perils of matrimony, both royal and personal, must often have
loomed large in the mind of the third Duke of Norfolk during the
late 1520s and into the next decade. His three surviving children
by his wife Elizabeth had been born despite the marriage having
irretrievably broken down soon after the wedding, because of her
anger at this loveless match being forced upon her by political and
dynastic expediency. She claimed, for example, that Norfolk had
displayed 'great cruelty' to her at the time of the birth of their
second child, Mary, in 1519.[2] Throughout her life, the shrewish
Elizabeth declared to all that would listen: 'I was born in an
unhappy hour to be matched with such an ungracious husband.'
Norfolk, in return, complained bitterly of her 'false and abominable
lies' and craftily questioned her sanity.

The couple drank deeply from their brimming cups of hatred
for each other and their frequently noisy and heated rows in public
embarrassed even the red-blooded courtiers strutting around them.

In May 1520, the Howards and their young family had been sent
to Dublin after he had been appointed Lord Lieutenant, or viceroy,
of Ireland. Within weeks, the plague was claiming hundreds and
the duke reported to Wolsey that 'the bodies lie like swine unburied'
and appealed for permission to send his family to safety:

Three of my household folks have sickened in my house and
died in the town within seven days past ... I am fain to keep my

wife and children here still for I know no place in this country where to send them in clean air. Most humbly, I beseech your grace to give me leave to send my wife and children into Wales or Lancashire to remain near the seaside until . . . it shall please God to cease this death here.

And I shall take such fortune as God will send, for whilst I live, fear of death, nor other thing, shall cause me to forbear to serve my master, where it shall be his pleasure to command me.[3]

This heartfelt plea to be recalled to London – together with frequent subsequent appeals – was ignored. For four months in the summer of 1521 Surrey had been afflicted by a bad dose of dysentery and he asked Henry to come home on 16 September:

I have be[en], am, and ever shall be, ready to serve your grace in whatever place so ever your pleasure shall be to command me. Beseeching your most noble grace so to look on me, your poor servant, that once, or I die, I do your highness' service in such business in your own presence.[4]

The Howards were eventually allowed home later that year. Henry took Surrey at his word; he then served in northern France and on the Scottish borders,[5] creating absences from home drearily familiar to any army wife. During the rare times they were together and not in the north, they lived in their houses at Stoke-by-Nayland in Suffolk, and Hunsdon in Hertfordshire, or at the Howards' main London base in Lambeth. Documents preserved in the Arundel Castle archives[6] show the lavish entertaining they laid on for visitors between 1513 and 1524 at their country manors. Dinner was eaten at ten in the morning and supper at five in the afternoon. The food provided at their table cost anything up to £6 a week, and consisted of simple, sound country produce: beer and bread; meat, fish and fowls. Their visitors not only included the many great and good, but, as befits a pious household, 'priests of London and Colchester', as well as monks and hermits, and also glovers, tailors, bakers and brewers – all tradesmen seeking to sell their wares.

No doubt a heroic front of normality was presented to their noble visitors at their houses for the sake of propriety, but below the surface the bad blood between husband and wife was already building a veritable volcano of hate.

On 20 February 1516 both attended the christening of Princess Mary in the chapel at Greenwich, with their little son Henry Howard bearing the ceremonial taper during the service.

In the sixteenth century wives were, by law, little more than chattels of their husbands who were free physically to punish them. They controlled their wives' finances, their freedom of movement and their contact with the world outside the marriage. The legal doctrine of *coverture* enforced women's subordination to their husband's every whim and prevented them, in their own right, from signing contracts, writing wills or initiating or defending a case in law. Wives also were denied reciprocal rights in their spouse's property.[7] The evangelical fire and brimstone preacher Hugh Latimer, Bishop of Worcester from 1535, had a black and white view of the state of marriage, and taught wives from his pulpit that it was 'part of your penance to be subjects unto your husband. You are underlings, underlings, and must be obedient.'[8] Norfolk and his fellow nobles doubtless shared this rather fundamentalist view, so his wife's vocal antagonism at her treatment at the hands of the duke scandalised the court and publicly shamed him.

Behind the king's own fickle form in the marriage stakes, the Norfolks were probably the most infamous married couple in mid-sixteenth-century England.

By 1527, their relationship was completely dead, mainly because Norfolk had sought love and comfort elsewhere in the willing arms of the voluptuous Bessie, sister to his secretary and chief steward, John Holland – the girl whom Elizabeth contemptuously dismissed as 'a churl's daughter ... of no gentle blood' and for eight years 'the washer-woman of her nursery'.[9] It was a bitter, obnoxious pill for her – and one she would not swallow meekly. She had never wanted to marry her husband and now he had deserted her for another woman; worse still, a woman of low birth. She became incandescent with rage, particularly when the mistress became a lady-in-waiting to another concubine – Anne Boleyn.

Her father's execution for treason isolated Elizabeth from help or sympathy from the crown, or from relatives with any influence or standing at court.[10]

Norfolk, never an individual noted for his sensitivity and tolerance, acted decisively to resolve his marital crisis – simply by throwing his irate wife out of his house.

He signed a legal document which blandly stated that the duchess, 'at the instance and device of the said duke, has departed with all such right and title ... interest and possession which she ... had in the name'.[11] The indenture, dated 20 June 1529, between the 'right high and mighty prince Thomas, Duke of Norfolk' and Henry Percy, sixth Earl of Northumberland, and Elizabeth's brother Henry, Lord Stafford, appointed them overseers of various properties, including the manor of Kelsale, near Saxmundham in Suffolk, and enabled her to recover her marriage jointure.

This unsubtle bribery may have been an unsuccessful attempt at ousting an unwanted termagant from his life; it was not until five turbulent years had elapsed that she was finally discarded. Norfolk must have looked on Henry's tumultuous attempts to achieve an annulment of his unwanted marriage with Catherine of Aragon with grave misgivings and considerable sympathy. The duke knew his wife only too well – and his forebodings were entirely justified.

Elizabeth, a lady blessed with great passion, pride and strong, unbending opinions, was not going to go quietly, even though two of her surviving children took their father's side in the bitter marital dispute that followed her shameful expulsion from her home. Social ostracism mattered little to her, because she shared her father's and husband's disparagement of the evangelical upstarts now increasingly acquiring royal office – and she cared not one jot for their harsh opinions of her.

Like some other women of the old noble houses, she had not behaved in a politically correct manner at the court of Henry VIII and thus became a continual and dangerous liability to the duke. She had been a faithful lady-in-waiting to Queen Catherine since 1509 and loudly supported her case in the king's 'Great Matter'. According to the gossipy Chapuys, in early 1530 she sent a message to Catherine pledging her absolute loyalty, despite some impassioned attempts, probably including some earnest appeals by her husband, to persuade her to switch sides in the royal *cause célèbre*:

Those of the opposite party were trying hard to win her over to their opinion, but if the whole world were to set about it they would not make her change. She was and would continue to be one of her party.

Elizabeth was eventually dismissed from the court in May that year for speaking 'too freely and declaring herself, (more than they liked), for the queen'.[12] Her removal became necessary to placate an increasingly irritated Anne Boleyn.

The following November, the duchess sent Catherine a present of a *volaille* – a tempting dish of glazed chicken – and an orange, and also a letter from the English representative in Rome, Sir Gregory Casale. Such was the atmosphere of intrigue and mistrust surrounding the whole question of the annulment that Chapuys doubted the queen's own belief that Elizabeth's gift was merely an act of kindness: 'I fear it was done with the knowledge of her husband, as a means of entering into some secret communication with her majesty more easily,' he reported to his master, Charles V, enclosing Casale's note.[13]

Her banishment from court did nothing to subdue her.

Elizabeth stubbornly refused to carry Anne's train when the king's mistress was created Marchioness of Pembroke in that sumptuous ceremony at Windsor Castle in September 1532 and it had to be borne, instead, by her thirteen-year-old daughter, Mary. She also unashamedly refused to attend Anne's coronation in June 1533,[14] although the queen's step-grandmother, Agnes, Dowager Duchess of Norfolk, was the chief lady among the royal attendants. She pointedly stayed away from the christening of Princess Elizabeth at Greenwich in September that year. Elizabeth also (unsuccessfully) opposed the new queen's ambitions to marry off her own daughter to Henry Fitzroy, Duke of Richmond, and was later to protest volubly about the king's failure to pay up the due marriage jointure to Mary.

Some time after August 1533, the king sent Elizabeth's brother-in-law, Lord Bergavenny, to 'make an arrangement between her and the duke, her husband'. Norfolk, who had just arrived back from a mission in France, was warily reluctant to meet his wife before Bergavenny could instil some sweet reason in her bitter heart. He failed, probably after pledging, more in hope than expectation, that the duke 'should henceforth be a good husband'. Both Elizabeth and her husband knew he had no intention of giving up the warmth and ample, bawdy comforts that Bessie Holland provided in his magnificent ducal bed.[15]

Before the Norfolks formally separated just before Easter 1534, the duke had cast around for somewhere comfortably distant where his wife would now live. Even he could not be seen to throw her out on the street, much as he would have liked to. He pleaded with her brother to house her (and a small number of her immediate attendants), but Henry, Lord Stafford, sensibly refused to become involved. Who could blame him? He was only too familiar with the 'sensual and wilful' character of his formidable sister and had tasted a full measure of her fearsome temper. Stafford prayed piously to God to 'send my Lady a better mind' but, more realistically, confessed to Norfolk: 'Her accustomed wild language does not lie in my power to stop, whereby great danger might ensue to me and all mine, though I never deserved it. In this matter, you know, by long experience, I can do no good,'[16] he plaintively added.

The same day – 13 May 1533 – Stafford also wrote to Cromwell.

> I received your letter today, by my lord of Norfolk's servant, touching the taking of my lady of Norfolk into my house, whereby you reckon that with my good counsel, tranquillity may be established between my lord and her.
>
> To be assured of that, I would not only receive her – but fetch her on my feet [from] London.

The only viable solution, he steadfastly maintained, lay not among her family, nor in 'the pitiful exclamations of her poor friends, praying her to remember what honour she has come to by her husband', or even through the king, 'who has showed her so great favour as might have won any alien's heart'. No, her own uncompromising attitude towards her husband had to change dramatically.

> What more could her enemies wish than this continual contention with her husband, which makes him forsake her

company, and besides the obloquy of this word, brings her into the king's displeasure, which to every true heart is death.

Despite all this, 'and the gentleness of her husband, she cannot be induced to break her sensual and wilful mind, and she takes me, and all others who have advised her to conformity, to be flatterers and liars'. Stafford added: 'I trust you will not reckon that I can do any good in this matter, but I should incur great jeopardy from her wild language.' Soberly, he concluded: 'It is my shame and sorrow, being her brother, to rehearse all this.'[17]

In the end, Elizabeth was ignominiously packed off to a bleak manor house, rented by Norfolk from the crown, at Redbourn in Hertfordshire, and permitted a twenty-strong household to display some small semblance of status for someone of such high, noble birth. Here she fruitfully occupied her time venting her ample spleen at her unfaithful husband through a series of virulent and sadly repetitive letters written to the king, his Council and, deviously perhaps, to Norfolk's arch-enemy in the king's administration, Thomas Cromwell.

She spared no blushes.

Heaven has no rage like a love turned to hatred, nor hell a fury like a woman scorned. The slights and humiliations allegedly inflicted upon her over many years by Norfolk were always as fresh and as painful as if they had been suffered only minutes before. Her vitriolic words tumbled off page after page as she angrily dictated to her clerk, although, at times, strong emotions clouded her memory for dates and places. It would have been a waking nightmare to find oneself sitting next to Elizabeth at a banquet.

Cromwell, who had usurped Norfolk's position as the king's closest councillor, seems happily to have assumed the improbable role of marriage counsellor. In appearing to be a sympathetic friend to the duchess, he doubtless envisaged sweet opportunity both to deflate the duke's rampant pride and profitably exploit his personal difficulties in the constant infighting for influence at Henry's court. In late August 1534, Elizabeth wrote to him, seeking his assistance to procure some venison for her table, 'as none was sent to her since her lord's displeasure'.[18] This was the beginning of a prolonged correspondence lasting until 1539 and its vituperative contents would be all too familiar to a divorce lawyer of today.

In the summer of 1535, the duchess journeyed to Dunstable, Bedfordshire, where the king was staying, to plead with a clearly unsympathetic Henry to order Norfolk to grant her 'a better living', or more simply, more cash for her to live on.

Another attempt at reconciliation followed in December 1536 when Elizabeth was again urged to return to Norfolk's bed and board. This unlikely plan was predictably rejected by the spurned wife, who later told the Lord Privy Seal that she could never bring herself to agree to this,

> for no ill-handling that he [Norfolk] can do to me – nor for no imprisonment. So I pray you show it to my lord my husband that he may [believe] it, seeing that I will not do it at the king's commandment, nor at your desire.
>
> I will not do it for [any] friend nor kin I have living. Nor, from this day forward, I will never sue to the king, or to none other, to desire my lord my husband to take me [back] again.
>
> I have made much suit to him ... and I made him no fault, [aside from] declaring ... his shameful handling of me.[19]

Even if he took her back, it would be more 'for the shame of the world than for any love he bears me'. After all, she now preferred a solitary existence at Redbourn: 'I have been well used, since I have been from him, to a quiet life, and if I should come to him, to use me as he did [it] would greet me worse now than it did before, because I have lived quiet these three years without brawling or fighting.'[20]

Her 'quiet life' also included estrangement from her elder son, Henry, and her daughter, Mary, who took their father's side in the protracted and bitter dispute. Elizabeth angrily branded them both as 'ungracious' and 'unkind' and in one letter, perhaps revealingly, referred to her offspring as 'his children'.[21]

The following year she returned to the attack over her pitiful income. On 26 June, she wrote to Cromwell asking both him and the king to speak to her husband about releasing funds from her jointure. 'My trust', she told the minister, 'is in you, next [to] God.' There was also the nagging matter of the settlement for the unconsummated marriage of her daughter with the king's bastard son (who had died in July 1536) and the 2,000 marks paid out at her own wedding by her father, the Duke of Buckingham,

> which ... my husband has forgotten now he has so much wealth and honours and is so far in doting love with that queen [Anne Boleyn] that he neither regards God nor his honour.
>
> He knows that it is spoken of far and near, to his great dishonour and shame.

Then the old, irrepressible burning resentment at her lost marriage to Ralph Neville welled up again: Norfolk 'chose me for love and I am younger than him by twenty years and he has put me away [three] years and a quarter at this midsummer':

> I have lived always a good woman, as it is not unknown to him. I was daily ... in the court sixteen years together, when he has lived from me more than a year in the king's wars.
>
> The king's grace shall be my record how I used myself without any ill name or fame and [was] the best in the court. There were at that time both men and women [who] know how I used myself in my younger days.
>
> Here is a poor reward I have in my latter days for my well doing![22]

– a less than subtle reference to the notorious promiscuity among the ladies of Henry's court. Her husband had confiscated all her jewels and clothes and left her like a prisoner – as no one could visit her without his express permission.

> I know, my lord, my husband's crafty ways of old. He has made me many times promises ... never [fulfilled]. I will never make more [pleas] to him.

Norfolk kept 'that drab ... that harlot' Bess Holland in his house at Kenninghall, Norfolk, and once had ordered his ladies to attack and to bind her, until her fingers bled from her frantic scratching at the wooden floorboards, in her anger and frustration. The ladies

> [chained] me and sat on my breast until I spat blood and he never punished them.

All this was done for Bess Holland's sake.

I know well, if I should come home again, my life should be but short.[23]

Elizabeth had heard how kind Cromwell had been to Princess Mary 'in her great trouble': could he not now help her by increasing her own lowly income? 'I live in Hertfordshire and have but £50 a quarter and keep twenty persons daily, besides other great charges. I could live better and cheaper in London than I do here.'[24]

Norfolk was notoriously mean. He may well have handed out alms and food to two hundred poor people every day – this was part and parcel of *noblesse oblige*, after all – and owned more than fifty jewelled rosaries, but he habitually refused to pay anything but the smallest pittances both to his estranged duchess and to his own son and heir, Henry Howard, Earl of Surrey.[25] Thus, poverty and penury came high on Elizabeth Howard's ever-growing list of grievances and became the most pressing of her complaints. In the same letter, she told Cromwell:

> I have but £50 [every] quarter and here I lie in a dear country. I have been from my husband, come Tuesday in the Passion week three years. Though I be left poor, yet I am content with all, for I am out of danger from my enemies and of the ill life that I had with ... my husband since he loved Bess Holland first ... [who] has been the cause of all my trouble.
>
> I pray you my lord when you have leisure, write me an answer whether I shall have a better living or not.

She was determined never to write to Norfolk again 'however poorly I live' as he had never bothered to answer her letters, even though they had been written by the king's commandment. (In this, she was a little harsh, as Norfolk was away, suppressing the Pilgrimage of Grace rebellion in the north.) She was, however, not to be diverted from the justice of her arguments:

> If he shall take me again, I know well it is more for the sake of the world than for any love he bears me, for I know well, my life shall be as ill as ever it was.

Elizabeth ended this letter to the Lord Privy Seal with fervent prayers for God to send him 'long life and health, as I would myself' and, finally, added a very barbed desire for divine intervention to help him to 'overcome your enemies'.[26]

No doubt she meant her husband.

Despite his best efforts, Cromwell could not get the parsimonious Norfolk to relent, even after Elizabeth came to London in yet another attempt to convince him and Henry to press her case. Norfolk quickly heard of her visit to the court and wrote immediately to the minister:

> It has come to my knowledge that my wilful wife is come to London and has [been] with you yesterday night ...
>
> I assure you as long as I live I will never come into her company ...

Over the years, the scandal seemed to wash off egotistical Norfolk's back, but one of Elizabeth's claims clearly nettled him – her allegation about his 'cruel' treatment of her during the birth of their daughter, Mary. It does seem unlikely that the duke, anxious for a second male heir, would risk the life of the child by attacking his wife at such a time. In his denials, he also did not mince his words. 'She has untruly slandered me in writing and saying, that when she had been in childbed of my daughter of Richmond two nights and a day',

> I [pulled] her out of the bed by the hair of her head, about the house, and with my dagger gave her a wound in her head.

Battered and insulted, Norfolk was aghast at the claim. 'My good lord,' he told Cromwell, 'if I prove not by witness, and that with many honest persons, that she had the scar on her head fifteen months before she was delivered of my daughter and that the same was cut by a surgeon of London, for a swelling she had in her head, [after pulling] two teeth, never trust my word after.'

> I think there is no man alive that would handle a woman in child-bed of that sort, nor, for my part, would I have done for all that I am worth.

He bemoaned the fact that she had written to Cromwell and had washed all his family's dirty linen in public: 'Whether I play the fool or no, [she has] put me in her danger, which so falsely will slander me.' The duke pleaded that the minister should not disclose his whereabouts to his wife – he was staying at Buntingford in Hertfordshire and was perhaps too close to his wife's home for comfort – 'for the same shall not ... put me to more trouble than I have (whereof I have no need)'. He added, ominously, that if their paths should cross, it 'might give me occasion to handle her otherwise than I have done yet'. This was a man not unknown to use his fists freely in a heated argument, so his threat should be taken seriously.

Norfolk then made what he saw as a handsome offer of conciliation.

> If she first write to me, confessing her false slander and thereupon sue to the king's highness to make any deed, I will never refuse to do that his majesty shall command me to do. But before, assuredly never.[27]

After he returned from his brutal repression of the northern counties, the tenacious Elizabeth renewed her pleas to the Privy Seal:

> I pray you my lord, now my ... husband is coming home, that you will be in hand with him for a better living [for me] ..., seeing he has taken away all my jewels and my apparel and had with me two thousand marks, which is more, by times, than ever [he had].
>
> He had but little to take to when he married me first but his lands and he was always a great player.
>
> My lord, I have been his wife twenty-five years and have borne him five children. But because I would not be content to suffer the harlots that bound me to be still in the house ... and all for speaking against the woman in the court, Bess Holland. Therefore, he put me out of the doors.
>
> It is [three] years come the Tuesday in Passion week that he came riding all night and locked me up in a chamber and took away my jewels ...

She added: 'By means of you, a word [from] the king's mouth, [and] my husband dare not say "nay".'

Elizabeth had lived 'very poorly' during the last three years and had suffered 'much sickness . . . at the fall of the leaf and at the spring' because of the physical effects of the earlier attacks upon her.[28]

On 10 November 1537, Elizabeth sent Cromwell 'a fair present' (or bribe) of 'partridges, twelve cocks and one hen'. Her 'special good lord and friend' learned of more complaints at her treatment. Darkly, she told him: 'They rule, my lord, as they lust.' Cromwell must have sighed with frustration as all the old grievances were trotted out again, as if brand new and freshly bleeding wounds.

This time, however, the duchess recalled that after she had been thrown out of her house Norfolk had sent two of his chaplains, called Burley and Thomas Seymour, to urge her to divorce him. In return for her assent, she would receive her confiscated jewels, 'a great part of his plate' and some of his household goods.

> I rebuked his priests and then he wrote with his own hand on the next day. Though my children are unkind to me I have always loved them for I know well . . . my husband did it but to provoke to put me to shame . . .
>
> His love I will never trust. He has deceived me so many times. He can speak fair as well to his enemy as to his friend and that I perceive by them that be dead and them that be alive.[29]

But not even Cromwell's famed powers of diplomacy, nor his considerable skills of manipulation, could bring the warring couple together.

Norfolk himself appealed to Cromwell in January 1538: 'I require you by your wisdom to find [the] means that my wife may sojourn in some honest place [?a hapless nunnery] and I shall help her with some better living if she so do – and surely if she does not and continues in her most false and abominable lies and obstinacy against me, if God bring me home again, I shall not fail, (unless the king's highness command me to the contrary), to lock up her.' The duke added that never had been such lies contrived by a wife of her husband.[30]

The duchess remained adamant. The following March, she told

Cromwell: 'They shall not rule me as long as I offend not the king. I pray you show my last letter to my husband and write me an answer, which I shall trust.' Norfolk had again suggested that she move in with her brother, or with Lord Bray. 'I would not be in my Lord Bray's houses of all the houses I know, and if I were disposed to *suggyn* [fall silent] as I am not, my husband would have sent to me two years ago ... that I would not do':

> I am of an age to rule myself as have done these five years since my husband put me away.
>
> Seeing that my lord my husband reckoned me to be so unreasonable, it were better that I kept me away and keep my own house still, and trouble no other body, as I am sure I should so.
>
> Be not displeased that I have not followed your counsel to come home again, which I will never do during my life.[31]

Norfolk was unlucky with the women in his life – very much a case of 'like mother, like daughter'.

Not only did he suffer all those years of stormy abuse from his estranged wife, but his daughter inherited some of her mother's dogged determination and temper. Her letters to him were often signed 'your humble daughter', but she was far from that, and did not hesitate to give him a vocal piece of her mind. In January 1537, she wrote to her father seeking assistance in an appeal to the king to 'have justice done' over her maintenance following the death of her husband, Henry Fitzroy.[32] Henry had conveniently forgotten about her jointure and had washed his hands of the issue. Mary was incensed and called in lawyers for advice on how to reclaim her legal entitlement. The marriage may not have been consummated, but they had been man and wife, as far as the law was concerned, she insisted. Norfolk was shocked to discover she had acted on her own initiative 'and be put in such comfort by learned men that her right is clearly good and that she has delayed so long (so she thinks) for lack of good suit made to the king's highness by me'. He told Cromwell: 'In all my life, I never commoned [talked] with her in any serious cause or now, and would not have thought she [would] be such as I find her, which, as I think, is but too wise for a woman.'[33]

Perhaps that was the root cause of his problems in the family home.

Mary blamed her father for her failure to enjoy her jointure and, in January 1538, told Cromwell – now weary of the Howards' family troubles – that she felt little confidence in her father's efforts and sought his permission for her to appeal to Henry in person. Norfolk was browbeaten by her 'weeping and wailing' into agreeing to her 'following her mind'. His daughter, therefore, came to court in May and the following March the king granted her substantial monastic properties and the reversion of some manors.[34]

Meanwhile, Elizabeth moved on resentfully into old age, her hatred and grievances rekindled every time she heard her husband's name mentioned.

She continued to be restricted in her movements on Norfolk's instructions. In 1541, she told another brother-in-law, her former love, Sir Ralph Neville, the Earl of Westmorland: 'I pray God that I may break my [im]prisonment that I have had this seven year and that I may come abroad and see my friends.'[35] Was she hoping to see him again and rekindle her old love?

She became, however, reconciled with her long-suffering brother, who bravely sent his daughters Susanne and Jane to stay with her in the 1540s, when she reported them in 'good health and merry and deserving your blessings'. Elizabeth also asked him to send 'my niece Dorothy, for I am well acquainted with her conditions already, and so I am not with the others. She is the youngest too and if she be changed, therefore, she is better to break as concerning her youth.'[36] She added the inevitable plea to speak to her husband 'that I may have the better living' before he went up to the Scottish borders yet again.

There is something uncomfortable about the use of that word 'break' which suggests that Elizabeth was not a lady to tolerate idly childish pranks or independence. In this may lie her children's decision to side with their father.

So perhaps we could allow ourselves just a *soupçon* of sympathy for her estranged children – if not for bluff old Norfolk himself, for all his manifold faults and wickedness.

'DREADFUL EXECUTION'

———◆———

'[I] shall rather be torn in a million pieces than to show one point of cowardice or untruth to your majesty'

Norfolk to Henry VIII, 25 October 1536¹

After Anne Boleyn turned Norfolk's dreams and ambitions to bitter ashes, Henry VIII's bastard son, Henry Fitzroy, Duke of Richmond, had represented another chance for him to forge politically vital family bonds with the Tudor dynasty. Fitzroy had been placed in the duke's custody after the downfall of Wolsey, and he took care that his son Henry Howard, now Earl of Surrey, and Richmond became inseparable friends. They lived together at Windsor Castle for two years from 1530 and in October 1532 accompanied the king at his meeting with the French king Francis I in Calais and Boulogne. They remained in France afterwards for a year, staying at Fontainebleau and Avignon, and living happily with Francis's three sons.

Norfolk then joyfully secured Richmond's marriage with his daughter Mary. As they were considered to be related within the forbidden degrees of consanguinity, he obtained a dispensation for the formal wedding on 26 November 1533 at Hampton Court.² Surrey went to live with his wife Frances in 1535 and a son was born in March the following year and christened Thomas.

The third duke could now sit back, content that the Howard line stretched safely forward through his son and heir Surrey, and a grandson. He may have rid himself of Anne Boleyn, but after the marriage of Jane Seymour her family shone brightly in Henry's favour, and now threatened his political ambitions.

It was to become a bad time for the House of Howard.

Norfolk's youngest half-brother, the twenty-four-year-old

courtier Lord Thomas Howard,[3] had been wooing Lady Margaret Douglas, the daughter of the king's sister, Margaret, and half-sister to James V of Scotland, since the end of 1535 – two years after he had arrived at court. Theirs was a heady, whirlwind romance and some time before the middle of 1536, probably at Easter, they married secretly. But her uncle Henry was enraged when he heard of their betrothal in early July 1536. There is no sign of his gently lyrical and courtly 'Past-time and Good Company' here; Lord Thomas was immediately arrested for treason and both he and his twenty-one-year-old bride were carted off to the Tower.

Their clandestine marriage came at an unquestionably importune time for the Tudor monarchy. As both Princesses Mary and Elizabeth had been declared bastards by Acts of Parliament in 1534[4] and 1536,[5] the children of Margaret Tudor had now become the only legitimate offspring in the dynasty, until the new queen, Jane Seymour, could produce any lawful heirs herself. It is impossible to determine whether, in pursuing the match, Lord Thomas Howard was either being ambitious (a normal family trait) or just simply, stultifyingly stupid in being oblivious of the political implications. As far as Henry was concerned, marrying a niece was too close to his throne and he decided promptly to cut the family down a peg or two.

To legalise Howard's incarceration, a Bill of Attainder against him was swiftly passed by both Houses of Parliament on 18 July. Its ponderous preamble accused him of having been 'led and seduced by the Devil, not having God before his eyes, [and] not regarding his duty of allegiance that he owes to ... our king ... his most dread sovereign lord'. He had 'contemptuously and traitorously contracted himself by crafty flair and flattering words to and with the Lady Margaret Douglas'. Moreover, the Act added, it was 'vehemently suspected and presumed' that he was 'maliciously and traitorously minding and imagining to put division in this realm' and to 'interrupt, impede and let the ... succession of the crown contrary to the limitation thereof mentioned in the said act'. The Attainder sentenced him to death.[6]

The ever-vigilant Chapuys, while deprecating the licentiousness rampant at Henry's court, told Charles V that the vengeful king had also planned initially to execute Lady Margaret. But she

> for the present, has been pardoned her life, considering that copulation had not taken place. Certainly, if she had done much worse [in being promiscuous] she deserved pardon, seeing the number of domestic examples she had seen and sees daily, and that she has [been] for eight years, of age and capacity, to marry.
>
> Since the case has been discovered, she has not been seen and no-one knows whether she be in the Tower, or some other prison.[7]

Lord Thomas, held in atrocious conditions, suffered more the sharp pangs of love and separation than the filth and discomfort of his surroundings. He wrote a number of sad, lovesick poems that survive in a small quarto volume in the British Library, the name of 'Lady Margaret Howard' inscribed in her own hand on its flyleaf.[8]

Even the charms of poetry cannot always quieten fears for your life. Margaret soon saw sense and renounced her love for him, yet remained in the Tower, albeit in more comfortable conditions than her husband. In August, she thanked Thomas Cromwell for winning back Henry's favour towards her and sought his wise counsel on 'how to avoid again incurring his grace's displeasure'. She reported that two of Lord Howard's servants still attended her, but she would dismiss them 'since she is to keep none that belong to him, though she took them in consideration of their poverty'. Margaret begged the minister not 'to think that any fancy remains in me' about Lord Howard, and, rather pathetically, added that she now received no visitors except gentlewomen, as 'it would not become her, as a maid, to keep company with gentlemen'.[9]

Aside from separating the illicit lovers, another dynastic worry for Henry was the health of his bastard son Henry Fitzroy, Duke of Richmond, hitherto fit and athletic. He had attended the opening of Parliament on 8 June, but a month later had fallen sick at his apartments in St James's Palace, just across the deer park from Westminster. His condition deteriorated day by day, and caused mounting concern among his physicians. John Husee wrote to his master, Lord Lisle, in Calais on 18 July: 'My lord of Richmond [is] very sick, Jesu be his comfort!'[10]

Then, on the morning of 23 July, he died from what appears to have been a pulmonary infection – a cause of death that finished off many of the Tudors – and one that now claimed Henry's only living son. He was aged just seventeen. After all the years of his marital travails, the king must have truly believed that God's hand still lay heavily upon his dynasty.

At the time, many thought Richmond's death deeply suspicious. The contemporary chronicler Charles Wriothesley commented:

It was thought that he was privily poisoned by the means of Queen Anne and her brother Lord Rochford, for he pined inwardly in his body long before he died. God knows the truth: he was a goodly young lord and [forward] in many qualities and feats.[11]

He added that Richmond had 'never lain by his wife, [who was the same age], and so she is maid, wife and now a widow. I pray God send her good fortune.'

The king ordered that Richmond's goods should be listed and valued and that his only son should be buried secretly, to avoid any speculation over the shaky future of the Tudor line. The arrangements for his funeral were assigned to Norfolk.

Five days after the death, the inventory was completed by one of Cromwell's henchmen, John Gostwick, who often worked for him on delicate financial matters,[12] except for 'certain parcels which remain with the duchess, delivered long ago by indenture'. The estate was not inconsiderable, and most went directly into the king's jewel house at Westminster.

I have examined Mr Stringer, almoner to the ... duke [about] what ready money he has and he confesses to about £300, besides £190 delivered by him on Sunday last to Mr [George] Cotton, controller of the same household.

None of the revenues due at our Lady's day in Lent were paid to my lord's use; so that by Michaelmas a whole year's profit will be due to the king's use.

Gostwick had some concerns about the substantial holdings of precious metal owned by Richmond.

> I have been at the Tower to prove the four wedges of gold, which are so hard and egre,[13] they will not abide the hammer and must be new [re]fined.
>
> One of them does not come up to the weight noted by 140 ounces [3.97 kg.] I have caused the Master and Controller of the Minister to weigh and certify every piece. The blocks of silver hold their weight pretty well.
>
> The great chain of seventy-two links, weighing 138.5 ounces, is valued by the Controller at forty shillings ... I mention this because Ralph Sadler[14] tells me the king valued it at £500 or £600.
>
> Let me know your lordship's pleasure for this gold ... [that] weighs 538.5 ounces [15.26 kg.] and will weigh less when toughened.[15]

On 31 July – eight days after his death – Richmond's body was unceremoniously dumped on a wagon and covered with straw to conceal the nature of what must have become a rather malodorous cargo in the summer heat, for the long journey from St James's to Thetford, where the duke planned to bury him among the Howards. Only two attendants, dressed in green, followed this strange bucolic cortège, and then only at a distance.[16] Norfolk and Surrey hurried to Kenninghall for the funeral,[17] which was conducted decently, but quietly, with no pomp or ceremony, at the Cluniac abbey in the Norfolk town at the end of July.

Surrey grieved deeply at the sudden loss of his old school friend. A year later he was still in mourning, 'very weak, his nature running from him abundantly', whenever Surrey 'thought of my lord of Richmond',[18] according to his father, in a rare display of sympathy.

Ever mercurial, Henry was infuriated at what he now saw as the disreputable burial of a royal son, whom at one stage he envisaged as king of Ireland, if not of England, if all else failed, and there were no other royal progeny.

Norfolk very quickly learned at his palace at Kenninghall of the king's terrible rage over Richmond's parsimonious funeral and hurriedly dashed off a letter to Cromwell at ten o'clock at night on 5 August, writing with his 'hand ... full, full, full of choler and agony':

> This night at eight o'clock came letters from friends and servants about London, all agreeing that the king was displeased with me because my lord of Richmond was not buried honourably.
>
> The king wished the body conveyed secretly in a closed cart to Thetford ... and so buried. Accordingly, I ordered both the Cottons to have the body wrapped in lead and in a close cart provided, but it was not done, nor was the body conveyed very secretly.

'I trust the king will not blame me undeservedly,' he added, probably more in hope than sorrow. Norfolk had heard of the rumour sweeping London that he would shortly be arrested and thrown into the Tower of London to join his half-brother Thomas. He ranted to the newly appointed Lord Privy Seal:[19] 'When I shall deserve to be there, Tottenham[20] shall turn French!' What's more, if the duke ever discovered who invented and spread that story, 'he being a gentlemen, and I, were only together on Shooter's Hill,[21] [we would] see [who] should prove himself the more honest man'. Presumably, if the rumour-monger was not a gentleman, Norfolk would have found other, less genteel, ways of silencing him.

Despite all the familiar bluster and his threats of duels to defend his honour, troublesome, nagging doubts about his future must have haunted him, and that night he sat down and twice rewrote his will. The king was to supervise its implementation and Cromwell was to be his principal executor: 'If I die, and when I shall die, I doubt not [that] you both will consider [that] I have been to the one a true poor servant and to the other a true faithful friend,' he pompously told the minister.[22]

His fears of imminent royal retribution were increased greatly by two more letters from London the following day from 'such as would not write without some ground'. Norfolk ordered the immediate packing of his bags in preparation for a hasty journey to court to plead his defence in person. He asked Cromwell to tell

him the truth about the king's opinion of him 'by this bearer, who
shall meet me ere I come to London'.

> Spare not to be plain with me. I thank God for His strokes
> [blows], having deserved infinite more of His Godhead, but
> never of the king.
>
> On Thursday by noon I shall be in London. Send word where
> you will then be, for sorry I would be to come to the court, before
> I spoke with you.[23]

There was, however, no royal vengeance. Norfolk survived, but
he and his family remained firmly destitute of the king's favour.
Cromwell, a self-made man brought up in the hard school of
knocks with a violent, drunken brewer for a father, was not
someone who would shrink from kicking an opponent when he
was down. By timely, malicious comments whispered in the royal
ear, probably over the duke's stance on religious issues, he ensured
that Henry's resentment towards the Howards burned ever
brightly. Norfolk was forced to spend the remainder of the summer
and autumn in East Anglia, in morose exile from court.

Having been in and out of the king's esteem all too frequently,
after a while he philosophically shrugged off the king's disfavour.
Norfolk knew perfectly well that his fickle sovereign's moods could
swing like a weathercock. He was now more preoccupied with
getting his hands on the spoils from the smaller monasteries being
dissolved by Cromwell, as a canny means of severing any remaining
links with Rome and augmenting the riches of Henry's always
hard-pressed exchequer. As soon as news of the legislation authorising the suppressions spread among England's devout nobility,
Cromwell (who had been appointed Vicar General and Vice-
Regent of the king in matters spiritual) was inundated with pleas
to grant this or that monastic property. Norfolk was in the vanguard
of this unseemly scramble for monastic riches – very anxious not
to appear too grasping, but 'where others speak, I must speak' –
and registering his particular desire for the Benedictine nunnery
at Bungay and the Augustinian abbey at Woodbridge, both in
Suffolk.[24]

Therein lies an obvious incongruity. Even in the diverse morality

of Tudor England, how could the devout and religiously conservative Norfolk enrich himself on the proceeds of the dissolved
monasteries? The answer is twofold: firstly, he was always driven
by a need for ever greater power and status and the monastic
properties would bring incomes and lands that would enhance his
position. Unlike upstarts such as Cromwell and his cronies, his
ancestors had piously endowed these religious houses, so he was
merely reclaiming his family's own wealth before it fell into the
undeserving hands of the *nouveau riche*. Secondly, on the political
front, the duke was a firm believer in authority; if suppression of
the monasteries was Henry's policy, so be it. The old ingrained
Howard loyalty towards their monarchs still held sway; as Norfolk
held office under the king, he must unswervingly support him.
Today we would call it 'cabinet collective responsibility', although
in the fevered, conspiratorial cockpit of Henry's court, few others
would recognise the concept.

So, as the months went by, the third duke's claims became more
strident as he lost patience at his lack of reward. In September
1536, he wrote to Cromwell complaining that he still had not been
favoured by any grant. 'Where you write to me to take patience till
you ... may perfect my affairs, I have never laboured to any but
you. I trust shortly to hear you have obtained my suits, for the time
of sowing is at hand and every other nobleman has already [had]
his portion. I trust well for Bungay and Woodbridge.' A few days
later came another demand: 'I know no nobleman but [who] has
their desires and if I shall now dance alone, my back friends
[enemies] shall rejoice. Help me for my old service to be advanced
as soon as those that have yet little served his highness to have
farms [leases] for terms of years.'[25]

Very soon Norfolk would willingly slaughter hundreds of men
whose religious and political ideals he passionately shared, in a
cynical quest to win back Henry's favour and re-establish his pre-
eminent position at court.[26]

The monastic dissolutions were hugely unpopular among the
majority of Henry's subjects. In September 1536, Norfolk arrested
an organ-master in Norwich who was planning an insurrection
over the closure of the monasteries. His companion – a 'right ill

person', in the duke's opinion – was also clapped in jail.[27] A few weeks later, on Monday 2 October, a far more dangerous rebellion broke out at the prosperous Lincolnshire market town of Louth, triggered by rumours – untrue, as it turned out – that Cromwell was now about to loot the riches of the parish churches. Riots and disorder spread rapidly throughout the county, with the insurgents demanding they should keep their holy days, that suppressed monasteries should be reinstated and that they 'be no more taxed'.

They also wanted Cromwell dead.

The king had no standing army and his immediate blustering claim that 100,000 royalist troops were on the march to destroy the rebels was merely a psychological warfare weapon against them.[28] The truth about his immediately available military power was very different. Charles Brandon, Duke of Suffolk, arrived at Huntingdon on 9 October with 'neither ordnance nor men enough to do anything: such men as are gathered here have neither harness [armour] nor weapons'.[29]

Something akin to panic gripped Henry's administration.

Richard Cromwell, the nephew of the minister, scurried around London gathering men, armour and weapons, and even pressed seventy carpenters and masons into military service who had been working on extensions to his uncle's palatial home at Austin Friars.[30] Having been ordered to commandeer every horse he could find, Sir Ralph Warren, the Lord Mayor of London, went from stable to stable, telling the owners the cover story that their animals were required for a fictitious visit of 'Count Nassau' to the capital. Thirty-four small cannon were taken out of storage at the Tower on Sunday 8 October but the poor horses dragging the artillery train gave up the ghost before they had got very far out of London, and thirteen of the guns had to be sent back. Letters were expressed out to the nobility and gentry in the Home Counties and southern England, ordering them to muster their retainers and followers at Ampthill, in Bedfordshire, to form Henry's army. It was not always easy to obey. Lord William Howard, Norfolk's half-brother, reported to Cromwell from his house at Chesworth, near Horsham in West Sussex:

I have received the king's letter to [bring] one hundred men against the 15th. instant, of whom thirty must be archers and all on horseback. I cannot do it because the land is in division between my lady Russell's daughter and me and I am sure Mr Russell has taken up the best of them already.

I beg therefore, that my lady, my mother [the Dowager Duchess of Norfolk] may have a letter to furnish me with one hundred men, for I cannot make forty without her help.[31]

Henry needed a general to destroy the rebels and, as was the Tudor habit, wreak merciless reprisals upon them. He initially planned to lead them himself – two harnesses, or suits of armour, were sent up the Thames from Greenwich for his use on the battlefield – but was persuaded otherwise. Cromwell, although a mercenary soldier in his youth in Italy, was not an experienced or inspiring military commander. Given his unenviable reputation in the realm, he probably faced assassination by his own soldiers if he was to lead the royalist forces.[32]

The king 'unwillingly' ordered Norfolk from Kenninghall to command the army as High Marshal. The Spanish ambassador Chapuys reported: 'The Bishop of Carlisle ... [said] he never saw the duke in such spirits as he is at present; which I take to be caused either by his reconciliation with the king or the pleasure he feels that it will ultimately work the ruin and destruction of his competitor and enemy Cromwell, whom the rioters designate the chief cause of these troubles and whose head ... they actually demand.'[33]

The problem over the choice of Norfolk as general was that he was widely suspected of sympathising with much of the rebels' manifesto, and there was persistent gossip that, at the right moment, he would reveal himself as their leader. If Chapuys knew it, so did Henry:

Perhaps ... the duke fancies that the rebellion will be the means of arresting the progress of the demolition of churches and monasteries, and putting an end to religious innovations, which are not to his taste.

It was supposed that it was partly owing to his having expressed his views on that subject that he did incur the king's indignation, suggested the ambassador. He recalled his conversation with old John, Lord Hussey, in September 1534, when there was unguarded and dangerous talk of Charles V of Spain intervening in England to restore the true faith and safeguard the life of Princess Mary. Hussey's ill-thought-out plans included Norfolk, as 'one of those on whom he counted ... to support the cause of Faith and Church, though it must be said that owing to the said duke's versatile and inconstant humour, the good old lord ... did not much rely upon him'.

Norfolk may have been merry, but Henry was 'dejected' and, according to Richard Cromwell, in 'great fear' of the rebellion.[34] The duke, even though he was sixty-three, was his ablest general, but his half-brother remained imprisoned in the Tower for treason, and doubts about his general's true allegiance loomed large in Henry's mind. The king summoned Norfolk to Windsor Castle for a private discussion about religion and he boldly offered up Surrey as a hostage 'to be pledge for my truth, which by my dealing may give occasion to be suspected, shall never be deserved'.[35] The offer was refused.

Here was a unique opportunity for Norfolk to regain his monarch's favour. He bustled off back to East Anglia, pausing only to ask John Kite, the Bishop of Carlisle, and an anonymous rich merchant to buy a huge quantity of woollen cloth in London to provide work for those who might otherwise be unemployed and tempted to join the rebel forces. Norfolk firmly believed that the Devil found work for idle hands. As a piece of lateral thinking, it leaves something to be desired, but at least the duke felt he was being seen to do something to protect the king's realm. What is more, it was not his money. The bishop promised to lend five or six thousand crowns – about £500,000 at current values – to buy up the surplus bolts of cloth. At the same time, a large number of criminals and debtors who had sought sanctuary in churches and the larger monasteries were rounded up and imprisoned, for fear that they, too, could go over to the insurgents.

Initially, Norfolk scornfully dismissed the Lincolnshire insurrection as a trifling local difficulty and one easily put down by a police action.[36] This failure to appreciate the gravity of the situation, or lingering doubts over his loyalty (perhaps inspired by Thomas Cromwell), lay behind a message from Windsor Castle which overtook him when he was halfway home, at Kelvedon, in Essex. His son Surrey was ordered to take a handful of cavalry north but he was to stay behind in his own region to maintain law and order. His hopes of military glory cruelly and unexpectedly dashed, the duke immediately penned a grumpy reply to the king:

> Alas sir, shall every nobleman save I only either come to your person or else go towards your enemies? Shall I now sit still like a man of law? Alas, sir, My heart is near dead, as would to God it were.

His course was now clear: he would disobey his orders and march immediately towards Lincolnshire, rather than be shamed by sitting impotently at home. But after hearing reports of unrest among the East Anglian cloth workers, he had a change of heart and promised the Privy Council that he 'dared not leave these parts without the king's command'.[37]

By 9 October, Norfolk had paid for 600 troops and was equipped with five of his own 'falcon' cannon,[38] but had no gunners. He also possessed twenty brass hackbushes, or infantry firearms.[39] The duke also organised for '1,400 or 1,500 tall men out of Suffolk [to be ready] at an hour's warning'. Realistically, he warned Henry: 'I think it unwise to be too hasty in giving them [the rebels] battle' as royalist forces were, as yet, too weak 'to meddle with them'.[40] He had also taken firm action against local sedition: 'I have set such order that it shall be hard for anyone to speak an unfitting word without being incontinently taken and sent to me.' Although the words must have choked him, he offered to 'gladly serve' under the Duke of Suffolk and promised the Privy Council: 'My lords ... I shall set forward towards his highness tonight, as the moon rises.'

The duke headed northwards with 3,000 troops, but sought two favours from Cromwell on the way. First, that as Marshal of England, he should command the vanguard in any battle – military glory was still uppermost in the old warhorse's mind – and, second, could his fellow commanders help him out with some bows and arrows, please? He needed 100 bows and 500 sheaves of arrows:

'These were better than gold and silver, [as] for money, I cannot get bows and arrows.'[41]

He was ordered to Ampthill, in Bedfordshire, where a 20,000-strong army was gathering, and reported to Henry on 11 October that he had secured the counties of Norfolk and Suffolk, with hastily assembled scratch forces under the command of the local gentry. He had, naturally, not forgotten to protect his own home at Kenninghall:

> I will leave in my house my son Thomas, with three or four hundred tall fellows and Roger Townsend and Robert Holdish, my steward.

He was anxious, he wrote, to 'joyfully show' Henry 'what I can do to serve your highness'.[42]

Then, unexpectedly over the two days 11–12 October, the rebellious commons of Lincolnshire melted away like spectres at dawn.

Richard Cromwell, relishing his new career as a soldier, regretted their disappearance: 'I lament nothing so much as that they fly thus, as we had hoped to have used them as they deserved,' he robustly told his uncle back in London.[43] At Lincoln, he snorted, he had found 'as obstinate persons as ever I saw, who would scarce [re]move their bonnets' to their betters.

Henry despatched orders to Norfolk on 14 October, commanding that his son with his contingent should remain at Cambridge, while the situation became clearer. Surrey wrote to his father, enclosing the instructions:

> As they declare the submission and retirement of most of the traitors, [they] import a commandment of stay to your company [of soldiers] (which is judged by those here who have seen many musters, the finest raised on such short warning).
>
> I have consulted [Sir Richard] Southwell and the treasurer of your house alone (lest if it were generally known, the companies might withdraw without the king's command) and decided to hold the musters here tomorrow ... so that you may give orders for the payment of the soldiers and appoint me a council, for otherwise they give their advice with diffidence.

Surrey had paid his troops arrears of 3s 4d (16p) 'as you commanded at Thetford, Bury and Newmarket, and this day the gentlemen [commanders] of the companies have been importuned by them for an advance of wages as they have spent all their money, which is not unlikely considering the great price of victuals . . .'.[44]

The Lincolnshire insurgents may have drifted home but the threat of rebellion remained as serious as ever. The beacon fires flickering along the ridge of the north Lincolnshire Wolds that heralded their uprising had been seen further north, across the River Humber, and the commoners in the East Riding of Yorkshire belatedly rose in support. Confirmation of the new emergency arrived in London on 15 October. A report reached Cromwell that 'the greater part of Yorkshire [is] . . . up, and the whole country favour[s] their opinions. The matter hangs like a fever, one day good, another bad.'[45] The Yorkshire insurrection posed a far graver threat to Henry's throne because it was more widespread and better led. Within days, the northern capital of York had been taken and the major seaport of Hull surrendered after a rebel siege of five days. On 20 October, Pontefract Castle capitulated. More than 40,000 insurgents were on the march and the rebellion spread west and north, infecting the counties of Lancashire, Westmorland and Cumberland.

The Yorkshire rebels called themselves the 'Pilgrimage of Grace' and were led by banners embroidered with the Five Wounds of Christ on the Holy Cross, with the sacred monogram 'IHS' shown with the image of a chalice below.[46] Their leader, or captain, was Robert Aske, a one-eyed lawyer in his early thirties who had previously been a servant to Henry Percy, sixth Earl of Northumberland. All swore an oath of fidelity to their cause on the Holy Bible:

> You shall not enter to this our pilgrimage of grace for the common wealth[47] but only for the maintenance of God's Faith and Church militant, preservation of the king's person and issue and purifying the nobility of all villains' blood and evil counsellors; to the restitution of Christ's church and suppression of heretics' opinions by the holy contents of this book.

They were now 'pilgrims', defending the old, familiar and comfortable faith of their forefathers, and their emotionally powerful message rallied many, including gentry, minor lords and the religious, to their banners. Ironically, theirs was a vow which Norfolk could, in his heart, have willingly signed up to.‾

He was again ordered north, in command of the army gathered at Ampthill, but denied the forces he required. Henry may have been unwilling to commit all his forces to Norfolk, in case his fears over his loyalty proved justified.

The king was also keen to avoid spending any more than he had to, although his lieutenants were warned that any talk leaking out of 'want of money would be most injurious'. Norfolk was rarely a happy general and now complained about having to dip into his own bulging purse to pay the king's troops. But the old warrior also scented the smoke of battle and pledged to the Privy Council that he would rather now be alongside the Duke of Suffolk in Lincolnshire, 'furnished with money', than win 10,000 marks (about £7,000 in money of the time) in a wager.[48] The same day, he wrote to Henry acknowledging that 'we cannot be at Doncaster before [Thursday 26 October] for our horses are too weak to go more than twenty miles [32.2 km.] a day'. He had at last received £10,000 in cash for his soldiers' pay but this would not 'despatch the army here and pay those who go northwards till Sunday next. We cannot advance further than they may be paid without disorder ensuing.' 'All,' he added, 'complain they cannot live on 8d [just over 1.5p] a day.'[49]

By 20 October, Norfolk had reached Cambridge and late that night sent the king his assessment of the military situation in the north. His letter is lost, but its import may be reconstructed by Henry's reply. The duke must have counselled that gentle persuasion should be used to disperse the rebels to play for time until enough royalist troops could be concentrated to defeat them in battle. If soft words did not work, George Talbot, fourth Earl of Shrewsbury, with his force of only 7,000 men, should hold the bridges across the Rivers Trent and Don at Newark and Doncaster to prevent further rebel advances but should keep his distance, until reinforced.[50]

Shrewsbury, indeed, sent a letter to the insurgents passing on Norfolk's request to have four 'discreet' men from the north to meet him at their forward base at Doncaster and explain to him the causes of the revolt. The thrust of the government's public strategy was that negotiation must be better than shedding Christian blood.

Norfolk, riding ahead of his troops, arrived at Newark early in the morning of Wednesday 25 October, complaining 'I have not slept two hours these two nights and must take some rest'. He had little chance of slumber. Lord Talbot, Shrewsbury's son, rode in to brief him on the situation at Doncaster and promised that his father would not give the rebels battle until Norfolk's forces could join him.

That night – 'in bed and not asleep' – a letter was received from Shrewsbury, summoning him to Doncaster to talk to the rebel delegation. Norfolk was anxious about the consequences but mounted up and, accompanied only by a small party of horsemen, set off into the dangers of the night. At Welbeck, 14 miles (22.5 km.) from Doncaster, just before midnight, he dashed off a note to Henry. The duke was convinced it could be the last letter he wrote to his sovereign:

I have taken my horse accompanied only with my [half-]brother William and Sir Richard Page, Sir Arthur Darcy and four of my servants to ride towards my Lord Steward [Shrewsbury] according to his desire, not knowing where the enemies be, nor of what number ... wherein I am so far pricked that whatsoever be the sequel, I shall not spare [my] poor little carcass that for any ease or danger other men shall have cause to object ...

Sir, most humbly, I beseech you to take in good part whatsoever promise I shall make unto the rebels ... no oath nor promise made for policy to serve you mine only master and sovereign can disdain [corrupt] me, who shall rather be torn in a million pieces than to show one point of cowardice or untruth to your majesty.

Sir, I trust the sending for me is meant to God's purpose and if it chance to me to miscarry, most good and noble master, be good to my sons and to my poor daughter.

Then Norfolk added a sting in the tail of his letter. He sniped at
the wisdom of Shrewsbury's earlier tentative advance from Newark
to seize bridges across the River Don: 'If my Lord Steward had
not advanced from Trent [Newark] until my coming ... then I
might have followed the effect of my letter written you from
Cambridge [and] these traitors, with ease, might have been
subdued. I pray God that hap [this mischance] turn not to much
hurt.'[51]

Norfolk's meeting with the rebel representatives seems to have
agreed that their army concentrated on Doncaster should disperse
under a general pardon and that two delegates should accompany
the duke to court where their complaints would be explained to
the king.

Reinforcements had now arrived including 100 gunners, who
were posted to defend the bridge at Doncaster. Very soon the rebels
began slowly to trudge home, under the protection of their royal
pardons, and Shrewsbury and some of his colleagues also started
to demobilise their troops.

Some time on or after 26 October, a letter was despatched to
underline the message the royalists had brought to the negotiating
table, signed by Norfolk, Shrewsbury and others who were the
king's lieutenants. Its contents suggest it was the handiwork of the
duke, as it did not waste words in any gesture towards conciliation.
The letter challenged the insurgents to return home, or else expect
the worst from the king. Addressing them as 'unhappy men', it
castigated them for the folly which seduced them 'to make this
most shameful rebellion against our most noble and righteous king
and sovereign, who is more worthy, for his innumerable graces and
noble virtues ... to be king, master and governor of all Chris-
tendom, than of so small a realm as England?':

> If you find fault, that he has had much good of you, then you
> ought to consider and think the same to be well employed. He
> has not only spent the same, but also an infinite sum of his own
> treasure to maintain and keep you in peace against all enemies.
>   Fie for shame!
>   It is now your choice whether you will abide the danger of

battle against us, or else go home to your houses, submitting yourself to the king's mercy. If you go home, you may be assured to have us [as the] most humble suitors to his highness to you.

And yet, you have occasion to say, that we deal like honest charitable men with you to give you this warning – more gentle than your deserts do require.[52]

Norfolk, now at Tuxford, in Nottinghamshire, was exhausted, apprehensive and gloomy. He complained to the Council on Sunday morning, 29 October:

I came to this town this night late and found the scantiest supper I had for many years. I am weary with anxiety and have been in bed three hours, during which time I have been twice wakened, once with letters from my lord of Suffolk and again with letters from the king ...

I have served his highness many times without reproach and now am forced to appoint [meet] with the rebels, my heart is near broken. Yet every man says I never served his grace so well as in dissolving the enemy's army without loss to ours, yet I am the most unquiet man of mind living.

All others here [are] joyful and only I sorrowful.

The tone of the duke's letter then moved to a mixture of truculence, self-pity and hasty explanations to justify his actions. He again showed his contempt for Shrewsbury's poor tactical manoeuvres:

Alas that the valiant heart of my Lord Steward [Shrewsbury] would not suffer him to have tarried about Trent [Newark] but with his fast hastening forwards to bring us into the most barren country of the realm, whereof has caused the effect that I saw long before would fall.

It was not fear that which caused us [to meet] with the enemy but the cold weather and the want of room to house more than a third of the army and of fuel to make fires.

Pestilence in the town [Doncaster] is marvellously fervent and where I and my son lie, at a friar's, ten or twelve houses are infected within a[n archery] butt's length. On Friday night, the mayor's wife and two daughters all died in one house. Nine soldiers are dead.

There is not within five miles of the town one load of hay, oats, peas or beans left.

It is therefore impossible to give battle or to retreat as we had no horse and they all the flower of the North.

He also doubted the loyalty of his own troops: 'Never a prince had a company of more true noblemen and gentlemen, yet right few of the soldiers ... think their quarrels [with the rebels] to be good.' Norfolk could not resist the opportunity of yet another dig at his fellow general:

Woe! Woe! Woe, worth the time that my Lord Steward bent so far forth. Had he not, you should have heard other news.

Finally, if the king should write to me to gather the army again, it is impossible.

To preserve the terms of the truce, he begged: 'For God's sake [ensure] that his highness cause not my lord of Suffolk to put any man to death [before] my coming.'[53]

Norfolk continued in his negotiations with the insurgents into December, in pursuance of a policy that banked on the harsh weather reducing rebel numbers and weakening their tenacity for the cause. But soon the pilgrims realised that all along they had been deceived by the weasel-worded promises of both king and duke.

In January 1537, the glowing embers of rebellion burst into flames again, fanned by rumours that Henry was reinforcing Hull and the Yorkshire town of Scarborough to create bases from which he could subdue the country and make them safe havens for the loyal local gentry. This new revolt was quickly put down and the ringleaders of the Pilgrimage of Grace and others caught up in the insurgency rounded up. In the middle of the following month there was renewed fighting in Cumberland and Westmorland, led by a man with the egalitarian *nom de guerre* of 'Captain Poverty'.

Norfolk had wearily journeyed to Kenninghall for much-deserved rest and recuperation after Christmas. At the end of

January, he sent a newly written will to Cromwell for safekeeping[54] in preparation for his return north. On the way back, on 2 February, he faced some delicate issues over alleged subversion close to home. He thanked Cromwell for interceding with the Duke of Suffolk over his indictment of some of Norfolk's feudal bondmen – 'my folks', as he called them cosily. 'I never knew till my first going to Doncaster [that] he bore me any grudge. But, as you write, the better we agree, the better the king shall be served.' He added: 'Some lewd persons do not yet cease to speak ill of us, as you shall perceive by a prophecy framed of late.'[55]

Despite Norfolk's earlier boasts that he had crushed sedition in East Anglia, there were still worrying signs of unrest and agitation. Cromwell received a report later that month of an itinerant fiddler called John Hogan who was going around Norfolk, drawing the crowds with his witty, tuneful treasons. In the butcher's home at Diss, on the 'Thursday after Ash Wednesday' he sang a ditty mentioning Norfolk, his son Surrey and the Earl of Shrewsbury. When he finished, a cautious soul called John James told him:

> Beware how you sing this song in Suffolk. [Hogan] asked [him] why, for he had sung it twice before my lord of Surrey at Cambridge and at Thetford Abbey at which Thomas Beck replied if he had sung before [Surrey] he would have set him by the feet for slandering him.

Hogan steadfastly maintained that if the Duke of Suffolk had allowed the Lincolnshire rebels to 'join the Northern men, they would have brought England to a better stay [state] than it is now'.[56]

Henry's patience had long since ebbed away. The king, who loathed even the thought of negotiating with rebellious subjects, now demanded blood. Norfolk was the man to wreak pitiless retribution on the north. On 22 February, Henry sent him a chilling instruction: he must now impose martial law in the north and mercilessly slaughter all traitors.

> You shall cause such dreadful execution upon a good number of the inhabitants, of every town, village and hamlet that have

offended in this rebellion, as well as by the hanging of them up on trees, as by the quartering them and setting their heads and quarters in every town, great and small, as may be a fearful spectacle to all hereafter that would practice any like matter.

The king required the duke to kill them 'without pity or respect ... Remember that it shall be much better that these traitors should perish in their wilful, unkind, and traitorous follies, than that so slender a punishment should be done upon them as the dread [of it] should not be a warning to others.'

Henry also thanked Norfolk for his loyalty:

We shall not forget your services and are glad to hear also from sundry of our servants how you advance the truth, declaring the usurpation of the Bishop of Rome [the Pope] and how discreetly you paint those persons that call themselves religious[57] in the colours of their hypocrisy and we doubt not but the further [that] you wade in the investigation of their behaviours, the more you shall detest the great number of them and the less esteem the punishment of those culpable.[58]

The duke had some old grudges, and he cuttingly wrote to Cromwell: 'Now shall appear whether for favour of these countrymen I forbore to fight with them at Doncaster as, you know, the king's highness showed me it was thought by some I did. Those that so said shall now be proved false liars.'[59]

At Carlisle there were so many prisoners that Norfolk did not know how to incarcerate them all: 'You will hardly believe the trouble I have to keep the prisoners, there are so many,' he lamented. There was not a lord or gentleman of Cumberland or Westmorland whose servants and tenants had not joined the insurgency. He informed the Privy Council that he would 'proceed by the law martial, for if I should proceed by indictments, many a great offender might fortune [to] be found not guilty, saying he was brought forth against his will'.[60] In a postscript, he jocularly told Sir William Paulet, Comptroller of the Household:

And good Mr Comptroller, provide you of a new bailiff at Embleton for John Jackson your bailiff, will be hanged Thursday

or Friday at the [latest] and I think some of your tenants will
keep him company.

On 24 February, he ordered that seventy-four 'principal offenders'
should be hanged, pointing out 'had I proceeded by the trial of
twelve men, I think not the fifth ... of these should have suffered,
for the common saying here [is that] "I came out of fear of my life
... I came forth for fear of burning of my house and destroying of
my wife and children". [Such] a small excuse will be well believed
here, where much affection and pity of neighbours does reign.'[61]
As normal, their bodies were hung up and displayed until they
rotted or were picked clean by carrion crows. But the number of
executions was so great that the local chain manufacturers could
not fulfil Norfolk's order in time, so several corpses were left
hanging on gibbets by rope.[62] When Henry heard that several
wives and mothers had cut down the bodies to give them Christian
burial, he was enraged and insisted on the women being rooted
out and punished.[63] He was also disappointed that Norfolk had
not quartered the corpses.[64]

Norfolk moved on, hanging as he went. Cromwell drove him
on to even greater cruelty, taunting him that he was soft on the
suppression of the monasteries and lenient in his punishment of
traitors. The duke retorted: 'Neither here, nor elsewhere, will I be
reputed Papist or a favourer of naughty religious persons' and
disclosed that he had been warned 'to take heed of what he ate or
drank in religious houses for fear of poison' being used against
him.[65]

Despite Cromwell's jibes, the king's harsh injunctions to be
ruthless were always in the forefront of Norfolk's mind. Before
moving on to the north-east and Yorkshire, he eagerly reported to
Henry: 'Folks think the last justice at Carlisle great and if more
than twenty suffer at Durham and York it will be talked about' and
politely inquired how many the king wanted executed in York.[66]

In Durham, while presiding over a commission of oyer and
terminer to try twenty-four rebels in March, he discovered that
the county palatine was not covered by the legal instrument setting
up the process, so he and his fellow judges were 'driven to the

extremity of our simple wits [as to] what we should do'. As Norfolk wanted to arraign thirteen accused the following day, he decided to swear in the jury 'keeping secret from them our lack of authority and I ... thought to have proceeded by the law martial and to have taken the indictments as evidence'. But their offences were committed before his appointment as king's lieutenant, so he could not employ martial law against them. It was all rather embarrassing.[67]

At York, William Levening, of Acklam, who was involved in the January rebellion, was acquitted on 23 March 1537, much to Norfolk's chagrin. Two jurymen – Thomas Delariver and Sir Henry Gascoigne – were empanelled by the duke himself to ensure the right verdict. With four others, Delariver was convinced that Levening was 'worthy to die' but seven said he was their neighbour and they 'knew better his conversation'. The jury debates continued and an impatient Norfolk sent in his usher to ask 'whether they were agreed or no'. When no unanimous verdict was forthcoming, an angry duke 'took away from them all that might keep them warm' and refused them food and water.[68] But all was to no avail and Levening was freed after more than thirty-six hours of jury deliberations.[69] Norfolk had learned a hard lesson from this second fiasco: in future trials at York, he packed the jury with compliant gentry.

Overall, Norfolk was thoroughly satisfied with his efforts, 'though the number be nothing as great as their deserts did require to have suffered, yet I think the like number has not been heard of put to execution at one time', as he commented at Carlisle. Almost two hundred and twenty had been executed in the north and, in London, forty-four of them from monasteries, including the abbots of Kirkstall, Jervaulx, Fountains, Sawley and Whalley. One of the abbots he executed was Dr Matthew Mackerell[70] of the Premonstratensian abbey at Barlings, Lincolnshire, who had preached that startling homily at the funeral of his father, the second Duke of Norfolk, back in 1524. Robert Aske, the pilgrims' leader, had been hanged in chains at York Castle. A self-satisfied Norfolk summed things up: 'These countries, thanked be God, [are now] in such order that I trust never in our life, no new commotions shall be attempted. Surely, I see nothing here but fear.'[71]

Unsurprisingly, Norfolk's punitive progress through the north made him an unpopular figure. The thirty-two-year-old widow Mabel Brigge began a three-day 'Black Fast of St Trynzan' (St Trinian) in Yorkshire in March 1538 to cast a curse on the king and the duke. She had done it once before 'for a man and he broke his neck and so she trusted [the same would happen] to the king and this false duke'. It did not work and she was executed at York in early April that year.[72]

Despite the slaughter he had inflicted, there was still malicious gossip at Henry's court about Norfolk's self-interest in doing his duty for the king. One malevolent rumour suggested he had brought his twenty-four-year-old son Surrey north in order to train him as his deputy in ruling the region – not such a far-fetched idea, given the Howards' earlier experience on the borders. Heaven forfend! Norfolk was disingenuously aghast and protested to Henry: 'Sir, on the troth I owe to God and you my sovereign lord, I never had such a thought.' Surrey was there merely to keep him company during those dark, cold nights in the northern counties:

> I am very affectionate to him and love him better than all my children and would have gladly had him here with me, both to have me company, in hunting, hawking, playing at cards, shooting and other pastimes, and also to have entertained my servants to the intent they should have been the less desirous to ask leave to go home to their wives and friends.
>
> If I minded any other thing in sending for him than these, and especially if ever I thought other false surmises matter, God let me shortly die in the most shameful death that ever man did.

Norfolk vowed to lay down his 'poor body' to defend his reputation against these 'false caitiffs'[73] that were too afraid to show their faces.[74]

Surrey returned to court at the beginning of that August and almost immediately came up against a courtier who suggested, mischievously, that he was sympathetic to the pilgrims' cause. The hot-headed and proud Howard heir struck the man viciously in the face with his fist. Legend has it that the other protagonist was Edward Seymour, Viscount Beauchamp, one of the queen's brothers, but there is no real evidence to support this identification. Violence, or the shedding of blood within the precincts of the king's court, was a serious felony, normally punished by the loss of the right hand in a gruesome ceremony.

Norfolk was horrified at the incident, but even more so at the prospect of how justice against his son would be meted out. He immediately wrote to Cromwell on 8 August, his heart pierced 'by a multitude of pricks', especially the fear of Surrey's maiming. The 'informations [about] my son [are] falsely imagined, no man knows better than you . . .' and he sought reassurance 'to amend the [fear] in my heart by chance of likelihood to be maimed of his right arm'. Norfolk added in his own handwriting: 'The loss of a finger would not cause me as much sorrow.'[75] The Lord Privy Seal duly intervened and Surrey was packed off to Windsor Castle for two weeks' imprisonment to cool his heels, and his temper.[76] There he consoled himself by writing the poem *When Windsor Walls Sustained my Wearied Arm* and the elegy *So Cruel Prison*, which recalled his friendship with Richmond.

Norfolk, who was feeling the effects of his punishing itinerary on his advancing years, frequently asked permission to return to London – but each time was refused. In September, Henry thanked him for his congratulations on Jane Seymour's pregnancy, and asked him to stay just a little longer in the north:

> Touching your suit for your return; albeit your wisdom and circumspection is such as we think we could hardly devise to be so well served there as . . . by your continuance in those parts.
>
> Yet, minding to grant your desire, for your better quiet, satisfaction and recovery of your health, (which we do more tender and regard than we can almost express), we do purpose shortly to revoke you and to establish a standing Council there for the conservation of those countries in quiet . . .[77]

The king's letter was double-edged. Norfolk's recall may have become imminent, but any dreams he had of becoming the powerful magnate controlling the north of England had vanished. The 'Council of the North' with Cuthbert Tunstall, Bishop of Durham, as its president, was duly created and Norfolk returned to London in time for the long-awaited birth of a lawful son to Henry and his queen Jane, on 12 October 1537.

He was one of the godfathers to Prince Edward at the christening at midnight on Sunday 15 October in the splendours of the newly decorated Chapel Royal at Hampton Court.[78] But three days later, the queen fell ill. Her condition rapidly worsened and, during the evening of 24 October, Norfolk dashed off a hasty note to Cromwell, still at Westminster:

> My good lord: I pray you to be here tomorrow early to comfort our good master, for as for our mistress, there is no likelihood of her life – the more pity – and I fear she shall not be alive at the time you shall read this.
> At eight at night, with the hand of [your] sorrowful friend.
>   T. NORFOLK[79]

She died just before midnight that night, aged twenty-eight.

With the queen scarcely cold in her coffin, on 3 November the duke pressed the king to take another wife as quickly as possible during a conversation at Hampton Court – advice that carried, unspoken, the need for a 'spare heir', a Duke of York. But Norfolk had another critical matter to settle with the grieving Henry: his personal share of the wealth and lands of the Cluniac priory of St Pancras, in Lewes, East Sussex, one of the richest monasteries in England.

One might think that Norfolk was insensitive, grasping, even bovine, in raising this issue when Henry had just lost a wife he genuinely loved. Truthfully, he could be all that and more. Certainly, he risked the king's unpredictable and violent temper, which may be a measure of his greed. The next day the duke wrote to Cromwell, who also had an interest in the proceeds from the same religious house:

> Thanks for your venison. By your letter, you [wanted to] know how I sped [fared] with the king yesterday.
> First (peradventure [perhaps] not wisely, yet plainly) I exhorted him to accept God's pleasure in taking the queen and

[to] comfort himself with the treasure sent to him and this realm (namely the prince) and advised him to provide for a new wife.

After that, I thanked him for being content to give us Lewes, if we might conclude the bargain, rehearsing of your service to him, as I told you in your garden, and saying I was content you should have two parts.

Henry distractedly replied: 'As you showed to me' – a vital indication of royal approval, Norfolk surmised, that the priory's property was 'well bestowed'.[80] Three months later, the duke got his wish: he was granted the priory's valuable properties at Castleacre in Norfolk and a total of 126 manors and lordships, together with the rectories and advowsons[81] of twenty-nine parishes in the same county. Cromwell got the priory site itself and some other properties.

Norfolk, as Earl Marshal, should have been concentrating on the arrangements for Queen Jane's funeral on 12 November at St George's Chapel, Windsor. A funeral for a 'lawful' queen had not been held since that of Henry's mother, Elizabeth of York, in 1503. Then, Norfolk told Cromwell, there were seven marquises and earls, sixteen barons, sixty knights and 'forty spirituals, besides the ordinary of the king's household. Therefore, we have named more persons that you may choose from ...'[82] He no doubt ensured that Surrey, now rehabilitated at court, was one of the principal mourners in the procession. The duke also issued instructions for 1,200 Masses to be said in the city of London churches for the soul of Queen Jane.[83]

Norfolk, for all his enthusiasm in delivering the king's brutal revenge on the north, was no nearer to regaining real political influence. The Privy Council seat still eluded him because the powerful figure of Thomas Cromwell blocked his advancement at court.

The sentence of death was never carried out on Norfolk's half-brother Lord Thomas Howard. Tradition speaks of another poisoning, but he died of an ague, or fever, in the Tower on All Hallows Eve, 31 October 1537,[84] and his body was given to his mother, the Dowager Duchess of Norfolk, for burial 'without pomp' at Thetford Abbey.

Lady Margaret Douglas remained in the Tower until her former lover's death, was pardoned, and despatched for a time to the Bridgettine house at Syon Abbey, at Isleworth on the banks of the River Thames, for her physical and spiritual health. In 1544, she married Matthew, fourth Earl of Lennox, and gave birth to a son, Henry Stuart, Earl of Darnley, who grew up to become the distinctively unattractive husband of Mary Queen of Scots, who was to have her own dire impact on the House of Howard.

6

'PROSTRATE AND MOST HUMBLE'

---◆---

'When so ever two false knaves ... secretly accuse a man ... ,
he must die. Death, death, [comes] even for trifles, so that
they follow the high priests in crucifying Christ'

**The London religious radical Henry Brinklow,
on the Act of the Six Articles**[1]

The crisis of the northern rebellions safely and bloodily resolved,[2]
the way now lay clear for the king's chief minister, Thomas
Cromwell, to pursue the three policy priorities at the top of his
agenda: enriching still further Henry's revenues by still more dissolutions of monastic houses; continuing religious reform in
England; and, after the premature death of Jane Seymour, finding
a suitable new queen for his royal master.

The easiest to implement (and most pleasantly profitable) was the
total eradication of monastic life from the English landscape. The
surrenders of abbeys, priories and nunneries had continued
unabated and the larger, wealthier houses fell after a second Act of
Suppression was passed by Parliament in the spring of 1539.[3] This
process was much more than recycling monastic wealth into hard
cash, to the benefit of the king, the noble houses and an emerging
breed of gentry. Cromwell's policy was also gratuitous, wanton vandalism on a grand scale. At many of the more remote abbey sites,
such as Tintern, Fountains and at Rievaulx, the great churches were
stripped of the commercially desirable lead from their roofs and left
open to the skies in a deliberate act to deny permanently their use as
places of worship. Swept away on a tide of brutish iconoclasm were
also their works of art and the monastic libraries of incalculable intel-
lectual value. The brooding stone ruins to this day remain eloquent
witnesses to Tudor governmental greed and ruthlessness.

As the dissolutions progressed, Norfolk continued to eye the potential spoil as greedily as anyone else of his class. While in the north during the bleak aftermath of the Pilgrimage of Grace, he spoke approvingly of the Augustinian priory at Bridlington, East Yorkshire, which had 'a barn all covered with lead, [with] the largest, widest and deepest roofs that I ever saw'. The richness of its shrine of St John excited him still further: 'If I [dared] be a thief I would have stolen [three carved retables⁴] to have sent ... to the Queen's grace.'⁵ At long last, he had been granted the Benedictine nuns' house at Bungay, which fell like an over-ripe plum into his lap on 18 December 1537, at a modest rental of £6 4s 3d per year – only a tenth of its regular annual income. But the duke's hopes had been frustrated at Woodbridge, where the priory site was granted to Sir John Wingfield and his wife Dorothy, of Letheringham, Suffolk.⁶ At least he had the consolation of the prime catch of Lewes Priory's substantial possessions in East Anglia, notably Castle Rising, another huge bargain.⁷ Other houses also came Norfolk's way: he was keen to secure the Franciscan friary in Norwich and told Cromwell on 21 September 1538 that he had intended to ride into the city from Kenninghall the previous day to take the surrender of the house, but fell ill and so sent Surrey instead. The duke took pity on the 'very poor wretches' he had expelled and gave the grey friars forty shillings each to buy clothes for their new secular life.⁸ He systematically demolished the friary buildings, sold off the materials for a quick profit and left the site barren and empty.⁹

His receipts for 1537 show considerable profits. Cash that 'remains to me clear' totalled £2,638 (or more than £1 million at 2009 prices) after deductions of £400 to his estranged wife and son and other costs. That year, he sold lands worth £568 and purchased new property worth £1,739.¹⁰

Norfolk, however, was faced with the uncomfortable problem of the Cluniac abbey of Our Lady at Thetford, the resting place of his ancestors, which faced an uncertain future after its surrender. In 1539, the duke suggested its conversion into 'a very honest parish' church of secular canons, governed by a dean and chapter. He proposed the first dean should be the existing prior, William

Inxworth. With an eye to the religious reforms under way, with their focus on the importance of God's Word, Norfolk also suggested the appointment of a doctor or bachelor of divinity to act as a preacher in the new church, to be paid an annual stipend of £20.

He petitioned Henry for approval of his plans, astutely pointing out that the priory church held the remains of the king's natural son, the Duke of Richmond, Norfolk's first wife Lady Anne (Henry's aunt), as well as the tombs of his own father (the second duke) and his grandfather. Norfolk was at pains to point out that he was spending £400 in erecting an impressive monument for Richmond and another for himself, ready for when he shuffled off his own mortal coil.

His arguments struck a chord of pious resonance in Henry's normally grasping heart, and Thetford was included in a list of five new collegiate churches to be created by the king himself. But then Henry unexpectedly changed his mind and insisted that the priory should, like all the others, be dissolved.

This duly followed on 16 February 1540, when Prior William and his thirteen Cluniac monks signed the deed of surrender.[11] Prudently, the duke had already seized the conventual seal, without which no transactions concerning the priory could be legally completed. On 9 July, Norfolk acquired the site and the priory's extensive lands and properties throughout East Anglia on exceptionally favourable terms as the king's 'special gift'. He paid up £1,000 in cash and faced an annual outlay of £59 5s 1d in rent.[12]

Although he ensured that the priory church was still maintained, Norfolk remained uneasy about what could happen in the future. Accordingly, he began planning a new family mortuary chapel at the parish church of St Michael, at Framlingham in Suffolk, where the remains of his first wife and ancestors could be safely re-housed.

Cromwell, meanwhile, was intent on driving through a programme of religious reform and launched state attacks on shrines and relics, probably sparked by Henry's belief that such 'idolatry' was the last vestige of Rome's spiritual hold on his subjects. As Norfolk was to point out later, on issues of religion he had promised Henry that 'I shall stick to whatsoever laws you make and for this cause, diverse [people] have borne me ill will, as appears by casting libels abroad against me'.[13]

If the king wanted to rule over the spiritual as well as the temporal lives of his subjects, Norfolk was perfectly content. The Latin phrase *Deo et regi fidelis* – 'faithful to God and king' – aptly sums up his rather self-righteous beliefs, even if confronted by the unpalatable, as in May 1535, when his former chaplain Robert Lawrence was executed for treason at Tyburn, still scandalously wearing his Carthusian robes.[14] Hence the duke's enthusiastic persecution of Anthony Browne, in July 1538, who had chosen the life of a hermit after leaving his community, that hotbed of sedition, the Friars Observants in Greenwich.[15]

Browne had declared his opposition to Henry's supremacy and had pleaded guilty to the indictment for treason when he appeared before the Norwich justices. His execution was delayed for ten days to allow Norfolk and one of his own gentlemen, Sir Roger Townshend,[16] to win some political capital by persuading him to publicly recant. However, their attempts proved unsuccessful as the friar insisted that 'no temporal prince was *capax* [able to hold] that name and authority'. The duke then summoned reinforcements – a reformed grey friar and the retired Bishop of Norwich, the theologian Richard Nykke – to dispute with the recalcitrant prisoner. Even though the bishop's arguments, according to Norfolk, were 'sufficient to have turned the opinion of any man not given to wilfulness as this fool', Browne remained obdurate. The duke wrote to Cromwell, inquiring whether the friar should be sent to London to be 'more straitenly examined and . . . put to torture' in the Tower.

The friar's fate is unrecorded but he was probably executed at Norwich.[17]

The supremacy was thus a rigidly enforced fact of life, although Norfolk believed that Henry did not support further radical religious change.[18] Growing fears of an impending revolution in doctrine spawned a faction at Henry's court, led by the duke and Stephen Gardiner (appointed Bishop of Winchester back in November 1531), who opposed any more liturgical reform, particularly some ideas espoused by Archbishop Cranmer.[19] In Norfolk's and his fellow conservatives' view, it was high time to halt the damaging drift from the much-loved and secure religion of their forefathers.

They may have been mirroring the king's own concerns. By late 1538 and early the following year, Henry began to disapprove of suggested further reforms. Many of his subjects shared the traditionalists' standpoint on the liturgy and one London radical reformer, Henry Brinklow, lamented how the city's 'inordinate rich, stiff-necked citizens processed through the filthy streets during epidemics, calling upon the saints with their cries of *ora pro nobis* [Pray for me ...]'. They refused to have the English translation of the New Testament in their homes, 'nor suffer their servants to read it, neither yet gladly read it, or hear it read'.[20]

The first sign of Henry's obsession with religious orthodoxy was the proclamation, issued in late 1538, that reaffirmed that heretics were not to be tolerated. These included Anabaptists, who recognised only the baptism of adults, and the so-called 'sacramentaries' who denied Christ's corporal presence in the holy wafer and wine of the Eucharist. Upholding their beliefs meant death by being burned alive at the stake.

A more rigorous legal regime followed that stopped the evolutionary religious reforms dead in their tracks.

Cromwell was laid low with a fever and missed the opening of Parliament on 28 April 1539 but had recovered enough to take up his seat on 10 May. The new Speaker was one of Norfolk's protégés, Sir Nicholas Hare,[21] and the stage was set for a policy coup against the minister, which could only have been approved by the king himself. On 16 May Norfolk stood up in Parliament and, after accusing Cromwell of 'slothfulness' in his role as Vice-Regent in matters spiritual,[22] announced that Henry desired legislation to create new tenets of religion in England 'to abolish diversity in opinion'. He posed six profound questions to their temporal and spiritual lordships (fully anticipating six conservative answers) which later formed the meat of the Bill. These were probably the handiwork of the irascible Gardiner, but a surviving copy of them, profusely amended in Henry's own hand, indicates his own close involvement as God's own deputy on earth. He edited the description of his own title in the Act's preamble – amended from 'Supreme Head of this

Henry VII, who seized the throne at Bosworth, kept two Howard sons
hostage, as pages at his court, to guarantee the loyalty of
their father, Thomas, Earl of Surrey, after he was freed from
the Tower of London.

John Howard, first Duke of Norfolk, painted in the late sixteenth century for Lord Lumley. The first Duke died valiantly at Bosworth, leading Richard III's vanguard.

Thomas Howard, second Duke of Norfolk. His loyal service to Henry VII and his son, Henry VIII, including the crushing defeat of the Scots at the Battle of Flodden in 1513, brought back the dukedom and his lands. In his hand, he holds the wand of office as Lord High Treasurer of England, an office he passed to his son in 1522.

Henry VIII, painted around 1535. His uncertain temper, and the
constant conspiracies of those jockeying for position around him
at court, made life uncertain and perilous for those serving him
in high office – not least the Howards.

THOMAS · DVKE · OFF · NORFOLK · MARSHALL ·
AND · TRESVRER · OFF · INGLONDE
THE · LXVI YERE · · OF · HIS · AGE ·

Thomas Howard, third Duke of Norfolk. He was arrogant, ambitious, and willing to sacrifice those close to him in order to survive. A conservative to the last, he was one of the last great landowners to maintain the old feudal system on his estates in East Anglia.

Anne Boleyn, niece of the third Duke of Norfolk. Her tantrums and failure
to provide Henry VIII with his longed-for male heir were her undoing.

Henry Fitzroy, Duke of Richmond, Henry VIII's bastard son, who married Mary Howard, daughter of the third Duke of Norfolk, but their marriage was never consummated.

SAT
SVPER
EST

Henry Howard, Earl of Surrey, eldest son of the third Duke of Norfolk. He may have been one of the greatest poets of the sixteenth century, but his temper and anti-social behaviour stemmed from the haughty arrogance of the Howards.

Church in England' to the resounding 'by God's law, Supreme Head of this Church and Congregation of England'.[23]

The Bill seemed draconian. It came to be called the 'Six Articles' or, in Protestant eyes, the 'whip with six strings' or the 'Bloody Act'. In its final version, it laid down:

1 That in the most blessed Sacrament of the Altar, by the strength and efficacy of Christ's mighty word, it being spoken by the priest, is present really, under the form of bread and wine, the natural Body and Blood of Our Saviour Jesu Christ, conceived of the Virgin Mary, and that after the consecration, there remains no substance of bread or wine, nor any other substance but the substance of Christ, God and man.

2 Communion in both kinds is not necessarily *ad salutem* [the way to salvation] by the law of God to all persons and that it is to be believed and not doubted that in the flesh under form of bread is the very Blood and with the Blood under form of wine is the very Flesh as well apart, as they were both together.

3 Priests ... received [into the priesthood] as afore may not marry by the law of God.

4 Vows of chastity or widowhood by man or woman made to God advisedly ought to be observed by the law of God and that it exempts them from other liberties of Christian people which without that they might enjoy.

5 It is meet and necessary that private masses be continued and admitted in this, the King's English Church and Congregation, as whereby, good Christian people, ordering themselves, do receive both godly and goodly consolations and benefits and it is agreeable to God's law.

6 Auricular [private] confession is expedient and necessary to be retained and continued, used and frequented in the Church of God.[24]

Anyone who scorned, refused or abstained from confession or to receive the Sacrament 'shall suffer such imprisonment and make such fine and ransom to the king'. On a second offence, they 'shall suffer pains of death and forfeit all ... goods, lands and tenements, as in cases of felony'.

There is much talk here of 'God's law' – but this was very much Henry's law, and there were grievous secular penalties for breaking it, the severity of which bear Bishop Gardiner's own individual stamp of intolerance.[25] Transgressors faced death by hanging, drawing and quartering, and forfeiture of goods and estates – exactly the same punishment as that for traitors. Those trying to escape the new law by fleeing England would be automatically guilty of treason and therefore also liable to suffer the same terrible fate after capture.

The Act consolidated existing laws against religious dissent and deviation: heresy was now a secular offence and closely redefined. Any person 'by word, writing, imprinting, ciphering or any other ways to publish, teach, say, affirm, declare, dispute, argue, or hold contrary opinion' who, together with their aiders and abettors, would be 'adjudged heretics and therefore had [to] suffer judgement, execution, pain, and pains of death ... by burning'.

The debate on Norfolk's proposals continued vociferously over three successive days, 19–21 May 1539. Henry attended each day's debate and spoke strongly in support of the Six Articles on each occasion. Inevitably, he 'confounded them all with God's learning'. His presence in the House of Lords and his personal interventions meant that opposition by the likes of Archbishop Cranmer and his six reforming bishops had become nugatory. Only 'that lewd fool', Nicholas Shaxton, Bishop of Salisbury, persisted in his dissent, but he missed the final vote because his household was infected with the plague.[26] The Act duly passed into English law on 28 June by royal assent.[27]

The next morning the king joined Norfolk, Cromwell and the Duke of Suffolk at what was planned to be a conciliatory dinner with an apprehensive and bruised Archbishop at Lambeth Palace. After a strained and difficult meal at the high table, punctured by long silences, Cromwell decided to lighten the conversation.

Courteously, he favourably compared his friend Cranmer with Wolsey, claiming that the Cardinal had 'lost his friends by his haughtiness and pride' but the Archbishop 'gained on his enemies by his gentleness and mildness'. From there, the conversation went downhill very quickly.

Norfolk, who bitterly recalled that he had saved the minister from political oblivion after the Cardinal's downfall, sneered that at least Cromwell could speak well of Wolsey, as 'he knew him well, having been his man'. Cromwell snapped back that, yes, he had worked for Wolsey, 'yet he never liked his manners'. Furthermore, he 'was never so far in love with Wolsey as to have waited on him in Rome, as he thought Norfolk would have done', adding mischievously that, if the Cardinal had become Pope, the duke would have served him as his Lord Admiral.

Norfolk, who had hated Wolsey with a passion, retorted 'with a deep oath' that Cromwell had lied.[28]

A few days after the Act of Six Articles came into force, the minister's own chaplain, Henry Molet, panicked over its provisions. He tried to recall a biblical tract from the printers, as he feared its contents would bring the full force of the law down upon him: 'I dare not be so bold over such statutes as I can be with doctors upon scriptures,' he bleated.

The reformist bishops found themselves in an equal measure of distress. There were wild rumours that Hugh Latimer, Bishop of Worcester, had been arrested in disguise at Gravesend in Kent, illegally trying to flee England for the friendlier regime of the Lutheran states in Germany. The gossip was groundless, but Latimer and his fellow evangelical bishop, Shaxton, resigned their bishoprics within the week and quickly found themselves under house arrest in London.

Within days, a barber-surgeon, a soldier and two priests, all from Calais[29] and suspected of heretical sacramentary views, were interrogated in London. The Bishop of Winchester attended the examination of the soldier, Ralph Hare, at Lambeth on 6 July. When the prisoner was warned that his opinions would cost him his life, unsurprisingly he was transfixed by terror. Gardiner told him bluntly:

By my troth [faith] I pity you much. For in good faith I think you a good simple man … [and well-meaning], but you have had shrewd and subtle schoolmasters … It is a pity that you should be burned, for you are a good fellow, a tall man, and have served the king right well in his wars.

You know my lord of Canterbury's grace here is a good, gentle lord, and [who] would be loath [that] you should be cast away. Tell me, can you be content to submit yourself to him?

The soldier fell to his knees, crying piteously, and willingly submitted.[30] As his and the other prisoners' heresy dated from before the Six Articles had entered law, they were spared, after making full recantations. They were still paraded through the London streets as a public humiliation, each one carrying a symbolic faggot, or bundle of firewood – the fuel for heretics' pyres – before beginning various terms of imprisonment.[31]

The Act's provisions struck very close to home for Cranmer. He had married Margaret, the niece of the Lutheran divine Andreas Osiander, at Nuremberg, while serving there as ambassador to Germany in 1532 – the year before his appointment as Archbishop of Canterbury. Then, as seven years later, clerical marriage was illegal. Cranmer plainly believed in the wisdom of 'out of sight, out of mind' and so he packed Margaret off, back to Germany.

He also was unable to conceal his opposition to the Six Articles, and spent many hours writing down closely reasoned arguments, supported by relevant citations from the Bible, to present to the king. His secretary, Ralph Morice, made a fair copy of his master's treatise in a small notebook, and departed by boat from Lambeth for the short journey downriver to Westminster, to deliver it to Henry. But he faced an alarming emergency en route:

Some others that were with him in the wherry[32] needed to go to the Southwark side to look at a bear-baiting that was near the river, where the king was in person.

The bear broke loose into the river [with] the dogs after her. Those who were in the boat leapt out and left the poor secretary alone.

But the bear got into the boat, with the dogs about her, and sank it. The secretary, apprehending [that] his life was in danger, did not mind his book, which he lost in the water.

But being quickly rescued and brought to land, he began to look for his book and saw it floating on the river.

So he desired the bearward [bear-keeper] to bring it to him:

who took it up, but before he could restore it, put it into the hands of a priest that stood there, to see what it might contain.[33]

The illiterate bear-keeper, who was employed in Princess Elizabeth's household, was told by the priest, after a swift glance through its sodden pages, that whoever claimed the book would face certain death. The rank smell of ample reward filled the bearward's nostrils and 'no offers or entreaties could prevail on him to give it back'. The Archbishop's secretary panicked, sought out Cromwell for assistance, and next day they discovered the bearward at the Palace of Westminster, seeking to hand over the book to Cranmer's enemies, Norfolk or the odious Gardiner. The minister snatched it 'out of his hands [and] threatened him severely for his presumption in meddling with a Privy Councillor's book'. Cranmer was safe.

It was surprising that Cromwell could spare the time to retrieve compromising books, preoccupied as he was with the unfamiliar role of marriage broker in a delicate quest to find a fourth wife for Henry. Choosing a successor to Jane Seymour from the great aristocratic houses of England was too risky politically, and, after a number of princesses from the Habsburg and Valois dynasties in Europe were unsuccessfully solicited, the minister at last secured the dimpled, podgy hand of twenty-two-year-old Anne of Cleves, from a north German ducal state,[34] at the beginning of October 1539.

When the king met his new bride, he was aghast at both her pockmarked appearance and deplorable personal hygiene. After much angry prevarication, he reluctantly, unwillingly and resentfully went through with his marriage to her at Greenwich Palace on 6 January 1540. Inevitably the wedding night was a disaster and after four nights of grudging effort, Henry had not consummated the marriage. Very soon, he decided he wanted rid of his 'Flanders Mare'. He turned on Cromwell for arranging the match – 'I am not well handled,' he growled – and there may have been occasions when, as gossip suggested, the enraged and frustrated king slapped and pummelled his minister about the head.[35]

Norfolk and Gardiner watched the discomfiture of their enemy at court with something approaching glee, if that is a sentiment either would allow themselves.

They devised a sophisticated entrapment that would finally overthrow the despised and hated Cromwell, restore everything they cherished in the old liturgy, and provide them with an inestimably powerful political weapon at court.

The trap came in the shape of another of Norfolk's nieces, pretty eighteen-year-old Catherine Howard, the giddy, empty-headed daughter of the duke's recently deceased spendthrift brother, Lord Edmund Howard,[36] and his second wife, Joyce Culpeper, who had died in the 1520s. Catherine had been brought up by her step-grandmother, Agnes, Dowager Duchess of Norfolk, at the Howard seats at Lambeth and at Chesworth, in Horsham, in Sussex. The new French ambassador, Charles de Marillac, described her as more graceful than beautiful and short of stature. She was auburn-haired, with hazel eyes, and Norfolk ensured that she was appointed one of the twelve maids in waiting to the unwanted queen.

Use of the word cannot be avoided, shameful as it sounds.

To all intents and purposes, Norfolk and Gardiner were pimping.

They hoped to make Catherine at least Henry's mistress, but, better still, his fifth queen, who then would be malleable to their influence and compliant to their wishes.

They succeeded, beyond their wildest expectations.

Henry first met Catherine at Gardiner's sprawling fourteenth-century Gothic palace in Southwark, on the south bank of the Thames, in the spring of 1540. As he watched the youthful dancers pirouette in the bishop's great hall, his rheumy old eyes alighted on the laughing and giggling Catherine, dressed fashionably in the French style and dancing 'wilfully'. Always flirting, she knew full well how to please men.

The king was then frequently invited to banquets at Winchester House and to 'entertainments' by the dowager duchess to Norfolk House in Lambeth that spring and early summer. Very soon, he 'did cast a fancy' to Catherine and she was put on a royal pedestal, to be adored, 'a blushing rose without a thorn'.[37] How much the teenager understood the ramifications of her uncle's plot must be a matter of debate. Anyway, she shamelessly accepted Henry's geriatric attentions. As early as Easter, he was showering expensive jewellery on the Howard girl and granting her the lands of two convicted felons. Ralph Morice, Cranmer's secretary, observed that Henry's 'affection was so marvellously set upon the gentlewoman as it was never known that he had the like to any woman'.[38]

The king had fallen madly, deeply in love with yet another niece of the Duke of Norfolk. They made a grotesque couple. He was now forty-nine, and, at six feet three inches tall, towered over the diminutive girl. The mismatch was accentuated by his huge and rapidly increasing girth, probably caused by the early stages of an acute endocrine abnormality called Cushing's syndrome.[39] Catherine was also thirty years younger than him and six years younger than his daughter, Princess Mary.

As Henry's appetite for her girlish charms sharpened that hot summer of 1540, his sour distaste for his queen changed into a restless impatience to banish her from his life. He wanted rid of poor Anne of Cleves as soon as possible and, as Cromwell had got him into this marital nightmare, now he could get him out of it. As the king's resentment grew, he listened to the devious siren voices of those around him who had other agendas, particularly Norfolk and Gardiner.

Cromwell recognised that Anne of Cleves could become his stolid if unwitting nemesis, and so she proved. He also knew where the danger came from: the minister warned Richard Pate, about to embark on a diplomatic assignment to Germany, that association with the duke was dangerous.[40] Cromwell therefore moved to neutralise his enemies.

His prognosis was quite justified. Norfolk, now back on the Privy Council, felt his political power waxing just as Cromwell's was waning. The duke returned to London on 1 March after a three-week-long diplomatic mission to France, and had mischievously repeated Francis I's belief that Cromwell's removal from office would improve Anglo-French relations. With startling effrontery, on 11 March Norfolk also wrote to Cromwell seeking information about future policy towards France. The duke had been receiving a generous pension from the French government and if this was going to be cut off, he would like to trim his household spending by firing a few superfluous servants.[41]

The minister relied upon Wolsey's tried and trusted formula of finding work for his enemies far away from court to silence their conspiracies. Three days later, he sent Norfolk to the north to superintend the destruction of an abbey and then sought to confine him to Kenninghall because of an infectious disease afflicting one of his servants.[42]

All his efforts were to no avail.

The French ambassador reported on 10 April that Cromwell and Cranmer 'do not know where they are'. He predicted:

> Within a few days, there will be seen in this country a great change in many things which this king begins to make in his ministers, recalling those he had rejected and degrading those he has raised.
>
> Cromwell is tottering. All those recalled, who were dismissed by his means, reserve [not] *une bonne pensée* [one good thought] for him – among others, the bishops of Winchester, Durham and Bath, men of great learning and experience, who are now summoned to the Privy Council.[43]

Norfolk ordered one of his dependants at court, Sir Anthony Wingfield, the captain of the King's Guard, to the Parliament House early on the morning of Saturday 10 June 1540. He instructed him to bring a file of halberdiers to the Palace of Westminster and to arrest Cromwell after dinner, during a meeting of the Privy Council at the king's house. The officer was stunned by the mission, but the duke told him peremptorily: 'You need not be surprised. The king orders it.'[44]

The duke's relationship with Cromwell over the years had swerved, back and forth, between lukewarm friendship and bitter enmity. In September 1534, they had argued publicly over policy on Ireland, yet on Ascension Day, 6 May 1535, he had written: 'Since I saw you last, you have most lovingly handled me. You will always find me a faithful friend, grudge who will.'[45] Two years later, when the widower minister[46] stayed with Norfolk, the rough old soldier joked pruriently that if he lust not to dally with my wife [?a reference to his correspondence with Elizabeth, Duchess of Norfolk] he could find him a young woman with pretty proper tetins [breasts] for his entertainment.

In March 1539, the duke had added a postscript to a letter to Cromwell, surprisingly dropping an important formality: 'my lord, I require you to [call me your] grace no more in your letters, for surely it is not convenient that one of your sort should do so'.[47]

Behind Norfolk's chameleon façade, however, was his deep-seated hatred and contempt for a brewer and fuller's son who now pulled the levers of power in England. An Act, passed the previous year, gave Cromwell, as the king's secretary, precedence over everyone, be they barons, bishops, or commoners.[48] It was legislation that proud and arrogant Norfolk found impossible to stomach. Henry's grant of the Earldom of Essex to Cromwell on 17 April and his appointment as Lord Great Chamberlain of England – both positions held down the centuries by the great noble houses – swelled still more his resentment and umbrage. He despised Cromwell. He envied his wealth, status and influence with the king. He loathed everything this jack-in-office stood for.

The duke had brought down another of that ilk, Cardinal Wolsey, and now, at long last, he was to add Cromwell's scalp to his belt. Norfolk was going to savour this day for years to come.

When an unsuspecting Cromwell walked into the Council chamber at about three o'clock that afternoon, the duke snapped the jaws of his trap. He stood up, a smile of triumph creasing his fleshy features, and shouted at the minister: 'Cromwell! Do not sit there! That is no place for you!'

All the pent-up antagonism and jealousy over low-born upstarts occupying the pinnacles of power burst out in Norfolk's snarling sneer: 'Traitors do not sit among gentlemen!'

Wingfield, listening at the door, then entered the chamber with six halberdiers and arrested Cromwell. The minister dashed his cap on to the floor in fury, glared at the duke and cried out reproachfully: 'This, then, is the reward for all my services.' He appealed to the other councillors, now crowding round him: 'On your consciences, I ask you, am I a traitor?'

If he was looking for sympathy, he found it wanting. Their answer was robust. Scenting blood, some shouted 'Yes' and chanted 'Traitor, traitor, traitor' – their fists beating on the Council table in time with their chants.

Wingfield, fearful that his prisoner was going to be attacked, began to push and tug a protesting Cromwell out of the room, but a jubilant Norfolk wanted to humiliate and debase his fallen enemy still further. 'Stop, captain,' he ordered, 'traitors must not wear the Garter.' He marched up and pulled the glittering Order of St George from around Cromwell's neck and threw it to the floor. The minister's one-time friend Sir William Fitzwilliam, Earl of Southampton, tugged at and finally ripped the Garter insignia off Cromwell's gown. As they stood back panting from their exertions, he was bundled out of the room and taken by boat to the Tower.[49]

Norfolk and Gardiner were now paramount at court and took a leading role in how Cromwell's downfall was to be presented for propaganda purposes and in drawing up the charges against him. Religion was to be the hook upon which they hung him.

Hours after the arrest, a 'gentleman' of the court brought a letter from the king to the French envoy Marillac. Henry wrote that despite his 'wishing by all means to lead back religion to the way of truth, Cromwell, as attached to the German Lutherans, had always favoured the doctors who preached such erroneous opinions'.

Recently, warned by some of his principal servants to reflect that he was working against the intention of the king and of the Acts of Parliament, he had betrayed himself and said he hoped to suppress the old preachers and have only the new, adding that the affair would soon be brought to such a pass that the king with all his power could not prevent it.

His own party would be so strong that he would make the king descend to the new doctrines even if he had to take arms against him.

These plots were told the king by those who heard them and who esteemed their fealty more than the favour of their master.[50]

The next day, compromising letters between him and the German Lutherans were conveniently discovered at his house at

Austin Friars – possibly planted by Norfolk's agents. Henry was so 'exasperated' at their content 'that he could no longer hear [Cromwell] spoken of, but rather desired to abolish all memory of him as the greatest wretch ever born in England'.[51] The minister was stripped of all titles and it was decreed that he should henceforth be called merely 'Thomas Cromwell, shearman'.

The French king Francis I wrote to Henry on 15 June, praising God for the minister's downfall, and for revealing 'the faults and malversations[52] of the unhappy person Cromwell, who alone has been the cause of all the suspicions conceived against not only [Henry's] friends but his best servants'. Henry would soon realise 'how much the getting rid of this wicked ... instrument will tranquillise his kingdom, to the common welfare of church, nobles and people'.[53] The French king's comments indicate the trouble Norfolk had taken to poison his mind about Cromwell. As we have seen, a few months earlier Norfolk had cheerfully reported Francis's views about the minister. Indeed, the king added in his letter: 'Norfolk will be able to remember what I said', so *he* clearly recalled the duke's complaints about his treatment at Cromwell's hands.

On 17 June, Norfolk and Gardiner introduced a Bill of Attainder against Cromwell in the House of Lords.[54] It was a spiteful document, short on facts but long on invective. The fallen minister, whom Henry had raised 'from a very base and low degree', had become 'the most false and corrupt traitor, deceiver and circumventor' of the king's reign, as had been proved by many 'personages of great honour, worship and discretion'. He was accused of being a 'detestable heretic' who sowed sedition and 'false and erroneous books' that discredited the Blessed Sacraments.

The religious charges were the work of Gardiner, but Norfolk now had a chance to vent his spleen, accusing Cromwell of holding

the nobles of the realm in great disdain, derision and detestation ... and being put in remembrance [by] others of his estate ... said most arrogantly, willingly, maliciously and traitorously, on 31 January 1540 in the parish of St Martin's in the Fields [London] that if the lords would handle him so, he would give them such a breakfast as never was made in England and that the proudest of them should know.[55]

The Bill declared that he should suffer death as a heretic or traitor at Henry's pleasure and should forfeit all property granted or held since 31 March 1539. It was passed, without dissent, on 29 June, just before Parliament adjourned.[56]

Henry needed Cromwell's evidence to win his annulment of the loveless marriage with Anne of Cleves. Norfolk gloatingly led a small delegation of senior councillors to question him in the Tower, charging him to declare 'as he would answer God at the day of judgement and also upon the extreme danger and damnation of his soul' what he knew of the match. Cromwell quickly supplied the necessary evidence and Henry himself swore that 'I never for love to the woman consented to marry, nor yet if she brought maidenhead with her, took any from her by true carnal copulation'.[57] The duke was among a group of notables, including Cranmer and Bishop Tunstall, who also produced some rather bland testimony, signing himself 'T Norfolk'.[58]

The Clerical Convocation of two archbishops, sixteen bishops and one hundred and thirty-nine learned academics therefore annulled the king's fourth marriage on 9 July, their decision confirmed by Parliament four days later.[59] Anne was pensioned off and awarded an annuity of £500, or £220,000 a year at today's prices, and a handsome portfolio of property, some of which came from Cromwell's forfeited estates.

There was much popular curiosity about what kind of dreadful means would be employed to kill Cromwell. Norfolk promised that his enemy's demise would be 'the most ignominious use in the country'. By this, he may have been referring to the decision – was it his? – to execute the disgraced minister with the clearly mad Walter, Lord Hungerford, who had been condemned for a whole raft of heinous crimes: sodomy, raping his daughter, paying magicians to predict when Henry would die and, finally, employing a chaplain who sympathised with the rebels in the Pilgrimage of Grace.[60] His presence on the scaffold was an attempt publicly to humiliate Cromwell at his last hour.

That came on the morning of 28 July at Tower Hill. The king had decided, in his infinite mercy, that Cromwell would suffer death by simple decapitation.

Perhaps deliberately, a clumsy or at least inexperienced headsman called Gurrea was employed for the grisly task. One account talks of him and his assistant 'chopping the Lord Cromwell's neck and head for nearly half an hour'.[61]

Norfolk's eldest son, Surrey, sneered: 'Now is the false churl dead, so ambitious of others' [noble] blood. These new erected men, would by their wills, leave no noble man a life.' Acts of Attainder – Cromwell's own device to destroy traitors – had become the instrument of his own demise: 'Now he is stricken,' Surrey crowed triumphantly, 'with his own staff.'[62]

On the same day that Cromwell was executed, Henry married Catherine Howard in a private ceremony at Oatlands Palace, near Weybridge, in Surrey.

The Queen of England was now a Howard.

Not everyone was jubilant about Cromwell's death. In September, on his return to court, one of the king's sewers,[63] John Lassells, met three reformist friends, called Jonson, Maxey and Smethwick, in the king's great chamber. He asked: 'What news is there pertaining to God's Holy Word, seeing we have lost so noble a man [Cromwell] which did love and favour it so well?' Lassells did not believe that Norfolk and Gardiner loved the Bible. Maxey said the duke was not ashamed to declare 'that he had never read Scripture in English, nor ever would. Only yesterday I overheard him say "It was merry in England before this new learning came up."' There were rumours around the court that Norfolk had rebuked a bureaucrat in the Court of Exchequer for marrying a nun, who had been expelled from her religious house. Her new husband had told him simplistically: 'Well, I know no nuns or religious folk, nor such bondage, seeing God and the king have made them free.' His response infuriated Norfolk: 'By God's sacred Body, that may be, but it will never be out of my heart as long as I live,' cried the duke as he stormed off.

Lassells said the evangelicals at the court should not be 'too rash or quick in maintaining the Scriptures, for if we let them [Norfolk and Gardiner] alone and suffer a little time, they would (I doubt not) overthrow themselves. They stand so manifestly against God and their prince that they cannot long survive.'

With an element perhaps of wishful thinking, the four courtiers then discussed whether Norfolk's words could possibly be construed as treasonable and the next day Smethwick repeated them to an official who advised him to speak to a member of the king's Council. Nothing, of course, came of it. Lassells underestimated Norfolk and six years later he was to be burned at the stake for heresy.

Meanwhile, Henry was still captivated by his bride. In September, Marillac said the king was 'so amorous of her that he cannot treat her well enough and caresses her more than he did the others'.[64] He was determined to show her off and that summer took her on a whirlwind progress through the counties of Surrey, Berkshire, Buckinghamshire and Oxfordshire, hunting and feasting all the way.

The sun was now smiling again on the House of Howard and honours and positions were heaped upon them. Surrey was created a Knight of the Garter and appointed Cupbearer to Henry. His sister Mary became a member of the queen's household and Catherine's brother Charles was made a Gentleman of the king's Privy Chamber. Marillac believed that Norfolk 'nowadays has the chief management of affairs' in the realm.

The following year the royal couple went north for a long-promised progress, reaching York on 16 September, where their subjects cherished hopes, subsequently unfulfilled, that Catherine would formally be crowned queen. By now, the frivolous, flighty queen was bored with her obese husband's fumbling, flatulent attentions and began to look elsewhere for affection.

Henry returned to Hampton Court at the end of October and gave instructions that on 1 November 1541 – All Hallows Day – there would be special prayers offered for 'the good life he led and trusted to lead' with 'this jewel of womanhood', his queen.

Unbeknown to him, John Lassells, whom we have just met, had been talking to his married sister, Mary Hall, a nurse to one of the children of Lord William Howard, Norfolk's half-brother, and from 1533, chamberer to the dowager duchess. Her disclosures about the queen's earlier nocturnal shenanigans at Chesworth and Lambeth sent Lassells running hotfoot to the Archbishop of Canterbury, with the most scandalous news.

Cranmer was astonished, havered for a while, and finally screwed up enough courage to scribble a letter to his sovereign, which he left sealed in Henry's pew in the Chapel Royal. On the note's cover, the Archbishop prudently asked him to read it in private.

The king was incredulous, disbelieving, and, unusually, struggled for words. Cranmer's letter informed him that his beloved wife had behaved licentiously with Henry Monox, a lute player from Streatham in Surrey who had taught her the virginals when she was just fifteen while she stayed at the Norfolk house in Horsham. Unfortunately, she learned more from him than just nimble finger work on the keyboard. Two years later, she had a lusty affair with a gentleman page called Francis Dereham – the same man whom the queen had recently appointed her secretary and usher of her chamber. Henry asked Southampton, now Lord Privy Seal, secretly to investigate the allegations.

Worse was to come.

Under interrogation at the Tower, Dereham named Thomas Culpeper, one of the king's especial favourites in the Privy Chamber, as having 'succeeded him in the queen's affections'. Marillac later commented dryly that here was a young man who shared the king's bed who now 'wished to share the queen's too'.[65]

A week later, at Gardiner's palace at Southwark, a hesitant and apprehensive Council laid out the evidence that was accumulating against the queen before a still sceptical Henry. It must have been a tense, torrid meeting; it went on all day and most of the night, but finally the king was convinced of his wife's past debauchery and her current betrayal of him – with Culpeper of all people.

The effect was so terrible that his councillors, Norfolk among them, cowered in their robes. Henry treated them to the most terrifying of all rages. He called for a sword so that he could kill Catherine 'that he loved so much'. And that 'wicked woman' had 'never such delight in her incontinency as she [will] have torture in her death', he screamed at the courtiers. They believed his anger had driven him insane, and they shrank from his rage, as he blamed them for 'soliciting' him to marry her. His frenzy eventually broke down into tears and, blubbing like a child, he sobbed about his 'ill-luck in meeting with such ill-conditioned wives'.[66]

They departed the meeting looking 'very troubled, especially Norfolk, who is esteemed very resolute and not easily moved to show by his face what his heart conceives', reported the perceptive Marillac.

On 12 November, the Privy Council wrote to Sir William Paget, ambassador to France, reporting 'a most miserable case lately revealed'. Dereham had confessed that he had known her carnally 'many times, both in his doublet and [hose between] the sheets and in naked bed'. The 'puffing and blowing' emanating from the heaving blankets on Catherine's bed had tiresomely kept the others awake in the girls' dormitory on several nights. Monox admitted he used 'to feel the [secret parts] of her body before Dereham was familiar with her'. The king's heart 'was pierced with pensiveness, so it was long before he could utter his sorrow and finally, with plenty [of tears] (which was strange in his courage) opened the same'. The letter added pessimistically: 'Now you may see what was done before her marriage. God knows what has been done since.'[67]

The investigation gathered speed, as a devastated king shunned his wife at Hampton Court. Marillac said the queen

who did nothing but dance and amuse herself, now keeps her apartments without showing herself ... when musicians with instruments call at her door, they are dismissed, saying it was no longer time for dancing.

Her brother Charles Howard was also exiled from court. Marillac added:

The Duke of Norfolk must be exceedingly sorry and troubled for the queen happens to be his own niece and the daughter of his brother, just as Anne [Boleyn] was also his niece on his sister's side and his having been the chief cause of the king marrying her.[68]

Norfolk interrogated Catherine roughly but it was Cranmer's gentler manner, plus his promise of mercy, that made her admit her licentious romps with Dereham.[69] There were further distressing questions, and she refused 'to drink or eat and weeps and cries like a madwoman, so they must take away things by which she might hasten her death', according to her uncle.

Witnesses recounted how the dowager duchess discovered Dereham in Catherine's arms, 'and she beat her and gave Joan Bulmer a stroke who stood by. Often she blamed him ... for keeping company together, saying he would never be out of Catherine Howard's chamber.' On another occasion she asked where he was, muttering 'I am sure he is sleeping in the gentlewomen's chamber.'[70]

Piece by piece, the evidence against the queen was mounting. The Privy Council was told that when the royal party was at Lincoln, Culpeper had entered her chamber 'by the backstairs' at eleven o'clock at night and had remained there until four the next morning. Another tryst had occurred in the cramped and noisome surroundings of the queen's stool chamber, or lavatory. Hardly romantic. Her servant, Margaret Morton, testified that she never mistrusted the queen until at Hatfield, when she saw her glance out of her chamber window 'on Mr Culpeper after such a sort that she thought there was love between them'.[71]

Culpeper himself admitted 'many stolen interviews' with Catherine, which had been arranged by her lady of the Privy Chamber, Lady Jane Rochford, widow of Anne Boleyn's beheaded brother, George. The queen clearly had a liking for intrigue and in every house during the northern progress would 'seek for the back doors and back stairs' herself. At Pontefract, she feared the king 'had set watch at the back door' and her servant 'waited in the court to see if that were so'.[72]

The Howards were soon compromised in the investigation and many were dragged off to the Tower. The Lieutenant there warned the Privy Council that there were not enough rooms to 'lodge them severally' unless the king and queen's own lodgings were used. The king agreed to this, but his keys to the apartments could not be found and accommodation for some prisoners had to be arranged elsewhere.

Lord William Howard and Margaret, his wife, were among

those arrested. He admitted that he knew of his niece's behaviour with Dereham and, when told of it, had exclaimed: 'What mad wenches!' The dowager duchess and her daughter, the Countess of Bridgewater, were also imprisoned. All were accused of misprision of treason.

Norfolk desperately tried to distance himself from his niece, telling Marillac 'with tears in his eyes, of the king's grief' who had loved Catherine 'much and the misfortunes to his house in her and Queen Anne [Boleyn], his two nieces'.[73] Despairingly, he told Chapuys, the Spanish ambassador, 'I wish the queen was burned.'[74]

The duke sat uncomfortably as one of the judges at the trial of Culpeper and Dereham for treason at the Guildhall. Marillac commented:

A strange thing has been noted that Norfolk ... in examining the prisoners laughed as if he had cause to rejoice. His son, the Earl of Surrey, was also there, and the brothers of the queen and Culpeper rode about the town.

It is the custom and must be done to show that they did not share the crimes of their relatives.[75]

After a hearing lasting around six hours, Dereham and Culpeper were found guilty. Both were executed at Tyburn on 10 December, with the king unexpectedly commuting the sentence to simple beheading for Culpeper, rather than the hanging and evisceration cruelly suffered by Dereham. The heads of both men were displayed on London Bridge.

Norfolk was, above all else, a survivor in the cut and thrust politics of Henry's court. Now was the time speedily to abandon his kith and kin to save his own neck. The duke had prudently moved to Kenninghall, well away from the hullabaloo in London. On 15 December 1541, he picked up his pen and 'scribbled' a sycophantic, obsequious letter to his king:

Most noble and gracious Sovereign Lord: Yesterday [it] came to my knowledge that my own ungracious [step] mother my unhappy brother and his wife, with my lewd sister of Bridgewater were committed to the Tower.

By long experience, knowing your accustomed equity and justice (used to all your subjects) [I] am sure [this was] not done but for some [of] their [faults] and traitorous proceedings against your royal majesty.

Which, revolving in my mind, with also the most abominable deeds done by two of my nieces against your highness, has brought me to [the] greatest perplexity that ever [a] poor wretch was in.

[I] fear that your majesty, having so often and by so many of my kin been thus falsely and traitorously handled, might not only conserve a displeasure in your heart against me and all other of that kin, but also . . . abhor to here speak of any of the same.

Norfolk, already 'prostrate and most humble' at the feet of his monarch, now sought to win credit for the discovery of his family's crimes:

I beseech your majesty to [remember] that a great part of this matter is come to light by my declaration to your majesty, according to my bounden duty, of the words spoken to me by my mother in law [stepmother], when your highness sent me to Lambeth to search Dereham's coffers.

Without the which, I think she [would] not be further examined, nor consequently her ungracious children.

Moreover, the dowager duchess – as well as his 'two false traitorous nieces' – had not shown any love towards him, and this rancour, together with his honest endeavours in the matter, gave him some 'hope that your highness will not conserve any displeasure in your most gentle heart against me'.

Still 'prostrate at your royal feet [and] most humble', Norfolk pleaded with Henry to tell him 'plainly' how 'your highness do weigh your favour towards me'. He assured the king:

Unless I know your majesty [continues] my good and gracious lord (as you were before their offences [were] committed), I shall never desire to live in this world any longer but [would] shortly to finish this transitory life, as God knows, who sends your majesty the accomplishments of your most noble heart's desires.[76]

There is no sign of drafting here. The words spill off the page, pleading, beseeching and grovelling for mercy. In Norfolk's mind, the incarceration and probable death of his immediate family was plainly a small price to pay for his survival and the achievement of his ambitions.

On 22 December, Lord William Howard and his wife, the wife of Catherine's elder brother Henry, and others of the Howard household were sentenced to 'perpetual imprisonment' for their misprision and their goods and estates confiscated. They and the dowager duchess were eventually freed in August 1542.

Norfolk returned to Lambeth at the turn of the year amidst continuing doubts about his own survival. By mid-January, however, he had returned to court 'apparently in his full former credit and authority'.[77]

No such mercy was shown to Catherine and her procuress, Lady Rochford. On 11 February 1542, the queen was found guilty of treason by Act of Attainder.[78] The following day she asked for the block to be delivered to her room in the Tower and spent the evening bizarrely rehearsing her own execution. The next morning at nine o'clock she was swiftly despatched on Tower Green. Lady Rochford, who had been thought mad during her questioning, immediately followed her to the scaffold and met the same fate. Always anxious to endow his actions with a veneer of legality, Henry had hurried an Act through Parliament allowing the execution of insane persons who had committed treason.[79]

Surrey watched his diminutive and terrified cousin die, 'so weak, that she could hardly speak'. But she did manage to confess 'in a few words that she merited a hundred deaths for so offending the king'.[80] One eyewitness, the merchant Ottwell Johnson, said both ladies 'made the most godly and Christian end that was ever heard tell of'.[81]

Norfolk and his son had survived a huge scandal.

Henry had not yet worked out when his time of reckoning would come for them.

7

DOWN BUT NOT OUT

——◆——

'His majesty, like a prince of wisdom, knows that who plays
at a game of chance must sometimes lose'

Sir William Paget to the Earl of Surrey, 18 January 1546[1]

After the execution of a second niece who had loved and lost her
royal bedmate, Thomas Howard, third Duke of Norfolk, was
languishing in another valley of dark despair in the roller-coaster
of Henry's regard. In early April 1542, the French ambassador
Marillac reported him still in disfavour, but two months later his
prospects had changed for the better. Maybe the derring-do of a
famous military exploit could rescue him from prolonged political
disgrace.

Henry, after the dark emotional turmoil of Catherine Howard's
betrayal and confronting advancing years and declining health,
also sought the glory of military adventures to rebuild his battered
self-esteem and cheer his old heart. Should Scotland or France
become his target? Egged on by the young bloods at his court, and
spurred by an embarrassing defeat during a skirmish at Hadden
Rig near Berwick on 24 August (when a small English force of
raiders was routed with the loss of 500 prisoners), Henry plumped
for war with the old foe across his northern border. With an
admirable diplomatic sleight of hand, he claimed feudal suzerainty
over James V of Scotland and objected to his nephew's failure to
reform his own Church and abjure the Pope's supremacy.

Conflict is expensive, and Norfolk was one of the 300 richest in
the realm who now faced hefty tax bills – both he and Suffolk had
each to find 6,000 crowns, or £1.3 million at current prices, to help
create a war chest of 300,000 crowns to pay for Henry's martial

ambitions. No wonder the duke was depressed and Marillac commented:

> The duke departed ... to refresh himself at his own house
> [Kenninghall], as he has been languishing all this Lent ... [being]
> very ill in body besides being mentally worried.[2]

Every head of state needs reliable, dependable generals and Norfolk
was again recalled to the colours, as 'Lieutenant and Captain-
General of the North'. Memories of Flodden, all those years before,
were kept alive by the late-night fireside boasts of veterans who
had fought the Scots on that bloody day. The duke found himself
happily returned to the king's grace and 'all men who have heretofore served in war are ordinarily at his house, reckoning to be
soon employed', the French envoy reported.[3]

Norfolk could never be described as a compliant general. There
were unquestionable shortcomings in the logistical support for
Henry's armies, but when reading Norfolk's despatches we can
detect not only overt impatience over poor planning, but also a
frequent, instinctive desire to justify in advance any future failure
on his part. Such insecurity, such lack of confidence was born out
of the king's unpredictable and violent temper, and the certain
knowledge that Norfolk had enemies aplenty at court, only too
pleased to point accusing fingers over the disgrace of military
blunders.

He wrote to the Privy Council from Kenninghall on 11 September 1542, his mind buzzing with the arrangements for the
expedition to Scotland. As far as the old campaigner was concerned, an army marched not only on its stomach, but refreshed
by beer. Likely shortages of this vital beverage for his troops were
his chief worry.[4] He told the councillors:

> I wrote of late to send 1,000 tuns[5] [barrels] of beer to Berwick
> and also wrote to Sir George Lawson [the Treasurer of Berwick]
> to know what he could furnish. His answer shows that he could
> do nothing towards furnishing so great an army for eight days
> going towards Edinburgh.
>
> These parts cannot help for lack of foists.[6] I am leaving here

in two or three hours and so cannot help ... but at York I will do my best. Hull and York should be written to, to brew as much as they can (1,500 tuns above that [sent] from London would not do too much).[7]

Norfolk's misgivings over the expedition were scarcely eased by Lawson's rather torpid reply a week later:

There are no tents of the king's in these parts. It is impossible to prepare so much bread against [your day of arrival]. I have set workmen to prepare 100 spears and sent to Newcastle for spearheads. I trust to provide forty bullocks and 100 wethers' [castrated sheep] against your coming.[8]

One hundred spears do not make an army. Norfolk and Sir Anthony Browne, the Master of the Horse, decided to speak out frankly about the shortcomings in supplies.[9] On 20 September, they wrote to the Privy Council:

Lawson's [letters] show how little of the victuals prepared in Norfolk, Suffolk and London is arrived and there is no knowledge of the ships of war, although the wind on Saturday, Sunday and Monday ... was as fair as could blow and now, with the rain yesterday, is so contrary that no man can come northward.

My Lord Privy Seal [Sir William Fitzwilliam, Earl of Southampton] does not sign this because he has been ill all night, which we think is for melancholy, because the victual ships are not arrived and that we are likely to lack bread and drink at Berwick for lack of foists and mills to grind wheat.

It is impossible to invade Scotland or ever pass Newcastle without victuals, although never men would more gladly accomplish the intended journey than we would.[10]

Norfolk, now labouring under 'a great agony of mind', was keen to protect his back in London, telling Gardiner and the king's secretary, Sir Thomas Wriothesley, that if he was blamed for the delays in supplies, he hoped they would be his 'buckler' [shield] of defence. He also had a keen sense of his own mortality. In what had become his custom before going into action, the duke had written a new will and had handed it over to Cuthbert Tunstall, Bishop of Durham, for safekeeping 'if the case requires'. He was suffering misgivings about his chances of success in this campaign:

> The Lord Privy Seal [Sir William Fitzwilliam, Earl of South-ampton] has been ill these eight or nine days and came hither this day in a litter. The fear of not being able to [take on] this journey troubles him and I would rather have an arm broken than miss his company, for without him [and Sir Anthony Browne] I [would be] all naked.[11]

But Norfolk, who had arrived in Newcastle in time for Fitzwilliam's subsequent death, was also fretting about other issues. On 12 October, he wrote again to Gardiner and Wriothesley, this time troubled by worries about his own future. He was now aged sixty-nine, not enjoying great health, and the thought of a late blossoming of his career in the service of the crown in the bleak border country, away from the comforts of court and the seat of power, horrified him. He begged them to make 'intercession with the king, when the time comes, not to name him Warden of the Scottish Marches'.

> In my old age, the winter here would kill me.
>
> I would rather lose the small substance of goods I have, than lie this winter in any house this side of Doncaster, save only Leconfield [Yorkshire] where the air is nothing so vehemently cold as it is here.

After all, he had more than served his time in the north: 'About twenty years past, I was the king's lieutenant here, when the Marquis of Dorset was Warden, who when the winter came, was discharged and I was charged with both offices.'[12]

His plea was successful: six days later, Henry wrote, somewhat sniffily, that he intended 'not to trouble Norfolk with the Wardenry' and, on 25 October, he selected Edward Seymour, first Earl of Hertford, to take up the post.[13] Paradoxically, Norfolk's relief was tinged with irritation that, by this appointment, the Seymour clan had continued their inexorable advancement in the public affairs of the realm. But on balance, the duke must have embarked on his latest military expedition with a lighter heart, knowing that administering the inhospitable heather-clad bogs, moors and mountains of the borders would be someone else's problem in the months ahead.

It was not that he did not relish fighting the Scots. He and his father, the second duke, had been the glorious victors at Flodden and he believed absolutely that his family had been 'appointed by God to be to the Scots a sharp scourge and rod'.[14] Now with Surrey, his son, and his half-brother, Lord William Howard,[15] riding beside him, Norfolk was determined to teach the unruly Scots another harsh lesson with steel and fire. 'We shall do as much as is possible for men to do,' he promised sombrely, 'to make the enemies speak according to the king's pleasure, or else make them such a smoke as never was in Scotland these hundred years.'[16]

On 19 October, Norfolk reported that his army would 'lie tomorrow in the field'. But his orders that with every 100 men 'there should be two carts laden with drink and with every ten, a spare horse with victuals' had been completely ignored. '[They] say it is impossible, as the carriages they did bring were destroyed by the foul ways and the weather.' Despite his instructions 'that no horse that should come past Newcastle, ... serve for a spear[man], a javelin or archer; all have come on naughty nags, saying they could not travel on foot and keep the day.'[17]

His 20,000-strong force of levies from the northern counties of England finally crossed the Scottish frontier three days later at Berwick.[18] The Duke of Suffolk and Bishop Tunstall soon heard of him, from near Coldstream, still complaining about the lack of food. His note, brought in by panting horseback messenger, urged Suffolk 'to warn all Northumberland to bake and brew for the army at their return'. Local reports suggested that Norfolk and his troops had headed off in the direction of the small town of Kelso 'from whence much gunshots [were] heard and [he] has done great harm'.[19]

It all sounded very encouraging. But the reality was very different.

On 28 October, Norfolk reported from Kelso, built on a bend of the River Tweed, that he had been 'forced to turn homeward and the next night shall be our last in Scotland'.

The principal cause is our lack of victuals, for few of the army found bread and drink between York and Newcastle and [it was] much worse in the four days' journey from Newcastle to Berwick.

Since entering Scotland, [for] the most part [we] have drunk nothing but water these five days and eaten no bread . . .

I never thought Englishmen could endure with so little and yet be willing to go forward.

I have come through such ill passages that the wains [wagons, drawn by horses or oxen] are broken . . . and ordnance and carriages have been with difficulty brought hither.

This day and yesterday nineteen men have died with drinking puddle water and lack of victuals and many more are like to follow.[20]

It was all a litany of accidents, worsened by 'horrible rains'. Five of his soldiers, for example, drowned when a bridge collapsed. On the positive side, his troops had looted and burned Kelso and its Romanesque abbey to the Blessed Virgin and St John, belonging to the Tironensian order.[21] Eight Scots had also been hanged for stealing his cavalry horses. That same day he sat down before dawn to assure his allies in London, Gardiner and Wriothesley, that 'his was the goodliest army I have [ever] seen'. Then came the nip: 'Had we set forth with victuals two months earlier, we might have done what we would, without great resistance.' The old warhorse was exhausted and ill with the distressing affliction of 'the lax' which was 'marvellously sore on me, as my lord of Hertford . . . knows'. One shudders to think how.

He begged his friends to obtain Henry's permission for him to return to court. His fervent plea was not only influenced by the debilitating effects of his uncontrollable bowels. A stronger motivation was his desire to snap up some of the choice property, belonging to his comrade-in-arms, the recently deceased and barely cold Fitzwilliam, which was now available. Others might profit by exploiting his absence in the benighted Scottish borders!

I hear that the king has distributed the late Privy Seal's things. I pray that the house of Bath Place[22] may light upon me, for I have no place in London, for I have no entry in Exeter Place but only of lending [?leasing].[23]

Just in case there were any lingering doubts at court as to his loyal service, Norfolk stressed that his 'cost and pain in this journey has been treble any other man's'.[24]

For all his suffering, Norfolk had lost none of his bravura: he claimed that his troops had so devastated the corn crops (?in late October) and the countryside that 'they shall not be able to recover [from] this displeasure [for] many years hereafter'.[25]

He was plainly scrabbling around, seeking to find tangible military benefits from his all too brief sojourn in Scotland. In truth, his much vaunted punitive expedition achieved almost nothing. A contemporary document talks of the twenty 'towns' he put to the torch around Kelso, but most were mere hamlets, some too small to appear on large-scale maps of the area. They may just have been single dwellings. At Kelso,

> A tall man of ours that was above in the abbey looking forth was killed by one of our gunners in mistake for a Scot. Certain of our men were taken and some slain.[26]

After just eight days wandering in enemy territory, he and his army were back in England. Norfolk, Hertford and Browne adroitly sensed they would not be viewed in London as all-conquering military heroes. Clearly rattled, they begged the king to believe that 'we have done all in our power'. Henry, naturally, was far from impressed, and they knew it. Norfolk feared that 'his highness is not pleased with proceedings. Assuredly, we could do no more as we will show when the king pleases to hear us.'[27]

A disgruntled Henry did require some hard facts on what glories his expensive attack on the Scottish borders had added to the lexicon of English military prowess. On 2 November, he sent an acerbic, caustic letter to Norfolk, which must have made uncomfortable reading:

> We wish that such a costly and notable enterprise had been more displeasant to [our] enemies.
> We marvel you have not sent the names of the towns, villages

and castles which you have destroyed, with an estimate of the spoil done that it might be set forth and magnified to the world.[28]

His generals became defensive, pointing out that no castles had been destroyed because 'they were thrown down by Norfolk twenty years past, and as for the towns and villages, we do not know the names'. But, they added, somewhat feebly, 'the country will not recover ... these many years'.[29]

The duke's sufferings and worries increased by the hour. An old man needs his comforts. He admitted to Wriothesley that 'I was never more vexed [afflicted] with my disease. Please forward my letter, enclosed, to my servants at [Chesworth in] Horsham to make provisions for my house this winter as I desire not to be far from court. I dare not take great journeys.'[30] Two days later, he wrote again to Wriothesley, describing his ailment in almost scatological detail:

> Since I wrote last, I have been so very ill of the lax that if medicines had not stopped it, I think I should never have seen you. I had incredible purging from six o'clock on Friday until ten o'clock in the morning but am now well.[31]

Despite his 'incredible purging', Norfolk was still anxious about his chances of acquiring Bath Place, and, indeed, whether the king still held a good opinion of him. 'I have had no letter from you or the Council for a long time' was the cry of a man a long way from home and uncertain of the welcome awaiting his return. He added plaintively, with a rare hint of honesty: 'I am sure that no man could have done more to give satisfaction, though all things may not have been [done] as well as could have been wished.'[32]

The duke's growing agitation over his perceived sins of omission in Scotland must have deepened still further at the end of November, when Sir Thomas Wharton, the Warden of the Western Marches, although hugely outnumbered, routed an invading Scottish army of 18,000 men on the tidal marshes of the Solway Moss near Longtown in Cumbria with the loss of only seven men. As the Scots retreated, they were caught up by the oncoming tide and many were drowned in the sea, the River Esk or horribly in the surrounding bogs, the weight of their armour dragging them down in the choking, filthy mire. Wharton captured more than 1,200 prisoners, including two earls and five barons; 3,000 horses and twenty-four 'great pieces' of artillery; four carts of booty, ten pavilions and thirty standards. Here were some real spoils of war that Henry could celebrate and crow over.[33] When he heard the news of Solway Moss, a triumphant grin spread across his moon-like face and the Spanish ambassador Chapuys noted that, for the first time, the sadness and dejection that had cursed him 'since he learnt the conduct of his last wife' had disappeared. Henry felt so chipper that the diplomat believed he was toying with the idea of finding a sixth wife and he began to invite ladies to entertainments at court.[34]

After Hertford had burned and pillaged Edinburgh in May 1544, Henry felt secure in his northern borders and free to turn his martial attentions to his old adversary France. He secured an alliance with the Imperial Emperor Charles V of Spain, under which both pledged to invade the realm of that 'Most Christian' king Francis I. Spanish forces had been fighting the French in the Low Countries to further imperial claims to Burgundy and to end France's relations with the Turks, the 'inveterate enemy of the Christian name and faith'. The Spanish had been reinforced by 5,600 English troops (including Surrey) under Sir John Wallop for the siege of Landrecies (near the border with present-day Belgium) and Henry had contributed cash to pay foreign mercenaries. Now England and Spain were committed to fielding armies, each totalling 42,000 strong, which would launch a twin-pronged offensive aimed at the French capital – the so-called 'Enterprise of Paris' – from English-held Calais and the Emperor's territories to the north.

Norfolk, despite his inglorious expedition to Scotland in 1542, was appointed Captain of the English vanguard, initially commanding 9,606 infantry and 370 cavalry. His son, Surrey, was made Marshal of the Field under him. The Howards supplied one of the largest contingents to the English invasion force, comprising 500 foot and 150 horsemen.[35]

The duke landed in Calais on 9 June 1544 and immediately

complained about the 'marvellous scarcity of hay and oats and no new hay cut because, by the great rains, much of the hay [fields are] under water'.[36] The supply wagons were too small; the prices for food far too high. 'I have been to the market place and found great complaints that the soldiers cannot live off their wages with victuals at such excessive prices ... The soldiers will go hungrily to bed or else spend more than their wages if such prices continue.'[37] A few days later, even the bovine and tactless Norfolk began to detect his unpopularity among his colleagues in the Privy Council:

> I forebear to molest you ... fearing that I have troubled you with too many things because I have received no answer of any part of them.
>
> I had rather be busy in writing than slothful, and yet I have enough to do besides writing, and for lack of a good secretary, I must draw every minute [document] with my own hand.[38]

The duke was also vexed about being kept in the dark over Henry's grand strategy for the invasion of France – even accusing his fellow general Suffolk of deliberately concealing the king's objectives from him.[39] At last, on 7 July, the Privy Council informed him of the plans, adding, unnecessarily, that it should be 'kept secret to your lordship'.[40] The king, he was told, intended 'to lay siege to Boulogne' and thus Norfolk's projected attack on Montreuil[41] had been relegated into a mere sideshow, a diversionary tactic to allow the real military glory to be won elsewhere – and by someone else. True, in strategic terms the walled town was the main French staging area for action against the English Pale of Calais, but Boulogne was thought an easier and symbolic target for Henry to take quickly.

On 15 June, Norfolk and his son led out their soldiers from Calais. Their column made slow progress across the hostile country towards Montreuil, even though they were escorted by their imperial allies:

> We might have been at Montreuil three or days past, but we, knowing no part of the country, nor having no guides but such as they gave us, have been brought such ways as we think never

[an] army passed – up and down the hills, through hedges, woods and marshes and all to cause us to lodge on French ground and save their own friends [from English looting].[42]

By 9 July, Norfolk, commanding a small force of cavalry and infantry, reconnoitred the defences of Montreuil, with its garrison of 4,000 seasoned troops, and gloomily reported that he had 'never seen so evil a town to approach'. The walled town, with its eight churches and a castle, sat atop a 134 foot (40 m.) high chalk hill dominating the surrounding flat, featureless fields which provided little cover for any attacking force. Furthermore, its fortifications had recently been strengthened after an unsuccessful siege in 1537. There was no suitable site for an English camp within a mile of its walls and the duke foresaw problems in crossing the River Canche: it was impassable without his pioneers building bridges of planks laid across boats 'which are not so easy set up as the king was informed'.[43]

Henry was growing impatient with Norfolk's persistent stream of gripes about just how difficult everything was proving. His generals had been appointed to achieve famous military victories, not to grumble. His secretary Sir William Paget instructed Suffolk to spell out to the duke, rather patronisingly, the obvious. Norfolk should know that

every frontier town is made as strong as possible and if, because they are strong, no man has courage to essay the winning of them, little good is to be done in France [by the English army].

As for the strength of the Montreuil garrison, the duke should be aware 'how Frenchmen count their numbers which vaunt [boast] always commonly by two for one'. Even if there were so many, after all, 'they are mostly Frenchmen and Norfolk has Englishmen with him'. Moreover, if Boulogne and Montreuil were regarded as impregnable, 'his majesty [could] return home without doing anything, which shall neither be to him honour[able]', nor, Paget added, somewhat pointedly, '[to] the reputation of those in charge of such things under him'.[44] The duke must have ground his teeth in frustration after receiving this condescending, sharply worded missive, and, old soldier that he was, became determined to pursue the siege, come what may.

He instructed his engineers to dig trenches so his men could move closer to the walls of Montreuil protected from defending fire. He began construction of a high earthwork from which his limited artillery could batter the French into submission. Unfortunately – and disastrously to his chances of a successful mission – Norfolk signally failed to block the approaches to the town and two gates remained thereafter always open to allow French supplies and reinforcements to enter freely by night.

Despite the duke's appeals, Henry refused to bolster the besieging English force by diverting men from his own operations to capture Boulogne, which fell after six weeks' siege on 18 September, after an English mine spectacularly blew up the castle.

Reinforcements belatedly departed Boulogne on 25 September but by that time Henry's ally, Charles V of Spain, had perfidiously made a separate peace with France and the English were left to fight on alone.[45] The Dauphin, heir to the French throne, was now freed of an imperial threat to Paris, and able to concentrate a 36,000-strong army to march on Montreuil, still forlornly besieged by Norfolk and his starving, sick troops. The duke mounted an eleventh-hour, last-ditch attempt to storm the town before the siege could be raised. On 19 September, Surrey led a hopelessly inadequate force to storm Montreuil's Abbeville Gate. After a 'right warm fight', he broke through to the adjacent walls, but Surrey was wounded and the English were forced to retreat, pell-mell, to their muddy trenches, carrying their injured commander back with them.[46]

These were the last shots to be fired in Norfolk's preposterous siege of Montreuil. Henry, busy supervising the rebuilding and strengthening of the Boulogne fortifications, ordered him to withdraw to the Pale of Calais in the face of the approaching French threat. The English broke camp on 28 September, destroying much of their equipment, and then headed wearily back to the coast. There were no tunes of glory for them or, yet again, for their general.

The Dauphin launched a surprise attack on Boulogne on the

night of 9 October 1544 and was narrowly repelled, even though Norfolk and Suffolk had stupidly retired to Calais, leaving only a small garrison under Sir Thomas Poynings to defend it. Henry, whose sole war prize had been the capture of the town, was furious. On 14 October he told his generals that he:

> well understood your humble submission . . . to us to forget your late proceedings. These suits . . . [demonstrate] you being indeed penitent for that is past, so [do not] doubt but this shall be a warning for you from henceforth.[47]

Almost a year later, the Howards were given another chance to demonstrate their military leadership.

At the end of August 1545, Surrey was appointed Lieutenant of Boulogne.[48] He proved an enthusiastic and zealous commander, always seeking military action, always seeking fame on the battle-field. In this he mirrored Henry's restless ambitions, but he was out of kilter with the Privy Council, which was becoming increasingly apprehensive about the cost of retaining Boulogne and maintaining so many men under arms. The invasion of France the previous year had drunk deep of Henry's revenues: more than £700,000 had been spent (well over £200 million at today's prices), compared with the budgeted £250,000. Furthermore, up to the beginning of September 1545, a further £560,000 had disappeared on war costs.[49]

Henry, for his part, was determined to hold on to Boulogne. He told the new Spanish ambassador, Francis van der Delft, that he had captured the town honourably 'at the sword's point and he meant to keep it'.[50] But Wriothesley, now Lord Chancellor, had investigated the king's finances and discovered, to his horror, that the exchequer was nearly empty, while the royal debts were still climbing. He warned Paget:

> If you tarry for more money to be sent to Boulogne at this time, you may tarry too long before you have the sum desired . . .
>
> I assure you Mr Secretary, I am at my wits end, how we shall possibly shift for [the] three months following and specially for the two next.

> For I see not any great likelihood that any good sum will come
> in till after Christmas . . .[51]

Norfolk, as Lord Treasurer, shared the fears that England was
sliding into bankruptcy. He wrote to his son from Windsor, with
dire warnings about the taste and tone of his despatches to London.
For his own good, the duke said, he should stop his braggart claims
about small-scale victories over the French, or just how easy it was
to hold Boulogne. Surrey should

> animate not the king too much for the keeping of Boulogne, for
> who does so, at length shall get small thanks.

Sir William Paget had urged him to pass on this caution, 'upon
what grounds he spoke it, I know not, but I fear you wrote something too much therein to somebody'.[52] He also informed Surrey
that his request to bring his wife and children to Boulogne had
been denied. But the dashing, devil-may-care Earl of Surrey would
not come to heel.

His love of splendour and luxury had cost him dear. The previous
year, he had built a new, grand house on the site of the Benedictine
priory of St Leonard's,[53] just outside Norwich. Its ambitious construction in the Italian Renaissance style and lavish furnishings
had thrown him into painful debt – he had been forced even
to borrow from his own servants, such as his steward Richard
Fulmerston, to meet the spiralling costs of his fashionable tastes.

Norfolk was proverbially tight-fisted and he decided to use
Surrey's embarrassing impecuniosity as a bludgeon with which he
could knock some sense into his son and bring him into line with
the Privy Council's policy.

It was blackmail, pure and simple.

On 26 October, the duke's own treasurer, Thomas Hussey, told
Surrey about his difficult conversation with Norfolk about his
mounting debts. The duke asked him: 'What way takes my son
for payment of his debts?' and he replied: 'I know not.' Well, said
Norfolk, 'he owes Fulmerston an honest sum, what does he owe
you?' Hussey answered: 'So much as I can forebear in respect of
his necessity.' The treasurer promised Surrey he was willing to

borrow money himself 'upon my credit in this town' to help him, but warned: 'I cannot see how you can both pay your whole debts and finance your necessities at present.'

The implication was stark: Norfolk would not help his son unless he sang the same tune as the Privy Council. 'By these means and others, you will be made weary of your will of Boulogne,' explained Hussey, who finally cautioned Surrey: 'As my trust is in you, burn this letter.'[54]

The duke then attempted to block the sale of one of Surrey's manors, at Rochford, Essex, to tighten the screw on his son's depleted finances. On 6 November, Hussey wrote again to Surrey about his renewed efforts to convince Norfolk to help:

I moved my lord touching your silver vessel, hangings and loans of money but his grace is clearly resolved to refuse. My advice is to devise some other ways to furnish your necessities.

My lord, to be plain with you, I see my lord's grace somewhat offended in seeing your private letters to the king ... of such vehemency as touching the animating of the king's majesty for the keeping of Boulogne, especially considering his diverse letters [to you] ...

What his grace and the rest of the council works is the render [hand-back] of Boulogne and the concluding of a peace, in six days, you with your letters set back in six hours – such importance be your letters in the king's opinion at this time ...

As to Boulogne, every councillor says 'Away with it' and the king and your lordship says 'We will keep it.'

But the ministers were too afraid to raise the matter with the king: 'There is not remaining in the council (my lord of Norfolk being absent, who will bark in it to his dying day), a member that dare move [propose] the render.'

Hussey warned that 'there was no hope' that Surrey's expenses could be repaid by the exchequer but promised that, if 'Boulogne be rendered', Norfolk would use his influence to ensure his son's appointment to either the captainship of Guisnes Castle or as deputy governor of Calais.

A generous bribe was on the table. If Surrey did not accept it, the treasurer had heard Norfolk declare that 'he had rather bury you and the rest of his children before he should give his consent to the ruin of this realm, not doubting that you should be removed in spite of your head [stubbornness], work what you could'.

Hussey hoped to push up the sale price to £1,000 for the manor at Rochford, but added that there was little hope of immediate financial assistance from Norfolk, who himself was facing debts of his own, unless, of course, a request for cash came from his mistress 'Mrs Holland, whom I think you will not trouble for the matter'.[55]

Surrey ignored his father's bile and threats. Almost every day there were skirmishes with the French in his attempts to take the fortress at Chatillon and his vivid reports of the fighting captivated the king as much as they annoyed his hard-nosed Privy Council.

Then, in early January, Surrey pushed his luck just a little too far.

His spies reported on the evening of 6 January 1546 that the French were attempting to resupply the fortress opposite Boulogne. Around 100 wagons, escorted by more than 600 cavalry and 3,000 mercenary foot soldiers, were intercepted the following evening by Surrey's outnumbered forces. His mounted men-at-arms drove off the French horse and began to burn and loot the wagons. The first and second lines of his infantry also charged, their pikes levelled at the enemy formations. Suddenly, the second wave broke ranks and fled for their lives. Surrey and his council at Boulogne put a brave face on it as they admitted to the king: 'There [was] loss and victory on both sides.'

By the time our first rank and the second were come to push of the pike, there grew a disorder in our men and without cause, the second line fled. At which time, many of our gentlemen were slain ...

So started, our fleeing footmen could not be halted in any position that we could use till they came to our trenches on St Étienne's Hill. But even after being well settled there ... our soldiers forsook these trenches and crossed the river. This gave the enemy courage to follow them, [but] the night drawing on, they followed not far beyond ...

The 'fury of the English footmen's flight' was so rampant that all attempts to rally them failed and they did not stop running until they were safely inside the gates of Boulogne. Surrey and his colleagues emphasised that

> The enemy took more loss than we, but for the gentlemen, whose loss is much to be lamented. This day, we have kept the field from break of day for the enemy retired to Montreuil immediately after the fight and left their carriages distressed behind them. Not twenty carts entered into the fortress – and that [carrying only] biscuit.

They begged Henry 'to accept our poor service, albeit the success in all things was not such as we wished, yet was the enterprise of our enemies disappointed ... If any disorder there were, we assure your majesty it was no [fault] in the rulers [commanders], nor lack of courage on their part. It was the fault of a humour that sometimes reigns in Englishmen.'[56]

Surrey had lost more than 200 men (including his own second-in-command) and, shamefully, a number of his standards.[57]

Soon afterwards, he was relieved of his command and replaced by Edward Seymour, Earl of Hertford. Paget sought to soften the blow in a much rewritten note:

> The latter part of your letter, touching the intended enterprise of the enemy, gives me occasion to write to you, frankly, my poor opinion; trusting your lordship will take the same in no worse part than I mean it
>
> As your lordship wishes, so his majesty wants to do something for the damaging of the enemy and for that purpose has appointed to send over an army shortly and that my lord of Hertford shall be his highness' Lieutenant General – whereby I fear your authority as Lieutenant should be touched ...

The king's secretary urged Surrey to seek another appointment to regain Henry's favour:

> In my opinion, you should do well to make sure betimes by petitioning his majesty to appoint you to some place of service

in the army: as to the command of the [vanguard] or [rearguard], or to some other place of honour as should be meet for you.

So should you be where knowledge and experience may be gotten, whereby you should the better be able hereafter to serve and also, [perhaps] to have occasion to do so notable service which should be to your reputation in the world, in revenge of your men lost in the previous encounter with the enemy.[58]

Although Norfolk's son was chosen to lead the rearguard of a new army mobilising for service in France, Hertford's appointment as the new general could not have been more unfortunate, or untimely. Surrey had long nurtured a deep grudge against the Seymours, whom he regarded as hardly of noble blood and mere noisy upstarts. Moreover, he saw Hertford as a personal enemy, his own *bête noire*, and his irrepressible anger against him led Norfolk to fuss lest 'his son would lose as much as he [Norfolk] had gathered together'.[59] Now, to cap it all, that social parvenu Hertford announced allegations of corruption against Surrey during his time in Boulogne and promptly purged many of his appointees to offices in the town. Surrey furiously denied the claims, saying there were 'too many witnesses that Henry of Surrey was never for singular profit corrupted nor never yet bribe closed his hand, which lesson I learnt from my father'.

He was recalled to London and on 27 March 1546 arrived at court, 'but was coldly received and did not see the king. His father ... is absent from court.'[60] Observers noted he had 'lost greatly in reputation' because of the English losses at Boulogne.

A few months later Norfolk hit upon a plan to defuse the growing hostility between the Howards and the Seymour brothers, Edward and Thomas, who were uncles to Henry's precious heir to the throne, Prince Edward. Given Surrey's vocal hostility to these arrivistes, the duke's design was hopelessly optimistic, or, more likely, his insensitivity towards others' feelings, plus his overarching ambition, blinded him to his son's predictable objections.

He played the marriage card again.

On the Tuesday of Whitsun week, Norfolk proposed to marry his daughter Mary, the flirty widow of the Duke of Richmond, to Hertford's younger brother, the roguish soldier of fortune Sir Thomas Seymour, an idea he had unsuccessfully raised in 1538.[61] He also suggested marrying off Surrey's two sons to Sir Edward's daughters to secure a powerful alliance between the old nobility and those close to the throne during the last years of Henry's reign and the next.[62] The king smiled upon Norfolk's plan, doubtless because his sixth wife, the matronly widow Katherine Parr, had previously been head over heels in love with Seymour and Henry wanted him safely married off and out of harm's way.[63]

Surrey was enraged when he heard the news and searched the Palace of Westminster for his father to remonstrate with him. He came across his sister Mary in one of the anterooms and, unforgivably, urged her to lure Henry into a liaison with her. 'Thus by length of time it is possible the king should take such a fancy to you that you shall be able to govern like Madam d'Estampes' (the French king's mistress) in France, he told her.[64] Mary was disgusted at her brother's suggestion and screamed angrily that all the Howards should 'perish and she would cut her own throat rather than ... consent to such a villainy'.[65]

With a dysfunctional family such as the Howards, it is hardly surprising that the Seymours were uninterested in Norfolk's marriage plans. Well aware of the king's increasing bad health and that his end was drawing nigh, they had their own agenda for the future.

Surrey, known as the 'Poet Earl', may have been capable of writing some of the most poignant and touching verse in the English language, but his genius also possessed a darker side. From a teenager, he was always a hothead: impetuous, swift to anger, prickly and intensely jealous of his rank and lineage. It was small wonder that John Barlow, the Dean of Westbury in Wiltshire, described him in 1539 as 'the most foolish proud boy that is in England'.[66] So it continued throughout his short adult life. Following his imprisonment at Windsor for striking a courtier in 1537, he was in trouble again in July 1542 for challenging a member of the royal household, John Leigh, to a duel. He was promptly clapped in the Fleet Prison,[67] with two of his servants to look after him. Seemingly penitent, he sought the Privy Council's help in restoring him to the king's grace, writing 'from this noisome prison, whose pestilent airs are not unlike to bring some alteration of health'.

> If your good lordships judge me not a member rather to be clean cut away, than reformed, it may please you to be suitors to the king's majesty on my behalf.
>
> Albeit no part of this, my trespass, in any way do me good, I should yet judge me happy if it should please the king's majesty to think that this simple body [that] rashly adventured in the revenge of his own quarrel shall be without respect always ready to be employed in his service.[68]

After pledging that he would 'bridle my heady will', freedom came on 7 August but only after his punitive payment of almost £7,000 as a surety for good behaviour. Surrey was bound over from committing 'neither by himself, his servants or any other at his procurement, any bodily displeasure, either by word or deed [against] John Leigh esquire'.[69]

The earl returned frustrated from his father's ignominious campaign in Scotland in the early winter of 1542. The following January, he was accused of rowdy and violent disorder in the capital. Today, he would probably have an anti-social behaviour order slapped upon him. In 1543, he was sent back to prison.

His fresh disgrace – and his eventual downfall – began with a trivial incident. On 24 January, Alice Flaner, a maid servant of one Mistress Millicent Arundel, who ran an inn off St Lawrence Lane, near Cheapside, had complained that a butcher in St Nicholas Shambles[70] had 'deceived her with a knuckle of veal'. In future, she wanted 'the best for "peers of the realm should thereof eat, and besides that a prince"'. What prince did she mean? She answered: 'The Earl of Surrey.' Surely, the earl was 'no prince, but a man of honour and of more honour like to be?' The serving girl replied: 'Yes, and if ... ought came to the king otherwise than well, he is like to be king.' She was firmly told: 'It is not so', but defiantly, she maintained: 'It is said so.'[71]

The Privy Council became curiously interested in the case and questioned Mistress Arundel. She disclosed a baleful tale of wanton vandalism and hooliganism in the streets of London. On 21 January, Surrey, together with Thomas Clere and Thomas Wyatt, had left her house at about nine o'clock at night armed with crossbows (used to shoot stones in hunting birds). Their servants carried cudgels. Every one of them was probably drunk or at least tipsy. They did not return until after midnight.

> Next day was a great clamour of the breaking of glass windows, both of houses and churches, and shooting of men in the streets, and the voice [word] was that those hurts were done by my lord and his company ...
>
> She heard Surrey 'the night after, when Mr [George] Blagge rebuked him for it, say that he had [rather] than all the good in the world it were undone, for he was sure it would come before the king and his council.
>
> 'But we shall have a maddening time in our youth and there-fore, I am very sorry for it.'[72]

Surrey and his fellow roisterers had smashed the windows in the home of a former Lord Mayor, Sir Richard Gresham, in Milk Street, off Cheapside, and then had moved east, via Lombard Street, to Fenchurch Street, where they had broken the windows of the merchant Alderman William Birch. What jolly japes! They rounded off their exciting and enjoyable evening by taking a boat out on to the Thames and firing their crossbows at the whores plying their trade on Bankside, Southwark. She also testified that Surrey, and his two servants, Thomas Clere and William Pickering, together with Norfolk's treasurer, Hussey, had eaten meat during Lent.

Surrey's enemies on the Council, particularly Hertford, were not going to turn a blind eye to such mischief. In later evidence, Mistress Arundel talked about the earl's anger over the purchase of some cloth. She had told her kitchen maids 'how he fumed' and added:

> 'I marvel they will thus mock a prince.' 'Why' asked Alice, her maid, 'Is he a prince?' 'Yes ... he is ... and if ought to come at the king but good, his father [Norfolk] should stand for king.'[73]

Another maid, Joan Whetnall, testified that the coat of arms above the earl's bed 'were very like the king'.

Surrey was summoned to a Privy Council meeting at St James's Palace on 1 April 1543. Fortunately, he appeared before Bishop Gardiner, Wriothesley, John Russell and Anthony Browne, then his father's close allies at court. He was charged

> as well as eating of flesh [in Lent], as of a lewd and unseemly manner of walking in the night about the streets and breaking with stone bows of certain windows.

The earl claimed he had permission to eat the meat, but 'touching the stone bows, he could not deny but that he had very evil done therein, submitting himself to such punishment as should to them be thought good'. So he was packed off to the Fleet Prison again, as were Clere and Pickering the next day.[74] Gardiner had focused on the religious issue of breaking the Lenten fast and, strangely, there was no mention of Surrey's dangerous aspirations on the crown. After eight days, he was free again.

The earl was still struggling with his burden of debt. In October 1546, he sought the award of a cloister and dorter (dormitory) of a Norwich monastery which was 'unserviceable to their church, saving for a memory of the old superstition and will ... discharge me out of the misery of debt'. If Henry agreed to the grant, 'I will faithfully promise never to trouble his majesty with any suit of profit to myself hereafter and spend the rest [of his life] in his majesty's service with the old zeal that I have served with always.'[75]

As the day of Henry's death grew nearer, the conspiracies at court became more fevered and intense. Who would control the realm as regent to the boy king, Edward?

Norfolk and Gardiner's faction held sway for the first nine months of 1546, instituting fierce crackdowns on religious reformers, although the duke attended few council meetings. One of those to die in the heretic's fire on 16 July was John Lassells, who had earlier exposed Catherine Howard's teenage promiscuity. At one point in late June or early July, Henry's sixth queen was herself in danger of arrest for heresy and only escaped through her feminine guile.[76] Norfolk's younger son, Thomas, was admonished by the Privy Council at Greenwich in May for 'disputing indiscreetly of Scripture with other young gentlemen of the court'. He was offered mercy if 'he would frankly confess what he said in disproof of sermons preached in court last Lent and his other talk in the Queen's chamber and elsewhere in the court concerning Scripture'. After meekly promising to 'reform his indiscreet ways', he was dismissed.[77]

The tensions between the traditionalist and evangelical factions culminated in the admiral John Dudley, Viscount Lisle, quarrelling with Gardiner during a Council meeting at the beginning of October and angrily striking him full in the face.[78] Hertford and Lisle also used 'violent and injurious' words to Wriothesley and Sir William Paulet, Lord St John, the Lord Steward of the Household.[79]

Norfolk's great ally, Bishop Gardiner of Winchester, was the first casualty, being banished from the Privy Council over a simple misunderstanding about an exchange of episcopal land, which the king wanted to tidy up the boundaries of one of his many estates. Gardiner refused him, overconfident of his relationship with his royal master. He realised his enemies had exploited the situation and rushed to soothe Henry's anger:

If for want of circumspection, my doings or sayings be otherwise taken in this matter of lands wherein I was spoken with, I must and will lament my own infelicity and most humbly, on my knees, desire your majesty to pardon it.

I never said 'nay' ... to resist your highness' pleasure, but only ... to be a suitor to your highness' goodness, as emboldened by the abundance of your majesty's favour heretofore shown to me.

Because I have no access to your majesty, not hearing of late any more of this matter, I cannot forebear to open truly my heart to your highness with a most humble request to take the same in the most gratuitous part.[80]

Gardiner feared this letter would be intercepted by Hertford and Lisle so begged his old friend Paget to deliver the note personally to Henry and pass on his request for an audience for the bishop.

But Paget had turned against him. The king responded with a cold and unforgiving letter on 4 December:

> Had your doings ... been agreeable to such fair words as you have now written ... you should neither [have] had cause to write this excuse nor we to answer it.
>
> But we marvel at your writing that you never said 'nay' to any request for those lands, considering that to our chancellor [Wriothesley] secretary [?Paget] and chancellor of our court of augmentations [Sir Edward North], both jointly and apart, you utterly refused any conformity, saying that you would make your answer to our own person.

Henry told Gardiner with dreadful finality: 'We see no cause why you should molest us further.'[81]

With the bishop exiled to his palace at Southwark, Hertford held the Privy Council meetings at his own home. He and his allies could now shift their sights on to Norfolk and his son, who had become rivals for the looming regency of England.

First to fall was Henry Howard, Earl of Surrey.

He had come to court some time in November to press his case for the Norwich monastic site. He seemed oblivious to the king's declining health or the change in the balance of power among his councillors.

At the beginning of December, the Privy Council received damaging information about him from the courtier and Member of Parliament (MP) Sir Richard Southwell, a former friend to the earl and his comrade-in-arms at Boulogne.[82] Southwell told them 'he knew of certain things of the earl that touched his fidelity to the king'.[83] They detained the MP for further questioning and ordered Surrey's arrest, by Sir Anthony Wingfield, captain of the king's guard. The next day, Thursday 2 December,

> after dinner, [Wingfield] saw the earl coming into the palace [of Westminster] whilst he was walking in the great hall downstairs.
>
> He had a dozen halberdiers waiting in an adjoining corridor and approaching the earl, said: 'Welcome, my lord, I wish to ask you to intercede for me with the duke your father in a matter in

which I need his favour, if you would deign to listen to me.'

So he led him to the corridor and the halberdiers took him ... without attracting notice.[84]

Surrey was taken to Lord Chancellor Wriothesley's house at Ely Place in Holborn, opposite the church of St Andrew, for questioning.[85] The new French ambassador, Odet de Selve,[86] heard whispers that the earl faced two charges: 'that he had the means of attempting the [French] castle of Hardelot when he was at Boulogne and neglected it; the other that he said there were some who made no great account of him, but he trusted one day to make them very small'.[87] His accuser was also held at Wriothesley's house and Surrey wanted to fight him as a matter of honour. True to form, the earl 'vehemently affirmed himself a true man, desiring to be tried by justice, or else offering himself to fight in his shirt with Southwell'.[88]

But this was no time for duels.

Norfolk had been at Kenninghall since the beginning of November and word quickly reached him of his son's arrest. On 3 and 4 December he wrote urgently to friends at court for news, including Gardiner, who he did not know had been disgraced. The duke was also unaware that his letters were intercepted, read and held as potential evidence against him. He hastened to London and on his arrival, on Sunday 12 December, was arrested and humiliatingly degraded of his rank as Lord Treasurer. His white wand of office and the Garter insignia on his gown were removed from him at Westminster. Memories of his own similar treatment of Cromwell in the same palace must have troubled even his insensitive mind. He was taken by boat down to the Tower, and Norfolk 'both in the barge and on entering the Tower' publicly declared 'no person had ever been carried thither before who was a more loyal servant [of the king] than he was and always had been'. His protests were ignored.

The Seymour coup against the Howards had been carefully planned. At the same time that his father was making his forlorn journey down the river, Surrey was marched under close guard through the crowded streets of London from Ely Place to the

Tower, his progress marked by his anger and 'great lamentation'.[89]

The king must have been a party to their arrests and, in the knowledge that he would soon meet his Maker, wanted to remove the last surviving dynastic threat to his nine-year-old son's succession. He now believed the Howards' vast feudal resources and ambitions made them potential risks for the security of his son's forthcoming reign. Like Buckingham and others before them, they had to be cold-bloodedly snuffed out.[90]

Between three and four that Sunday afternoon, a small group of horsemen left London and rode post-haste for Norfolk. The party was led by John Gates, the thuggish fixer who undertook many unpleasant tasks for those who now controlled Henry's Privy Chamber, his brother-in-law Sir Wymond Carew, and Sir Richard Southwell, who, tellingly, had been freed from custody. Their destination was the Howard palace at Kenninghall. They reached Thetford on Monday night and were at the gates of the duke's mansion, seven miles (11.3 km.) away, by dawn the next morning.

News of the arrests had not yet reached the pastoral calm of Norfolk. They hammered on the doors of the sleeping palace and eventually were admitted. The steward, Robert Holdish, was away 'taking musters', and the trio instead met Henry Symonds, the duke's almoner, 'a man in whom [Norfolk] reposed a great trust for the order of his household and expenses of the same'. All entrances being secured, they ordered Symonds to summon Mary, Duchess of Richmond, and the duke's mistress, Bessie Holland, who had been awoken by the clamour, down to the dining room for interrogation.

Mary was 'sore perplexed, trembling and like to fall down', they reported to Henry that evening. She fell on her knees and 'humbled herself to your majesty', saying:

> Although nature constrained her sore to love her father, whom she had ever thought to be a true and faithful subject and also to desire the well-[being] of his son, her natural brother, whom she noted to be a rash man, yet, for her part, she would, nor will, hide or conceal any from your majesty's knowledge.[91]

Gates and his colleagues, 'perceiving her humble conformity', advised her not to despair. The polite niceties over, they demanded to see her chambers and coffers, but they discovered 'no writings worth sending'. Her possessions were not worth much: clearly, her mean father had not dipped into his purse to brighten her life:

> Her coffers and chambers so bare, as your majesty would hardly think. Her jewels, such as she had, [all] sold or [pawned] to pay her debts ...

Then the searchers turned their attentions on the blowsy Bessie Holland, who had benefited considerably from Norfolk's doting largesse. She possessed a wealth of pretty trinkets and baubles, including a number of gold brooches bearing pictures of 'Our Lady in Pity', the Holy Trinity, and, a nice touch this, Cupid:[92]

> We have found girdles, beads, buttons of gold, pearl and rings set with stones of diverse sorts, whereof, with all other things, we make a book to be sent to your highness.

Both the Duchess of Richmond and Bessie were told to travel to London for further interrogation 'in the morning or the next day at the latest'.

Gates and his team confiscated and inventoried all the duke's possessions, down to the horses in the stable, including one old nag called Button. They also sent 'our most discreet and trusty servants' to all Norfolk's other houses in East Anglia to ensure that 'nothing shall be embezzled until we have time to see them, among which, we do not omit Elizabeth Holland's [house] newly made in Suffolk which is thought to be well furnished with stuff'.[93] They confiscated all Norfolk's 'writings and books, which we shall diligently peruse', and listed the members of his household.[94]

Surrey's wife, Frances, pregnant with their fifth child, who was 'looking her time to lie in at this next Candlemas' (2 February), also lived at Kenninghall with her children and 'the women in the nursery attending upon them'. What should Gates do with them? Eventually it was decided to break up the household and she was sent away, one of Norfolk's worthless old nightgowns, 'much worn and furred with coney and lamb', draped across her lap for a vestige of warmth during her journey.[95] Her eldest son Thomas was placed in the care of Sir John Williams, the Treasurer of the Court of Augmentations, and the others dumped on old Sir Thomas Wentworth, a local magnate.

Back in London, Surrey had heard of his father's arrest and wrote to the Privy Council:

> Since the beginning of my durance [imprisonment] the displeasure of my master, much loss of blood with other distemperance of nature, with my sorrow to see the long approved truth of mine old father brought into question by any stir between Southwell and me has sore enfeebled me as is to be seen.

Surrey recalled his appearance before the Privy Council of nearly four years before, over his nocturnal high jinks in London, and wanted the same sympathetic quartet of councillors to examine him again.

> My desire is you four and only you may be sent to me, for so it sh[ould be best for his] majesty's service, to whom I intend to discha[rge my conscience] ... Trusting in your ho[onourable lordships that] ... you will make report of my tale to his majesty according as you shall hear.[96]

Sadly, he did not know that Gardiner was now out in the cold and Wriothesley had changed sides, deciding that his future prosperity now lay with the Seymour clan.

Norfolk, in another part of the Tower, also took up his pen and wrote to his sovereign, begging for mercy. He was astonished by his arrest and could not for the life of him understand why he now languished in prison:

> I, your most humble subject, prostrate at your feet, do most humbly beseech your highness to be my good and gracious lord.
>
> I am sure some great enemy of mine has informed your majesty of some untrue matter against me.
>
> Sir, God knows, in all my life I never thought one untrue thought against you, or your succession, nor can no more judge

... what should be laid at my charge than the child that was born this night.

Let his accusers confront him in front of his king or before the Privy Council, then, if he was found guilty, he would accept his punishment according to his just deserts.

At the reverence of Christ's passion, have pity on me and let me not be cast away by false enemies' informations.

I know not that I have offended any man ... unless it were such as are angry with me for being quick against such as have been accused for Sacramentaries.

As for all causes of religion, I say now and have said to your majesty and many others, I do know you to be a Prince of such virtue and knowledge that whatsoever laws you have in past time made ... I shall to the extremity of my power stick unto them, as long as my life shall last.

So that if any men be angry with me for these causes, they do me wrong.

Henry could take all his lands and goods, as long he may 'know what is laid to my charge' and 'may hear some comfortable word from your majesty'.[97]

Fear of the unknown is a powerful, nagging emotion. Norfolk had every reason to be worried. Both he and his son now confronted a march to the scaffold.

8

THE GREAT SURVIVOR

'Who knows the cares that go to bed with statesmen?'

Thomas Howard, third Duke of Norfolk[1]

While Norfolk and his son sat brooding in the Tower, the Privy Council, now firmly under Hertford's sway, began an assiduous search to uncover the evidence necessary to support indictments of treason against them. Two days after their imprisonment, the Spanish ambassador, Francis van der Delft, reported the political gossip pervasive at Westminster that 'they entertained some ambiguous designs when the king was ill at Windsor six weeks ago to obtain control of the Prince [Edward] or the country and their chance of liberation is small . . .'.[2]

One of the first witnesses to supply information to the Council was Surrey's steward, Richard Fulmerston,[3] who had recently been repaid all but £140 of the money he lent to his master. The Howards' 'most earnest drudge and servant' provided faithful testimony on their behalf:

> I have searched my conscience and knowledge to answer you what I knew of my lord of Norfolk . . . and the Earl of Surrey . . . in anything that might prove treason to the king, my lord prince, the Council or the commonwealth of this realm.
>
> I cannot accuse either of them, nor ever mistrusted either's truth [honesty].
>
> Knowing the king's goodness and justice and your lordships' discretion, I cannot but think that [something] is amiss. Before their last coming to the city, I never heard . . . them talk [of] any of these matters.[4]

No luck there, then, for the industrious investigators. The bland-ness of his statement was hardly surprising: Fulmerston realised that if he acknowledged his masters' treason, he would be vul-nerable to charges of misprision himself.

Norfolk was questioned in his two rooms in the Tower by Sir William Paulet, the Lord Steward of the Household, and Sir William Paget, the king's secretary. Their interrogation left him no wiser as to what lay behind his arrest. He emphatically denied writing his own letters in code or that he supported the Pope: 'If I had twenty lives, I would rather have spent them all, than that he should have any power in this realm, for no man knows better than I . . . how his usurped power has increased. Since he has been the king's enemy, no man has felt and spoken more against both here and in France and also to many Scottish gentlemen.'

That night, he penned an impassioned six-page letter to the Council, pleading to know 'what the causes [against him were]', adding defiantly, 'if I do not answer truly to every point, let me not live one hour . . .'. He remembered the terrible fate of others close to the king: 'My lords, I trust you to think [that] Cromwell's service and mine [be] not alike . . . He was a false man and surely, I am a true poor gentleman.' Repeatedly, the duke demanded to confront and face down his accusers: 'I will hide nothing. Never [was] gold tried better by fire and water than I have been, nor have had greater enemies about my sovereign lord than I have had and yet, God be thanked, my truth has ever tried me as, I doubt not, it shall do in these causes.'

The faces of his many enemies down the years appeared in his mind's eye like so many spectres, as he wrote his letter in the spluttering candlelight, each page brimming with pathos. Cardinal Wolsey had 'confessed to me at Esher' that for 'fourteen years' he had sought 'to destroy me . . . [and] unless he put me out of the way, I should undo him'. Cromwell was his most implacable foe who, when eliminating the last survivors of Plantagenet nobility, had questioned the wife of the Marquis of Exeter 'more strictly' about Norfolk's loyalty 'than of all other'. There was his discarded and spurned wife, of whom Cromwell had often slyly told him: 'My lord, you are a happy man that your wife knows no hurt [of] you, for if she did, she would undo you.' Her father, the Duke of Buckingham, had confessed at the criminal bar so long ago, 'my father [the second Duke of Norfolk] sitting as a judge, that of all men living, he hated me the most'. His brother-in-law, Thomas Boleyn, Earl of Wiltshire, also 'confessed the same and wished he had found means to thrust his dagger in me'. Finally, the 'malice borne me by both my nieces, whom it pleased the king to marry', was well known to those ladies who attended them in their last hours in the Tower.

This was a veritable litany of hate directed at just one man and some of it came from those once close to him. In the face of such relentless odium, some may have pondered the shortcomings in their own characters or even become quite paranoid. However, Norfolk was not like other men: his blood, his ambition, his lust for power, all smothered any frail, human sensitivity. But apart from his wife, all these adversaries were dead. Who was now his secret enemy in the shadows? Who had struck him down? And why? The duke's bafflement was palpable: his abundant loyalty and fidelity to the crown was evident for all to admire. After all, who was it who had diligently hunted down all those traitors during what he called the 'commotion time' – the 'Pilgrimage of Grace' rebellion? It was, of course, Norfolk. He asked:

Who showed his majesty of the words of my [step]mother [Agnes, Dowager Duchess of Norfolk] for which she was attainted of misprision but I?

In all times past unto this time, I have shown myself a most true man to my sovereign and since these things done, have received more profits of his highness than before.

Alas! Who can think that I, having been so long a true man, should now be false to his majesty?

Poor man as I am yet, I am his ... near kinsman. For whose sake should I be untrue?

Piteously, the duke appealed to the Council to show 'this scribbled letter' to the king and 'beg him to grant its petitions and remit out of his noble, gentle heart, the displeasure conceived against me'. He signed it 'By his highness' poor prisoner, T. NORFOLK'.[5] A poor prisoner indeed: he was aged seventy-three and suffered from bouts of indigestion and acute rheumatism, the latter made worse by the damp, dank conditions of the Tower.

What is more, he was a badly frightened old man.

The emotional shock of his arrest must have dulled his senses and blunted his normally astute political instincts. Norfolk knew of Henry's rapidly declining health – van der Delft had seen the king at Oatlands Palace at Weybridge, Surrey, on 5 December when the king told him he had suffered 'a sharp attack of the fever which lasted in the burning stage for thirty hours, but now he was quite restored'. The ambassador doubted Henry's chances of recovery: 'His colour does not bear out [this] statement and he looks to me greatly fallen away.'[6] It was only too obvious that the fifty-five-year-old king had few days remaining to him and that time was running out for Edward and Thomas Seymour to seize the regency of England when their nephew ascended the throne.

The Howards should have recognised their peril. They were clear targets for the king, worried over his son's succession, and for those who now made their bid for supremacy. Norfolk's and Surrey's dynastic pride and inbred arrogance had spawned an absurd complacency. In Henry's dangerous court of conspiracies, no man – no matter how important, how influential – was entirely safe from being suddenly and unexpectedly cut down.

Outside the walls of the Tower, their fate was being sealed. The government propaganda machine cranked up a gear. Lord Chancellor Wriothesley sent a helpful message to van der Delft on 16 December disclosing that Norfolk and Surrey 'planned by sinister means to obtain the government of the king, who was too old to allow himself to be governed' and that

their intention was to usurp authority by means of the murder of all members of the council and the control of the prince [Edward] by them alone.[7]

It was deplorable, said Wriothesley, that 'persons of such high and noble lineage should have undertaken so shameful a business as to plan the seizure of the government of the king by sinister means'. The courts of Europe were stunned by the arrests. Nicholas

Wotton, English ambassador to the court of Francis I, told the French king of the 'most execrable and abominable intent and enterprise' of Norfolk and Surrey. Francis – while frankly surprised at the news – replied merely that if their guilt was proved they should both be put to death.[8] Thomas Thirlby, Bishop of Westminster, abroad on a diplomatic mission to the court of Charles V, was horrified:

> Those two ungracious, ingrate and inhuman *non humines,*[9] the Duke of Norfolk and his son, the elder of whom I do confess that I did love, for I ever supposed him a true servant to his master. Before God, I am so amazed!

He had informed one of the Emperor's chief secretaries, Josie Bauar, of the development, 'not forgetting' to mention 'the great benefits which these two ungracious men had received'. The Spanish official, during their discussion, talked of 'the busy head of the father and the pride of the son'. The bishop felt he should write a consoling letter to Henry, but prudently had second thoughts, believing it 'unwise to renew the memory of this great malice'.[10]

Inevitably, garbled versions of the alleged plot circulated. The Protestant refugee John Bourchier wrote triumphantly from Strasbourg: 'The news is agreeable ... Norfolk, whose authority extended to the north of England – a most bitter enemy of the Word of God – has been imprisoned with his son, with whom he made a secret attempt to restore the Pope and the monks, but their design was discovered. Nothing is wanting now but that [Gardiner, Bishop of] Winchester be caught, without which evangelical truth cannot be restored.'[11]

In London, the witnesses were stumbling over themselves to tell all. Norfolk's conceited and free-spending nephew, Sir Edmund Knyvett (the son of the naval commander killed at Brest), had fallen out with the duke and, in protest, had quit Kenninghall. He met Surrey soon after and 'declared that because of his father and his unkindness, I would go from my country and dwell here and wait as [I am] unable to bear the burden of their malice'. Surrey had hastened to reassure Knyvett that he bore him no ill will: 'No, cousin Knyvett, I malice not so low; my malice is higher – my malice climbs higher.' After Cromwell's death, 'whom he and his father suspected [to be] my friend against the duke, he said: "Now is that foul churl dead, so ambitious of others' blood [nobility]".' When he was sharply reminded it was a sin to speak ill of souls departed, Surrey retorted: 'These new erected men would by their wits leave no noble man a life.' Knyvett was also suspicious of the Italians in his cousin's household and believed the earl's conversations with them 'had therein some ill device'. One of Surrey's servants had been with the traitor Cardinal Reginald Pole in Italy 'and was received again on his return'. He also kept an Italian jester called 'Pasquil', who 'was more likely a spy, and so reputed'.[12]

Surrey's friend Sir Edward Warner, a 'king's servant' from Norfolk,[13] testified that during the summer, 'Master [Richard] Devereux [son of Lord Ferrers] did tell me . . .'

> of the pride and vain glory of the said earl [but] that it was possible it might be abated one day. I asked what he meant thereby and he said: 'What if he be accused to the king that he should say if God should call the king to his mercy, who were so meet to govern the Prince as my lord, his father?'
>
> I asked then if there were any such thing and he said 'It may be so.' Whereupon I gathered it was so and looked every day to see the earl in the case that he is now in, which, I thought, with those word[s] he well deserved.[14]

This was all hearsay, but was doubtless welcomed by the Privy Council. More evidence at second hand came from another friend, Edward Rogers, who recalled a conversation with George Blagge, an esquire of the body to Henry,[15] about nine months before. Blagge had recounted a talk with Surrey when he told him that the king should appoint regents 'to rule the prince' after Henry's death. The earl held that his father 'was the meetest' for the job, 'both for good services done and for estate'. Blagge, who opposed everything that Norfolk stood for in religion, retorted that if that happened,

> then the Prince should be but evil taught . . . Rather than it should come to pass that the Prince should be under the government of

your father or you, I would bid the adventure to thrust this dagger in you.

Surrey suggested he was very hasty and, using an aphorism much favoured by his father, added: 'God send a shrewd cow short horns.'

Yes my lord (quoth Blagge) and I trust your horns also shall be kept so short as you will not be able to do any hurt with them.

Afterwards, Surrey – who was unarmed during what had become a noisy quarrel – 'took sword and dagger and went to Blagge's house' and repeated menacingly 'that of late he had been very hasty with him'. Unfortunately, Rogers could not remember what happened next.[16]

Sir Gawen Carew was a bemused witness to Surrey's unseemly row with his sister at Westminster, and gaily reported the heated words that passed between them. He added:

The Earl of Surrey has said to me, place and time now out of my remembrance, 'Note those men which are made by the king's majesty of vile birth have been the distraction [undoing] of all the nobility of this realm' and again that the Cardinal and Lord Cromwell sought the death of his father. Mr Edward Rogers has told me of the earl's saying: 'If God should call the king's majesty to his mercy (whose life and health the Lord long preserve) that he thought no man so meet to have the governance of the Prince as my lord, his father.'[17]

All this contributed little to the case against the Howards, save perhaps a tenuous charge of 'maliciously wishing, willing or desiring by words' the death of the king, which had become treason under Cromwell's Act of 1534.[18] It merely confirmed, if it was a surprise to anybody, the depth of Surrey's contempt and hatred for those not born of the old aristocratic blood.

Then Mary, Duchess of Richmond, and Bessie Holland, Norfolk's long-standing mistress, were called in and examined.

Norfolk's daughter had longed to savour the sweet taste of revenge for Surrey's treatment of her. She confirmed her father's plan to marry her off to Sir Thomas Seymour and her brother's vehement opposition to it. Mary said the duke had tetchily warned Surrey that if the wedding did not go ahead, he 'would lose as much as he had gathered together'.

> Moreover, that the earl, her brother, should say 'These new men loved no nobility and if God called away the king, they should smart for it.'
>
> Her brother hated them all since his being in custody in Windsor Castle but that her father seemed not to care for their ill-will, saying 'the truth will bear him out ...' [He] never said that the king hated him, but his counsellors.
>
> And that her brother should say, 'God save my father's life, for if he were dead, they would shortly have my head.' And that he [Norfolk] reviled some of the present Council, not forgetting the old Cardinal.

Mary repeated some 'passionate words' spoken by Surrey, 'and also some circumstantial speeches, little [to] his advantage, yet they seemed to clear her father'.[19]

Mrs Holland's testimony painted an unattractive portrait of her ageing lover as a self-righteous, conceited prig. If it was pillow talk, it hardly showed him in a good light. She repeated Norfolk's belief that 'none of the council loved him because they were no noblemen born themselves, [and] also because he believed too truly in the Sacrament of the Altar [the Eucharist]'.

> The king loved him not, because he was too much loved in his country ... [Norfolk] would follow his father's lesson which was that the less [that] others set by him, the more he would set by himself.
>
> The duke complained he was [no longer] part of the most secret (or as it is there termed, the privy Privy) Council.

Then came the meat of her evidence – and the most damaging to the duke. He had told her that 'the king was much grown of his body and that he could not go up and down stairs, but was let up and down by a device'.[20]

> And that his majesty was sickly and could not long endure and

that the realm like to be in an ill case through diversity of opinions.

She offered a further, telling sidelight about the duke's religious beliefs: 'If he were a young man, and the realm in quiet, he would ask leave to see [the] *Vernacle*, which he said was the picture of Christ given to women by Himself as he went to death.'[21] In a burst of honesty, she acknowledged that the earl 'loved her not, nor the Duchess of Richmond him and that she addicted herself much to the said duchess'.[22]

Like his father, the image of Surrey that was emerging was of a bumptious, self-opinionated individual. But the earl did not rely on mere words to buttress his own rarefied status: he had changed his coat of arms to reflect his royal origins, based on an old shield carved in stone he had discovered in a house in Norfolk. One report suggests that his sister had secretly already informed the king of her brother's new – and potentially treasonous – heraldic pretensions.[23] She now told the investigators that on his arms:

> instead of the duke's coronet, was put ... a Cap of Maintenance[24] [in] purple, with powdered fur, and with a crown, much like to a close crown.
>
> Underneath the arms was a cipher which she took to be the king's cipher 'HR' [*Henricus Rex*].[25]

Surrey had reassumed the arms of their attainted and executed grandfather, the Duke of Buckingham. These were the royal arms and lilies inherited from Thomas of Woodstock, a younger son of King Edward III. By this seemingly innocuous act, he had implicitly repudiated Buckingham's attainder and reinstated a claim to the throne.[26]

He also included the arms of St Edward the Confessor, which had been granted to Thomas Mowbray, first [Mowbray] Duke of Norfolk, by Richard II, of whom the Howards were heirs and successors. Furthermore, Surrey's secretary Hugh Ellis remembered the earl saying that the ancient arms of England had been given to his ancestors 'by King Edward – that is St Edward'.[27]

Bessie Holland said the duke did not like his son's new arms,

'and that he had gathered them himself knew not from whence ...
He had placed the Norfolk arms wrong and had found fault with
him. And therefore, that she should take no pattern of his son's
arms to work with them with her needle in his house ...'

This seemingly obscure heraldic issue was to be Surrey's final
undoing. Three years earlier, the Council had heard of his claims
to be a prince and the maids' gossip that if 'ought came to the king
otherwise than well, he is like to be king'. Now he seemed to be
publicly flaunting his aspirations to the crown of England.

Lord Chancellor Wriothesley's grandfather, father and uncle
were all heralds. He immediately realised that Surrey's heraldic
pretensions would provide the strongest case against him. He now
drew up some hard questions to be put to the earl:

- Whether you bear in your arms the escutcheon and arms of
  King Edward that was king before the [Norman] Conquest,
  commonly called St Edward?
- To what intent you put the arms of St Edward in your coat?
- Why [do] you bear them at this time more than your father at
  other times before?
- If the king should die in my lord prince's tender age, whether
  you have devised who should govern him and the realm?
- Whether you have at any time determined to fly out of the
  realm?
- Whether you acknowledge yourself the king's true subject?
- Of what degree [do you] take yourself to be in this realm?
- What inheritance [do] you think you ought of right to have
  therein?
- Whether you procured any person to dissemble [deceive] in
  anything with the king's majesty [with] the intent the same
  might grow in his favour for the better compassing your purposes.

This last question had been amended. Wriothesley's first attempt
read: '... procured your sister or any other woman to be the king's
concubine or not?'[28] Was he being prudish – or did he believe such
a starkly posed question would simply push Surrey into a rage and
stop any further useful interrogation?

The Lord Chancellor also jotted down some thoughts in an *aide-mémoire* to himself. The tantalisingly brief notes included: 'My lord of Surrey dissembling [lying or deceiving].' 'Fulmerston.' 'Mr Paget.' '... Surrey's pride and his gown of gold. Departure of the king's apparel.' 'The duke's will.' In most cases, we can only guess at their true import and, unfortunately, the earl's probably blustering answers in his interrogation have not survived. The reference to the king's secretary, Sir William Paget, could relate to claims that Surrey had already been distributing high offices of state on the promise of his regency and had offered Paget the Lord Chancellorship.[29] Another note – 'Riding with many men in the streets' – refers to the earl's habit of travelling around London at the head of a considerable number of mounted retainers, sparking suspicions of possible insurrection.[30]

Wriothesley was a busy man. He ordered inquiries into Norfolk's annuities from a host of sinecure jobs: 'By the king for the Office of High Treasurer, £365. Earl Marshal, £20. Steward of Suppressed [monastic] Lands on this side [of the river] Trent, £100.' The list included stewardships awarded by various bishops and nobles. The duke's total income from all these various offices was more than £700 a year, or £190,000 in 2009 purchasing power. Surrey's, by comparison, was more modest: just £20 a year for the stewardship of the Duchy of Lancaster, the same amount for his earldom, and £50 as the king's cup-bearer at court.[31]

Henry arrived back in London from Windsor, via his huge new palace at Nonsuch, near Ewell, Surrey, on 23 December, still suffering from 'some grief of his leg' and the fever it caused.[32] The next day, Christmas Eve, van der Delft reported to Mary, the Dowager Queen of Hungary, and his master, Charles V:[33]

> The king is so unwell that, considering his age and corpulence, he may not survive another attack such as he recently had at Windsor.
>
> The court is closed to all but the Privy Council and some gentlemen of the Privy Chamber, the rumour being that the king is busied about the affair of Norfolk and his son.
>
> It is understood that he will be thus occupied during the

holidays and some days in addition, the Queen [Katherine Parr] and all the courtiers having gone to Greenwich, though she has never been known before to leave him on solemn occasions like this.

Henry, said the ambassador, was 'deeply engaged and much perplexed in the consideration of this affair'. He noted the ascendancy of the evangelical Seymours at court, 'and it is even asserted here that the custody of the prince and the government of the realm will be entrusted to them'. Their supporters also

> do not conceal their wish to see the Bishop of Winchester and other adherents of the old faith sent to the Tower to keep company with the Duke of Norfolk.[34]

Wriothesley presented his summary of the charges against father and son to Henry. The king, spectacles perched on the end of his nose,[35] struggled with the arcane complexities of heraldic law, custom and practice. He amended and corrected the document in a faltering hand, but his thoughts were as incisive as ever:[36]

> If a man coming out of *the collateral line to the heir of* the crown, who ought *not* to bear the Arms of England *but on* the second quarter ... do *presume* to change his right place and bear them in the first quarter ... *how this man's intent is to be judged, and whether this* import any danger, peril, or slander to the title of the Prince or very Heir Apparent ...
>
> If a man *presume to take into* his arms an old coat of the Crown *which his ancestor never bore, nor he of right ought to bear* ... whether it may be to the peril and slander of the very Heir of the Crown or be taken to his disturbance ...
>
> If a man compassing *with himself to govern the realm, do actually go about to rule the king and* should, for that purpose, advise his daughter or sister to become his harlot, *thinking thereby to bring it to pass, and so would rule both father and son, as by this next article does more appear; what this importeth* [mean]?
>
> If a man say these words: 'If the king die, who should have the rule of the Prince, but my father or I', what it importeth?
>
> The depraving of the King's Council.

> If a man shall say these words of a [nobleman] … of the realm,
> 'if the K[ing] were dead, I should shortly shut him up,' what it
> importeth?[37]

As evidence of conspiracy against Norfolk and Surrey became
less credible, the charges concerned with purely heraldic offences
became the focus of the indictments.

Meantime, the duke, in another letter, asked the privy councillors for some homely comforts as he awaited his fate. He
requested that some books should be brought from his library in
his Lambeth house 'for unless I may have books to read ere I fall
on sleep and after I awake again, I cannot sleep, nor did these
dozen years'. Other titles could be purchased in London – St
Augustine's *de Civitate Dei* (City of God),[38] Flavius Josephus's *de
Antiquitatibus ac de bello Judaico*[39] and another by Eduard Wilhelm
Sabell 'who doth declare most of any book, how the Bishop of
Rome [the Pope] from time to time has usurped his power against
all princes, by their unwise sufferance'.[40] Norfolk also asked for a
priest (a 'Ghostly Father') to say Mass for him but he promised
'upon my life to speak no word to him that shall say Mass which
he may do in the other chamber and I to remain within'. Could he
also have more freedom of movement to ease his aching old limbs?

> To have licence [permission] in the day time to walk in the
> chamber without and in the night to be locked in, as I am now.
> At my first coming, I had a chamber without [in the] day.

Finally, and pathetically, he requested some clean sheets.[41]

With events (and the Seymours) conspiring against him, Surrey
must have been desperate with frustration and fury, pacing up and
down in his room, possibly located in the western section of St
Thomas's Tower. Within its west wall was a vertical shaft, built as
a garderobe, or lavatory, that emptied into the tidal moat.[42] One
contemporary report suggests he attempted a daring escape. The
source – Antonio de Guaras, a Spanish merchant in London – says
that the earl asked his servant, Martin, to smuggle a dagger into
his room, hidden in his breeches. Surrey told him: 'Go to St
Katherine's [dock] and take a boat, no matter what it costs and

wait for me there. I hope to be with you at midnight.'

> The earl was confined in a room overlooking the river [Thames] and he saw that he could escape through a retiring room, if he killed the two men who slept in it . . .
>
> He arose from his bed and went to see if the tide was low and found that it would be quite midnight before it was low water.
>
> So, when midnight came, he went and took the lid off the closet and saw there was only about two feet of water. As he could not wait any longer, he began to let himself down.
>
> But at that instant, the guards came in and seeing that he was not in the bed, ran to the closet and one of them just reached his arm. The earl could not help himself and the guards [raised the alarm] . . . The other guards came and put some shackles on his feet. The servant who had taken the boat went away with the money and nothing more was heard of him.[43]

The accounts of Walter Stonor, the Lieutenant of the Tower, include an 'allowance for the said earl's irons – £13 6s 8d' – possibly the shackles mentioned in the story. They also cover the cost of his board: attendants, candles, coals and a small sum for hangings and plate in his room, totalling £24. This also included the cost of a new coat of black satin, trimmed with rabbit fur, purchased by Stonor 'against his arraignment'.[44]

Norfolk and Suffolk were indicted for treason at a hearing at Norwich Castle on 7 January 1547.

Five days later Norfolk confessed, 'without compulsion, without force, without advice or counsel'. But his statement would either have been dictated to him, or written beforehand – all he had to do was to sign it.

> I, Thomas, Duke of Norfolk, do confess and acknowledge myself most untruly, and contrary to my Oath [of] Allegiance, to have offended the king's most excellent majesty, in the disclosing and opening of his private and most secret counsel at diverse and sundry times, to the great peril of his highness and disappointing of his most prudent and regal affairs.

T.N.

Also, I likewise confess that I concealed High Treason in keeping secret the false and traitorous act, most presumptuously committed by my son Henry Howard, Earl of Surrey, against the king's majesty and his laws, in the putting and using of the arms of St Edward the Confessor, king of the realm of England before the Conquest, in his escutcheon or arms, which said arms ... pertain only to the king of this realm, whereto the said earl ... could make any claim or title, by men, or any of mine or his ancestors.

T.N.

I likewise confess, that to the peril, slander and [disinheritance] of the king's majesty and his noble son Prince Edward, his son and heir apparent, I have, against all right, unjustly and without authority, born in the first quarter of my arms, ever since the death of my father, the arms of England, with a difference of three labels of silver,[45] which are the proper arms of my said prince ... [This] gives occasion that his highness might be disturbed or interrupted of the crown of this realm and my said lord prince might be destroyed, disturbed and interrupted in fame, body and title ... which I know and confess by the laws of the realm to be treason.

T.N.

For ... my said heinous offences, I have worthily deserved ... to be attainted of High Treason and to suffer the punishment, losses and forfeitures that appertain ... Although I be not worthy to have or enjoy any part of the king's majesty's clemency and mercy to be extended to me ... yet I most humbly and with a most sorrowful and repentant heart, do beseech his highness to have mercy, pity and compassion on me.

I shall most devoutly and heartily make my daily prayer to God for the preservation of his most noble succession, as long as life and breath shall continue.

T.N.[46]

Those who witnessed the confession included Hertford, Wriothesley, Paget and Sir Anthony Browne, Master of the King's Horse. To add legal respectability, the two chief justices, Sir

Richard Lister and Sir Edward Montague, also subscribed their names.

His first offence – disclosing state secrets – probably emanated from the testimony of a spy named John Torre who had claimed that Norfolk and his half-brother William had paid secret visits at night to the home of the French ambassador Charles de Marillac.[47] Norfolk was notoriously pro-French in his political beliefs and, indeed, received an annuity from France over many years. But these meetings, between May 1541 and late 1542, were made on the king's orders and everyone knew about them.[48] The second offence – bearing the three lions of England with a label on his arms – is even more nonsensical, as the Howards had used this coat for centuries.[49]

Norfolk was neither a fool nor a coward, but he was patently too old and sick to fight his enemies any longer. Despite the very long odds, he gambled his last card from the poor hand destiny had dealt him: that his past loyalty would prompt a generous act of mercy from his sometimes malevolent sovereign. However, his confession also deliberately prejudiced his son's fate, due to be decided the following day, 13 January.

Because he was not a lord of Parliament, Surrey was to be humiliatingly tried by a common court at the Guildhall.[50] The earl was popular in London, despite his previous hooligan escapades. An eyewitness reported it was 'fearful to see the enormous number of people'[51] watching as Surrey was taken through the capital's early morning streets guarded by 300 halberdiers, commanded by Sir John Gage, Constable of the Tower, who was responsible for delivering him safely to trial.[52]

The earl was brought to the bar of the packed court at nine o'clock, preceded by the black-coated headsman, carrying the execution axe, its sharp edge turned away from the prisoner. Surrey directly faced his judges sitting alongside Lord Mayor Hobberthorne – they included his enemies Hertford and Wriothesley and the king's secretary Paget, sitting as a commissioner. The earl would also have recognised many of the twelve-man jury, as its membership of knights and gentlemen were drawn from an area twelve miles (19 km.) around his father's palace at Kenninghall.

His indictment was then read out – the first time Surrey would have heard the charges against him. It was based on section twelve of the Second Succession Act of 1536:

> Whosoever, by words, writings, printing or other external act, maliciously shall procure anything to the peril of the king's person or give occasion whereby the king or his successors might be disturbed in their possession of the crown shall be guilty of high treason.
>
> And whereas Henry VIII is true King of England and Edward, formerly king of England, commonly called St Edward the Confessor, in right of the said realm ... used certain arms and ensigns, namely, *azure, a cross fleury*[53] *between five merletts*[54] *gold* belonging to the said king of England and his progenitors in right of the crown of England, which arms and ensigns are therefore appropriate to the king and no other person.
>
> And whereas Edward, now prince of England, the king's son and heir apparent, bears ... the said arms and ensigns with three labels, called *three labels silver* ...
>
> Nevertheless, one Henry Howard, late of Kenninghall, Knight of the Garter, otherwise called ... Earl of Surrey, on 7 October 1546 at Kenninghall, in the house of Thomas, Duke of Norfolk, his father, openly used and traitorously caused to be depicted, mixed and conjoined, with his own arms and ensigns, the said arms and ensigns of the king, with *three labels silver*.[55]

With a firm voice, Surrey pleaded: 'Not guilty.'

The prosecution opened their case. 'My lords, for either of the offences the earl has committed, he deserves death. First, for usurping the royal arms which gives rise to suspicion that he hoped to become king, and the other, for escaping from prison, whereby he showed his guilt.'[56] Surrey, 'with manly courage', interrupted:

> You are false and to earn a piece of gold would condemn your father. I never sought to usurp the king's arms, for everybody knows that my ancestors bore them.
>
> Go to the church in Norfolk and you will see them there, for they have been ours for 500 years.

He did not name the church, but he was talking about the Howards' mortuary chapel attached to the church of All Saints, East Winch, which had an arched monument to Sir Robert Howard (died 1388), and his wife Margaret, which bore the arms of St Edward.[57] Paget retorted:

Hold your peace my lord! Your idea was to commit treason and as the king is old, you thought to be king.

Surrey snapped back, a sneer on his face:

And you catchpole! What have you to do with it? You had better hold your tongue, for the kingdom has never been well since the king put mean creatures like you into government.

The jibe was born out of the earl's disdain for the low-born – 'catchpole' was street slang for a bailiff. Paget's father was said to have been a humble constable and the cutting insult silenced the king's secretary, leaving him 'very much abashed'. John Dudley, Viscount Lisle, then tried to trip up the prisoner with a question about his attempted escape, but Surrey retorted:

I tried to get out, to prevent myself from coming to the pass in which I am now and you, my lord, know full well that however right a man may be, they always find the fallen one guilty.[58]

One witness described an argument with Surrey, who had used 'high words' to him, and he had retaliated with a 'braving', or insulting, answer. The prisoner again interrupted and demanded of the jury:

Is it probable this man should speak thus to the Earl of Surrey and he not strike him?[59]

He then faced questions about his plan to make his sister the king's mistress, an allegation he emphatically denied: 'Must I be condemned,' he asked angrily, 'on the word of a wretched woman?'[60]

The trial continued until late in the afternoon. Surrey, 'of deep understanding, sharp wit and deep courage, defended himself in many ways, sometimes denying their accusations as false, and together weakening the credit of his adversaries'.[61] Amidst the gloom of a January afternoon, the jury retired at five to consider their verdict after eight hours of cross-examination. Paget scurried away to report on the trial's progress to the king at Westminster. An hour later he returned, possibly with a message from Henry to the jury.

They came back soon afterwards. With all of them standing and staring at Surrey, they pronounced their verdict: 'Guilty' – a brief pause – 'And he should die.' The court erupted into a noisy tumult, 'and it was a long while' before silence could be restored.[62]

The headsman now turned his axe so that the blade pointed at the earl, a sinister indication of his condemnation. The prisoner at the bar was still defiant:

Of what have you found me guilty? Surely you find no law that justifies you! But I know the king wants to get rid of the noble blood around him and employ none but low people.[63]

Wriothesley, his voice raised above the babble of voices, then pronounced sentence: that Surrey was to be taken 'back to the Tower and thence led through the City of London to the gallows at Tyburn[64] and hanged and disembowelled' and his body quartered. He was led out of the Guildhall and back to the Tower, the halberdiers struggling to push back the crowds, with Surrey still angrily declaring his innocence. One eyewitness said it was 'shocking to hear the things he kept saying and to see the grief of the people'.[65]

On 19 January, the sentence against this 'foolish proud boy' having been commuted to mere beheading, Surrey was executed on Tower Hill and buried immediately in the church of All Hallows, close by in Upper Thames Street.[66] On the scaffold 'he spoke a great deal but said he never meant to commit treason. They would not let him talk any more.'

The British Library holds a sketch of his arms, drawn by the Garter King of Arms in 1586, and headed 'Drawing of Arms of Howard, Earl of Surrey, for which he was attainted'. Its complexity – and inaccuracies in the twelve quarters – demonstrates that the earl was probably doing little more than careless, wistful doodling.[67]

Just over a week later, on 27 January, Wriothesley presided over a joint session of Parliament and announced the Royal Assent to the Bill of Attainder[68] of both Surrey and Norfolk, as Henry was too ill to attend in person. It was the last document signed in the king's reign.[69] As traitors, Norfolk and Surrey were automatically degraded from the Order of the Garter.[70]

Norfolk, still in the Tower, anxiously awaited his own lonely march to the scaffold. At least now he was relatively comfortable, lodged in the Constable's apartments. Walter Stonor's accounts for 12 December to 6 February show that £210 (£58,000 in today's money) was spent on the duke's board and lodging, including the cost of coals and candles.[71]

Henry VIII died dumbly, probably from renal and liver failure, coupled with the effects of his obesity,[72] at around two o'clock on the morning of Friday 28 January 1547, his hand clasped by the faithful Thomas Cranmer, Archbishop of Canterbury.

Later that morning Norfolk was due to be executed. He had probably been told the time of his last hour and as it passed – together with the days that followed – he must have puzzled at the reprieve.

The king's huge body lay within his apartments at Westminster for three days while the power brokers on his Council fashioned the shape of the government of the new nine-year-old king, Edward VI. Normal ceremonies were maintained as the news of Henry's death remained secret; the royal dishes were greeted at mealtimes by a flourish of trumpets as usual.

On 31 January, Wriothesley, his voice choking with emotion, announced the death of the king to a grieving Parliament. Edward, under Hertford's close protection, rode into London and was proclaimed king at the Tower amid the roar of cannon salutes from the ramparts and from ships moored in the Thames. Norfolk now knew the reason for his survival: if he shed any tears, they would have been of relief rather than remorse over the death of his old master.

Hertford was created Duke of Somerset and Lord Protector.

Norfolk's death warrant, already signed, was never fulfilled, probably because it was felt the threat he posed was effectively neutralised by his continued imprisonment.

Two months later, the plain, stark truth about Surrey's arraignment and execution emerged during a conversation between Jean de St Mauris, the Spanish ambassador to France, and his English counterpart, Nicholas Wotton. The English diplomat declared that 'God had shown mercy to the late king and to his people in that the Earl of Surrey had died before him',

> for otherwise he would have given the government trouble ... [Wotton] greatly censured the earl's insolence and hinted that he had been put out of the way because it had been feared he might stir up some commotion.[73]

In July 1547, six months after Surrey's trial, some of the evidence against him turned up, tantalisingly only to be lost again. Privy Council records show that Sir Robert Southwell, Master of the Rolls – the younger brother of the informer against the earl –

> delivered up a bag of books, sealed with his seal, wherein were contained writings concerning the attainder of the Duke of Norfolk and the Earl of Surrey his son, to the said Sir Robert and other learned men heretofore delivered to peruse. [The] bag was hereupon ordered to be stowed in the study at Westminster Palace, where other records do lie.[74]

Surrey left two sons and two daughters and his wife, Frances, gave birth to a third daughter, Jane, three weeks after his execution. Their custody was granted by the government to his sister, Mary, Duchess of Richmond, who was allowed £100 a year, paid quarterly, for their upkeep. Thomas, aged ten, Henry, six, and the eldest daughter Katherine were lodged at Reigate Castle in Surrey, which had been forfeited, with the rest of Norfolk's and Surrey's possessions, to the crown.[75] Frances remarried by 1553; her new husband was Thomas Steyning, with whom she had two children.[76]

The duke's second son, Thomas, was pardoned and restored to the rank of baron in mid-April.[77] Norfolk's half-brother, Lord

William Howard, was the only member of the family not tainted by disgrace. The general pardon issued to 'all who had offended the king' deliberately excluded Norfolk. Cannily, he sought assistance from the Archbishop of Canterbury, whom he asked to visit him in the Tower. They talked for two hours, both weeping – one in sympathy, the other in self-pity – and Cranmer agreed to lobby for the duke's release. His mission failed.

To the victors, the spoils. Edward Seymour, Duke of Somerset, received Norfolk's clothes and apparel 'however much worn: his parliamentary robes, jewels, gold chains, the French order of St Michael and the Garter regalia; crosses, brooches, rings, bracelets' and 'most of his chapel plate'. The duke's livestock and provisions were divided between Somerset and Princess Mary.[78]

Claims by Bessie Holland, his mistress, for the return of all her glitzy jewellery were allowed, no doubt as reward for testifying against father and son. The Duchess of Richmond also received 'a good many things'. Surrey's widow was allowed a small quantity of plate and furniture but the pictures and furnishings from their home at Mount Surrey were passed over to the earl's creditors in payment of his still sizeable debts.

The Duchess of Norfolk received a considerable quantity of clothes, soft furnishings and some of her other possessions: 'a little coffer of ivory . . . [with] a silver gilt lock; a little flat casket, having a silver lock'. Neither had their keys. Her smile of satisfaction must have been terrible to see.

The summer of 1549 brought rebellion to Devon and Cornwall, the southern Midlands and elsewhere, over the imposition of the Book of Common Prayer. In Norfolk, the population rose in reaction to the end of the Howards' conservative – if not reactionary – domination of East Anglia and their maintenance of medieval feudalism. In the mid-1540s, of four manors in Norfolk which still maintained bondmen or serfs three belonged to the duke, and, in adjacent Suffolk, five of the six manors retaining villeins were owned by him.[79] The East Anglian insurrection was led by a tanner called William Kett and, among more general damage, it destroyed the fences around Kenninghall Park and sacked Surrey's house in Norwich. One of the rebels' demands was: 'We pray that all bondmen be made free – for God made all free with his precious blood shedding.'[80]

The rebellion was crushed at the end of August and Norfolk's feudalism continued, with complaints to Somerset that the duke had used his serfs 'much more extremely than his ancestors did'. The accounts for the Howard estates are liberally sprinkled with references to 'bondmen' and payments for *chevage*, a poll tax levied on villeins, including fines paid for permission for their daughters to be married. At Bungay in Suffolk, the manor court records show that on 25 May (no year, but during the later reign of Mary),

> It is informed that where Robert Spark, bondman of blood to the manor there, fled from them at the rebellion and commotion upon Mousehold, besides Norwich, to Colchester in Essex and dwells at the sign of the George there.
>
> And being spoken to and desired to return and compound to pay his chevage yearly, and does not, that therefore he be seized before the day of my lord's delivery out of the Tower.[81]

And at Bressingham, on the 'vigil of St Luke' (17 October) 1552, 'to this court comes John Bartram of Palgrave, bever[82] and acknowledges that he is a villein of the lord and he pays a fine, for chevage 12d'.[83] At Kenninghall 'came William Foster and Joan Baxter, the widow of William Baxter and daughter to William Glede and asked licence to marry together, which for 3s 4d of fine to be paid to my lord at the next account ... for the manor ... I granted'.[84]

Back in London, conditions of Norfolk's confinement slowly eased. He was now housed in the Beauchamp Tower, adjacent to the Lieutenant's lodgings. In March 1548, Sir Ralph Sadler, Master of the Great Wardrobe, was authorised to deliver 'apparel and beddings' to Sir John Markham, the new Lieutenant, for Norfolk's use.[85] The following month, the Treasurer of the Exchequer was authorised to pay Markham an annual sum of £73 5s 4d towards the duke's apparel, and £80 as 'his spending money' so long as he remained his prisoner.[86] Accordingly in June, a tailor called Bridges was paid £9 9s 9d for making clothes for Norfolk.[87] A total of £5 was allowed for food and drink and 6s 8d each for boarding five servants, each paid 6s 8d a week.

There were other benefits of a less material nature. In February 1549, the Privy Council agreed that the duke's daughter and wife may 'have recourse to the late duke' who 'could have liberty to walk in the garden and gallery when the Lieutenant shall think good'.[88] The duke's reaction to meeting his estranged wife in the Tower can only be imagined.

His freedom of movement continued to be extended: on 20 July 1550, the Privy Council ordered the Lieutenant and Sir Ralph Hopton, Knight Marshal, to 'suffer the late Duke of Norfolk to have the liberty to walk and ride within the precincts of the Tower [so long as] one of them [was always] present'.[89] Nine months later came another concession to make the old man's life more bearable. On 8 April, the Council wrote to the Lieutenant instructing him 'to suffer for this once, the Lord Thomas Howard [Norfolk's grandson] to speak with the late duke . . .'.[90]

He may have watched in smug satisfaction as Sir Thomas Seymour was marched out of the Tower for execution for treason on 20 March 1549 and, better yet, on 22 January 1552, the same lonely walk undertaken by his brother Somerset, who took his death 'very patiently'.[91]

The duke's sufferings finally ended after the death of Edward VI and the accession of his Catholic half-sister, Mary, in August 1553, who swept aside the Protestant candidate for the throne, Lady Jane Grey. On the evening of 3 August, Mary arrived at the Tower after a triumphal progress through London, escorted by 1,000 retainers dressed in velvet coats. She was met at the gates by Sir John Gage and, arriving at the green, she saw Norfolk and Gardiner (who had also been imprisoned during Edward's reign) kneeling humbly on the grass, amidst the joyful salvoes of gunfire ringing out from the fortress. Mary kissed them, declared 'these be my prisoners', and bid them rise up and stand.[92] The following day Norfolk and Gardiner were formally freed.

Norfolk's revenge on his captors was swift and ruthless.

On Friday 18 August, Norfolk, as High Steward of England, sat beneath a canopy of gold cloth of estate in Westminster Hall in judgement on Sir John Dudley, now first Duke of Northumberland, his eldest son John, Earl of Warwick, and Sir William

Parr, Marquis of Northampton, on charges of treason. North-umberland objected, claiming there was no crime in him having supported Lady Jane Grey as his sovereign, but Norfolk declared the charges just.[93] But after the indictments were read, they meekly pleaded guilty and 'without passing of any jury of their peers, had judgement to be drawn, hanged and quartered'. The duke was among the official witnesses at Northumberland's execution on 22 August[94] and a month later had the satisfaction of recovering his gold ducal coronet, the collar and badge of the Garter and his jewels and plate from Northumberland's estate.[95] The duke also presided over the trials of Cranmer, Lady Jane and her husband.

As Earl Marshal, he organised Mary's coronation at West-minster Abbey on 1 October. As his customary fee, he claimed 'the queen's horse and palfrey, with all the furniture that is on the horse and he claimed to be high usher on the day of the coronation and to have the table cloth of the high dess [desk] and the cloth of estate that was behind the queen'.[96]

Norfolk's attainder was reversed in October and his grandson Thomas Howard, now the Earl of Surrey, was restored in blood.[97] He had trouble reclaiming his forfeited lands, which had been disposed of by Edward VI. Eventually, two-thirds were restored, worth £1,600, and early in 1554 he held a manorial court at Fram-lingham.[98]

The duke's warlike duties were not over – and his last campaign was probably his most ignominious. In January 1554, Kent rose in rebellion, under Sir Thomas Wyatt, over Mary's plans to marry Philip of Spain, the son of Charles V. Norfolk, as an eighty-one-year-old Lieutenant General of the army, was despatched to Kent to assault the rebel headquarters at Rochester with a small force of 1,000 white-coated London troops. From Gravesend, he con-fidently promised the Privy Council: 'I doubt not you shall shortly hear of their repulse out of . . . Rochester.'[99]

His confidence was misplaced.

Without securing his lines of communication, Norfolk hastened on to Strood and opened fire with his artillery on Rochester Bridge. One of his captains, called Bret, suddenly turned to face his 500-strong battalion and drew his sword. He shouted:

Masters, we [are] about to fight against our native countrymen of England ... in a quarrel unrightful and partly wicked for ... we shall be under the rule of the proud Spaniards ... [and] if we should be under their subjection, they would, as slaves and villeins, spoil us of our goods and lands, ravish our wives before our faces and deflower our daughters in our presence.

The troops responded by crying 'A Wyatt, a Wyatt' and 'We are all Englishmen'. They turned their cannon on the remainder of Norfolk's little army and the duke, sensing discretion to be the better part of valour, hastily departed, leaving behind him eight brass guns and his honour.[100] Fortunately for him, perhaps, Wyatt's rebellion foundered in Fleet Street at the gates of the city of London in early February.

Norfolk attended his last Privy Council meeting on 7 May but was too ill to be present at the preparations for his grandson Thomas's marriage to Mary Fitzalan, daughter of the Earl of Arundel, a fortnight later.

Back at Kenninghall on 21 July, he dictated his last will to George Holland, his secretary:

I Thomas Duke of Norfolk, Earl Marshal of England, being [moved] by the goodness of God and by merciful pity shown and extended towards me for and concerning my deliverance out of and from my long imprisonment by the most gracious lady Queen Mary, by the grace of God, Queen of England, France and Ireland, Defender of the Faith, and on earth, the supreme head of the church of England[101] ... of that name the first.

Calling now into remembrance the great age I am now grown into and feeling myself thereby to be fallen into great weakness of my body, albeit, thanks to almighty God, having my full, whole and perfect memory, [I] here[to]fore declare my last will and testament in form following.

First, I bequeath my soul to almighty God, having sure trust and confidence that through and by the merits of Christ's death and Passion, to have that remission and forgiveness of my sins and trespasses and to be a partaker and one of the inheritors of the kingdom of God.

His grandson Thomas was named heir 'to all and singular, my manors, lands, tenements, possessions . . . whatsoever which I have within the realm of England'.[102] Among the other bequests was £500 to Mary, Duchess of Richmond, for bringing up her brother's children and 'her great costs and charges in making suit for my deliverance out of my imprisonment'. Each of Surrey's daughters were also to receive £1,000 on their marriage or when they reached the age of twenty-one.

There was no mention of his wife, or Bessie Holland. But there was one surprise: £100 was left to his lawyer and steward 'Sergeant [Thomas] Gawdy and John Gosnold', to bring up 'the child which [is] in my house now commonly called Jane Goodman' – quite probably his bastard daughter.'[103] A clue to this may lie in a document detailing his properties which includes the annuities paid by the duke. Among them is: 'Item. To Thomas Goodman, gentleman, out of the manor of Shelfhanger, £20.'[104]

His last act was to give his blessing to the wedding of his granddaughter Katherine and Henry Lord Berkeley, who were married a month later at Kenninghall.[105]

Norfolk died in his bed on 25 August 1554 at Kenninghall. There were many who would say there was no justice in his peaceful end. But after all his conspiracies, intrigue and the tumult of his life, he ended up the great survivor.

The London mercer and undertaker Henry Machyn recorded the duke's funeral at Framlingham on 2 October:

There was a goodly hearse [with] wax [candles] as [ever] I have seen in these days, with a dozen of bannerols[106] of his progeny [ancestral descent] and twelve dozen pensels,[107] two dozen of escutcheons and with [a] standard and three coats of arms, and a banner of damask . . . and many mourners and a great dole and after, a great dinner.

[Mourners were fed on] forty great oxen and a hundred sheep and sixty calves, besides venison, swans and cranes, capons, rabbits, pigeons, pikes and other provisions, both flesh and fish. There was also a great plenty of wine and of bread and beer as great plenty as ever been known, both for rich and poor and all the country came thither and a great dole of money [was bestowed on the poor].[108]

That marital thorn in Norfolk's side, Elizabeth Howard, died at Kenninghall during the evening of Thursday 4 September 1558, aged sixty-five – no doubt delighted that she had outlived her much despised husband.[109] Her will, signed when she was 'sick and diseased in body', asked that she should be buried in the Howard chapel at St Mary's church, Lambeth, in Surrey. Even in death, her proper status as widow of a duke must be observed, even though she hated most of her Howard in-laws.

She left her brother's wife Ursula her jewels and most of her clothes, and her grandson, now the fourth Duke of Norfolk, some tablets carved with religious iconography. A 'gown of crimson velvet' went to his wife. Her granddaughter, Margaret, was bequeathed 'two gowns of taffeta' and her younger son, Thomas, created Viscount Bindon in 1559, was left a silver gilt cup and cover. After a few gifts to her servants, the rest of her 'goods, cattle and debts' she left to her brother Henry, Lord Stafford.[110] After years of her husband's parsimony, there was not much for her to bequeath.

Elizabeth was buried at Lambeth in December and an epitaph, written by Stafford, was erected over her grave:

Farewell good lady and sister dear
In earth, we shall never meet here
But yet, I trust, with God's grace,
In heaven we deserve a place
Yet thy kindness shall nere depart
During my life out of my heart
You were to me both far and near
A mother, sister, a friend most dear.

It ends: 'God thy soul preserve from pain.'[111]

Elizabeth's effigy was placed incongruously on her husband's tomb at Framlingham when it was completed in 1559.[112] In life, they were noisily divided. In death, they were reunited, if only for the sake of appearances.

PART 3

CAUGHT IN THE RELIGIOUS SNARE

9

AN EQUAL OF KINGS

———◆———

'She wept and blubbered, saying "Woe is me! That [noble] house [of Howard] has suffered so much for my sake"'

Mary Queen of Scots at her trial, October 1586¹

Thomas Howard, fourth Duke of Norfolk, was aged just eighteen when he inherited the title from his grandfather – together with a handsome bequest of fifty-six manors, thirty-seven advowsons and 'many other considerable estates', to make him probably the greatest landowner in the realm.² His legacy also included the hereditary title of Earl Marshal of England.³ The Howard lands in East Anglia were lumped together as 'the Liberty of the Duke of Norfolk' administered by the duke's own courts and covering four hundreds,⁴ together with fourteen other manors in Norfolk and nine parishes in Suffolk. The fourth duke also owned the rapes⁵ of Lewes and Bramber in Sussex, the Surrey manors of Dorking and Reigate, and other estates in Devon, Shropshire and in Ireland, and even a coal mine in South Wales.⁶

These were happier, golden times for the Howards. After the arrest of his father, the Earl of Surrey, Howard had been placed in the custody of Sir John Williams and lived at his sumptuous Tudor palace at Rycote, near Thame in Oxfordshire.⁷ Then, after Surrey's execution, his aunt, Mary, Duchess of Richmond, had taken responsibility for the ten-year-old and his siblings at Reigate Castle and placed him in the care of the Protestant polemicist John Foxe, as tutor. Later, after the accession of the devout Mary, he joined Bishop Gardiner's household at Southwark – something of a contrast in religious ambience – and his education was completed by the pious Catholic John White, Bishop of Lincoln, in 1554–6. Little wonder that doubts about his religious allegiance dogged him throughout his life.

As the new duke was underage, he became a ward of the queen and required royal permission to marry Mary, the daughter of Sir Henry Fitzalan, twelfth Earl of Arundel, on 30 March 1555, who became his heir when her brother died in 1556.

Young Thomas had lost nothing of the Howard flair in picking an appropriate wife: Mary added Arundel Castle and substantial estates in Sussex to her young husband's bulging portfolio of property.[8] In the same year as his wedding, a private Act of Parliament was passed empowering Norfolk to make sales and grants of his own property in his own right, but under the guidance of the Lord Chancellor (now Gardiner, who died shortly afterwards), the Earl of Arundel and Thomas Thirlby, Bishop of Ely since 1554.[9]

The Norfolks enjoyed high favour at Mary's court. A month after Mary's accession, Thomas was restored to the title of Earl of Surrey,[10] created a Knight of the Bath and in July 1554 he became the first gentleman of the chamber of King Philip, the queen's new Spanish consort, and he attended their wedding at Winchester Cathedral on 25 July 1554, just two days after the royal couple's first meeting.

The duke survived an unfortunate accident on 26 June 1557 when he was riding in Stamford Hill, London. His pistol, 'hanging on his saddle bow … by misfortune' was fired 'and hit one of his men' whose horse panicked, threw him, and the retainer 'was hanged by his stirrup, so that the horse knocked his brains out with flinging out of his legs'.[11]

The new king was godfather to the Norfolks' child, Philip, born two days later, and named after him.[12] Sadly, the duchess died eight weeks afterwards, aged only seventeen, and was buried in the church of St Clement Danes in London.[13]

With the continuation of his dynasty resting precariously on the life of a young baby, he moved smartly to find another wife to produce other heirs, and found a suitable candidate in his cousin, Margaret, Lady Dudley. She was the daughter and sole heiress of Lord Audley of Walden[14] and the eighteen-year-old widow of Lord Henry Dudley, who had died without issue in 1557. The fourth duke needed a papal dispensation for the marriage, and his lawyers predictably spent months in Rome negotiating to win the necessary permission. However, after Queen Mary's death at St James's Palace on 17 November 1558, and the accession of her Protestant half-sister Elizabeth, the Vatican's authority over his prospective nuptials vanished like a puff of incense.[15] His second marriage was duly ratified by the new queen's first parliament in 1559 and it brought him yet another fine mansion – Audley End in Essex.

The duke and his new duchess, together with his four-year-old son, Philip, Earl of Surrey, attended a magnificent feast laid on by William Mingay, the mayor of Norwich, on 5 June 1562 for members of the nobility visiting the duke's home in the city. The twenty-two guests, the last named being Sir Richard Fulmerston, the old family retainer now made good, sat down to a meal of truly Johnsonian proportions. Certainly, no one went home hungry, unless they were vegetarians. The toothsome menu included 112 lb (50.8 kg.) of beef, four collars of brawn, a hind quarter of veal, a leg, breast and loin of mutton, six pullets, four brace of partridges, two guinea fowl and two mallard ducks, together with thirty-four loaves. To wash all this down were a barrel of double-strength beer and two gallons of white wine.[16]

Margaret provided him with three children: firstly a daughter, Margaret (or Meg), then two sons, Thomas, on 24 August 1561, and William, born on 19 December 1563. The tragedy of his first wife was now repeated: three weeks after William's birth, on Sunday 9 January, she too 'departed this transitory world' at 'about seven of the clock [in the] afternoon' in Norwich.[17]

Kenninghall remained a popular country home and his principal seat, and there were also several houses owned by the Howards in Norwich, then the prosperous second city in England. But as the premier peer of the realm, Norfolk felt the need for another palatial home to firmly stamp his mark as a regional magnate, if not a prince. Indeed, he had inherited his father's and grandfather's overweening pride in his own dynasty, calling himself in legal documents 'the right honourable and noble prince, Thomas, Duke of Norfolk . . .'.[18] Some time around 1561, he began to build a huge new ducal palace on the banks of the River Wensum, in the parish of St John Maddermarket in Norwich,[19] using building materials brought by river from the demolished Benedictine abbey of St Benet's at Holm.[20] It was to become the greatest house outside London, equipped with its own bowling alley, 188 feet (55.4 m.) long, a covered real tennis court and a theatre – the duke had his own company of actors.[21]

He was not content with the old ancestral home at Lambeth and so sold it in 1558 to Richard Garth and John Dister for £400.[22] The fourth duke purchased the former Carthusian monastery of the Charterhouse, on the northern outskirts of London, from Edward, first Baron North, for £2,000 in 1564 and embarked on an extensive rebuilding programme. It was proudly renamed Howard House.[23]

With his exalted position and ancestry, it was inevitable that he would be called upon for military service. Like his great-grand-father and grandfather before him, he accepted the appointment of Lieutenant General of the north in 1559, in his case somewhat reluctantly. Norfolk's mission was to prosecute Elizabeth's government's policy of ousting the French military and political presence from Scotland by defending the border town of Berwick and striking up alliances with the Scottish Protestant lords. He was not happy in his work. Although he played no part in the fighting, he wrote of his fervent desires, both to return south, 'because this country and I can ill agree',[24] and an earnest wish 'to finish this war now begun'.[25] Norfolk also amply demonstrated his Protestant credentials by his disapproval of the old religion's remaining deep roots in the border area. 'I find the town and country hereabouts far out of order in matters of religion, the altars still standing in the churches, contrary to the queen's majesty's proceedings,' he reported to Sir William Cecil, on 10 January 1560, and rec-ommended that James Pilkington, Bishop of Durham, should make some urgent reforms.[26]

Just over six weeks later, he signed a military agreement with the Scots and, later, the Treaty of Edinburgh in July 1560 ensured the withdrawal of French troops from Scotland.

Norfolk returned to London soon afterwards. He had lost nothing of the Howards' love of showy pomp and circumstance. A contemporary diarist records the duke and duchess's grand entry into the capital on 8 October 1562:

> My lord the Duke of Norfolk and the Duchess, my good lady, his wife, came riding through London and through Bishopsgate to Leadenhall [Street] and so to [St Katherine Cree] church [next] to his own place, with one hundred horse[men] in his livery ... gentlemen [with] coats [of velvet] and with four heralds [riding] before him.[27]

The following month, he was appointed a member of the Privy Council. Like the third duke, he soon acquired a taste for political intrigue and a thirst for power. Ranged against him at court, however, were some powerful adversaries: Cecil, Elizabeth's omnipotent minister, and Robert Dudley, who was created Earl of Leicester in 1564. Norfolk and Leicester soon clashed over the seemingly eternal question of Elizabeth's marriage – the duke opposed Leicester's own ambitions for the queen's hand and instead promoted the diplomatic benefits of her marrying Archduke Charles of Austria, inconveniently a Catholic. He wrote a three-page letter to the queen from Norwich in November 1567, about 'my opinion in these matters' as sickness had prevented him coming to London; he may have had an infected hand. He was hesitant to commit his ideas to paper:

> If it please your highness for me, being one of the youngest of your majesty's most honourable council, as also one that has least experience or understanding to weigh the depth of so weighty a cause ... though a man sometime in speech utters that which is not so well to be allowed, yet speech be easier forgotten. What a man ... commits to writing, wherein there is any error, it is ever open evidence of a man's folly.

He knew the Archduke's request to practise his religion privately after marriage to Elizabeth was a 'matter of such weight ... nor yet how [a] great difference there is for your highness' husband, upon whom all men's eyes [would] be set, to keep a contrary religion to yourself and your realm'.

If he should show himself an open maintainer of papistry, it might both bring danger to your self and your realm, for let your highness assure yourself that England can bear no more changes in religion.

It has been bowed so often that if it should be bent again, it would break.

Norfolk believed that the Archduke 'is not very careful of religion' and he nursed high hopes that she 'may persuade him afterwards to change [his faith]'. Norfolk underlined his hopes that 'she may marry soon, [as] the people desire it'.[28]

But, like all other suitors for the hand of Elizabeth, the Archduke was not found suitable as a consort for the Virgin Queen.

The duke was a widower again and on 29 January 1567 married his third wife, Elizabeth, daughter of Sir Thomas Leyburn and the widow of Thomas, Lord Dacre of Glisland, a powerful northern landowner. She already had four children – five-year-old George, Anne, Mary and Elizabeth. Norfolk married off his stepdaughters to his sons by his first two wives, in a less than subtle attempt to secure the substantial Dacre properties for his male offspring. Anne Dacre married his eldest, Philip; Mary, his second son, Thomas (later Earl of Suffolk); and Elizabeth wed William. Unfortunately, little George Dacre died in May 1569 at Thetford after being crushed by a wooden vaulting horse which fell on top of him, and Mary Dacre also died young.

All Norfolk's marriages, though happy, were blighted by heartbreak. His third wife died in childbirth on 4 September 1567, nine months after their wedding. Her baby was also born dead. The duke was stricken by grief and must have felt his family cursed. He fell ill and did not recover until the spring of the following year.

Events elsewhere were to trigger his downfall.

In May 1568, Mary Queen of Scots fled to England after her defeat in a brief civil war in Scotland, without money, or even a change of clothes. She was the widow of, firstly, Francis II of France, then of Henry Stuart, Lord Darnley, and latterly became the wife of the dashing James Hepburn, fourth Earl of Bothwell.

For her personal heraldry she had quartered the arms of England with those of Scotland and France in what was tantamount to a claim to the crown of England, based on her descent from her grandmother, Henry VIII's elder sister Margaret, who had married James IV of Scotland. Many English Catholics saw her as Elizabeth's replacement and Mary therefore spent the remainder of her life as a prisoner, sequestered from English politics and public life.

On top of all this, the Scottish queen had arrived as a refugee under a dark cloud of criminal suspicion. Elizabeth was persuaded by her Privy Council to investigate the Scots' allegations of her complicity in the murder, in February 1567, of her drunken, wastrel husband, the syphilitic Darnley. He had been brutally strangled after escaping from a house at Kirk o' Field, on the outskirts of Edinburgh, which had been destroyed in an explosion set off in an attempt to assassinate him.[29]

Norfolk was one of the English commissioners appointed to meet, at York, their Scottish counterparts, sent by James Stewart, Earl of Moray, and Regent to the infant James VI of Scotland, Mary's son by Darnley.

During a break in the deliberations on 16 October 1568, the duke went hawking with the Scottish Secretary of State, William Maitland. As they rode along the banks of the River Ouse, near Cawood, eight miles (4.87 km.) south-west of York, Maitland suddenly suggested that Norfolk should marry the Scottish queen as a convenient way of uniting the two nations in a powerful alliance, as well as securing her claim as an heir to the English throne. Although the duke suspected that Mary had been culpable in her husband's murder, the old Howard ambitions for power and status overwhelmed any qualms. The notion had considerable, almost irresistible, allure; marrying Mary could one day make Norfolk king consort, with sovereignty over all the British Isles, wearing the crown imperial.

Not unnaturally, he became sorely tempted by the marriage plan, and suppressed any nagging doubts by the sure knowledge that Elizabeth herself had suggested his name, together with those of Leicester and Darnley, as appropriate husbands back in December 1564, ten months after the duke lost his second wife.

The murder investigation was inevitably adjourned without a decision and Elizabeth summoned her commissioners back to London – telling the duke on 3 November he should 'repair thither as soon as he may'[30] – so they could continue their inquiries away from the machinations of the Scottish delegation. During the conference, resumed at Westminster, Norfolk discussed the possible marriage with Moray during a clandestine meeting in the park of Hampton Court.[31]

His attempts at secrecy failed dismally. The French ambassador had already reported rumours about the marriage to Paris,[32] and Elizabeth herself was becoming suspicious about her cousin's ambitions. She suddenly asked him point-blank that November whether he intended to marry Mary Queen of Scots, a match, she now believed, which threatened both her sacred person and her crown. Rather too smoothly, Norfolk replied that

> no reason could move him to like her that has been a competitor to the crown and if her majesty would move him thereto, he would rather be committed to the Tower, for he meant never to marry with such a person, where he could not be sure of his pillow.[33]

These were foolish, rash words that would return to haunt the fourth duke in the months to come. Daringly, recklessly, he had met Mary on the pretext of visiting his sister Margaret, who was married to Henry Scrope, ninth Lord Bolton, the Scottish queen's temporary jailer at Bolton Castle, north Yorkshire.[34] By early 1569, Norfolk became determined to marry her, even though Mary was still married to Bothwell.

She enthusiastically pledged her love for the duke, seeing him as the key that would free her from perpetual, tedious imprisonment. She petitioned the Pope to annul her union with Bothwell, which was invalid, she claimed, as it was by Protestant rites. Hedging her bets, she also sought more physical means of freedom, secretly writing to the Catholic Earls of Northumberland and Westmorland to seek their help in releasing her, by force of arms if necessary, from her new prison at Tutbury Castle in Staffordshire. She hinted at such an escape attempt in a letter to Norfolk on 31 January 1569:

I wrote to you before to know your pleasure if I should seek to make any enterprise [escape attempt]; if it please you, I care not for my danger, but I would wish you would seek to do the like, for if you and I could both escape, we should find friends enough.

Mary understood very well that Norfolk could forfeit his vast estates if attainted as a traitor, and sought to reassure him:

And for your lands, I hope they should not be lost, for being free and honourably bound together, you might make such good offers to the countries [Scotland and England] and the Queen of England, as they should not refuse.

You have promised to be mine and I yours. I believe the Queen of England and the country should like of it . . .

If you think the danger great, do as you think best, and let me know what you please that I do; for I will ever be, for your sake, perpetual prisoner or put my life in peril for your [well-being] and mine . . .

I pray God preserve you and keep us both from deceitful friends.

> Your own, faithful to death,
> Queen of Scots, my Norfolk.[35]

These were beguiling, but hazardous words. Mary was said to have an 'alluring grace, a pretty Scotch speech and a searching wit clouded with mildness'. She was also a natural conspirator, with intrigue running through her very veins.

On 19 March, after a long pause, she wrote again to Norfolk, 'in respect of the dangers of writing, which you seemed to fear'.

I will live and die with you. Your fortune shall be mine, therefore, let me know, in all things your mind . . .

I trust in God you shall be satisfied with my conditions and behaviour and faithful duty to you, whenever it shall please God I be with you.[36]

Norfolk gave her a rich diamond as a token of his love and she later described it as something 'I have always held very dear, having been given to me ... as a pledge, of his troth, and I have always worn it as such'.[37]

The duke became despondent about his chances of marriage and uneasy that the couple's covert correspondence could be revealed. He wrote to the Earl of Moray on 1 July declaring that he could not 'with honour proceed further till such time as you should remove all stumbling blocks to our more apparent proceedings'.

> My very earnest request is that you proceed with such expedition as the enemies (which will be in no small number) to this good purpose, of uniting this land into one kingdom in time coming, and the maintenance of God's true religion, may not have opportunity, through delay given them, to prevent our pretensed determinations.[38]

However, Moray was also having second thoughts about the match. Could Mary seek immediate restoration to the throne of Scotland? Would he therefore have to flee for his life and live in exile overseas? Would Norfolk use his wife's claim to the English crown to destroy that fledgling Protestant state? Fatally, and treacherously, he sent Elizabeth a copy of the duke's letter announcing his intention to marry Mary.

Three times during a royal progress that summer she had asked Norfolk to confirm his marriage plans with Mary Queen of Scots. Three times he could not summon up the courage to reveal his projected match to Elizabeth. Once, when they dined alone at her invitation, 'she gave him a nip, saying, "that she would wish me to take a good head to my pillow"'. This 'abashed' him, but he 'thought it not a fit time or place there to trouble her'.[39] Leicester, pursuing his own political agenda, assured Norfolk that the queen would surely accept his proposals if she heard them from her special favourite, the earl himself. Like a gullible fool, Norfolk believed him.

Leicester was lying on his sick bed at Titchfield in Hampshire on 6 September when he told Elizabeth. The words had scarcely escaped his trembling lips when he was treated to a vintage Tudor tantrum. The queen furiously forbade any idea of such a marriage and, later that day in the gallery, solemnly charged Norfolk, on his allegiance to her, 'to deal no further with the Scottish cause'. She commanded him 'to free himself of it, for the sake [of the] fidelity and loyalty which he ought to bear unto his sovereign'.[40] He hastily assured Elizabeth that he 'had a very slight regard' for Mary and that her rank and the fortunes of the Scottish crown meant nothing to him.

With the flawed, foolish pride that was part and parcel of the Howard genes, he went too far in his hurried reassurances. The duke boasted cheerfully that his revenues 'were not much less than those of Scotland ... and when he was in his tennis court at Norwich, he thought himself equal with some kings'. This was not a sentiment to calm the proud and always parsimonious queen and he soon found himself shunned, if not completely ostracised, at court.

Elizabeth, meanwhile, wrote to Mary's jailers on 15 September warning them of a possible attempt to rescue her from captivity.

> We find that she, and such as solicit and labour most for her cause, intend to proceed in it otherwise than is meet or than we can consent for our honour.
>
> We have cause to doubt that when she and her friends perceive their purpose not agreeable to us, there will be some secret device to procure her escape, both perilous and dishonourable to us.[41]

Norfolk decided that a spell in the country would allow time for things to quieten down at court, particularly after receiving a warning from Leicester that he was destined for the Tower.[42] He wrote to Cecil and Leicester after hearing that the queen planned to go to Windsor, 'whither her pleasure is he should repair. At my coming to Howard House, I found myself disposed to an ague, (malarial fever) [which] to avoid I took a purgative yesterday which continued working even this night in my bed ... I am afraid to go into the air so soon. But within four days, I will not fail to come to court.'[43]

Then Norfolk suddenly panicked. He left London without permission and arrived at Kenninghall, still sick with fever. From there, he wrote a long letter to Elizabeth, seeking to excuse his impulsive departure.

To my great grief . . . your majesty, I am told . . . [is] sore offended
with me . . . I did, with all humility, [hope] that I might recover
your majesty's favour but my enemies found such comfort of
your majesty's heavy displeasure that they begin to make of me
common table-talk [and] my friends [are] now afraid of my
company.

When I found this, I complained of my miserable state to
some of . . . [the] council and thought no way so good as privily
to withdraw to my sorrowful house . . .

It was no small grief that . . . every townsman could say my
house was beset [and] − a nipping to my heart − that I should
become a . . . suspected person.

Besides this, all the town reported (and some in noble houses)
. . . that I would be committed to my own house, [and after] a
while, to the Tower, which is so great a terror for a true man.

Yet, though daunted by these sharp reports, knowing not what
ground they had, my whole mind was to abide them till Tuesday,
between four and five at night, when I understood by more than
common friends that my overthrow and imprisonment were
determined.

He thought it 'good to withdraw' to win time to write 'this humble
declaration' to his sovereign and protested 'on my honour' that
he never dealt in the case of the Scottish queen 'further than I
declared'.[44]

Elizabeth was becoming impatient − and increasingly suspicious
about what the duke was up to. Was his disappearance sinister?
Would he become a figurehead in a rebellion by her disaffected
Catholic subjects in the northern counties? Her fears of revolt had
led her to seek the protection of the high walls of Windsor Castle.

From there, she issued categorical instructions to Norfolk on 25
September to come immediately to court:

We have received your letters . . . finding by the same that upon
a pretence of fear without cause, you have come to Kenninghall,
contrary to our expectations . . . [and] as you wrote to certify . . .
that you would, without fail, be at our court in four days.

The queen commanded him 'without delay, upon sight of this letter' to 'repair to us here at this our castle of Windsor, or wherever we shall be' upon 'your allegiance'.[45]

As ill luck for the house of Howard would have it, the duke never received this royal charge – or so he claimed.

Suspicions over Norfolk's loyalty and intentions multiplied at court. There were fears that his popularity might spark disorder if he was arrested and trigger the very insurrection the queen most feared. On 26 September, the Council sent a circular letter to lord lieutenants explaining the position:

> It is likely you may hear how the Duke of Norfolk is gone of late from London to Kenninghall, which by his letter to us signified to be upon fear of the queen's majesty's displeasure, where he avows that he remains a faithful subject and so we heartily wish and trust he will considering there is no other cause.
>
> Yet because we are not ignorant what disposition there is in evil disposed persons to take occasion, upon small matters, to move seditious bruits [rumours], we have thought good to signify to you that her majesty has not meant any wise [action] toward the Duke ... any manner to him offensive, but only upon his coming to the court to understand the truth of a certain matter that has been moved to him for a marriage with the Queen of Scots.

The circular's honeyed words hastened to stress that 'we know not of any manner of intent in him but that which belongs to an honourable person and a just and true servant to the queen's majesty'. Indeed, Elizabeth was anxious to avoid 'such a nobleman [being] abused with unkind reports' and so had sent for Norfolk 'to repair to here, as is most likely he will'.

> Meantime, because we know not how evil-disposed persons will upon such a matter raise sundry lewd and false rumours, we have thought good to advise you hereof and require you forthwith to communicate this, our letters, with the justices of the peace and have good regard to stay all seditious rumours by apprehending the authors thereof.[46]

On 28 September, there still was no sign of Norfolk at Windsor and he used his sickness to explain his tardiness. Elizabeth was more than exasperated and wrote again to the duke:

> We have by your letters and by this bringer, our trusty servant Edward Garrett, we understand the cause of your not coming to us presently … [to be that] you were entered into a fever, but that you would very shortly take your journey to us. We return this bringer, [*inserted*], with all haste and do charge you as before to immediately make your repair hitherwards.
>
> For avoiding the peril you doubt [fear] by your ague, if it continue, you may come by some shorter journey than accustomed, and in a litter[47] rather than delay further.
>
> So shall you make a demonstration to the world of your loyalty and humbleness that by your letters and speeches you do profess.

Elizabeth's anger then boiled over. As she dictated her letter, she did not mince her words.

> [Your] manner of answer, we have not been accustomed to receive from any person.
>
> Neither would we have you think us … as to allow an excuse by a fever, having had so strait a commandment from us and your case being so notorious, first by your departure, now by your delay, that our estimation [of you] cannot be in some discredit, except that you immediately repair to us, though in a litter.[48]

The same day, Cecil, who was playing his own canny game of politics, wrote to Norfolk in a more persuasive tone. The minister was 'grieved at your sickness, so I was glad to see your resolve … to come to her majesty according to her commandment which was very earnest and strait, according to her majesty's special direction'. Norfolk, he said soothingly, should not be troubled by the reports of any offence being taken by Elizabeth, and he trusted that nothing more would come of the affair but mere words – or at worst a temporary banishment from her presence. Cecil could not resist adding a pointed postscript:

> The queen's majesty was very much offended with Mr Garrett

[the messenger] for his coming away without your grace and has
suffered some reprimand for him.[49]

On 30 September, Norfolk acknowledged the receipt of the latest
angry missive from Elizabeth, but still reported in sick, 'whereby I
am not able to attend on her majesty according to my bounden
duty. My desire is that you give her majesty to understand thereof
and to make my humble excuse. [As] soon as I may, without peril
of further sickness, I shall wait upon her, before Monday or Tuesday
at the furthest.'[50]

Amazingly – or perhaps his fever really was bad – Norfolk did
not set off for Windsor until 1 October, with a deliberately small
retinue of thirty riders, sleeping overnight at Newmarket, and
taking the journey by easy stages.[51] On arrival at Windsor, he was
arrested on suspicion of treason and taken by Sir Francis Knollys
to the Tower of London. There, he was confined in the very
same rooms occupied by his grandfather during his imprisonment
between 1546 and 1553.

While he mused at this unfortunate coincidence, or indeed his
family's all too frequent stays in the Tower, a virulent propaganda
pamphlet was published in London attacking any marriage
between Norfolk and Mary Queen of Scots.

Its author was almost certainly the Calvinistic Francis Walsingham, later to become Elizabeth's frighteningly proficient Secretary of State and the adept organiser of a pervasive intelligence
network at home and overseas.[52] The polemic *Discourse Touching
the Pretended Match Between the Duke of Norfolk and the Queen
of Scots* was aimed at the enthusiastic and receptive audience of
England's Protestants. Mary, it declared, was in league

> with the confederate enemies of the gospel by the name of the
> Holy League, to root out all such princes and magistrates as are
> professors of the same.
>
> Of [her] nation, she is a Scot, which nation I forebear to say
> what may be said, in a reverend respect of a few godly of that
> nation.
>
> Of inclination ... let her own horrible acts,[53] publicly known
> to the whole world witness, though now of late, seduced by

practice [to] seek out to cloak and hide the same . . .

> In goodwill to our sovereign, she has showed herself [in] sundry ways very evil affected, whose ambition has drawn her by bearing the arms of England, to decipher herself a competitor of the crown, a thing publicly known.

Norfolk's religious beliefs were unctuously left to 'God and his own conscience'. But, said the book, poison oozing from every page, he was inconsistent and inconstant in his Protestant beliefs, as shown by five reasons:

> First, his education of his son [is] under the government of a Papist.
> Secondly, the corruption of his house, his chief men of trust being Papists.
> Thirdly, the reposed trust and confidence he has in the chief Papists in this realm.
> Fourthly, his last marriage with a Papist, and lastly, this pretended match.

Was it likely, asked Walsingham, raising the phantom of the murdered Darnley, that any man who professed religious belief or respected honour, 'or regards his own safety, would match with one detected of so horrible crimes in respect of love?' The Scottish queen could solemnly swear on oath that she posed no threat to Elizabeth or 'confirm anything that may tend to the queen's safety' but, the pamphlet added ferociously, 'If she [falsifies] her faith, no pleading will serve. The sword must be the remedy.'[54]

If Mary Queen of Scots was the hapless Norfolk's nemesis, so the Florentine banker Roberto Ridolphi was the ominous figure that finally brought him to his doom. Although the duke's annual income was around £4,500 – more than £1.1 million at 2009 prices – he found that the extravagances of life at court and his public duties cost him dearly.[55] It may have been a temporary need for hard cash that led to a fateful introduction to Ridolphi in 1569.[56] The Italian had come to London eight years earlier and in 1566 had been charged with channelling the secret funds provided by Pope Pius V to the English Catholics to help overthrow Elizabeth.

Both the French and Spanish ambassadors were involved in the conspiracy, as were a number of English Catholic nobles and Mary's representative in London, John Leslie, Bishop of Ross.

Cecil's agents had Ridolphi under surveillance and monitored his visits to Howard House. On 7 October, the banker was arrested and held at Walsingham's house for questioning.[57]

This was all unknown to Norfolk in the Tower of London. His friends and associates were being interrogated about him, but there was little hard evidence on which charges of treason could be brought against him. One note of Cecil's about the investigation is significant:

> The duke was advertised of the intent of conveying away the Queen of Scots to Arundel Castle by letters of the Scottish queen to the Bishop of Ross.
>
> The Earl of Arundel's [Philip Howard] cook to be examined of his knowledge.[58]

Wary of simmering discontent among the Catholic population, it was too dangerous to free the duke, as far as Elizabeth was concerned – so he continued to suffer in prison. On 16 October he wrote to the Privy Council beseeching them to procure the return of Elizabeth's favour to him and assuring them that if 'I knew what to do [which] should be to [her] satisfaction, no good would be found wanting in me'. Norfolk complained that his 'health doth decay every day and I am falling into the disease I had before going to the baths'.[59]

Under close questioning in fluent Italian over many days, Walsingham investigated Ridolphi's activities, particularly his dealings with Mary Queen of Scots and Norfolk. He admitted dealing with the Bishop of Ross and giving both him and the duke cash from overseas. Suddenly, on 11 November, the banker was ordered to be released as Elizabeth was now 'disposed to act with clemency'.[60]

The reason for his sudden release was that Walsingham had 'turned' the Italian into an agent for Cecil. The antiquary and herald William Camden, who probably knew Walsingham well, described him as 'a most subtle searcher of hidden secrets, who knew excellently well how to win men's minds unto him and apply them to his own use'. We shall see more of Ridolphi shortly and how he was used to snare the naive and trusting Norfolk.

In November 1569, the Catholic magnates in the north – Thomas Percy, seventh Earl of Northumberland, and Charles Neville, sixth Earl of Westmorland – armed 7,500 of their tenantry and marched on Durham. On the 14th, they broke into the city's cathedral and destroyed the English bibles and prayer books within and banned further Protestant services there. They then marched south, planning to free Mary Queen of Scots from her confinement at Tutbury Castle. But their bold advance was stopped in its tracks by approaching royalist forces and the rebellion disappeared in the withering cold of the northern winter. Elizabeth meant to teach her Catholics a harsh lesson. About 750 insurgents were executed to satisfy her strident calls for vengeance.[61]

On 25 February 1570, Pope Pius V published the Bull *Regnans in Excelsis* which excommunicated Elizabeth and deprived this 'pretended' queen of the English throne – as well as absolving her subjects from any allegiance or loyalty to her. This was a decisive tactical error by the Vatican in its campaign against Protestant England, as the Bull made each and every one of Elizabeth's Catholic subjects potentially an individual threat to her life. The Pope had, in effect, offered up his blessing upon their treason. As far as the queen and her staunchly Protestant government were concerned – particularly after the jolt to the body politic of the northern rebellion – all English Catholics were now latent enemies within their own country.

But with the lessons of the harsh retribution wreaked upon the north still fresh in Catholic minds, they felt safe enough to free Norfolk, after ten months of incarceration, in early August 1570, although the plague that raged in and around the fortress may have been a factor.[62] There remained grave uncertainties about his trustworthiness and he was confined in his London home in Charterhouse Square, under the charge of Sir Henry Neville, and kept under close surveillance.

Norfolk dutifully wrote to the queen acknowledging his offence 'and by my voluntary offering to make amends for the same with a determined mind, never to offend your majesty either in the same or in any matter ... And where I did unhappily give ease to certain motions made to me in a cause of marriage to be prosecuted for me with the Queen of Scots ... I will also willing confess ... I did err.'[63]

In such circumstances – his narrow escape from a treason charge, his grovelling apology and his house arrest – it is simply breathtaking that the duke was so stupid as to become involved again with Mary Queen of Scots and Roberto Ridolphi.

Only days after his release from the Tower, the audacious Florentine was back inside Howard House. One would think that a hardly more unwelcome visitor could be conceived. Nor was his mission more palatable. He asked the apprehensive Norfolk to write to the Duke of Alva, the Spanish Captain General in the Low Countries, and appeal for funds for Mary Queen of Scots. With rare perception, Norfolk shunned him – 'I began to mislike him,' he said later and, 'sought ways to shift me from him.'

Mary's love of intrigue and her lack of any sense of reality also added to his nervousness. On 31 January 1571, she wrote to him, encouraging his escape from house arrest – 'as she would do [herself] notwithstanding any danger' – in order that they could be married.[64]

The final chapter in Norfolk's meteor-like life began with the arrest on or about 12 April that year of Charles Bailly, a young Fleming who had entered Mary's service in 1564 and latterly worked for the Bishop of Ross. Cecil's agents had detained him in Dover after finding letters and books from English Catholic exiles in his luggage. Two of the missives, addressed to the Bishop, were from the ubiquitous Ridolphi, now in Brussels.

Brought to London, Bailly was soon strapped to the rack in the Tower of London, and, under torture, admitted tearfully that Ridolphi had departed England on 25 March with appeals from Mary to the Duke of Alva in the Low Countries, the Spanish king, Philip II, and the Pope, to fund and organise an invasion of England. The objective was to overthrow Elizabeth, replace her on the throne with Mary and return the realm to Catholicism. Earlier that month, Ridolphi had returned to Howard House and left Norfolk a document that detailed the invasion plans and listed forty nobles and officials who secretly supported Mary's claims to the English crown. Each name was identified by a number for use in coded correspondence.[65]

Meanwhile, Ridolphi had failed to convince the Spanish governor about the chances of success of the invasion plan. He talked confidently that Spain could contribute 6,000 infantry and twenty-five cannon to reinforce a populist army of English Catholics, led by Norfolk, to oust Elizabeth.[66] Hard-nosed Alva was not impressed, and clearly believed the plan was founded on wild flights of military fantasy. He urged the Spanish king to provide military assistance only after the English Catholics had successfully rebelled and Elizabeth 'was already dead . . . or else a prisoner'. He added: 'We may tell [Norfolk] that these conditions being fulfilled he shall have what he wants.'[67]

The duke was swimming in very dangerous waters indeed. He was now serenely approaching a vortex which would suck him down into oblivion. On 29 August, his two secretaries, William Barker and Robert Higford, handed over a bag purporting to contain £50 in silver coin to a Shrewsbury draper called Thomas Browne. They instructed him to deliver it to Laurence Bannister, the steward of the Dacre estates in the north. Once out of Howard House, the curious Browne opened the bag and found £600 in gold and a number of letters written in cipher. Being a cautious man, and aware of the suspicions still surrounding the duke, he took it immediately to the Privy Council.

Norfolk must have been either an innocent babe in matters of espionage and subversion, or supremely incompetent. Not only could the cash be linked directly to him – worse, it could be traced back to its source, de la Mothe Fénelon, the French ambassador in London. In reality, it was to be sent to Scotland to be used by the faction supporting Mary Queen of Scots.

Cecil's agents were soon hotfoot to Charterhouse Square, to search Howard House. Their efforts were quickly rewarded:

The cipher, or key to his [Norfolk's] correspondence on this subject, [was] found under the tiles of the roof of the Charter-

house and some particular papers deciphered by the duke's secretary Higford and which he had ordered him to burn, [were]
discovered under the mat leading to the duke's bedchamber.[68]

On 4 September, Sir Ralph Sadler checked on new tightened
security measures imposed at Howard House, arriving there at
eight o'clock in the morning. He found that Neville had 'discreetly
ordered all things'.

> The duke is committed to his chamber, all his servants secluded
> from him out of the house, saving two to attend upon him in his
> chamber and four or five necessary officers to provide and dress
> his meat.

Sadler expected to be 'on the spot all day' and at night, when he
departed to his lodgings in the Savoy, he would leave at least six
men to secure the house. He stressed that 'Neville guards so wisely
and well that my presence is not needful'.[69]

He was back three days later to warn the duke that 'for his
obstinate dealing and denial of his great faults, her majesty was
sore offended with him and had determined to use him more
severely'.

Sadler told a 'submissive' Norfolk that he was to be 'removed to
another place by her highness' command' and took him, between
four and five o'clock in the afternoon, by 'footcloth nag' to the
Tower. Their journey across the city was troubled by a 'number of
idle rascal people, women, men, boys and girls, running about him
and . . . gazing at him'. The Spanish ambassador, however, reported
that 'the concourse of people was so large and the shouts so general,
that a very little more, and he would have been liberated'.

Sadler and his companions left Norfolk in the custody of the
Lieutenant of the Tower, with two servants to attend to his needs.[70]
The queen instructed his jailer in the 'strict keeping' of the duke,
and ordered: 'You shall do well presently to shut up in close prison
for a time, all prisoners that are thither committed for obstinacy in
religion or such as you may conjecture will deal for intelligence in
favour of the duke.'[71]

Norfolk's secretaries were arrested and questioned. Old William

Barker was 'three or four times examined but hitherto showed [himself] an obstinate and a fool' reported Sadler.[72] Then, threatened with the rack, his resistance crumbled. The secretary said that many English nobles favoured the duke's marriage with the Scottish queen; he doubted the Earl of Derby's support 'for he was but a soft man'. Fatally, he talked of Ridolphi's invasion plans: Spanish military assistance would land at Dumbarton 'if from Flanders', at Leith [and at] Harwich in Essex.

> Last Lent he brought Ridolphi to the Duke of Norfolk, who talked with him. Ridolphi found no great good disposition in the duke because he would not write to Alva, which the duke afterwards told him, saying: 'I do not like it, nor will not write.'[73]

The keeper of Howard House, John Sinclair, alias John Gardener, who had served the duke for a decade, was also caught up in the inquiry and found himself in the Tower. He denied everything, but his inquisitors produced a man called Archie Inglis, who recounted a conversation with him that proved damning:

> He knew from Sinclair how the Queen of Scots should have got away before it was known in England ... After several knights and gentlemen had resorted to the duke by one or two together, certain men should have gone and taken her away where she should have been at hunting and companies of men should have been laid to have received her every ten or twelve miles.
>
> The duke should have gone away that same day and met her.
>
> The queen's [Elizabeth's] power had been nothing to the duke's; he would have had so many partakers.
>
> He who is the duke's keeper is of the duke's counsel and privy to this enterprise.
>
> The duke might leap on horseback at his back door, ride his way and send the queen word that he was gone and she should not be able to fetch him again.[74]

Sinclair acknowledged that 'there was talk among the yeomen of the house that the duke and the Scottish queen were assured together; that their goodwill remained still and that he would marry if he might'.[75]

Elizabeth Massey, wife to the parson of the Tower, was also questioned. She related that during Norfolk's first imprisonment there, 'one Jervis, serving there, sent his little daughter of seven years, almost daily unto the duke's chamber with nosegays' and she returned 'sometimes with a golden groat [4d]'. She did not like these visits and had seen Jervis talking to papists.

> And now lately on All Hallows night he counselled her husband to put her away with many evil words betwixt them ...
>
> That same evening, about eight of the clock, Jervis met her, saying: 'Whither goest thou?' She answered: 'To go to the Lieutenant to complain of him.' Then he struck her upon the arm with his halberd and did overthrow her into the myute [moat].
>
> She suspected also my Lady Eleanor because she spoke diverse times at the window with the duke at his first imprisonment and sent one of her children to him almost every day.
>
> Further, the said Elizabeth says that she ... was procured by certain signs to deliver and receive letters from the duke secretly by his [*underlined*] laundress. The same said to her that she should serve God and pray for the duke, whereby she should lack nothing for 'he thinks well of you'.
>
> As for the queen, [she] shall not be long queen, being a bastard.[76]

Of course, Norfolk faced a barrage of questions on many occasions.[77] At times, his memory conveniently failed him on tricky issues, but on others he was remarkably frank. On 13 October, he confirmed his knowledge of no less than three plots to free Mary Queen of Scots – but he denied any knowledge of Ridolphi's invasion plans.

By January 1572, the Council had different concerns. Catholic supporters of Norfolk had come up with a series of harebrained schemes to rescue him from the Tower, using a portable canvas bridge across the moat, and also planned to murder Cecil, now created Lord Burghley. Kenelm Berney and his accomplice Edmund Mather planned to assassinate the minister – 'the chief cause of [Norfolk's] trouble' – at Charing Cross with an arquebus (or musket), the killer crossing the Thames by waiting boat and then fleeing by horse into Surrey. They also plotted to rescue the duke at his arraignment, armed only with pistols.[78]

Another plan was to take Burghley's sons hostage, 'for pawns for us, which should be sent to the Duke of Alva ... that if we miscarry here, they might die the same death'. They would communicate with Norfolk by writing on some Holland cloth and then get his Italian tailor to line his breeches with the fabric. A new pair had recently been delivered and Norfolk had mournfully told his tailor: 'It is said, I shall not live to wear these hose out.'

He might well be dejected. Burghley was now planning his trial, prudently placing great emphasis on security. His roughly scribbled notes estimated how many men would be necessary to thwart any rescue attempt or to subdue disorder:

> The Lieutenant [Sir Owen Hopton] with the guard of the court.
> Sir Peter Carew with fifteen of the guard.
> Sir William Drury, with ten ... Sir Humfrey Gibbon with six;
> Henry Knollys with ten of the guard; The Knight Marshal with twenty of the guard to attend [Norfolk]; Mr Ireland – thirty of the Pensioners.[79]

Norfolk knew he was doomed. He was tried by his peers at Westminster Hall on 16 January 1572, with George Talbot, sixth Earl of Shrewsbury, sitting as Lord High Steward. Just after half past eight, the court went into session and Norfolk was brought to the bar with Hopton and Carew on each arm, preceded by the headsman's axe, now appearing at another Howard's trial for treason. Then

> the Duke, with a haughty look and oft biting his lip, surveyed the lords on each side of him

as the indictment was read out to him:

> That Thomas, Duke of Norfolk, as a false traitor ... not having the fear of God in his heart or weighing his due allegiance but seduced by the instigation of the Devil ... [intended] to cut off and destroy Queen Elizabeth on the 22 September at the Charterhouse.

That [he intended] to make and raise sedition in the kingdom of England and spread a miserable civil war ... and to endeavour a change and alteration in the sincere worship of God.

That [he knew that] Mary Queen of Scots had laid claim and pretended a title and interest to the present possession and dignity of the imperial crown of England ... [and] traitorously sought and endeavoured to be joined in marriage with Mary and had writ diverse letters to her and sent [her] several pledges and tokens ...

That [he] procured Roberto Ridolphi, a foreign merchant, to send to the Bishop of Rome and to the Duke of Alva to obtain ... certain sums of money towards the raising ... of an army to invade this kingdom.[80]

Norfolk asked for legal representation but was refused, and the duke answered bitterly: 'I am brought to fight without a weapon.' After pleading not guilty to the charges, he appealed for justice and a fair trial and admitted: 'My memory was never good. It is now much worse than it was, before troubles, before cares, before closeness in prison, evil rest, have much decayed my memory, so as I pray God, that this day it will not fail me.' He added: 'Another time I will forgive it.'

Written evidence was produced from his servants which included some testimony that had been falsified. They were not called into court, so Norfolk had no opportunity to cross-examine them. The duke admitted:

Touching Ridolphi's coming, I have indeed confessed that he came to me. In [the] summer, I was twelve month bound in recognisance for £1,800 to Ridolphi, for my lord of Arundel ... the day was passed whereby I stood in danger of my recognisance.

I sent to Ridolphi to entreat him to cancel my recognisance and I offered to give him twenty yards [18.2 m.] of velvet. Ridolphi would not be persuaded but desired to speak with me himself.

I was very loath that he should come to me ... [as] I thought [it] would be suspicious.

So Ridolphi came to me and I did what I could to entreat him about my recognisance and I could not persuade him, than to promise he would not sue me.

The banker spoke to Norfolk of his imprisonment at Walsingham's home; about Mary Queen of Scots and that he should 'treat with the Duke of Alva for money for her'.

> He prayed [for me to write] letters in the Scottish queen's favour to the Duke of Alva. I began to mislike him and was loath to write. I sought ways to shift me from him.
>
> I said I was not well at ease, I could not write – it was late – and I would not deal.

Norfolk had been trapped in a web partially of his own foolish making. There is little doubt that Ridolphi was a government *agent provocateur* who formed the bait for a trap and the duke's lack of foresight, or common sense, allowed him to be ensnared. The peers took an hour and a quarter to find him guilty of treason. Sentence was passed, and the axe blade was turned towards him. Norfolk had few words left to say:

> This is the judgement of a traitor and I shall die a true man to the queen as any man that lives.

Beating his chest he told his peers: 'I will not desire any of you to make any petition for my life. I will not desire to live. And my lords, seeing you have put me out of your company, I trust shortly to be in better company.'[81]

Norfolk, expecting imminent execution, scribbled a last letter to the queen on 21 January, signing the note 'with the woeful hand of a dead man'.[82] He also wrote a poignant letter to his children from the Tower, including, for their enlightenment, some final lessons about life. To his eldest son, Philip, Earl of Arundel, he insisted: 'Serve and fear God above all things. I find the fault in myself that I have been too negligent in this point.'

> Love and make much of your wife, and therein, considering the great adversity you are now in by reason of my fall, is your greatest comfort and relief.
>
> Though you be very young in years, yet you must strive to

becomc a man. When my grandfather died, I was not much above a year older than you are now, and yet, thank God, I took such order with myself . . .

Beware of high degree! To a vainglorious, proud stomach it seems at the first sweet. Look into all chronicles and you shall find that in the end, it brings heaps of cares . . . and most commonly, utter overthrow.

Assure yourself, as you may see by my books of accounts, and you shall find that my living did hardly maintain my expenses . . . I was ever a beggar.

Beware of the court, except it be to do your prince service . . . for that place has no certainty.

Norfolk believed his son 'Thom' would be made a ward of the queen, but Philip was sure to 'have your brother William left still with you, because, poor boy, he has nothing to feed cormorants with; to whom you will as well be a father as a brother'.[83] A separate enclosure urged Philip to make use of 'Sir Thomas Cornwallis' but 'beware of him, and all other Papists'. He commended Lord Henry Howard 'my brother and your uncle. There is no one who may stand you in better stead. He has been so natural, as for my sake, he has brought himself into trouble.'[84]

All these letters are signed plain 'Thomas Howard'. The dukedom was already attainted and all honours had been stripped from him. Sir Gilbert Dethick, Garter King of Arms, had ordered his heraldic accoutrements – banner, helmet, crest and stall plate – to be taken from St George's Chapel, Windsor, and hurled into the castle ditch, in his degradation from the Order.[85]

The duke also wrote a farewell to his faithful steward William Dix on a page of the fifth edition of the New Testament of Our Saviour Jesus Christ, printed and published in 1566 by Richard Jugge, 'printer to the queen's majesty'. Unsurprisingly, his thirteen lines form a harrowing letter:

Farewell good Dix. Your service has been so faithful to me as I am sorry that I cannot make proof of my goodwill to recompense it.

I trust my death shall not make no change in you towards

mine, but that you will faithfully perform the trust that I have reposed in you; forget me and remember me in mine.

Forget not with plainness to counsel and advise Philip and Nan's inexperienced years. The rest of their brothers and sisters' well-doing rests much upon their virtues and considerate dealings.

God grant them His grace which is able to work better in them than my natural well-meaning heart can wish unto them.

Amen, and so hoping of your honesty and faithfulness when I am dead, I bid you this, my last farewell, the 10 of February 1572.

T.H.[86]

On one of the book's endpapers is an ink inscription demonstrating that the duke disposed of a number of his books to his friends, writing a last message in each. The note relates to a quarto copy of Richard Grafton's *Chronicle or History of England*, published in 1570,[87] which had this letter, containing Norfolk's regrets about the recent history of the Howard family, written on a leaf:

Good friend George, farewell. I have no other tokens to send to my friends but my books and I know how sorrowful you are amongst the rest for my hard hap[88] whereof, I thank God, because I hope his merciful chastisement will prepare me for a better world.

Look well throughout this book and you shall find the name of a duke very unhappy.[89] I pray God it may end with me and that others may speed better hereafter. But if I might have my wish and were in as good a state as ever you knew me, yet I would wish for a lower degree.

Be a friend, I pray you, to mine and do my hearty commendations to your good wife and to gentle Mr Denny.

I die in the faith that you have ever known me to be. Farewell, good friend, 1572

Your dying as he was living
Norfolk.

God bless my godson – Amen.

Sadly it is not possible to identify the recipient.

On 26 February, he sat down to write his 'last confession and to my remembrance, true in all points upon the which I might take to my death'. He humbly recalled 'my life, my former misspent and ill-ordained life' and protested 'even before the Lord that I have been a Protestant [underlined] ever since I know'. But he confessed 'that my dealings have been given just suspicion that I should be a Papist or a favourer of Papists'.

> I did arrogantly presume ... to enter into dealing with the Queen of Scots ... nor is it any excuse for me to say that I was persuaded thereto if I had been mindful of my duty as I ought to have been.
>
> After her majesty had commanded me to the contrary and that I made promise [...] no further from it, I ... disobediently entered into the cause anew ... after I ... submitted to her majesty under my hand and seal never to deal further in that, my unhappy cause ... to my utter shame.

Norfolk agreed he had received letters about Ridolphi's mission and, when his secretary Barker brought two letters from the agent and the Pope, he had read and concealed them. The document ends:

> This is my sorrowful confession. Pity my hard fortune, in whose hands whoever this shall come. I myself will sufficiently lament and repent it during my short life. By the woeful and repentant hand, but now too late of
>
> Tho: Howard.[90]

He also wrote a lengthy will and attached to it a chequer roll listing the houses he thought 'fit for my children to keep ... and also what number of persons I find convenient to attend them'. Five houses are suggested: Framlingham Castle, Suffolk, Flitcham, Lopham and Thetford lodges in Norfolk and, of course, Kenninghall. The duke ordained that Philip should have 'two gentlemen to attend in his chamber' and one yeoman usher, together with a schoolmaster for his education. The Howard household should have a second tutor 'to teach the younger sons' and one more 'to teach them languages'. There was also a chaplain, two laundry men, one porter, four yeoman waiters, two grooms of the stables, an usher of the hall for William and three persons in the cellar, buttery and pantry.

Norfolk asked to be buried in the Howard mortuary chapel at Framlingham and 'there laid in that tomb whereat my loving wives are buried'. He asked his executors 'to bestow no further charge of any new tomb upon me, otherwise then, a statue of me set in the wall or laid upon that tomb as they shall think most fit'.[91]

Elizabeth hesitated and havered over the death warrant. She signed it on 9 February 1572 and then delayed its implementation. It was addressed to Sir Thomas Bacon, 'Lord Keeper of our Great Seal of England', and in the awful legal jargon of state retribution, it rehearsed that 'Thomas duke of Norfolk, late of Kenninghall ... for sundry treasons by him committed and done was the 16th day of January arraigned and tried ... by his peers and found guilty'.

He was sentenced to suffer the awful fate of traitors, but

> We being moved to pity of our grace especial, are pleased and contented to change such manner of execution as by our Steward of England was then pronounced against the said duke, minding nevertheless the surety and preservation of our person and realm ... and also to give example of terror, dread and fears for all others hereafter ...
>
> Forseeing always that no other execution of death be executed to the said duke but only to cause his head to be smitten from his body at the Tower Hill, the accustomed place of execution.[92]

In the middle of April, Alexander Nowell, Dean of St Paul's Cathedral, wrote to Burghley about the state of Norfolk's health – he suffered from an 'abundance of humours and [the] weakness of [his] stomach is growing upon him' because of the closeness of his prison and 'the lack of air in the warmness of the weather'.

On 31 May, the duke was warned to prepare himself for death and at eight o'clock on the morning of 2 June he was marched out of the Tower and up the slight slope to the scaffold on Tower Hill.

Norfolk had ordered a special suit for the execution – a white fustian shirt, worn beneath a black satin doublet. After prayers had been said, the duke told 'the multitude that stood around ...'

It is no new thing for men to suffer death in this place, though since the beginning of our most gracious queen's reign, I am the first and God grant I may be the last. That I treated with the Queen of Scots I freely confess ... Ridolphi I never talked to but once and that not to the prejudice of the queen for many men know I had dealings with him for money matters upon bills and bonds.

I found him to be a man that enjoyed the tranquillity of England and of a prompt and ready wit for any wicked design.

I have never been addicted to Popery ... but have always been averse from Popish doctrines ... Yet I cannot deny but that I have had amongst my servants and familiars some that have been addicted to Popish religion.

Dean Nowell told the crowd that the duke 'desires you to all join in a prayer to God to have mercy on him' and called for silence so he could compose himself. The executioner offered Norfolk a blindfold but he brushed it aside saying 'I fear not death'.

He knelt down and laid his head on the block.

It was cut off with one stroke of the axe, amid the tears of the sorrowful crowd and a small fight with some of the queen's gentleman pensioners.[93]

Mary Queen of Scots followed him to the block and was executed on 8 February 1587.

On 16 June 1572, Philip wrote to Lord Burghley, lamenting the death of his father and asking the minister to take him and the rest of Norfolk's family under his protection.[94]

Around 1600, Sir Walter Raleigh wrote to Sir Robert Cecil, son of Lord Burghley, with some good advice. Do not fear revenge: 'Your own father', he told him, 'was esteemed to be the contriver of Norfolk's ruin, yet his son followed your father ... and loved him.'[95]

IO
MARTYR EARL

———◆———

'If that be the cause in which I am to perish, sorry am I that I
have but one life to lose'

St Philip Howard before his death in the Tower,
October 1595[1]

Philip Howard, the only son of the fourth duke and his first wife,
was born at noon precisely on 28 June 1557, at Arundel House, just
off the Strand in London. Nicholas Heath, Archbishop of York
and Lord Chancellor, baptised him on 2 July in the Chapel Royal
of the Palace of Whitehall, using a 'gold' font, 'made [for the]
purpose and kept in the Treasury only for the christening of the
children of princes of the realm'.[2]

Philip's mother died from puerperal fever, an infection arising
from his birth. Two stepmothers rapidly followed her to the grave
and the eldest boy's care was entrusted to a 'grave and ancient
gentlewoman' before he was tutored in Greek and Hebrew by the
Oxford scholar Gregory Martin, at Audley End.[3] As part of his
father's grand plan to acquire extensive estates in the north for his
heirs, Philip, now Earl of Surrey, was betrothed to Anne Dacre
when both were aged twelve. Two years later, when they reached
the then age of consent, they were married by special order of
Norfolk while he was imprisoned in the Tower.

Fourteen-year-old Philip watched the royal commissioners
make their inventory of the Howard possessions at Kenninghall
and wrote to Burghley that their coming

> makes me afraid that the queen is very much displeased with my
> lord my father, which makes me no less heavy than duty binds
> me, or his unhappy chance does require.

Being assured of the great friendship that you bore to my
father in his former imprisonment, I now most earnestly desire
your lordship to continue the same and remember him who is
afflicted with grief and troubled with his unhappy state.[4]

Little did he know – perhaps he never guessed – that Burghley was
the chief architect of his father's downfall and execution.

In accordance with his dead father's last wishes, he and his two
brothers spent two years at St John's College, Cambridge, where
he proceeded MA in November 1576. Apart from a university
education, Philip Howard 'received no small detriment, partly by
the bad example[s] he saw there, partly by the liberty permitted
him, but principally by the flattery of some ministers [dons], which
was so palpable sometimes that his lady ... was ashamed to hear
it'.[5]

Meanwhile, his unattainted estates were being efficiently administered by a triumvirate of officials, including the fourth duke's
trusted auditor and receiver, William Dix. One of their early duties
was to recompense Laurence Bannister, the steward of the Dacre
estates, for his expenses when he was dragged into Norfolk's treason
case and confined in the Tower. This included his fine of £138 6s
8d, paid on his release; the £40 'to him which procured his pardon';
and £278 5s for his board while behind bars.[6] Among other administrative headaches, Dix was concerned about sureties for a flock
of 2,800 sheep that belonged to the late duke.[7]

Soon afterwards, Howard took up residence at court – keen, like
his forefathers, to capture the monarch's attention and favour. Now
aged eighteen, he swiftly forgot his father's solemn advice to be
wary of its dazzling glamour and dark-corner intrigues, and his
head was turned by 'corrupted immodest young women wherewith
the court in those days did much abound'.[8]

He selfishly neglected his young wife – indeed, cast doubts on
whether she was truly his spouse – in the cynical knowledge that
the jealous and cantankerous Elizabeth did not willingly bestow
her goodwill on dashing but married courtiers. Anne, or 'Nan', was
left marooned, destitute in the country while he occupied Howard
House, so handy for the palaces at Greenwich and Westminster.

He lavished money on the showy tournaments held on the anniversaries of Elizabeth's coronation. And he entertained the queen at his palaces at Norwich and Kenninghall during the royal progress to East Anglia in August 1578, 'where for diverse days, he lodged and feasted not only herself ... but the [Privy] Council, courtiers and all their company but all the gentlemen and people of the country'. A contemporary chronicler described how 'the Earl of Surrey did show most sumptuous cheer, in whose park were speeches well set out'.[9] His expensive New Year gift to Elizabeth in 1579 was a girdle 'of tawny velvet, embroidered with seed pearls, the buckle and pendant of gold'.[10]

Very soon he had drunk, gambled and spent his way through much of the Howard property revenues. Furthermore, Surrey fell into serious debt – totalling more than £14,000, or nearly £3 million at current values – and was forced to sell land to fend off his creditors. His behaviour shocked and affronted his grandfather, Henry Fitzalan, twelfth Earl of Arundel, and his aunt Jane (*née* Fitzalan), who had married John Lumley, Baron Lumley, both of whom partly disinherited him as a punishment for his spendthrift ways.

But when Arundel died on 24 February 1580, Howard still succeeded to the earldom and substantial properties, including Arundel Castle in Sussex. He now had two London homes – Arundel House, as well as Howard House in Charterhouse Square. His wife, as co-heir to the Dacre lands, had already brought manors and baronies in the north to the marriage. He demanded to be summoned to Parliament as Earl of Arundel but his title was questioned and he was not restored in blood until 15 March 1581 by private statute.[11]

His panache and ostentation remained undiminished: on 15 and 16 May 1581, he took part in a colourful 'triumph' before Elizabeth and the French ambassador which was intended as an elaborate, if not incomprehensible, allegory promoting the queen's marriage to yet another hopeful suitor, François d' Alençon, Duke of Anjou.

First the Earl of Arundel entered the tiltyard, all in ... engraven armour, with [horse] caparisons and furniture all richly and bravely embroidered, having attendant on him two gentlemen ushers, four pages riding on spare horses and twenty of his gentlemen ... apparelled in short cloaks and Venetian hose of crimson velvet, laid with gold lace; doublets of yellow satin, hats of crimson with gold bands and yellow feathers ...

Then he had six trumpeters that sounded before him and thirty-one yeomen that waited after him apparelled in cassock coats ...[12]

This may have been the last gasp of a misspent youth, for around this time the earl returned to his long-suffering wife and the couple belatedly set up home together. A daughter, Elizabeth, was born in 1583, and a son, Thomas, followed in 1585. The earl began to take his public duties seriously, aided by a prodigious, if not photographic, memory.[13] On 4 July 1581, he was asked to 'examine certain disordered persons in the town of Brithelmestone [Brighton]' and in August the same year arrested four south coast pirates called Daniel, Hunter, Page and Richards. Unfortunately, they escaped. He was also told in July 1580 that the queen needed his castle at Framlingham to imprison those recusants – obdurate Catholics – arrested in Norfolk and Suffolk.[14]

Shortly afterwards, the Countess of Arundel openly converted to Catholicism while living at Arundel Castle. The queen, who anyway had taken an unreasonable dislike to Anne, committed her into the custody of Sir Thomas Shirley, of Wiston House, on the other side of the South Downs, for a year. It was during this period that her first child was born.

The Howards, as a family, were slowly returning to the old faith of the third Duke of Norfolk. Arundel's favourite sister, Meg (who had married Robert Sackville, second Earl of Dorset, in 1580), was an early convert, as was his younger half-brother, Lord William Howard. Philip's uncle, Henry Howard (later Earl of Northampton), had become a Catholic in 1558 and was frequently in and out of prison because of official suspicions over his loyalty. Unwittingly, there was good reason as, unknown to Elizabeth's government, Henry Howard received 500 crowns (£125) in July 1582 from the Spanish ambassador, Don Bernardino de Mendoza, for information he provided about events at court. The envoy reported to King Philip of Spain:

> Milord Harry ... with a care which I can hardly describe ... informs me of everything he hears, which is of service to your majesty ... He has very good qualities and intelligence and much friendship with the ladies of the Privy Chamber, who inform him exactly what passes indoors.

Howard, younger brother of the executed fourth duke, also kept 'close correspondence with all the Catholic gentlemen of the kingdom, who, in turn esteem him, and show him all favour, both for his high qualities and for his influence with his nephew and he has offered to continue giving me constant information'. For this Howard received a handsome pension of 1,000 crowns a year from the appreciative ambassador.[15] Others saw him in a different light. In later years, the courtier Sir Anthony Weldon declared he had 'a venomous and cankered disposition' and described him as 'a great clerk, yet not a wise man, but the grossest flatterer of the world'.[16]

Then came one of those defining moments in life that unexpectedly and suddenly reveal a crossroads, both in terms of self-belief and personal values.

The Earl of Arundel witnessed one or more of the four disputations of religious issues staged between the condemned Jesuit priest Edmund Campion and a group of Anglican divines in the church of St Peter ad Vincula and later in the great hall of the Tower in September 1581. The debates gave Arundel grave pause for thought and he discovered, almost to his surprise, that Campion's arguments deeply impressed him.

These were perilous and treacherous times.[17] The Earl of Arundel's lengthy, deeply considered decision to become a Catholic was an act of enormous courage and commitment when adherents of the faith were being ruthlessly persecuted and missionary priests hunted down and slaughtered by the state. With the memory of his father's execution always haunting him, he struggled against changing his religious loyalties. It is claimed that the final call came to him one day when walking alone in the gallery[18] of his castle at Arundel, after long and great conflict within himself. Lifting up his eyes and hands to Heaven, he firmly resolved to become a member of God's church and frame his life accordingly.[19]

He kept his decision secret – not even telling his wife – until he met his Catholic half-brother William ('to whom he bore a special love') in London and told him of his conversion. Lord Howard lent him a Catholic treatise by Dr William Allen[20] and the earl was received into the Church by the fugitive Jesuit priest Father William Weston at Arundel on 30 September 1584.

In early November 1583, a Catholic zealot, twenty-nine-year-old Francis Throgmorton, was arrested by agents of Walsingham (by now Elizabeth's Secretary of State as well as her spymaster) for plotting to put Mary Queen of Scots on the throne. The Spanish ambassador, Mendoza, was expelled from England for his involvement, Throgmorton was executed at Tyburn on 10 July 1584, and Lord Henry Howard imprisoned yet again.[21]

Arundel feared he would be caught up in the fevered hunt for further conspirators and decided to flee England with his brother William. He despatched his secretary, John Momford, to Hull in south Yorkshire to hire a ship to take them to Flanders, but he was arrested, questioned and threatened with the rack in an attempt to extract information. The queen, her suspicions about the earl's loyalty growing by the minute, invited herself to Arundel House where an extravagant banquet was laid on for her. At the end of the evening Elizabeth declared her satisfaction at the delights of the evening and graciously thanked Arundel for her entertainment. She then told him bluntly that he was now a prisoner in his own house.[22]

His questioning began on Christmas Eve, 1583 and concerned his alleged involvement in the Throgmorton conspiracy and about sheltering another fugitive Jesuit priest, Jasper Heywood.[23] His other secretary, John Keeper, was also interrogated[24] as a suspected priest, by Sir Christopher Hatton, Elizabeth's Vice-Chamberlain.

The interrogations produced nothing that either Burghley or

Walsingham could use against him. Arundel was eventually released in April 1584 and his wife was freed from her confinement at Wiston House the following September.

The earl decided on a second attempt to flee England in April 1585 and made secret plans – not even telling his wife, who was heavily pregnant with his heir. He wrote a letter to Elizabeth explaining the reasons for his flight and entrusted it to his half-sister Meg Sackville until he arrived safely in France, when it could be delivered. He hired a small ship at Littlehampton, at the mouth of the River Arun, south of Arundel, and made several attempts to leave. Each time his departure was thwarted by adverse winds, according to the crew.

This may have been an excuse, a delaying tactic. Walsingham had laid a trap for the earl and his two companions, a servant called Burlace, and William Bray, who was a member of the covert network that smuggled Catholic priests and religious tracts into England. Bray was probably under surveillance and may have been the unwitting cause of the drama that now unfolded.

After a two-day delay, the ship finally put to sea at night and, after an hour, had made good headway out into the English Channel.

Arundel must have fondly believed that he was at last safe. In his delight, he probably did not notice that the crew had hoisted a lantern to the top of the ship's single mast.

It was a signal.

Soon afterwards, a small warship came alongside and its captain, Francis Kellway, clambered aboard Arundel's vessel. He 'pretended to be a pirate ... known to be a man of notorious, infamous life' and offered to permit the earl to continue his voyage – on payment of £100. He swore

> he would presently, without further stop, [allow] him [to] pass safely into France if he would write a word or two to any friend of his [from] whom he might receive [the money].

Arundel believed him. On the swaying deck he scribbled a few lines to his sister, asking her to speak to Edward Bridges, his chaplain at Arundel House, and to arrange for him to hand over

the cash, once the 'token', or password – 'black is white' – was
given to him.

Kellway read through the note approvingly and then revealed
his true colours.

He was no common pirate. He had been stationed on Walsingham's orders to intercept Arundel's ship and arrest him.

> The Earl was nothing but daunted with this so unexpected
> accident and not only with great patience and courage did endure
> it, but moreover carried it with a joyful and merry countenance.

Patience and fortitude may well be true Christian virtues. However,
given the circumstances, it is difficult to swallow entirely this
generous account of Arundel's unruffled calm, particularly when
Kellway relieved him of 'his money and all those things he had
about him, [such] as jewels and the like'.[25] Such events could test
anyone's sense of humour and find it wanting. Not only was he
heading straight for the Tower – rapidly becoming almost a second
home for successive generations of the Howards – but he had been
robbed by the rascal Kellway.

Once landed, Arundel was escorted under waiting heavy guard
to London, sleeping overnight in Guildford, Surrey. He was taken
straight to the grim fortress and committed as a prisoner there on
25 April 1585. His siblings William and Meg were also arrested and
put into the custody of Roger, second Lord North. So was the
usual suspect, his uncle Henry Howard, who once again faced his
all too familiar inquisitors in the Tower.

Bridges, the earl's chaplain, immediately published the four
quarto pages of the earl's unsigned and self-justifying letter to the
queen. It told the story of his past service at court, but, recently,
'the malice of my adversaries, by reason of your majesty's good
countenance towards me, began to be greater ...'

> I found little by little your good opinion declined and your favour
> somewhat estranged from me. I heard from time to time how
> your majesty in words took exception to many of my actions and
> how it pleased you daily in your speeches to betray hard and evil
> consent of me.

And though it pleased you at some times to talk with me, yet your majesty never charged me with the least fault or offence.

And thus my adversaries which did bark behind my back dared never accuse me, or once open their mouths to my face.

He heard of the queen's 'bitter speeches' and felt the finger of blame pointed at himself as a 'person whom you deeply suspect'.

I knew this smoke did betray a fire and I saw these clouds foretold a storm and therefore, with all patience, I prepared myself to endure whatsoever was the will of God by means of your majesty's indignation to lay upon me, being assured that my faults to you were none.

After his house arrest and questioning, 'I remained in the same estate fifteen weeks at the least, no man charging me with the least offence, nor my conscience being able to accuse me of the smallest fault'.

After I had escaped safely these storms and when I was clearly delivered from all my troubles, I began to call to remembrance the heavy sentence which had lighted upon those three of my ancestors who immediately went before me.

The first being my great grandfather [the third duke] who was so free from all suspicion of any fault, as because they had no colour of matter to bring him to his trial, they attainted him by Act of Parliament, without ever challenging him to his answer.

The second being my grandfather [Henry Howard, Earl of Surrey, who] was brought to his trial and condemned for such trifles as it amazed the bystanders at that time and it is ridiculous at this day to all that hear the same . . .

The last being my father [the fourth duke, who] was arraigned according to the law and condemned by his peers. God forbid that I should think but that his triers did that whereunto their consciences did lead them.

Howsoever he might unwittingly or wittingly be drawn into greater danger than himself did either see or imagine, yet all his actions did plainly declare and his greatest enemies must confess that he never carried any disloyal mind to your majesty . . .

At best, this was a pedigree of misfortune, and, at worst, one of hereditary treason. Arundel had grim forebodings when he considered 'the fortune of these three ... I called to mind my own danger and did not think it impossible that ... I might as well follow them ..., as I succeeded them in their place'.

> I perceived by my late troubles how narrowly my life was sought and how easily your majesty was drawn to a suspicion and hard opinion of my ancestors and ... how my innocence was [not] sufficient to protect me.
>
> I knew myself and besides was charged by your Council to be of that religion which they account odious and dangerous to your estate. ...
>
> When I considered in what continual danger I did remain here in England, both by laws established and by a new act lately made[26] I did think it my safest part to depart the realm and abide in some other place where I might live without danger to my conscience, without offence to your majesty, without the servile subjection to mine enemies and without this peril to my life.[27]

It is not known whether Elizabeth actually read this eloquent and piquant letter, but it provided Walsingham with some potent ammunition to use against the earl. The spymaster initially employed a tried and tested ruse for extracting information from unwilling prisoners – a forged and incriminating letter in hand-writing that 'very much resembled' Arundel's own. Its three pages were triumphantly waved before him but the earl was allowed to read only the first few paragraphs. The letter, addressed to his steward William Dix, began with a warning:

> Sir, this letter contains such matter as is fit for the fire to consume than be laid up in your study.

It went on to say that, although he departed England 'poorly, he would return in glory and land in Norfolk with a great power of men to trouble both the queen and state'. The note passed on to more mundane matters of business, such as instructions about a recent sale of cut timber, inserted to add credence to its content. Arundel was told the letter had been intercepted by Walsingham's agents 'at the very time of his going to sea'.[28] The earl vehemently denied writing it but the Council threatened him with arraignment for treason on its contents. Unconsciously echoing the words of his great-grandfather, the third duke, when he was in similar danger, Arundel said he was innocent of 'all kinds of treason, as a child newly-born'.

His nerve was not shaken and the letter mysteriously disappeared. The ruse had failed.

The interrogations in the Tower continued. On 1 May, Walsingham wrote to Hatton, suspecting there was someone, still more dangerous, that Arundel was concealing and drawing comfort from. He insisted that the earl's courage should be

> abated, and no advantage [should] be lost until he be drawn to use some other language, seasoned with more humility ... It cannot be that he receives some comfort and that not from mean persons that put him in this courage.
>
> No man is of his nature more fearful.[29]

Arundel himself wrote to Hatton on 7 May, acknowledging that he had written to Dr (later Cardinal) William Allen, the *de facto* leader of exiled English Catholics abroad. But he protested:

> that before God, [I] was so sorry for it after ... as when the messenger should have carried it, had not opportunity at the first to go over, I desired that it might be burnt. What was done with it, I know not, but Bridges told me it was burnt.
>
> I protest before God, as far as I can call to remembrance, I do utterly deny and disavow that ever was I privy to any plot or practice laid or made against her majesty or her state.

Arundel added: 'I must confess I was slipping, but not fallen. I call to God to witness she [the queen] has raised many that have slipped more and therefore I cannot despair but that she can raise me.'[30]

A bewildering variety of questions were put to him: How much did he know of the Throgmorton plot? What was the true reason behind his departure from England? For what purpose did he inspect Langstone Harbour, near Chichester – plainly, they believed he was reconnoitring possible south coast invasion sites. His half-brother William, who had joined the earl in the Tower, was also interrogated: was Bridges a priest? – 'he denies that ever he heard him say Mass'. How was he going to live overseas? – 'as he hoped ... [supported] by the earl his brother'.[31] His uncle Henry was reluctantly and regretfully acknowledged as probably innocent, as his inquisitors could 'find nothing to condemn him justly'.[32]

On 14 May, the earl's household of forty-six servants at Howard House were discharged, some of them going to 'my lady's house at Romford' in Essex.[33]

Probably because of failure to uncover hard evidence against him, Arundel had to wait another year before he faced any legal proceedings. He appeared in the Court of Star Chamber, within the Palace of Westminster, on 15 May 1586, to face three charges: that he tried to flee England without permission; he had been reconciled to the Church of Rome; and, finally, that he had been plotting with foreign powers in order to be restored as Duke of Norfolk.

John Popham, Attorney General, produced the letter that Arundel had written to Elizabeth and claimed it accused her 'very contemptuously and injuriously of partiality, alleging her highness had countenanced and protected his enemies to do him injury'. Among the earl's possessions when he was arrested was a 'clock bag wherein ... was a paper [on which] was written these words "Philip, Duke of Norfolk, Earl [of] Arundel"'. The earl, however, 'gave such sufficient answers to everything that was objected against him and behaved himself so discreetly, with such cheerfulness and alacrity, that he got that day much credit and reputation to his person and cause'.

Such demeanour could not go unpunished. The court fined him £10,000 and ordered that he 'shall return prisoner to the Tower of London from whence he came, there to remain prisoner at her majesty's pleasure'.[34]

Perpetual imprisonment! During his first thirteen months in the Tower, he had no servants of his own and was not allowed out of his room in the Beauchamp Tower or to walk in the Queen's Garden, in the south-east corner of the fortress, unless he was accompanied by a guard. Afterwards, he was allowed one or two servants, but they had to suffer the same strict regime and become prisoners as well. Walsingham's secretary, Francis Mills, complained that Arundel's friends 'daily resort to Tower Hill and as near to the view of him (... walking on the [roof] leads and the battlements) almost as [near] as a man may throw a stone'.

> I know right well the turret where the Earl is lodged and yesterday myself was an eye-witness of the Lord Henry and Lord William Howard, [with] one little page following them both, upon Tower Hill.
>
> This day again, these personages, I hear, have been there for an interview between them and the Earl.
>
> [If] his friends coming ... to view his prison, happen to be interpreters of signs only between these men, bad effects may follow.
>
> So better the Earl had another strong lodging where he might have air to walk in but no opportunity to view and be viewed as now he is.[35]

The Lieutenant of the Tower, Sir Michael Blount, was under orders to make life as uncomfortable as possible for the earl. Arundel complained that 'his injuries to me ... are intolerable, infinite, daily multiply, and to those who know them not, incredible'. He became ill and scratched on the wall over the fireplace of his room in the Beauchamp Tower the graffito: '*Quanto plus afflictionis pro Christo in hoc saeculo tanto plus gloriae cum Christo in futuro* Arundell, June 22 1587' – 'The more suffering for Christ in this world, so much more the glory with Christ in the next.'[36]

His wife had, meanwhile, given birth to a son, Thomas, at Finchingfield, Essex – the heir the earl was never to see. She and her two children were now eking out a meagre existence in one wing of Arundel House, on a pension of £8 a week. Anne, however, had scraped together £30 and used it to bribe the daughter of the Lieutenant to provide access to a nearby prisoner, an old priest named William Bennet, and two other incarcerated Catholics, the Lancashire landowner Sir Thomas Gerard and William Shelley, of Michelgrove in Clapham, Sussex, a near neighbour, in happier days, to the earl at Arundel Castle.[37] Bennet sometimes said Mass for all three in the earl's room, using smuggled vestments which were hidden behind a wall.

Another prisoner, John Snowden, a sailor who had traitorously served with the Spanish Armada during the thwarted invasion of England in July and August 1588, hoped to redeem himself by pretending to be a Catholic and revealing these secret Masses. He filched their missal and sent it to Walsingham as proof.

Bennet was immediately removed to another prison, The Counter, in Wood Street, one of the sheriff's prisons for the city of London, and there questioned in October 1588. His confession, 'written with his own hand', was damning. As the Armada had battled up through the English Channel,

> The Earl of Arundel [had] said 'Let us pray now, for we have more need to pray now than at any time. If it pleases God, the Catholic faith shall flourish. Now is the time at hand of our delivery.
>
> Moreover, the Earl said that he would make me Dean [of St Paul's], if the Catholic enterprise took place.
>
> I call to mind that when the said Earl [heard] of the discovery of the Spanish fleet, he desired me in the presence of Sir Thomas Gerard to say Mass of the Holy Ghost that it would please God to send them good success.
>
> So I said the Mass to his Lordship and he did help me say the same. At which Mass, Sir Thomas Gerard and Hammond, servant[38] unto the Earl were present.[39]

Gerard later told Bennet of Snowden's disclosure of their Masses, and 'charged me very earnestly and threatened me extremely in the earl's name, to confess nothing in such sort as the terrifying of me had like to have cost my life'.[40]

But Gerard made his own confession, reporting that the earl 'told us that the Spanish fleet was seen in the narrow seas, like unto a huge forest [of masts] and our fleet was not able to deal with them'.

The queen and the council were greatly afraid of their approach and then [he] sorrowfully said: 'God save my brother Thomas' [who had volunteered for service in the English fleet] ...

'And I hope,' said the earl, 'ere long ... to say Mass openly and to see the Catholic faith flourish again.'

Arundel also asked the priests held in the Tower to pray 'for the advance of the Catholic enterprise all the twenty-four hours of the day'.[41]

Burghley, Hatton and Henry, first Lord Hunsdon,[42] the Chamberlain, all questioned Arundel about these allegations. Hunsdon, enraged by his composure under interrogation, called him a 'beast and traitor, and said rather than he should not be hanged within four days, that he himself would hang him'. Burghley, rather more measured, said 'it was no marvel he was so settled in religion, because he read nothing to the contrary'.[43]

A new trial was now inevitable.

Like his forebears, Arundel now faced charges of high treason. Like his grandfather and father, the accused was grimly preceded by the execution axe, its blade pointing away from him, as he entered Westminster Hall on 14 April 1589. Arundel now had to undergo the same ordeal of a trial by his peers, this time presided over by Lord Derby, who sat under a cloth of estate, his three-foot long (0.91 m.) white wand of office as Lord High Steward lying before him.

Arundel was smartly dressed in a velvet gown, trimmed with fur and gold lace and fastened by gold buttons, worn over a black satin doublet with a tall black hat on his head. He was described 'as a very tall man, somewhat swarthy-coloured',[44] but his pallor was grey from the four years of confinement in the Tower.

As he arrived at the bar, he bowed twice to his twenty judges – one of them Burghley – 'but the lords never [re]moved their hats nor made any countenance'. The clerk then formally addressed him: 'Philip Howard, Earl of Arundel, late of Arundel in the county of Sussex, hold up thy hand.' The earl held his hand 'up very high, saying: "Here is as true a man's heart and hand as ever came into this hall."'[45] His comment goaded his old enemy, John

Popham, Attorney General, sitting near him, who sneered: 'That shall appear anon!'

The indictment comprised twenty-four separate counts, but focused on the old charge that alleged that he tried to flee the country without permission and a new accusation that he had prayed traitorously for the success of the Spanish Armada.

The earl asked: 'How [do] you prove me a traitor?' and Popham snapped back that 'because you have been reconciled to the Pope, there was a law made in the twenty-seventh year[46] of this queen, that whosoever was reconciled to the Pope from the obedience of the queen's majesty, was in case of treason'.[47]

The Attorney General turned to the charge against Arundel for fleeing England. After the earl had gone, he said, 'he found fault with her hard dealing in giving countenance to his adversaries and in disgracing him and that he was discontented with the injustice of the realm towards his great grandfather, his grandfather and his father'.

> It is apparent it was discontentment moved my lord, and not religion and fearing less his friends should think amiss of him, he left a copy of his letter with [the priest] Bridges, a traitor, to be dispersed to make the Catholics think well of him.
>
> Being discontented, he became a Catholic and being so great a man, he became a captain of the Catholics, which is as much as to be a captain over traitors.[48]

Arundel remarked dryly that there were some people 'who like the spider, can suck venom out of the sweetest flowers, and find materials for poison, where others would obtain matter only of a wholesome or harmless description'.[49]

Some of those who had made allegations against him were held in a room off the adjacent Court of the Queen's Bench, hidden by an arras, or screen. One was Sir Thomas Gerard, who was now summoned to give evidence. He was led in, his guards pushing away the onlookers, clearly amazed by the chattering crowds around him.

Once sworn in, Gerard found it difficult to look the prisoner in the eye and stared fixedly at the Lord High Steward. Arundel 'stood very stoutly in denial of what he witnessed [said], willing him to look him in the face and charging him as he would answer before God, in whose Presence he spoke, to tell him nothing but the truth'. Gerard, stumbling and hesitant, could only refer to the depositions which had been read in court earlier, 'to which I have been sworn, yes, twice sworn'.[50] He was quickly excused by the prosecution from further testimony.

The priest William Bennet was then called and again stuck by his confession. Arundel then produced a small piece of paper (a 'little ticket') hidden inside the sleeve of his doublet ('next to his skin', for fear of discovery if searched). It was a copy of a retraction written by Bennet.

> This he threw into the court and desired that it should be read. Bennet denied the same to be his handwriting and would not affirm that it did consent [agree] in all points with what he had ... scribbled.[51]

Some of the peers sitting in judgement muttered that the priest was 'a false man and no lawful witness'.[52] Two of them, Lords Grey and Norris, urged Bennet to explain why his two confessions contradicted themselves and asked if he knew of this letter: yes or no? The priest remained steadfast in his denials that he wrote the retraction.

The judges withdrew into the Court of the Queen's Bench to decide on their verdict and were back within an hour. Henry, Lord Norris, was the youngest of the peers, and he was asked first: 'Is Philip late Earl of Arundel of the several treasons whereof he is indicted, guilty or not guilty?'

Norris put his hand on his heart and replied: 'Guilty.' All the others said the same.[53]

Arundel was recalled to the bar and arrived 'cheerfully'. He was told of the guilty verdict and merely said in response: '*Sic voluntas Dei*' – 'God's will be done.'

The axe blade was turned towards him and he was sentenced to death by an anxious Lord Derby.[54]

The next day Howard wrote a letter to Burghley, pathetically full of gratitude for his 'honourable goodness always extended to

Catherine Howard, another niece of the third Duke of Norfolk, used as a bait in a trap to bring down Thomas Cromwell as Henry's chief minister. After becoming the King's fifth wife, her promiscuity led her to the executioner's block.

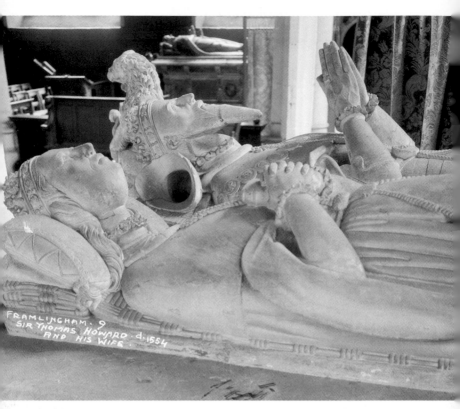

The French-style Renaissance tomb of the third Duke of Norfolk and his wife, erected at the new family mausoleum at Framlingham in 1559. Thomas Howard is shown in old age, with a long beard. His estranged wife was buried in the Howard chapel at Lambeth, but her effigy was included on her husband's tomb for the sake of appearances: in death, they were reunited at last.

Thomas Howard, fourth Duke of Norfolk, was aged eighteen when he inherited the title and immense estates from his grandfather. Like his father, Henry Howard, Earl of Surrey, he fell foul of the Tudors and was executed for his naive involvement in conspiracies surrounding Mary Queen of Scots.

vsyng thaduise and helpe of godly learned men, both in reducing the same
to the trueth of the Greke texte (appoyntyng out also the diuersitie wher
it happeneth) and also in the kepyng of the true ortographie of wordes,
as it shall manifestly appeare vnto them that wyll diligently and without
affection conferre this with the other that went foorth before. I haue (as
becommeth a true obedient subiecte, done all that in me dyd lye, to satis-
fie your graces moste godly zeale and commaundement: and with suche
submission, as it becommeth a subiect to his most drad soueraigne Lorde,
do nowe present it vnto your Maiestie, in most humble wyse desiring the
same, accordyng to your princely clemencie, to accepte my good en-
deuour. The geuer of all power, whiche is kyng of all kynges,
and prince of all princes, vouchsafe of his goodnes to pre-
serue your Maiestie, and in all your royall affaires so
to assist your gracious hyghnesse with his holy
spirite, that whatsoeuer your grace shall
thynke or do, may be to Gods glory,
the continuall floryshyng of
your hyghnesse ho-
nour, and the
common
wealth of your
subiectes.

Amen.

(∴)

The fourth Duke's farewell letter to his faithful retainer William Dix,
written from the Tower of London on a page of the Duke's copy of the
New Testament, before his execution.

Philip Howard, Earl of Arundel, painted in 1575 when he was aged eighteen.
He died of malnutrition in the Tower of London 1595, staunchly adhering to
the Catholic faith and was canonised by Pope Paul VI in 1970.

Charles Howard, second Baron Effingham and Earl of Nottingham. He was one of Mary Queen of Scots' judges at Fotheringay in 1586 and was the victor in the running battles against the Spanish Armada two years later.

Elizabeth I, daughter of Anne Boleyn, was beset by conspiracies to topple her from the throne of England. Some of the Howards were ensnared by the trap of religion and paid dearly for it.

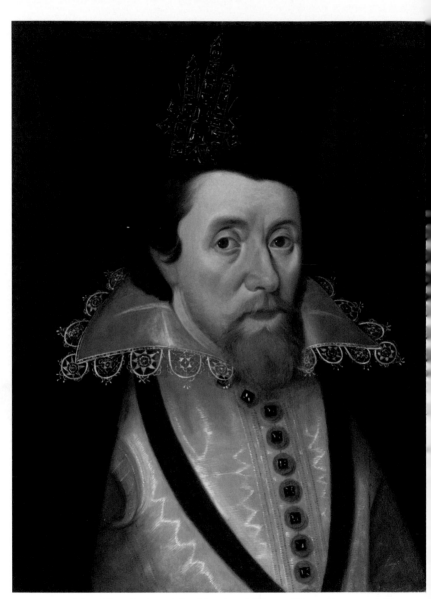

James VI of Scotland and I of England. Henry Howard was quickly rewarded for his role in bringing James to the English throne. Another Howard, Thomas, Earl of Suffolk, re-used an old family trick to win influence by introducing James, who had diverse sexual proclivities, to a striking youth, who was rejected as a 'vain forward boy'.

me'. Like his father before him, he wanted the minister to look
after his wife and children.

> And as a dead man to this world, and in all good will whilst I
> live ..., I humbly take my leave, beseeching God to send you all
> honour and happiness in this world to his glory and my poor
> soul a joyful meeting with yours in Heaven.[55]

He had already made his will, dated 12 June 1588: 'I Philip Earl of
Arundel, being a member of the true ancient Catholic and Apostolic Church ... [do] bequeath my soul into the hands of the
most glorious and inseparable Trinity, one true Almighty and
Everlasting God.' He asked that payment be immediately made of
'such money as my late lord and dear father gave to certain poor
towns by his last will and which I have not, by my negligence,
already performed, for which I am heartily sorry'. He also asked
that [Margaret] 'my sister's marriage money being the sum of
£3,000, be paid to her out of the money that shall come out of the
sale of the manor of [Castle] Rising [Norfolk] with all expedition
after my death ... For that I have done her so much injury in
withholding it from her so long.' Arundel left £2,000 to his
daughter Elizabeth on her marriage,[56] provided this was approved
by her mother, his half-sister Margaret and his executors, his
half-brother William and Lord Robert Sackville. Kenninghall was
bequeathed to his son. His wife and Margaret were both left
gold crosiers studded with diamonds.[57] In the event, none of his
instructions were carried out and most of Arundel's property,
including his wife's estates, went to the crown.

Sentence of death was also not carried out on the earl.

He lingered on for six more years in the Tower, unaware that
his execution warrant had not been signed by Elizabeth. The sword
of death was always hanging over his head. 'Not a bell sounded
but it might be his knell, not a footstep was heard, but that it
might be the messenger of death. Each morning as he arose, he
knew not that before night, he might be a headless corpse. Each
night, as he laid his head upon the pillow, he was uncertain whether
the morning might not summon him to another world.'[58]

His wife was still living in three unfurnished rooms on the

ground floor at Arundel House, but, if the court visited Somerset House next door, she was ordered to the country, because of the embarrassment of her presence. On one such occasion, when she was away, the queen saw an inscription about the sadness of life, scratched on the glass of one of the windows in Arundel House. Angered by its sentiments, she added a message beneath 'expressing much passion and disdain, on purpose to grieve and afflict the poor lady'.[59] Some time after his attainder she moved into a smaller house in Spitalfields, north of the city, and later to another at Acton, in Middlesex, where she retained a Catholic priest as a chaplain.[60]

Arundel was now growing weak and feeble from sickness. He spent much of his time at prayer or in translation of devotional works, such as the fifty-three pages of the Carthusian Johann Justus's *Epistle of Christ to the Christian Soul*.[61] A scrap of paper, addressed to him, was smuggled into the Tower, with two lines in Latin, intended to provide some religious comfort: 'Not always between two thieves did Christ hang! Truth will rise again in the Crucifix . . .'[62]

Some time in August 1595, he had got up at his usual time of 5.00 a.m., had breakfasted and was in reasonable health. At dinner (about ten o'clock) he had eaten some roast teal (duck) and had scarcely finished his plate before he began to retch violently. Soon after, he was afflicted with dysentery.

His doctors suspected poison and he made no recovery even after a few weeks. Arundel knew his last hour was nigh and appealed to the queen to be allowed to see his wife and two children.

The earl's letter was given to the Lieutenant, Sir Michael Blount, to deliver to court and at length he returned with Elizabeth's answer, which he repeated verbally. The queen said that if Arundel

> will but once go to the [established] church, his request shall not only be granted but he shall moreover be restored to his honour and estates with as much favour as I can show.

Resolute, if not stubborn, to the end, Arundel answered: 'On such condition, I cannot accept her majesty's offers. If that be the cause in which I am to perish, sorry am I that I have but one life to lose.'[63]

The earl was now confined to his bed. Blount visited him to seek pardon for the harsh treatment inflicted on the prisoner, and was duly forgiven. But Arundel had some sharp words of advice for him:

> You must think Mr Lieutenant, that when a prisoner comes to this place, he brings sorrow with him. Do not add affliction to affliction.
>
> It is a very inhuman part to tread on him, whom misfortune has cast down.
>
> The man that is void of mercy, God has cast down.
>
> Your commission is only to keep with safety, not to kill with severity.
>
> Remember, good Mr Lieutenant, that God, who, with his finger, turns the unstable wheel of this variable world, can, in the revolution of a few days, bring you to be a prisoner also and to be kept in the same place where you now keep others.[64]

His words were prophetic. Blount left the chamber weeping and within seven weeks had fallen into disgrace, lost his office, and had returned to the Tower a prisoner himself.

Sunday 19 October 1595 was the earl's last day of imprisonment in the Tower. He spent it in prayer, saying his rosary beads and reciting psalms off by heart. His servants were standing by his bedside weeping, and he asked them what time it was. They told him 'eight o'clock' (in the morning) and he replied: 'Why, then I have almost run my course and come to the end of this miserable and mortal life.'

He begged them not to cry any more, but his breath grew shallower and at length he could only mouth the names of 'Jesus' and the Virgin Mary. The earl died at noon, 'his eyes firmly fixed towards heaven and his long, lean and consumed arms out of the bed, his hand upon his breast, laid in cross one upon the other ... Without any sign of grief or groan, only turning his head a little aside, as one falling into a pleasing sleep, he surrendered his happy soul into the hands of Almighty God.'[65]

The state was to have its last vengeance.

His burial service, on 22 October in the chapel of St Peter ad Vincula in the Tower, was vulgarly amended to vilify him and his religion.

Blount was asked if the earl had relented in his obdurate espousal of Catholicism and, having been told 'no', the minister began the burial service.

'We are not come to honour this man's religion,' said the parson. 'We publicly profess and here openly protest otherways to be saved, nor to honour his offence. The law has judged him and we leave him to the Lord ...

'Man that is born of women is of short continuance and full of trouble. He shoots forth like a flower and is cut down. He vanishes also as a shadow and continues not. Thus, God has laid this man's honour in the dust ... We commit his body to the earth, giving God hearty thanks that he has delivered us of so great a fear.'

He ended with this prayer:

It has pleased Thee in mercy, to take this man out of the world. We leave him to Thy majesty, knowing by Thy word, that he and all other shall rise again to give account that which has been done in the flesh, be it good or evil against God or man.

We humbly beseech Thee, as Thou has hitherto very gloriously and in great mercy preserved Thy servant, our Queen Elizabeth [and] to preserve her despite of all her enemies, who either secretly or openly go about to b[ri]ng her life to the gra[ve, her] glory to the dust.

Confound still all Thine enemies and [hers] or convert them if they belong to Thee.[66]

He was buried in the chancel, in the same grave as his father was twenty-three years before.

The funeral costs were deliberately kept to a minimum. Ten shillings was paid for a coffin which was to be covered by just three yards of black mourning cloth, at a cost of £1 10s. The parson was paid 40s for his politically correct words and the clerk 13s 4d for digging the grave and paving over it afterwards. The Lieutenant wanted to know what should be done with the mourning cloth that had draped the coffin and was told to give it to the parson.[67]

His body was not to remain in the Tower.

In 1624 his remains were exhumed and reburied in the Fitzalan Chapel at Arundel. His coffin had a plate screwed to the lid with a Latin inscription recording that he had been 'wickedly sentenced to death ... for profession of the Catholic faith'.

The earl was named the 'Venerable Philip Howard' in 1886, beatified in 1929 and on 25 October 1970 was canonised as a saint by Pope Paul VI as a witness of Christ and an example of the Roman Catholic faith.[68]

The following year, his remains were placed in a shrine in the Catholic cathedral in Arundel.

II

RESURGAM

—◆—

'No other part of history [is] so considerable as what happened to his own family, in which ... there have been some very memorable people'

Thomas Howard, Earl of Arundel and Surrey, looking back on his own family in the 1600s[1]

For more than a century the vengeful hand of the English crown had frequently lain heavy on the Howards. Their colossal pride, egotism, ambition, or loyalty to their faith, had cost them dear. Two Dukes of Norfolk had been attainted as traitors and spent lonely years confined in the Tower of London. Another had been beheaded. An heir to the dukedom had been executed on trumped-up charges and one more had died piteously in prison. Two nieces had also been beheaded. Other members of the family had been frequently incarcerated on suspicion of infidelity to the throne. With the exception of Mary I, as far as the Tudor monarchy was concerned the Howards were very much a house of treason.

Amazingly, in the face of such adversity and distrust, the family fortunes survived, even prospered.

Charles Howard was the eldest son of William Howard, first Baron Effingham, one of the many progeny of Thomas Howard, second Duke of Norfolk, and his second wife, Agnes Tylney. Charles was born in 1536 and spent some time in the household of his half-uncle, the third Duke of Norfolk. His father was appointed Lord Admiral by Mary I in August 1555 and Charles was to follow him in this post and make a considerable reputation in naval affairs.

In 1563, he married Katherine Carey, eldest daughter of the queen's second cousin, Henry, Lord Hunsdon, who later played the role of one of the more brutal inquisitors of Philip Howard, Earl of Arundel.

When the Earl of Lincoln died in January 1585, Elizabeth's government cast around for a suitable candidate to replace him as Lord High Admiral and Howard was appointed the following May. Unlike some of the other Howards, his loyalty to the crown and the Protestant faith was unquestionable. His first duty was as one of the commissioners at the trial of Mary Queen of Scots at Fotheringay, Northamptonshire, in October 1586[2] and it was her execution on 18 February the following year that brought England closer to war with Spain.

On 15 December 1587, he was ordered to mobilise and command the English naval forces against the expected Spanish invasion of England. Elizabeth's tight-fisted control of cash for her fleet and her prevarication on the appropriate tactics frustrated and annoyed him. He warned Walsingham in January 1588, 'If her majesty would have spent but 1,000 crowns to have some intelligence, it would have saved her twenty times as much.'[3] On 10 March, Howard reported to the spymaster from his anchorage in Margate Roads, off the Kent coast, with news of the departure of the Spanish Armada:

> The Spanish forces by sea are for certain to depart from Lisbon the 20th. of this month with the light moon and that the number of the fleet, when they all meet, will be 210 sails and the number of soldiers, besides the mariners, are 36,000 ...
>
> I fear me ere it should be long, her majesty will be sorry that she has believed some as much as she has done, but it will be very late ...[4]

But this was a premature false alarm and, after being damaged by storms, the huge Armada did not depart for England until 12 July.

Unlike some of his family, Howard did not suffer from false pride. Vain he might have been, but he was fully aware that he was not an experienced sailor. Therefore, he appointed expert captains as his tactical advisers and Sir Francis Drake as his vice-admiral and second-in-command. However, with a whiff of nepotism, Thomas Howard, second son of the fourth Duke of Norfolk, and half-brother to Philip, Earl of Arundel, was appointed to command the *Golden Lion* in the English fleet.

Elizabeth's ever-present dread of catastrophic defeat at sea led either to a flurry of orders, or plain inaction, as she hesitated, undecided on how best to counter this approaching threat to her crown and her young Protestant state. 'For the love of Jesus Christ Madam,' Howard urged her on 23 June, 'awake thoroughly and see the villainous treasons round about you.'[5]

The Armada finally arrived off the south-west coast of England on 19 July. Howard, on board his flagship, *Ark Royal*, at Plymouth, wrote breathlessly to Walsingham of the first, inconclusive naval action:

> I will not trouble you with a long letter – we are at present otherwise occupied than with writing.
>
> Upon Friday ... I received intelligence that there were a great number of ships descried off the Lizard [peninsula]. Whereupon, although the wind was very scant, we first warped[6] out of harbour that night and upon Saturday turned out very hardly, the wind being [in the] south-west.
>
> About three in the afternoon, [we saw] the Spanish fleet and did what we could to work for the wind, which [by this] morning we had recovered, [observing] their fleet to consist of 120 sail, whereof there are four g[alleasses][7] and many ships of great burden.
>
> At nine of the [clock] we gave them fight which continued until one.
>
> [In this] fight we made some of them to bear room to stop their leaks. Notwithstanding, we dare not adventure to put in among them, their fleet being so strong.

The admiral added an urgent appeal for munitions in a hasty postscript:

> Sir, for the love of God and our country, let us have, with some speed, some great shot sent to us of all bigness, for this service, will continue long, and some powder with it.[8]

Howard's strategy was to push the advancing Armada further out to sea and away from any potential landfall on English soil. His smaller, lighter-armed warships could not hope to land a killer blow on the mighty Spanish fleet, so instead harried and snapped at its heels as the Armada sailed up the English Channel. The actions of 23 July, off Portland Bill, and, two days later, off the Isle of Wight, did not sink a single Spanish ship, but inflicted considerable battle damage.

The Armada anchored off Calais on 27 July, preparing to escort Spanish troops across the southern North Sea to planned invasion beaches in and around the Thames estuary. Howard now tried a new tactic: fireships. Eight vessels were packed with combustible materials – barrels of pitch and oil – to turn them into floating incendiary bombs. Just after midnight on 28 July, these were set ablaze and bravely steered in among the Armada. The Spanish, panic-stricken, cut their anchor cables, hoisted sail and headed out into the open sea in confusion.

The English were waiting for them beyond the horizon. As dawn broke, they attacked and battered the dispersed Armada off Gravelines, sinking twelve ships and forcing them eastwards until some were in danger of running aground on the treacherous sand-banks off the Zeeland coast. Then the wind suddenly veered and drove the Spaniards north, pursued by the English warships, like hunting dogs running down their prey.

Howard was forced to break off the chase as the Armada entered Scottish waters, not because of diplomatic niceties but because of his shortages of fresh water, food and powder and shot. The Spanish were left to limp home, around the north coast of Scotland and out into the tempestuous Atlantic, in the hope of steering a course home. After weeks of storms, only sixty ships survived. More than 20,000 Spanish sailors and soldiers had perished. It was a famous victory.

Characteristically, Elizabeth did not reward any of her commanders and left many of her sailors to die of disease and hunger. An epidemic of typhus, originating in the *Elizabeth Jonas*, swept through the fleet and killed hundreds. Howard was aghast: 'It would grieve any man's heart to see them that have served so valiantly, die so miserably.' He sold some of his own plate to raise cash to clothe his men and used his own money to pay some of the discharged sailors. 'It is a most pitiful sight to see how the men ... die in the streets. I am driven myself to come [ashore] to see them bestowed in some lodging. And the best I can get is barns and outhouses,' he complained.[9]

Eventually the parsimonious Elizabeth created Howard Earl of Nottingham on 22 October 1597, to become the second peer of the realm. Two years later, he was appointed 'Lieutenant General of All England' and finally retired from public duties, aged eighty-three, in January 1619. One of his favourite pastimes was hunting with dogs – he was a leading breeder of spaniels – and he continued to hunt enthusiastically right up to his final illness.[10] He died on 14 December 1624 at Haling House, Croydon, Surrey, and was buried in the Effingham family vault at Reigate, Surrey.

Henry Howard, younger son of the Earl of Surrey, had recurrently fallen foul of Elizabeth's government and had been imprisoned on at least five occasions. He returned to partial favour after the execution of his brother, the fourth Duke of Norfolk, in 1572, but found himself back within the noisome confines of the Fleet Prison in the aftermath of the Throgmorton plot in 1583. Even though she knew nothing of his perfidious reports to the Spanish about events at her court, or of his secret correspondence with Mary Queen of Scots, there seems little doubt that Elizabeth was convinced of his treachery and would cheerfully have signed his death warrant with a swift flourish of her quill pen. Howard's sworn enemy, Edward de Vere, seventeenth Earl of Oxford, told him that the queen reviled and detested him 'and sought his head more than any person living'.[11]

As the Virgin Queen sank into old age, the arch-conspirator Howard daringly began a secret correspondence with James VI of Scotland to facilitate his succession to the throne of England. Robert Cecil, son of Elizabeth's long-serving minister, Burghley, and also party to these negotiations, recommended Howard as 'long approved and trusty'.[12]

He bet on the right horse.

James became King of England and Scotland in March 1603 and, on hearing the news of his accession, sent Howard a jewel of three stones in reward for his efforts. He immediately appointed him a member of his Privy Council and on 13 March 1604, at the Tower – the scene of so much misery to his family – Howard was created Earl of Northampton. His notorious obsequiousness and flattery had not deserted him and this unpleasant trait earned him the less than happy nickname of 'His Majesty's earwig'.[13] Northampton's habitual duplicity also sometimes irked the new king, and James twice wrote to him in 1605 accusing him of disliking his sons, the princes Henry and Charles, and of 'innate hatred to me and all Scotland for my cause'. Moreover, he threatened to repay Howard 'for your often cruel and malicious speeches against Baby Charles and his honest father'.[14]

No one was quite sure of duplicitous Northampton's religious beliefs. He regularly attended the Chapel Royal and in 1604 served on the commission to expel seminary priests and Jesuits. He was one of the four privy councillors in October 1605 to whom Lord Monteagle handed the infamous letter warning of the Catholic Gunpowder Plot.

He erected new houses at Greenwich and at Charing Cross, north of Whitehall, where he died, aged seventy-four, on 16 June 1624 from gangrene in his thigh – but not before receiving extreme unction from a priest. His will, dated the day of his death, declared:

> I die ... a member of the Catholic and Apostolic church, saying with St Jerome '*in qua fide puer natus fui in eadem senex morior*' [I will die as an old man in the same faith in which I was born as a child].[15]

So, religiously, he had the last laugh on all those he had fooled over the years. He also left money to set up three almshouses or hospitals dedicated to the Holy Trinity at Castle Rising in Norfolk, Greenwich and Clun in Shropshire.[16]

Northampton's nephew, Thomas Howard, son of the fourth duke by his second wife Margaret Audley, who had served at sea against the Spanish Armada, also supported the accession of James I. He was almost immediately created Earl of Suffolk and appointed Lord Chamberlain. In the fifteen years that followed, he and his uncle enjoyed considerable political power.[17]

When the king, who was of diverse sexual proclivities, showed favour to the young, handsome George Villiers (later to be Marquis of Buckingham), Suffolk tried an old Howard trick to divert him and maintain their influence. They discovered a striking youth called William Monson with whom they 'took great pains in tricking and prancking up' and washed 'his face every day with posset-curd' to maintain his complexion. It did not turn out too well with Catherine Howard. It did not work in the seventeenth century either. James thought Monson to be a vain, forward boy and rejected him as any kind of royal favourite.[18]

Suffolk, now Lord Treasurer, was dismissed from all his offices in 1619 for corruption and fined £30,000. He died on 28 May 1626, leaving crippling debts. Another Howard was dishonoured.

The badly treated widow of Philip Earl of Arundel outlived her husband by thirty-five years and died in 1630 aged seventy-four.

Her son, Thomas, was restored in blood as Earl of Arundel and Surrey on 18 April 1604. As importantly, he was granted the lands in Norfolk, Suffolk, Cambridgeshire, Essex, Surrey and Sussex that had been enjoyed by his father, and the dignities and baronies lost by his grandfather, the fourth Duke of Norfolk.[19]

Two years later he married Alatheia, third daughter and later the sole heiress of Gilbert Talbot, seventh Earl of Shrewsbury, who died in 1616. She brought to the marriage huge estates in Derbyshire, Nottinghamshire and South Yorkshire, including the industrial town of Sheffield, with an annual income of £15,000, or £2 million at current values. Arundel took Holy Communion at the Chapel Royal that year and was quickly made a Privy Councillor. In August 1621, he was created Earl Marshal at a fee of £2,000 a year.

After all those years of bloodshed, all that intrigue, all that misery in the Tower of London, the Howards had at last retrieved their political fortunes.

In the future, they would enjoy industrial wealth and influence to add lustre to their once fatal family pride.

THE HOWARD HOMES AT KENNINGHALL, LAMBETH AND NORWICH

———◆———

The 'H'-shaped Palace of Kenninghall, fronting east and west, was built by Thomas Howard, third Duke of Norfolk, in 1525–7, around 250 yards (228 m.) north-east of an earlier doubled-moated manor house, East Hall,[1] which was demolished. The redbrick house, set in 700 acres (283.27 hectares) of deer park, was divided into two courts, named Ewery and Shelfhanger, with tall chimneys and Gothic traceried windows. It was further extended in 1532 at a cost of £348 1s 8d.[2]

It had seventy rooms, and later became the first house in England to be equipped with a bathroom, when the fourth duke fitted up a chamber there with 'twelve pieces of copper, great and small, to bathe in'. The clue to its purpose was in its decoration: hanging on the walls was a tapestry of ladies bathing.[3]

The third duke's own suite of rooms was situated on the second floor over the chapel. Conveniently, off the gallery on the floor above were the apartments of his mistress, Bessie Holland. In either court was accommodation for his children, and later their families, with the nursery on the ground floor, next to the wash-house. Space was reserved for the duke's stepmother, Agnes, Dowager Duchess of Norfolk, and more was later found for Mary, Duchess of Richmond, after the death of her husband.

The chapel walls were wainscoted and over the altar was probably a triptych of Christ's birth, passion and resurrection. It was staffed by six chaplains[4] – the oak presses in the vestry held forty-two embroidered copes, or ecclesiastical vestments – and had its own choristers, kept in order by their master. Music was provided by 'two pairs of organs' and the hymns and psalms were sung using illuminated Mass books.

The interior of the palace was hung with more than fifty rich tapestries with subjects including the Story of Hercules, the Siege of Paris and Christ's Passion. Others prominently and proudly displayed the Norfolk arms.[5] Of particular magnificence was the decoration of the 'public rooms' – the great hall and the presence chamber – as befitting the ducal style and title of 'right honourable and mighty prince ...'.

The palace also housed a number of officials: his secretary, Bessie's father; the steward, treasurer, comptroller of the household, seneschal,[6] auditor, tutor to the Howard children, almoners, and the physician, Adrian Junius.[7] There was also an armoury and a tennis court.

Household accounts for 1525 indicate the style of food served at table by the third duke's retainers, dressed in his personal livery of black and tawny velvet. On one day, Saturday 9 September, when the duke and his soon-to-be-discarded duchess were dining at home, doubtless with a host of household staff, they consumed: 400 oysters; 8 salt fish; 1 fresh pike; 2 tench; 30 eels and 286 eggs.

Those who brought presents were rewarded handsomely: two shillings were given to a man who brought a porpoise from the bailiff of Yarmouth and a similar amount given to the messenger from the Abbot of Langley who had carried three swans to Kenninghall. One must not imagine the Norfolks mere fish-eaters: a record of foodstuffs consumed over twenty-six days includes 12 oxen, 12 calves, 47 sheep, 3 bucks, 44 sucking-pigs and 263 rabbits. Poultry included 18 swans, 22 geese, 106 capons, 403 chickens and 406 pigeons, mallards, snipe, pheasants, partridges and lapwings. A crane and a bittern also went into the pot. Over the same period, the household consumed 2 porpoises; 1 sturgeon, 1 conger eel, 27 soles; 85 salt fish; 1 salmon trout, 840 other fish (cod, whiting, plaice, herring, flounders), 27 pike, 493 perch and roach; 3,200 oysters; 1,449 eels, 2,370 eggs, 134 dozen loaves. To wash all this down, they drank 58 barrels of beer, brewed on the premises.[8] Total cost of provisions for this period was £202 2s 7½d.

By the mid-seventeenth century the magnificence of Kenninghall had dulled and it fell into disrepair. It was demolished around 1650, leaving only one wing which remains today. The materials were used to maintain other buildings on the Norfolks' estates.

The second Duke of Norfolk built a London home in Lambeth, on Church Street, west of the palace of the Archbishop of Canterbury. Norfolk House had a fine library and substantial gardens and paddocks and Wenceslas Hollar's map of London of c. 1660 shows a high tiled lantern, topped by a weathercock, above the gabled roof, together with a bell cupola.

After the third duke's attainder and imprisonment, the property passed to William Parr, Marquis of Northampton, but in 1552, he exchanged it with the crown for the lordship of Southwark, which had been owned by the Bishop of Winchester.

After the house was returned to the Howards, it was sold in 1558 by the fourth duke to Richard Garth and John Dister for £400. Then it was described as a capital messuage 'wherein the ancestors of the said duke have accustomed to lye'. It included two inns, called the George and the Bell, the former annexed to the mansion on its west side. Bell Close, at the rear of the inn, comprised two acres and other paddocks included more than twenty-three acres in 'Cottmansfield', four acres near the Bishop of Rochester's house and eight acres of marsh called 'The Hopes' in Lambeth marsh.[9]

The mansion had a great gate on 'the king's highway leading from Lambeth to St George's Fields' which opened on to a paved yard. On the west side of the yard was the duke's chapel, which by 1590 had been partitioned into a hall, buttery and parlour. On the east side were the kitchens, with a 'great chamber' above for dining and a gallery, an oratory and several closets. Street frontage of the house was about 125 feet (38 m.).

The new owners divided the property into three, with one third, including Norfolk House and the Bell, sold first to John Glascock and then to Margaret Parker, wife of Matthew Parker, Archbishop of Canterbury. At her death in 1570, it passed to her younger son, also called Matthew, and the house was demolished in the seventeenth century.

Only Norfolk Row remains to remind us of the glories of the house: in 1610, it was a cartway to a lane, running behind the village of Lambeth.

The fourth duke focused his attentions on his new London home at Howard House, formerly the Carthusian monastery at the Charterhouse, and with building a new palace in Norwich, in the parish of St John Maddermarket, formerly called St Cross, from 1561. He had bought the land there from Alan Percy, third son of Henry Percy, fourth Earl of Northumberland, and warden of the Holy Trinity College at Arundel. He cleared the site and built the palace with materials brought by barge from St Benet's abbey.[10] An indenture of 1563 mentions 'my capital messuage new built with buildings, courts, orchards, gardens, ponds and yards'.[11]

The north and south boundaries of the site were the River Wensum and Wymer Street (now St Andrew's Street). The three-storey buildings formed a quadrangle with a great gateway in the south side. In the middle of the courtyard was a water conduit. Along the first floor of the south wing ran a gallery, with the duke's apartments at one end and his wife's at the other. The west wing held the great hall and presence chamber on the third floor and fifteen other rooms. The dining hall, with a ceiling as high as the roof, was on the north side, overlooking the river. This part of the house also contained a water gate, leading to a private quay, and the armoury. The mansion also included a theatre, a covered real tennis court and a bowling alley.[12]

Dr Edward Browne recorded a Christmas spent at the palace in 1663:

> I was at Mr Howard's, brother to the Duke of Norfolk [the insane Henry, fifth duke, who was living in Padua] who kept Christmas ... so magnificently that the like hath scarce been seen.
>
> They had dancing every night and gave entertainments to all that would come ...[13]

The diarist John Evelyn also visited the palace and described it as 'an old wretched building and that part of it newly built of brick is very ill understood, so as I was of the opinion it had been much better to have demolished it all and set it up in a better place than to proceed any further, for it stands in the very market-place and though near a river, yet a very narrow one and without any extent'.[14]

The palace was rebuilt by Henry, sixth Duke of Norfolk (who died in 1684), probably to the designs of Sir Robert Hooke. Thomas Baskerville, in 1681, referred disparagingly to the new mansion as 'a sumptuous new-built house not yet finished within but seated in a dung hole place, though it has cost the duke already £30,000 in building, as the gentleman as showed it told us'.[15]

It was never properly lived in and became something of an opulent embarrassment to the Norfolks. It was pulled down in 1711 by Thomas, eighth duke, after he became piqued with the then mayor of Norwich, over his 'ill-behaviour' towards him 'in not permitting his comedians to enter the city with their trumpets'.[16]

PEDIGREE OF THE TUDOR DUKES OF NORFOLK

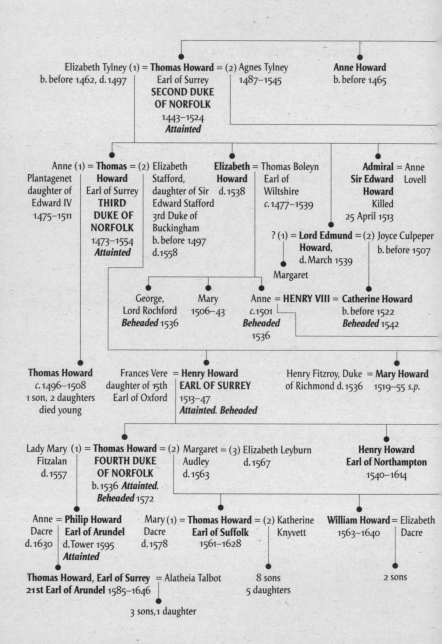

Elizabeth Tylney (1) = **Thomas Howard** = (2) Agnes Tylney
b. before 1462, d. 1497   Earl of Surrey   1487–1545
SECOND DUKE
OF NORFOLK
1443–1524
Attainted

Anne Howard
b. before 1465

Anne (1) = **Thomas** = (2) Elizabeth
Plantagenet **Howard** Stafford,
daughter of Earl of Surrey daughter of Sir
Edward IV **THIRD** Edward Stafford
1475–1511 **DUKE OF** 3rd Duke of
  NORFOLK Buckingham
  1473–1554 b. before 1497
  Attainted d. 1558

Elizabeth = Thomas Boleyn
Howard Earl of
d. 1538 Wiltshire
  c. 1477–1539

Admiral = Anne
Sir Edward Lovell
Howard
Killed
25 April 1513

? (1) = **Lord Edmund** = (2) Joyce Culpeper
  Howard, b. before 1507
  d. March 1539

Margaret

George,   Mary   Anne = **HENRY VIII** = Catherine Howard
Lord Rochford 1506–43 c. 1501   b. before 1522
Beheaded 1536   *Beheaded*   *Beheaded* 1542
          1536

Thomas Howard
c. 1496–1508
1 son, 2 daughters
died young

Frances Vere = **Henry Howard**
daughter of 15th **EARL OF SURREY**
Earl of Oxford 1513–47
  Attainted. Beheaded

Henry Fitzroy, Duke = **Mary Howard**
of Richmond d. 1536 1519–55 *s.p.*

Lady Mary (1) = **Thomas Howard** = (2) Margaret = (3) Elizabeth Leyburn
Fitzalan **FOURTH DUKE** Audley d. 1567
d. 1557 **OF NORFOLK** d. 1563
  b. 1536 *Attainted.*
  Beheaded 1572

Henry Howard
Earl of Northampton
1540–1614

Anne = **Philip Howard**
Dacre **Earl of Arundel**
d. 1630 d. Tower 1595
  Attainted

Mary (1) = **Thomas Howard** = (2) Katherine
Dacre **Earl of Suffolk** Knyvett
d. 1578 1561–1628

William Howard = Elizabeth
1563–1640 Dacre

Thomas Howard, Earl of Surrey = Alatheia Talbot
21st Earl of Arundel 1585–1646

8 sons
5 daughters

2 sons

3 sons, 1 daughter

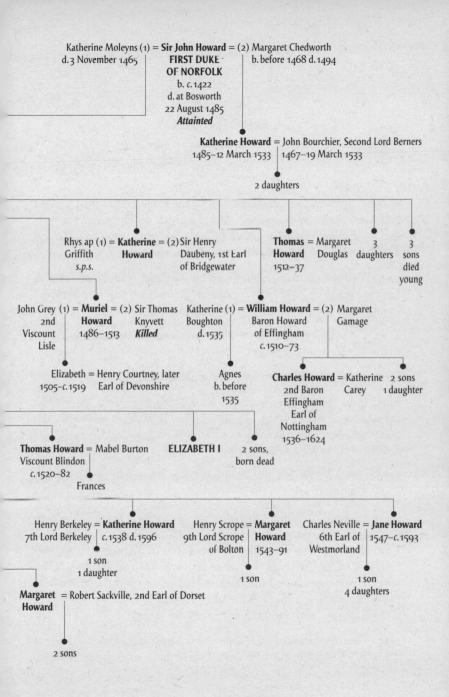

Katherine Moleyns (1) = **Sir John Howard** = (2) Margaret Chedworth
d. 3 November 1465   **FIRST DUKE**   b. before 1468 d. 1494
            OF NORFOLK
            b. *c*. 1422
            d. at Bosworth
            22 August 1485
            Attainted

Katherine Howard = John Bourchier, Second Lord Berners
1485–12 March 1533 | 1467–19 March 1533

2 daughters

Rhys ap (1) = **Katherine** = (2) Sir Henry   **Thomas** = Margaret   3   3
Griffith   **Howard**   Daubeny, 1st Earl   **Howard**   Douglas   daughters   sons
s.p.s.   of Bridgewater   1512–37   died
                                                       young

John Grey (1) = **Muriel** = (2) Sir Thomas   Katherine (1) = **William Howard** = (2) Margaret
2nd   **Howard**   Knyvett   Boughton   Baron Howard   Gamage
Viscount   1486–1513   *Killed*   d. 1535   of Effingham
Lisle   *c*. 1510–73

Elizabeth = Henry Courtney, later   Agnes   **Charles Howard** = Katherine   2 sons
1505–*c*. 1519   Earl of Devonshire   b. before   2nd Baron   Carey   1 daughter
                                1535   Effingham
                                                     Earl of
                                                    Nottingham

Thomas Howard = Mabel Burton   **ELIZABETH I**   2 sons,   1536–1624
Viscount Blindon   born dead
c. 1520–82

Frances

Henry Berkeley = **Katherine Howard**   Henry Scrope = **Margaret**   Charles Neville = **Jane Howard**
7th Lord Berkeley | *c*. 1538 d. 1596   9th Lord Scrope | **Howard**   6th Earl of | 1547–*c*. 1593
                               of Bolton | 1543–91   Westmorland

1 son
1 daughter

                                   1 son   1 son
                                                            4 daughters

Margaret = Robert Sackville, 2nd Earl of Dorset
Howard

2 sons

CHRONOLOGY

◆

c. 1422 Birth of John Howard, son of Sir Robert Howard (d. 1436) and his wife, Lady Margaret, elder daughter of Thomas Mowbray, first [Mowbray] Duke of Norfolk, Lord Mowbray and Segrave and Earl Marshal of England (who had died in 1399).

1443 Birth, at Tendring Hall, Stoke-by-Nayland, Suffolk, of Thomas Howard I, son of John Howard and his first wife, Katherine Moleyns (who died 3 November 1465, leaving six children).

1465: 3 November Death of Katherine, wife of John Howard, at Stoke-by-Nayland, Suffolk.

Late 1460s John Howard created Lord Howard.

1467 Lord Howard marries, as his second wife, Margaret Chedworth, the widow of John Norris esquire of Bray, Berkshire, previously the widow of Nicholas Wyfold, Lord Mayor of London, in 1450, and daughter of Sir John Chedworth.

1471: 14 April Thomas Howard I fights in the Battle of Barnet and is severely wounded.

1472: 30 April Thomas Howard I marries the rich heiress Elizabeth *née* Tylney, the widow of Sir Humphrey Bourchier (son of the first Lord Berners, who was killed at the Battle of Barnet in 1471), and daughter of Sir Frederick Tylney of Ashwell Thorpe, Norfolk. They have five children, including Thomas II, later third Duke of Norfolk, Edward, later Lord High Admiral of England (killed 25 April 1513), and Elizabeth, later the mother of Anne Boleyn.

1473 Thomas Howard II (later third Duke of Norfolk), son of Thomas Howard I and Elizabeth Tylney, born at Ashwell Thorpe, Norfolk.

1476: 17 January Sudden death of John Mowbray, fourth and last [Mowbray] Duke of Norfolk, at Framlingham Castle, Suffolk. Dukedoms of Norfolk and Earldom of Surrey become extinct.

1481 Lady Anne Mowbray, only daughter and heiress of the fourth [Mowbray] Duke of Norfolk, and wife to Richard, Duke of York, second son of Edward IV, dies aged nine, at Framlingham Castle, Suffolk, and is buried in Westminster Abbey. Lord Howard, as Lady Anne's cousin, is now the senior co-heir to Mowbray estates. York is later murdered in Tower of London.

1483: 9 April Death of the Yorkist King Edward IV. Richard, Duke of Gloucester, seizes throne on 26 June as King Richard III.

1483: 28 June John Howard created first [Howard] Duke of Norfolk and Earl Marshal of England by Richard III, who grants him the Mowbray estates. His son, Thomas Howard I, is created Earl of Surrey and appointed a member of the Privy Council and Knight of the Garter. The duke officiates as High Steward and Earl Marshal at the king's coronation on 6 July.

1483: 25 July The first Duke of Norfolk created Lord High Admiral of England, Ireland and Aquitaine and Steward of the Duchy of Lancaster for life.

1484 Thomas Howard II ?betrothed to nine-year-old Lady Anne Plantagenet, daughter of Edward IV and Elizabeth Woodville.

1485: 22 August Battle of Bosworth. Richard III killed and royalist army defeated. First [Howard] Duke of Norfolk is killed leading Richard's vanguard of archers. His body is buried at Thetford, Norfolk. His son, Thomas I, is wounded at Bosworth and taken prisoner. Succeeds his father as second Duke of Norfolk but is imprisoned in the Tower of London.

1485: 30 October Henry Tudor is crowned at Westminster Abbey as King Henry VII.

1485: 7 November John Howard, first Duke of Norfolk, and his son, Thomas I, Earl of Surrey, attainted for treason by Henry VII's first Parliament. Earl of Surrey degraded from Order of the Garter.

1486: 18 January Henry VII marries Elizabeth of York, eldest daughter of Edward IV.

1486: 20 September Prince Arthur, eldest son of Henry VII and his wife, Elizabeth of York, born at Winchester.

1489: March Thomas Howard I freed from Tower, his attainder is later reversed and he is restored as Earl of Surrey.

1489 Appointed Chief Justice in Eyre North of the Trent. Puts down a revolt in the north of England against new taxes imposed by Henry VII.

1490: 20 May Appointed Vice-Warden of the East and Middle Marches on the Scottish borders and, effectively, general of English forces in the region.

1491: 28 June Henry, second son of Henry VII, born at Greenwich Palace.

1492 Thomas Howard I suppresses fresh northern riots against taxation.

1494 Death of Margaret, widow of attainted first Duke of Norfolk. Her will is dated 13 May 1490 and is proved 3 December 1494.

1495: 4 February Henry VII allows marriage of Thomas Howard II to Lady Anne Plantagenet, the king's sister-in-law, at Greenwich. The four children of the marriage all die young – the longest lived being the only son, Thomas (c. 1496–August 1508).

1497 Thomas Howard I repels a Scottish attack on Norham Castle, Northumberland, and launches a raid into Scotland to seize Ayton Castle, Berwickshire.

1497: 4 April Death of Elizabeth Tylney, first wife of Thomas Howard I.

1497: 8 November Thomas Howard I marries his second wife, Agnes Tylney, daughter of Hugh Tylney of Skirbeck and Boston in Lincolnshire. They have six surviving children, including William, later first Baron Howard of Effingham, born c. 1510, and Thomas, died 1537.

1501: 16 June Thomas Howard I appointed Lord High Treasurer of England.

1501: 14 November Prince Arthur marries Catherine of Aragon.

1502: 2 April Prince Arthur dies from tuberculosis, aged fifteen, at Ludlow Castle.

1503: 25 June Henry, now Prince of Wales, is formally betrothed to Catherine of Aragon.

1509: 21 April Henry VII dies at Richmond Palace, Surrey. On his deathbed he restores the family estates to Thomas Howard I, Earl of Surrey, who is one of the executors of his will.

1509: 24 April Henry VIII proclaimed king; marries Catherine (11 June). Both are crowned on 24 June when Thomas Howard I serves as Marshal of England.

1510: 10 July Thomas Howard I created Earl Marshal of England for life.

1511: 12 November Anne Plantagenet, wife of Thomas Howard II, dies of consumption, aged thirty-six.

1513 Thomas Howard II marries Elizabeth Stafford, the unwilling fifteen-year-old daughter of Sir Edward Stafford, third Duke of Buckingham, and his wife, Eleanor Percy, daughter of the fourth Duke of Northumberland. They have three children: Henry, later Earl of Surrey, born 1513; Mary, born 1519; and Thomas, born c. 1520, later first Viscount Bindon.

1513: 25 April Admiral Sir Edward Howard drowned in attack on the French fleet at Brest, leaving the care of his two illegitimate sons to Henry VIII and Charles Brandon, later Duke of Suffolk.

1513: 4 May Thomas Howard II succeeds his brother as Lord High Admiral, an office he holds until 1525.

1513: July Thomas Howard I appointed Lieutenant General of English forces in the north.

1513: 9 September Thomas Howard I defeats Scots army at Battle of Flodden Field, Northumberland, killing James IV of Scotland and up to 12,000 of the invading Scots army.

1513   Birth of Henry Howard, later Earl of Surrey, eldest son of third Duke of Norfolk and second wife, Elizabeth Stafford.

1514: 1 February   Thomas Howard I created second Duke of Norfolk by a grateful Henry VIII and restored at a ceremony at Lambeth Palace on the feast of Candlemas (2 February). Thomas Howard II made Earl of Surrey for life. Both awarded grants and annuities.

1516: 18 February   Birth of Mary, daughter of Henry VIII and Catherine of Aragon, at Greenwich Palace.

1517: 1 May   Second Duke of Norfolk, as Earl Marshal, leads a private army of East Anglian retainers to suppress apprentice riots in London.

1519: June   Birth of Henry Fitzroy, later Duke of Richmond and Somerset, the bastard son of Henry VIII and his mistress, Elizabeth Blount, at priory of St Lawrence, Blackmore, near Ingatestone, Essex.

1520: 10 March–end 1521   Thomas Howard II, Earl of Surrey, serves as Lord Deputy of Ireland, based in Dublin.

1520: 31 May–18 July   Second Duke of Norfolk appointed Guardian of England during Henry VIII's absence in France.

1521: May   Second Duke of Norfolk, as Lord High Steward, presides over trial of Edward Stafford, third Duke of Buckingham (his son's father-in-law), for treason. Buckingham is beheaded on 17 May 1521 on Tower Hill.

1522: September   Thomas Howard II, Earl of Surrey, serves as Lieutenant General of Anglo-Burgundian army in France.

1522: 4 December   Second Duke of Norfolk resigns as Lord High Treasurer in favour of his son, Thomas Howard II, Earl of Surrey.

1523: 26 February–1524   Thomas Howard II, Earl of Surrey, serves as Lieutenant General of English forces on the Scottish border.

1524: 21 May   Death of Thomas Howard I, second Duke of Norfolk, aged eighty-one, at Framlingham Castle, Suffolk. He is buried at the Cluniac abbey of Our Lady, Thetford on 24 June. Thomas Howard

II succeeds as third Duke of Norfolk and his eldest son, Henry, becomes Earl of Surrey.

1525: July Henry VIII's illegitimate son, Henry Fitzroy, Duke of Richmond, appointed Lord High Admiral in place of Thomas Howard II, third Duke of Norfolk.

1527: Summer Henry VIII decides to seek annulment of his marriage to Catherine of Aragon.

1529: 18 October Cardinal Wolsey, Lord Chancellor, delivers Great Seal of England to third Duke of Norfolk and Duke of Suffolk at York Place.

1530: November Wolsey arrested on treason charges (4 November) and dies, probably from dysentery, on 29 November at Leicester Abbey, en route to the Tower of London.

1532: April Third Duke of Norfolk arranges the marriage of Henry Howard, Earl of Surrey, to Lady Frances de Vere (1517–77), daughter of John de Vere, fifteenth Earl of Oxford. They are married in the spring of the following year, although are too young to live together.

1533: 25 January Henry secretly marries Anne Boleyn, the third Duke of Norfolk's niece, in the high chamber over the Holbein Gate in the Palace of Westminster. She is crowned queen on 1 June at Westminster Abbey.

1533: 23 May Archbishop Thomas Cranmer grants divorce between Henry VIII and Catherine of Aragon at Dunstable, Bedfordshire.

1533: 28 May Third Duke of Norfolk created Earl Marshal of England.

1533: 7 September Birth of Princess Elizabeth, daughter of Henry VIII and Anne Boleyn, at Greenwich Palace.

1533: 26 November Henry Fitzroy, Duke of Richmond, Henry VIII's illegitimate son, marries Mary, younger daughter of third Duke of Norfolk. Marriage never consummated.

1535: 1 July Trial for treason of former Lord Chancellor, Sir Thomas More, in Westminster Hall. He is executed on 6 July on Tower Hill.

1536: 7 January   Death of Catherine of Aragon at Kimbolton Castle, Huntingdonshire.

1536: 26 January   Henry VIII injured in a jousting accident at Greenwich. Five days later, Anne Boleyn miscarries a male child when told of the accident by her uncle, the third Duke of Norfolk.

1536: March   Act for the Dissolutions of Minor Monastic Houses passed.

1536: 15 May   Third Duke presides over trial, at Tower of London, of Anne Boleyn and her brother George, Viscount Rochford, for incest and adultery. Rochford beheaded on Tower Hill on 17 May and Anne beheaded by a French executioner with a two-handed sword in the Tower of London, on 19 May.

1536: 30 May   Henry marries his third wife, Jane Seymour, in the Queen's Closet in the Palace of Westminster.

1536   Birth of Charles, eldest son of William Howard, first Baron Effingham (c. 1510–73), and his second wife, Margaret, daughter of Sir Thomas Gamage.

1536: 10 March   Thomas Howard III (later fourth Duke of Norfolk) is born to Henry Howard, Earl of Surrey, and his wife, Frances.

1536: 18 July   Bill of Attainder for high treason passed against Lord Thomas Howard, half-brother of the third Duke of Norfolk, for making a private marriage contract with Lady Margaret Douglas, niece to Henry VIII. Both he and Lady Margaret are imprisoned in the Tower of London.

1536: 23 July   Death of Henry Fitzroy, Duke of Richmond, Henry VIII's illegitimate son, at St James's Palace, London. Buried among the Howard tombs at the Cluniac abbey of Our Lady, Thetford, Norfolk.

1536: 2 October   Beginning of rebellions in Lincolnshire, spreading to Yorkshire, Lancashire, Westmorland and Cumberland – the Pilgrimage of Grace – later suppressed by third Duke of Norfolk as High Marshal.

1537: January   New rebellion in Yorkshire, quickly suppressed. Third Duke of Norfolk wreaks brutal royal vengeance on the rebels.

1537: 12 October Birth of Prince Edward, legitimate son and heir of Henry VIII and Jane Seymour, at Hampton Court.

1537: 24 October Death of Jane Seymour at Hampton Court from complications after birth of Prince Edward.

1537: 31 October Lord Thomas Howard, half-brother of the third Duke of Norfolk, dies inside the Tower of London. He is buried 'without pomp' at Thetford. His love Lady Margaret is pardoned and freed.

1539: 28 June Royal Assent granted to the Act Abolishing Diversity in Opinions – the so-called Statute of Six Articles – against Protestant practices.

1539: July Dissolution of major religious houses begins.

1540: 6 January Henry VIII marries, as his fourth wife, Anne of Cleves, at Greenwich Palace.

1540: 24 February Birth of Henry Howard, second son of Henry Howard, Earl of Surrey, and his wife, Lady Frances de Vere, at Shottesham, Norfolk.

1540: 10 June King's chief minister, Thomas Cromwell, arrested by third Duke of Norfolk at meeting of Privy Council at Westminster Palace.

1540: 9 July Henry VIII's marriage to Anne of Cleves is annulled by Clerical Convocation. The annulment is confirmed by Parliament on 13 July.

1540: 28 July Cromwell beheaded at Tower Hill. Henry VIII marries his fifth wife, Catherine Howard, another niece of the third Duke of Norfolk, at Oatlands, near Weybridge, Surrey.

1541: 10 December Execution of Thomas Culpeper and Francis Dereham, lovers of Queen Catherine Howard, at Tyburn, for treason.

1541: 22 December Third Duke of Norfolk's half-brother, Lord William Howard, and his wife, Norfolk's half-sister, Katherine, Countess Bridgewater, found guilty of misprision of treason over Queen Catherine Howard's adultery with Thomas Culpeper and of not disclosing her earlier affair with Francis Dereham. The Howards are sentenced to imprisonment in perpetuity and their possessions confiscated – but are later released. The queen's brother, Charles, is banished from court.

1542: January Agnes, Dowager Duchess of Norfolk, found guilty under Act of Attainder, of misprision of treason and sentenced to life imprisonment, but later released with the other jailed Howards.

1542: 13 February Execution of Queen Catherine Howard by beheading on Tower Green, witnessed by Henry Howard, Earl of Surrey.

1542: July Earl of Surrey imprisoned in the Fleet Prison for challenging John Leigh to a duel but released on 7 August on sureties for good behaviour.

1542: 22 October Third Duke of Norfolk leads English forces in a punitive expedition to lay waste Scottish lands just north of the border.

1542: 24 November English victory over the Scots at Solway Moss.

1543: 12 July Henry VIII marries his sixth and final wife, the twice-widowed Katherine Parr, at Hampton Court.

1543: 4 October Henry Howard, Earl of Surrey, joins the English contingent with Imperial Emperor Charles V's forces besieging Landrecies, which had been captured by the French the previous month.

1544: June Third Duke of Norfolk appointed Captain of the Vanguard of English forces in France. Surrey is also appointed Marshal of the Field and both are sent to capture the French fortress of Montreuil. Surrey is wounded on 19 September during an unsuccessful attempt to breach the town's gates.

1545: late August Henry Howard, Earl of Surrey, appointed Lieutenant of Boulogne and aims to subdue the French fortress of Chatillon.

1546: 7 January Earl of Surrey is defeated at a skirmish with French forces at St Etienne and is replaced as lieutenant general by the Earl of Hertford. He is summoned back to court on 21 March.

1546: June Third Duke of Norfolk proposes a series of marriages between the Seymours and Howards.

1546: 2 December Sir Richard Southwell makes allegations to the Privy Council about a conspiracy involving Henry Howard, Earl of Surrey. Howard is arrested as he finishes dinner at the Palace of Westminster and held at the Lord Chancellor's house at Ely Place, in Holborn, on the outskirts of London.

1546: 12 December Third Duke of Norfolk is summoned to London, is arrested, stripped of his offices and taken to the Tower of London by river. The same day, his son is led on foot through the streets of London to the Tower.

1547: 13 January The Earl of Surrey is found guilty of treason at a commission of oyer and terminer at the Guildhall, London, after a day-long trial, and is beheaded six days later.

1547: 24 January Bill of Attainder for treason passed against third Duke of Norfolk and Earl of Surrey by Parliament.

1547: 28 January Henry VIII dies at 2.00 a.m. in his Palace of Westminster only hours before the third Duke of Norfolk is due to be executed in the Tower. The king's son, Edward, is proclaimed king at the Tower on 31 January.

1547–53 The third Duke remains a prisoner in the Tower.

1553: 6 July Edward VI dies at Greenwich Palace of pulmonary tuberculosis after an attack of measles. Sixteen-year-old Lady Jane Grey proclaimed queen 9 July.

1553: 18 July Mary, Edward's half-sister, proclaims herself queen at Framlingham Castle and marches on London.

1553: 3 August Mary enters London and greets third Duke of Norfolk, and other prisoners, kneeling before her at the Tower of London. They are freed.

1554: 25 January Sir Thomas Wyatt raises his standard at Maidstone, Kent, in a rebellion against Mary's planned marriage with Philip of Spain.

1554: January Third Duke of Norfolk sent in command of a force of royalist troops from London to subdue rebels but they desert, forcing him to flee back to the capital. Wyatt's rebels defeated after a running battle along the Strand and Fleet Street at the gates of the city of London on 7 February. Lady Jane Grey executed on 12 February.

1554: 25 August Third Duke of Norfolk dies at Kenninghall, Norfolk. His grandson, Thomas, becomes fourth Duke of Norfolk.

1557: 28 June Birth at Arundel House, in the Strand, London, of Philip Howard, only child of Thomas Howard, fourth Duke of Norfolk, and his first wife, Mary, second daughter and co-heir of Henry Fitzalan, twelfth Earl of Arundel. He is baptised on 2 July in the Chapel Royal in the Palace of Whitehall. Among his godfathers is Philip of Spain.

1558: 17 November Elizabeth succeeds Mary as Queen of England.

1559: 16 January Mary Queen of Scots (daughter of King James V of Scotland and his second wife, Mary of Guise) and her husband, Francis, the Dauphin of France, assume the style of title 'Francis and Mary, by the Grace of God, of Scotland, England and Ireland, King and Queen' and include the arms of England in their heraldry.

1559: 10 July Mary Queen of Scots' husband becomes Francis II, King of France, but he dies on 5 December 1560.

1563: July Marriage of Charles Howard to Katherine Carey, eldest daughter of Lord Hunsdon, second cousin of Elizabeth I.

1565: 29 July Mary Queen of Scots marries her second husband – Henry Stuart, Lord Darnley, son and heir of the Earl of Lennox. He is proclaimed 'King of Scots'. Her only child James (later James VI of Scotland and, from 1603, James I of England) born in Edinburgh Castle on 19 June 1566. Darnley is murdered on 10 February 1567 and Mary marries James, Earl of Bothwell, according to Protestant rites, on 15 May.

1567: 24 July Mary Queen of Scots is forced to abdicate in favour of her one-year-old son, James, who is crowned James VI at Stirling five days later. Her half-brother, the Earl of Moray, is appointed Regent of Scotland.

1568: 13 May After escape from imprisonment, Mary's forces are defeated at the Battle of Langside, near Glasgow, by an army led by the Earl of Moray. Three days later, she crosses the Solway Firth and enters England as a refugee.

1568: 16 October Scottish Secretary of State William Maitland suggests to Thomas Howard, fourth Duke of Norfolk, that he should marry Mary Queen of Scots.

1569: October Thomas Howard, fourth Duke of Norfolk, is arrested on suspicion of treason and imprisoned in the Tower. Francis Walsingham writes a propaganda pamphlet, attacking any marriage between Norfolk and Mary Queen of Scots.

1569: 14 November The Earls of Northumberland and Westmorland rise in revolt, backed by a 7,500-strong army, with the twin aims of overthrowing Elizabeth I and re-establishing the Catholic religion in England. The rebellion is brutally suppressed, with 750 insurgents executed by royalist forces.

1569 Philip Howard betrothed to Anne Dacre, daughter of Thomas Dacre, fourth Baron Dacre of Glisland, and one of Thomas Howard, fourth Duke of Norfolk's stepchildren by his third marriage in 1567. Philip's marriage was solemnised after September 1571 when he and his wife had reached the age of fourteen, then the age of consent.

1570: 25 February Pope Pius V excommunicates Elizabeth I by the Papal Bull *Regnans in Excelsis*, depriving this 'pretended queen' of her throne and absolving her subjects of any allegiance or loyalty to her.

1570: August Thomas Howard, fourth Duke of Norfolk, is released from the Tower of London but kept under house arrest at his London home in Charterhouse Square. The Florentine banker Roberto Ridolphi visits him within days, asking him to write to the Duke of Alva, the Spanish Captain General in the Low Countries, to solicit funds for the Scottish queen.

1571: 7 September Thomas Howard, fourth Duke of Norfolk, is re-arrested and imprisoned in the Tower.

1572: 16 January Thomas Howard, fourth Duke of Norfolk, is tried by his peers at Westminster Hall on charges of treason.

1572: 2 June Thomas Howard, fourth Duke of Norfolk, beheaded at Tower Hill.

1574–85 Henry Howard, second son of beheaded Earl of Surrey, arrested five times during this period on suspicion of involvement in various conspiracies. The former Spanish ambassador to England, Don Bernardino de Mendoza, paid him an annual salary of 1,000 crowns in 1582–4, to send him 'confidential and minute accounts twice a week' of events at Elizabeth's court.

1580: 24 February Philip Howard becomes the thirteenth Earl of Arundel on the death of his Fitzalan grandfather, but his title is questioned and he is not restored in blood until 15 March 1581. His uncle, John Lumley, Baron Lumley, makes over to him his life interest in the castle and honour of Arundel in Sussex.

1583–4 Philip Howard, Earl of Arundel, is placed under house arrest, on suspicion of harbouring a Catholic priest and involvement in the Throgmorton conspiracy.

1584: 30 September Philip Howard, eldest son of Thomas Howard, fourth Duke of Norfolk, received into the Catholic Church by the fugitive Jesuit priest William Weston at Arundel Castle.

1585: 15 April Arrest of Philip Howard, Earl of Arundel, after he flees England in a ship from Littlehampton and is intercepted at sea. He is committed to the Tower on 25 April.

1585: May Charles Howard appointed Lord High Admiral of England.

1586: 15 May Arraignment of Philip Howard, Earl of Arundel, in the Star Chamber at Westminster on charges that he tried to leave England without royal permission, that he had been converted to the Church of Rome and was also plotting to be restored as Duke of Norfolk. He is fined £10,000 and is imprisoned in the Tower 'during the Queen's pleasure'.

1586: 11 October Elizabeth's commissioners arrive at Fotheringay Castle, Northamptonshire, to try Mary Queen of Scots for high treason. After further hearings in the Star Chamber at Westminster, she is condemned to death on 25 October.

1587: 18 February Mary Queen of Scots is beheaded at Fotheringay Castle.

1587: 15 December Charles Howard appointed to command English naval forces against the expected Spanish invasion of England.

1588: July–August Defeat of the Spanish Armada.

1589: 14 April Trial of Philip Howard, Earl of Arundel, in Westminster Hall, for arranging a Mass in the Tower for the success of the Armada. Attainted and condemned to death for treason. Elizabeth I does not sign his death warrant.

1595: 19 October Death from malnutrition – some claim he was poisoned – of Philip Howard, Earl of Arundel, in the Tower of London and his body buried in the chapel of St Peter ad Vincula in the Tower of London. His remains were reburied in 1624 in the Fitzalan Chapel at Arundel Castle and again in the Catholic cathedral at Arundel in 1971. He was beatified by Pope Pius XI in 1929 and canonised by Paul VI on 25 October 1970.

1597: 22 October Charles Howard created Earl of Nottingham.

1599 Charles Howard appointed Lieutenant General of All England and responsible for England's defences.

1601 Henry Howard, second son of beheaded Earl of Surrey, works with Robert Cecil in secret correspondence with James VI of Scotland to ensure his accession as King of England on Elizabeth's death.

1603: 24 March Death of Elizabeth I at Richmond Palace, probably from bronchopneumonia and septicaemia from tooth decay. James VI of Scotland succeeds unopposed as James I to the English throne.

1604: 6 January Henry Howard appointed Constable of Dover Castle and Lord Warden of the Cinque Ports.

1604: 21 January Thomas Howard, son of the fourth Duke of Norfolk, created first Earl of Suffolk.

1604: 13 March Henry Howard created Baron of Marnhull, Dorset, and Earl of Northampton.

1604: 18 April Thomas Howard, heir of Philip Howard, Earl of

Arundel, restored in blood by Act of Parliament and estates granted him.

1614: 16 June Henry Howard, Earl of Northampton, dies from gangrene of the leg, unmarried, at his house in Charing Cross, London. His will says that he died 'a member of the Catholic and Apostolic church' after being secretly received into the Catholic Church earlier in the year.

1619 Thomas Howard, Earl of Suffolk, dismissed from government office for gross corruption.

1624: 14 December Death of Charles Howard, second Baron Effingham and Earl of Nottingham, at Haling House, Croydon, Surrey.

DRAMATIS PERSONAE

◆

Richard III (1452–85). Youngest son of Richard Plantagenet, Duke of York, killed at the Battle of Wakefield on 30 December 1460. Created Duke of Gloucester at the age of eight. In 1472, he married the Prince of Wales's widow, Anne, younger daughter of Richard Neville, Earl of Warwick, 'the Kingmaker'. Edward IV died on 9 April 1483 and Richard was appointed Lord Protector over the heir to the throne, twelve-year-old Edward V, who, with his younger brother Richard, Duke of York, disappeared mysteriously in the Tower of London. Richard Duke of Gloucester seized power and was crowned on 6 July 1483 in Westminster Abbey. His army was defeated and he was killed at the Battle of Bosworth on 22 August 1485 by invading forces commanded by the Lancastrian pretender, Henry VII. Richard III was the last reigning English monarch to be killed on the battlefield.

Henry VII (1457–1509). Exiled in 1471 after the defeat of the Lancastrian cause in the Wars of the Roses and spent the following fourteen years under the protection of Francis II, Duke of Brittany. He snatched the throne of England after his defeat of Richard III at the Battle of Bosworth, Leicestershire, on 22 August 1485. Crowned as the first of the Tudor monarchs at Westminster on 30 October and married Elizabeth of York, daughter of Edward IV and Elizabeth Woodville, in 1486. They had two sons and two daughters: Arthur, who married Catherine of Aragon on 14 November 1501 but died six months later; Henry VIII; Margaret, who married first James IV of Scotland, then Archibald Douglas, sixth Earl of Angus, and finally Henry Stuart, Lord Methven; Mary, who married firstly Louis XII of France and then Charles Brandon, first Duke of Suffolk.

Henry VIII (1491–1547). Second son of Henry VII and Elizabeth of York. Succeeded to the throne 24 April 1509 and married six times – (1) his elder brother's widow, Catherine of Aragon (1485–1536), on 11

June; one surviving child, Mary Tudor, later Mary I. Marriage annulled by Thomas Cranmer, Archbishop of Canterbury, on 23 May 1533. (2) Anne Boleyn (c. 1501–36), niece of Thomas Howard, third Duke of Norfolk, on 25 January 1533. One surviving child: Elizabeth, later Elizabeth I. Anne Boleyn was executed on 19 May 1536 for incest and adultery. (3) Jane Seymour (?1509–37), daughter of Sir John Seymour of Wolf Hall, Savernake, Wiltshire. Died from puerperal fever and septicaemia following birth of Prince Edward, later Edward VI, at Hampton Court, 24 October 1537. (4) Anne of Cleves (1515–57), at Greenwich Palace, 6 January 1540; the marriage was annulled in July 1540 and she was pensioned off. (5) Catherine Howard, another niece of Thomas Howard, third Duke of Norfolk, on 28 July 1540 at Oatlands, near Weybridge, Surrey. Beheaded on 13 February 1542 for treason – adultery. (6) Katherine Parr (?1512–48). Married on 12 July 1543 at Hampton Court. Following Henry's death on 28 January 1547, she married Thomas Seymour, Lord High Admiral, probably early in June 1547. Died from puerperal fever following the birth of a daughter, 5 September 1548.

Henry Fitzroy, Duke of Richmond (1519–36). Illegitimate son of Henry VIII and Elizabeth Blount, a lady-in-waiting to Catherine of Aragon. Created Duke of Richmond on 18 June 1525. Under care of Thomas Howard, third Duke of Norfolk. Married, on 26 November 1533, Mary Howard, daughter of Norfolk. Died 23 July 1536 of a pulmonary infection at St James's Palace, London. The marriage was never consummated.

Edward VI (1537–53). Legitimate son and heir of Henry VIII and his third wife, Jane Seymour. Proclaimed king 31 January 1547 at the Tower of London. Died of tuberculosis after suffering attack of measles, Greenwich Palace, 6 July 1553.

Mary I (1516–58). Fourth and only surviving child (from at least six pregnancies) of Henry VIII and his first wife, Catherine of Aragon. Proclaimed queen 18 July 1553. Reintroduced Catholicism to England after the Protestant policies of the governments of her half-brother, Edward VI. Married Philip, son of Charles V of Spain, at Winchester, 25 July 1554. Died, childless, from ovarian or stomach cancer, St James's Palace, London, 17 November 1558.

Elizabeth I (1533–1603). Daughter of Henry VIII and his second wife, Anne Boleyn. Succeeded her half-sister Mary I as queen, 17 November 1558. Secured Protestantism as state religion. Died, unmarried, probably from bronchopneumonia and dental sepsis, Richmond Palace, 24 March 1603.

FOREIGN ROYALTY AND THEIR
AMBASSADORS TO ENGLAND
France

Louis XII (1462–1515). Succeeded his cousin Charles VIII in 1498. His first marriage to the pious Joan of France was annulled so that he could marry his predecessor's widow, Anne of Brittany. After her death in 1514, he married Mary Tudor, daughter of Henry VII of England, on 9 October. He died on 1 January 1515, reputedly through overexertion in the marital bed.

Francis I (1494–1547). Crowned at Reims, 1515, as the cousin of his father-in-law, Louis XII. Fought four wars against Charles V of Spain. Died at Château Rambouillet, thirty miles (48 km.) south-west of Paris, and succeeded by his son, Henry II.

Henry II (1519–59). Reigned 1547–59. Married Catherine de Medici (1519–89) on 28 October 1533. Became Dauphin when his elder brother, Francis, died after a game of tennis in 1536. Father-in-law of Mary Queen of Scots. Recaptured Calais from England, 1558. Died, following a jousting tournament to celebrate the marriage of his daughter Elizabeth of Valois to Philip II of Spain, 30 June 1559, in the Place des Vosges, Paris. A splinter from the broken lance of Gabriel de Montgomery, Seignour de Lorges, an officer in his own Scottish Guard, went through his visor, pierced his eye and penetrated his brain.

Francis II (1544–60). Reigned 10 July 1559–5 December 1560. Second son of Henry II. Became King Consort of Scotland after marrying Mary Queen of Scots on 24 April 1558 aged fourteen, in Notre-Dame Cathedral, Paris. Died 5 December 1560 at Orléans after an ear infection caused an abscess on the brain.

Charles IX (1550–74). Reigned 1560–74. Third son of Henry II and

Catherine de Medici. Witnessed the St Bartholomew's Day massacre of Huguenots in Paris on 24 August 1572.

Henry III (1551–89). Reigned 1574–89. Fourth son of Henry II and Catherine de Medici.

French Ambassadors to England

Louis de Perreau, Sieur de Castillon (c. 1487–1553). Ambassador November 1537–December 1538.

Charles de Marillac (c. 1510-60). Ambassador 1538–43. Later Bishop of Vannes (1550); Archbishop of Vienne (1557).

Odet de Selve (c. 1504–63). Ambassador 6 July 1546–50. Later served in Venice and Rome.

Bertrand de Salignac de la Mothe Fénelon (1523–89). Ambassador 1568–75. Returned briefly on a new embassy to London in 1582, but returned to France, via Scotland, the following year.

Michel Castelnau, Seignour de la Mauvissière (c. 1520–89). Ambassador 1575–85.

Claude de l'Aubespine de Châteauneuf. Ambassador from August 1585.

Spain

Charles V (1500–58). King of Spain and Holy Roman Emperor. Nephew of Catherine of Aragon, first wife of Henry VIII. Acceded to Spanish throne 1516. Abdicated in favour of his son, Philip (husband of Mary I of England), 1556. Retreated to monastery of Yuste, dying two years later.

Philip II (1527–98). King of Spain, 1556–98, and King of Portugal (as Philip I), 1580–98. Married four times – (1) on 15 November 1543, to his cousin, Princess Maria of Portugal, who died in 1545, a few days after giving birth to his only son, Don Carlos (1545–68); (2) Mary I, daughter of Henry VIII and Catherine of Aragon and Elizabeth I's half-sister, on 25 July 1559; she died 17 November 1558; (3) Elizabeth of Valois, daughter of Henry II of France, in 1559; she died 3 October 1568; and (4) his niece, Anne, Archduchess of Austria, in 1570. Despatched Spanish Armada against England, 1588.

Spanish Ambassadors to England

Eustace Chapuys (1489–1556). Lawyer, born in Annecy in Savoy. First embassy 1529–38, then served in Antwerp. Second embassy 1540–45. Retired to Leuven in the Low Countries and founded a grammar school.

Francis van der Delft. Ambassador from 1545.

Diego de Guzman de Silva. Canon of Toledo. Ambassador June 1564–68, and afterwards ambassador to Venice, November 1569–October 1577.

Guerau de Spes. Ambassador from September 1568 to December 1571 when he was expelled because of his involvement in the Ridolphi plot.

Bernardino de Mendoza. Ambassador 1578–84 and supporter of Mary Queen of Scots. Implicated in the Throgmorton plot and banished in January 1584. As Spanish ambassador in Paris from November 1584, he was involved in the Babington plot. Born before 1541, the son of the Count of Corunna, he served as a cavalry captain with Spanish forces in the Low Countries. Stricken by blindness in 1590, he died in the convent of San Bernardo of Madrid in 1604.

Scotland

James IV (1473–1513). Married Margaret, daughter of Henry VII of England, 1503. Signed treaty with France 1512 and sent a fleet to help Louis XII against Henry VII. Invaded Northumberland with a large army and captured Norham and other castles. Defeated by Thomas Howard, Earl of Surrey, at Flodden Field on 9 September 1513 and was killed.

James V (1512–42). Son of James IV and Margaret Tudor, succeeded on death of his father at Flodden. Married Madeleine, daughter of Francis I of France, in 1537 and after her death married Mary of Guise in 1538. Succeeded by Mary Queen of Scots, his only legitimate daughter.

Mary Queen of Scots (1542–87). Only daughter of James V of Scotland and Mary of Guise. On 7 August 1548, aged six, Mary sailed for France after being betrothed to Francis, son of Henry II of France and his wife, Catherine de Medici. They married on 24 April 1558 at

Notre-Dame Cathedral, Paris, and after the death of Mary I of England she quartered the arms of England with those of France and assumed the style and titles of the Queen of England. Her husband succeeded to the French throne on the death of his father but reigned only until 5 December 1560, when he died of a brain abscess. She returned to Scotland as queen and, in July 1565, married Henry Stuart, Lord Darnley, elder son of Matthew Stuart, fourth Earl of Lennox, and his wife Margaret Douglas (daughter of Mary Tudor). Darnley was an arrogant squanderer and sought equality with her as King of Scotland. Mary suffered his indiscretions and cruelty and a son, James (later James VI of Scotland and James I of England), was born in June 1566. Darnley became infected with syphilis and was sent, for his health, to a house outside Edinburgh, at Kirk o' Field. Early on 10 February 1567 the house was blown up, and Darnley's body was found outside; he had clearly been strangled before the explosion. Mary then married James Hepburn, fourth Earl of Bothwell, at Holyrood on 15 May 1567 and her forces were defeated by the Scottish Lords at Carberry Hill, near Edinburgh, the following month. She was forced to abdicate and escaped imprisonment in Loch Leven Castle in 1568 but another of her armies was defeated at Langside, near Glasgow, on 13 May that year. She fled to England and endured nineteen years of imprisonment at the hands of Elizabeth I, before being tried for treason in October 1586 and beheaded at Fotheringay Castle, Northamptonshire, on 8 February 1587.

James VI (later James I of England) (1566–1625). Son of Mary Queen of Scots and Henry Stuart, Lord Darnley. Crowned on his mother's abdication in 1567 and, after many years of bitter struggle between Catholic and Protestant factions among the Scottish nobility, assumed full powers. Although he made formal protests and intercessions for his mother, James quickly reconciled himself to her execution. Before the death of Elizabeth I on 24 March 1603, he engaged in secret correspondence with Robert Cecil and Henry Howard, second son of the beheaded Earl of Surrey. Succeeded to the throne of England, 1603.

THE HOWARD FAMILY

John Howard, first [Howard] Duke of Norfolk (c. 1422–85). Son of Sir Robert Howard and Lady Margaret, elder daughter of Thomas

Mowbray, first [Mowbray] Duke of Norfolk. Married Katherine Moleyns in the early 1440s, and son Thomas, born in 1443. Fought in the second Battle of St Albans and Towton in 1461 and created Lord Howard by Edward IV in the late 1460s. Lord Treasurer of the [royal] Household, 1466–74. After death of first wife in 1465, he married Margaret Chedworth in 1467. Commanded the English fleet in a successful action against the Scots in the Firth of Forth in 1482. Supported Richard, Duke of Gloucester, as Lord Protector and was one of the nobles who extracted Richard, Duke of York, from sanctuary in Westminster Abbey in 1483. Within days of the accession of Richard III to the throne was created first [Howard] Duke of Norfolk. Officiated at Richard's coronation on 6 July as Lord High Steward and Earl Marshal and on 25 July appointed Lord High Admiral of England, Ireland and Aquitaine and Steward of the Duchy of Lancaster for life. Killed at Battle of Bosworth, 22 August 1485, and attainted.

Thomas Howard, Earl of Surrey, and later **second Duke of Norfolk** (1443–1524). Married twice – (1) Elizabeth Tylney in 1472, who provided five surviving children, and, after her death in 1497, (2) her cousin, Agnes Tylney, who had six children. Badly wounded at Bosworth in 1485, attainted and imprisoned in the Tower of London. Freed in 1489 and appointed Chief Justice in Eyre, North of Trent, and, the following year, Vice-Warden of the East and Middle Marches on the Scottish borders. Lord High Treasurer of England from 1501 until his resignation in 1522, when he passed the position on to his son and heir, Thomas Howard. Victor of Flodden over the Scots army on 9 September 1513. Created second duke 1 February 1514.

Thomas Howard, Earl of Surrey, and, from 1524, **third Duke of Norfolk** (1473–1554). Eldest son of Thomas Howard, second Duke of Norfolk, and his first wife, Elizabeth Tylney. Married twice – (1) in 1495 to Anne Plantagenet, sister-in-law of Henry VII, and on her death in November 1511, with no surviving children, married (2) Elizabeth Stafford, one of the daughters of Sir Edward Stafford, third Duke of Buckingham. They had three surviving children: Henry, Mary and Thomas. Loyal servant of the crown in a number of military and naval campaigns of varying success and wreaked royal retribution in the north of England in 1537 after the Pilgrimage of Grace.

Arch-conspirator: instrumental in the downfalls of Cardinal Wolsey and Thomas Cromwell. Arrested and attainted for treason in the jockeying for position during Henry VIII's last illness, but saved from execution by the king's death on 27 January 1547. Imprisoned in the Tower until Mary I's entry into London in August 1553. After farcical last military adventure against the Kentish rebels in the Wyatt rebellion in 1554, he retired to Kenninghall, the grand palace he built in the Norfolk countryside, and died there in his bed.

Elizabeth Howard, *née* **Stafford, Duchess of Norfolk** (c. 1497–1558). Estranged wife of Thomas Howard, third Duke of Norfolk. Thrown out of his household in preference to his mistress, Bessie Holland.

Sir Edward Howard (1476–1513). Second son of Thomas Howard, second Duke of Norfolk, and his first wife, Elizabeth Tylney. Appointed a vice-admiral 7 April 1512 and Lord High Admiral on 19 March 1513. Killed on 25 April during a reckless, foolhardy attack on a French galley, leaving two bastard sons.

Lord Edmund Howard (d. March 1539). Third son of Thomas Howard, second Duke of Norfolk, and his first wife, Elizabeth Tylney. Commanded the English right wing at the Battle of Flodden in 1513. Wastrel and frequently heavily in debt. His daughter Catherine, by his second wife, Joyce Culpeper, became Henry VIII's fifth wife before being beheaded.

Thomas Howard (1512–37). Son of Thomas Howard, second Duke of Norfolk, and his second wife, Agnes Tylney. Condemned for treason after marrying Lady Margaret Lennox, daughter of Henry VIII's sister Margaret. Died of a fever in the Tower, 31 October 1537.

Henry Howard, Earl of Surrey (1513–47). Eldest son of Thomas Howard, third Duke of Norfolk, and his second wife, Elizabeth *née* Stafford. Poet and soldier. Married Frances de Vere, daughter of the fifteenth Earl of Oxford, and by her had five children, the last born posthumously. Arrested on trumped-up charges of treason and executed on 19 January 1547.

Mary Howard, Duchess of Richmond (1519–55). Daughter of Thomas Howard, third Duke of Norfolk, and his second wife, Elizabeth *née*

Stafford. Married Henry Fitzroy, Duke of Richmond and illegitimate son of Henry VIII, on 26 November 1533. The marriage was never consummated. After his death on 23 July 1536 she struggled to claim her marriage jointure.

Thomas Howard, fourth Duke of Norfolk (1536–72). Inherited the title from his grandfather, the third duke, on his death in 1554. Married three times – (1) Lady Mary Fitzalan, who died 1557; (2) Margaret Audley, died 1563; and (3) Elizabeth Leyburn, widow of Thomas, Lord Dacre of Glisland, died 1567. Too trusting and naive, he planned to marry Mary Queen of Scots and was executed for treason in 1572.

Henry Howard, Earl of Northampton (1540–1614). Younger son of Henry Howard, Earl of Surrey. Remained a bachelor and became a Catholic convert in 1558 and was in and out of prison at least five times afterwards. Involved in the secret negotiations to make James VI of Scotland king, after the death of Elizabeth. Created Earl of Northampton and a member of the Privy Council on 13 March 1604.

Philip Howard, Earl of Arundel (1557–95). Eldest son of Thomas Howard, fourth Duke of Norfolk. Became a Catholic in 1584. Imprisoned after attempting to escape England in 1585. Fined £10,000 and condemned to perpetual imprisonment on charges that he tried to leave England without permission and that he had been converted to the Church of Rome. Condemned to death for allegedly arranging Mass for the success of the Armada but not executed. Died in the Tower of London.

Charles Howard, second Baron Effingham and Earl of Nottingham (1536–1624). Eldest son of William Howard, first son of Thomas Howard, second Duke of Norfolk, and his second wife, Agnes Tylney. Married Katherine Carey, eldest daughter of Elizabeth's second cousin, Lord Hunsdon, in 1563. Appointed Lord High Admiral of England in May 1585 and a commissioner at the trial of Mary Queen of Scots in October 1586. Led the English fleet that harried the Spanish Armada as it sailed up the English Channel in 1588 and chased the survivors into Scottish waters. Created Earl of Nottingham in 1597 and appointed Lieutenant General of all England in 1599.

THE ROYAL HOUSEHOLD AND TUDOR GOVERNMENT

Charles Brandon, first Duke of Suffolk (?1484–1545). Appointed Warden of the Scottish Marches in 1542. Commanded English army invading France in 1544. Lord Steward of the King's Household, 1541–4. Died at Guildford, Surrey, 22 August 1545. Buried in St George's Chapel, Windsor.

Sir Anthony Browne (d. 1548). Master of the King's Horse, 1539–48.

Sir William Cecil, Baron Burghley (1520–98). Elizabeth's chief minister. Lord High Treasurer of England, 1572–98. Organiser of the queen's domestic and foreign intelligence network.

Thomas Cranmer, Archbishop of Canterbury (1489–1556). Supervised preparation and publication of first Prayer Book, 1548. Burned at the stake in Oxford, 21 March 1556, for repudiating his admissions of the supremacy of the Pope and the truth of Catholic doctrine.

Thomas Cromwell, Earl of Essex (?1485–1540). Legal adviser to Cardinal Wolsey; lawyer and money-lender. Later, Lord Privy Seal and Vice-Regent for religious affairs. Earl of Essex and Lord High Chamberlain of England. Beheaded for treason, 28 July 1540, on Tower Hill.

John Dudley (?1502–53). Created Viscount Lisle, 1542. Served as Lord High Admiral, 1542–7 and 1548–9. Governor of Boulogne, 1544–6. Created Earl of Warwick on Edward VI's succession and appointed Lord High Chamberlain of England, 1551–3. Duke of Northumberland, 1551. Married his son to Lady Jane Grey. Executed for treason – supporting Lady Jane as queen – 22 August 1553 at Tower Hill.

Robert Dudley, Earl of Leicester (?1532–88). Supposed by some to have caused the death of his wife, Amy, in 1560. English Privy Councillor. Queen Elizabeth's favourite and her Master of the Horse. Suggested setting up an association for the protection of the queen's person, 1584; and commanded the English expedition to support Protestant rebels against the Spanish in the Low Countries, 1585, and made absolute governor the following year.

Sir William Fitzwilliam, Earl of Southampton (d. 1542). Lord High Admiral, 1536–40. Later Lord Privy Seal. Died on active service while commanding the vanguard of Norfolk's expedition against Scotland, 1542.

Stephen Gardiner, Bishop of Winchester (c. 1483–1555). Secretary to Wolsey and later to Henry VIII until ?15 April 1534. Later ambassador to France. Imprisoned from 1547 during most of Edward's reign for sedition and failure in religious conformity. Appointed Lord Chancellor by Mary I on her accession in 1553. Died at Palace of Westminster, 13 November 1555.

Sir Christopher Hatton (1540–89). Vice-Chamberlain and later Lord Chancellor of England in Elizabeth I's government.

Sir Thomas More (1478–1535). Helped Henry VIII to write his book on the Seven Sacraments against Martin Luther. Chancellor of the Duchy of Lancaster, 1525. Lord Chancellor after fall of Wolsey. Refused to take Oath of Supremacy. Executed 6 July 1536.

Sir William Paget, later **Lord Paget of Beaudesert** (1505–63). Protégé of Bishop Stephen Gardiner. Appointed Secretary of State 1543 and later was one of Henry's chief advisers. Became an ally of radical reformers just before Henry's death. Imprisoned in 1551 and fined £6,000 for misconduct as Chancellor of the Duchy of Lancaster. Reinstated as a member of the Privy Council in 1553. Signed document transferring crown to Lady Jane Grey after Edward VI's death but was retained by Queen Mary as a Privy Councillor because of his administrative abilities and appointed Lord Privy Seal in 1556. He gave up all public office on Elizabeth's accession in 1558.

Sir William Paulet, Lord St John (?1485–1572). Treasurer of the Household, 1537–9. Lord Steward of the Household, 1545–50. Keeper of the Great Seal under Somerset, 1547. Created Earl of Wiltshire, 1550, and Marquis of Winchester, 1551. Proclaimed Mary queen on 19 July 1553 at Baynard's Castle, London. Appointed Lord Treasurer in 1549–50 and remained so until his death.

John, Lord Russell (?1486–1555). Comptroller of the Household, 1537–9. Lord High Admiral, 1540–42. Lord Privy Seal, 1542, 1547 and 1553. Created Earl of Bedford, 1550.

Sir Ralph Sadler (1507–87). Cromwell's servant and secretary. Made a Gentleman of the Privy Chamber in 1536 and one of the two joint

Principal Secretaries to the king (with Wriothesley) in 1540. He was then knighted and made a member of the Privy Council. Retired from public life during Mary's reign and became jailer to Mary Queen of Scots in 1572 and 1584 after Elizabeth came to the throne.

Sir Edward Seymour (?1506–52). Earl of Hertford, 1537; made Duke of Somerset on Edward's accession. Lieutenant General in the North, 1545. Lieutenant and Captain General of Boulogne, 1546. Lieutenant General of the English army in France, 1546. Lord Treasurer, 1546–7. Lord Great Chamberlain of England, 1546–7. Declared Protector by Privy Council, 31 January 1547. Arrested on charges of conspiracy to murder Warwick, October 1551, and beheaded on Tower Hill on 22 January 1552.

Sir Francis Walsingham (c. 1532–90). Staunchly Protestant diplomat, administrator, and organiser of Elizabeth I's effective network of spies and agents both at home and overseas.

Thomas Wolsey (c. 1473–1530). Cardinal Archbishop of York, Lord Chancellor, Papal Legate and Henry's chief minister 1515–29. Indicted under the Statute of Praemunire, 9 October 1529, and property confiscated. Died 29 November 1530 at Leicester after being arrested for treason.

Sir Thomas Wriothesley (1505–50). Joint Principal Secretary to Henry VIII, 1540. Created Baron Wriothesley, 1544. Lord Chancellor, 1544–7. Created Earl of Southampton, 1547. Deprived of office in 1547, fined £4,000 for acting illegally in his use of the Great Seal and put under house arrest at his London home. Reinstated to Privy Council in 1548. Struck off list of councillors, 1550.

NOTES

Prologue

1 Hall's *Chronicle*, p. 419, and Grafton's *Chronicle*, vol. 2, p. 154. 'Dicken' refers to the king, Richard III.

2 He was born on 28 January 1457 at Pembroke Castle and immediately assumed the title as his father, Edmund Tudor, had died a few months before.

3 Edward IV (1442–83), whose fondness for good food led to obesity, may have contracted a chest infection while fishing on the River Thames. This led to pneumonia, coupled with pleurisy, which was the probable cause of death, rather than the contemporary rumours that he was poisoned. See Clifford Brewer, *The Death of Kings*, London, 2000, pp. 97–8.

4 Both the father and grandfather of Buckingham (1455–83) were killed in the Wars of the Roses, supporting the Lancastrian cause. He was hastily executed for treason at Salisbury, Wiltshire, on Sunday 2 November 1483.

5 Thomas Stanley (?1435–1504) succeeded his father as second Baron Stanley in 1460. He was made Chief Justice of Chester and Flint by Edward IV in 1461. He married Henry Tudor's mother c. 1482 and was arrested at the Council table in Richard's *coup d'état* on 13 June 1483 for supporting Edward's teenage heir Edward V in 1483. Richard later made him a Knight of the Garter and appointed him Constable of England in an attempt to buy his loyalty.

6 Sir George Stanley, Lord Strange of Knockyn (c. 1460–1503), Constable of Knaresborough Castle and later Chief Justice of the Duchy of Lancaster. He died, allegedly as the result of poison, at a banquet at Derby House, off London's St Paul's Wharf, on 5 December 1503.

7 Gairdner, *The Paston Letters*, vol. 3, p. 320.

8 The wedge formation was designed to enable volleys with the maximum of arrows without its flanks being turned by the enemy – always a risk if the archers were deployed in long lines.

9 Sir Henry Percy (c. 1449–89) had been imprisoned in the Fleet Prison and the Tower of London by Edward IV but was restored to his earldom in 1473.

10 Hall, *Chronicle*, p. 420.

11 Dead, putrefying flesh.

12 Hall, *Chronicle*, p. 418, and Grafton, *Chronicle*, vol. 2, p. 151.

13 The site of the Battle of Bosworth has traditionally been thought to be the top of Ambion Hill. However, recent research, based on contemporary sources, has placed it on level ground at Redemore Heath, one mile (1.6 km.) south-west of Ambion Hill. Today's visitor centre is on the summit of the hill. See Brooks, pp. 266–7. For further discussion, see Peter J. Foss, *History of Market Bosworth* (Wymondham, 1983) and his later book, *The Field of Redemore: The Battle of Bosworth 1485* (Leeds, 1990).

14 Bill men were armed with a variety of long pointed, hooked, spiked and bladed staff or hafted weapons, including partisans, glaives, gisarmes, lugged spears and halberds, some of which were probably developed from agricultural tools. They were particularly useful for infantry to attack mounted horsemen, but were equally efficacious in hand-to-hand fighting on foot.

15 Hall's *Chronicle*, p. 418.

16 De Vere (1442–1513) was a distinguished and accomplished soldier. He was imprisoned as a suspected Lancastrian in 1468 and escaped to France after the Battle of Barnet in 1471. He was attainted for treason in 1475 and joined Henry Tudor in Brittany in 1484 and sailed with him from Honfleur.

17 Hall's *Chronicle*, p. 419.

18 Brenan and Statham, vol. 1, fn p. 54.

19 Hutton, *Bosworth Field*, pp. 100–106, and Brenan and Statham, vol. 1, p. 55.

20 Brenan and Statham, vol. 1, pp. 54–5.

21 From Sir John Beaumont's poem *Bosworth Field*, published in 1629.

22 Brenan and Statham, vol. 1, p. 56.

23 Northumberland's position was immediately in front of today's visitor centre on Ambion Hill.

24 Brooks, p. 269.

25 Vergil, p. 224.

26 Hall, *Chronicle*, p. 421.

27 Henry VII eventually arranged for a monument to Richard to be erected after his visit to Leicester in September 1495, paying £10 to James Keyley for carving an alabaster effigy or 'picture' of the dead king (BL Add. MS 7,099, fol. 129). After the Greyfriars surrendered on 10 November 1538 during the dissolution of the monasteries, the tomb was apparently wrecked, and the body removed from what was called 'a cattle trough' although this is likely to have been a re-used

twelfth-century stone coffin. Local tradition holds that Richard's remains were then thrown into the nearby River Soar. While there is no evidence to support this legend, a skeleton was found face up on the bed of the river, near Bow Bridge, in 1862. It was immediately suggested that these were the remains of Richard III, although it was difficult to determine the sex of the skeleton and its age at death may not fit. The skull, showing cranium damage, as if struck by sword blows, was taken into the safe-keeping of the Goddard family at Newton Harcourt, Leicestershire.

28 A bronze-gilt processional cross, bearing Yorkist motifs of incised sun-burst symbols, was found on the Bosworth battlefield site around 1778. It seems probable that it was carried by one of Richard's chaplains and abandoned in panic-stricken flight after the royalist forces were defeated. It is now in the possession of the Society of Antiquaries of London. See David Gaimster, Sarah McCarthy and Bernard Nurse (eds), *Making History: Antiquaries in Britain 1707–2007*, London, 2007, p. 119, where it is illustrated.

29 See Weever, p. 830, where he cites information provided by Francis Thynne, Lancaster Herald.

30 The choice of burial place is interesting; Norfolk's parents were buried in the church near their estates at Stoke-by-Nayland, Suffolk, as was his first wife Katherine (*née* Moleyns). Her monument must have been erected much later, after 1514, as its inscription referred to her as '... sometime wife unto the right high and mighty Prince, Lord John Howard, Duke of Norfolk, and mother unto the right noble puissant Prince Lord Thomas Howard, Duke also of Norfolk'. See Robert Hawes and Robert Loder, *History of Framlingham* (Woodbridge, 1798), p. 66. The first duke married, as his second wife, Margaret Chedworth, widow of John Norris of Bray, Berkshire, who died in 1494.

31 Grafton, *Chronicle*, vol. 2, p. 154.

32 Hall, *Chronicle*, p. 420.

33 Northumberland was assassinated at South Kilvington near Thirsk, Yorkshire, in 1489 in a skirmish with the peasantry who rebelled over his efforts to collect a newly imposed tax, intended to enable Henry VII to intervene on behalf of Brittany against the French crown. He was the only person to die during the commotion.

34 The Bill is contained in BL Add. MS 46,372, fols 1–50, and there is a copy in Arundel Castle Archives, G2/8. See also *Rot. Parl.*, vol. 6, pp. 275–8. It was based on the legal canard that Henry VII's reign began the day before Bosworth was fought. First named in the Bill was Richard of Gloucester himself, followed by Norfolk.

35 See, for example, the award, on 21 September 1485, to John Martindale, king's servant, for 'service done beyond the seas and on this side' of the office of keeper of the park of Kelsale, Suffolk, 'lately held by John, Duke of Norfolk'.

36 The award was made on 29 July 1486. See *Patent Rolls*, vol. 1, p. 121.

37 Campbell, vol. 2, p. 420.

38 See Gairdner, *Paston Letters*, vol. 4, pp. 87–8.

39 Head, *Ebbs and Flows*, p. 18. St Katherine's Dock was built on the site of the hospital in 1825.

40 Tucker, pp. 47–9. Her husband's attainder specified that she 'might freely enjoy ... all her own inheritance'. *Rot. Parl.*, vol. 6, p. 276. See also Howard, *Memorials*, appendix 6.

41 Robinson, p. 1. It is situated off the A47, the main Norwich–King's Lynn road. South of this road, near the appropriately termed Manor Farm, is a partially silted moat, the site of a long-vanished manor house that was the Howards' first home. Their mortuary chapel, dedicated to St Mary and built on the south side of the chancel of All Saints church, fell into disrepair, with the lead stripped off the roof. It was repaired by Thomas Howard, Earl of Arundel, the only son of Sir Philip Howard, in the 1630s. It became decayed again and was said to be the home of paupers in the nineteenth century before it was finally demolished by the architect Sir Gilbert Scott during his restoration of All Saints in 1875–8 and rebuilt by him. (See Pevsner and Wilson, p. 326.) The church still has the magnificent fourteenth-century octagonal font, with foliated panels, given by Sir John Howard II which bears his arms and those of his wife Alice de Boys. Sadly, the medieval cone-shaped cover of painted wood was lost by 1844 but was replaced by another designed by Sir Ninian Comper in 1913. For an illustration of the original, see Weever, op. cit., p. 849, and Robinson, p. 3. A drawing of the stained-glass image of the family's founder, Chief Justice Sir William Howard, once in the east window of the chancel and now lost, is in Arundel Castle Archives, MS 1638. The Howard monuments at East Winch are also all now destroyed. Blomefield, in 1805–10, records the remains of a monument to Sir Robert Howard, died 1388, and his wife Margaret, daughter and co-heir of Robert de Scales, Baron Scales, against the south wall of this chapel. In the early seventeenth century, the epitaph was defaced and 'a great part of the monument itself destroyed many years past' (Blomefield, vol. 9, pp. 152–3).

42 Towton, fought all day in snowstorms, caused official losses totalling 28,000 killed, and has the unenviable distinction of being the bloodiest battle fought on English soil.

43 Gloucester claimed the marriage of Edward IV and Elizabeth Woodville was invalid.

44 Weever, p. 835, and Casady, p. 13. He told the Lieutenant that he 'would not depart thence [until] such time as he that commanded thither should command him out again'.

Chapter 1: Rebuilding the Dynasty

1 Camden, *Remains* ..., p. 354. The quote may be apocryphal, but these words reflect the essence of Howard loyalty to the Tudor crown over several generations.

2 Howard's wife had also produced four other sons and a daughter, all of whom had died young.

3 See *Rot. Parl.*, vol. 6, pp. 410, 426. Casady, p. 14. His petition prayed for the repeal and making void of the act, passed 7 November 1485, against him and his father. The act of 'annullation and restitution' was limited to any 'honour but the Earldom of Surrey or to any other lands than those which the said Earl of Surrey had in right of his wife'.

4 Bacon, p. 68. The Commissions of Oyer and Terminer for the city and county of York were set up on 27 May. See *Patent Rolls*, vol. 1, p. 285.

5 *Patent Rolls*, vol. 1, p. 314.

6 *Patent Rolls*, vol. 1, p. 322.

7 Such as the pardon he granted the yeoman John Harrison, of the quaintly named Middleton-in-the-Mire, Yorkshire, on 11 October 1490, for the death of Thomas Metcalf. Surrey and other king's councillors investigated at the scene and decided that Metcalf had killed himself. See *Patent Rolls*, vol. 1, p. 332.

8 Plumpton Correspondence, pp. 95–7. After executing the leaders, he won a royal pardon for the remaining rioters. During the fighting, he lost a valuable gelding, taken by a soldier commanded by one of his captains, Robert Plumpton. He demanded its immediate return: 'Cousin, I have some proof that your servant Robert Beck has my gelding – one [who] knows him well told it me. I pray you cousin, fail not to send me the gelding.' Ibid., p. 96.

9 The Scots believed Surrey was absent at court in London. Teams of oxen had dragged the famous six-ton (6,040 kg.) cannon Mons Meg from Edinburgh to the village of Ladykirk, across the river from Norham Castle, for the siege, at a speed of three miles (4.83 km.) a day. The twenty-two-inch (56 cm.) calibre gun, which could fire stones weighing 390 lb (180 kg.) up to two miles, had been given to the Scots king James II by Philip the Good, Duke of Burgundy, in 1457. Surrey's arrival, with

about 9,000 men, forced the Scots to break off the siege and retreat. Mons Meg is today preserved in Edinburgh Castle.

10 The present-day Ayton Castle was built in 1851 by James Gillespie Graham, Scotland's leading Gothic revival architect.

11 Pope Alexander VI granted Surrey a dispensation to marry, since his new bride was within the prohibited degrees of marriage and also because the banns were only published once. See Tucker, fn, p. 94.

12 Sheriff Hutton Castle, thirteen miles (22 km.) north of York, is situated on a minor road off the A64. After Bosworth, the castle became the property of Henry VII and, in 1525, Henry VIII granted it to his illegitimate six-year-old son, Henry Fitzroy, Duke of Richmond, who had been appointed Warden-General of the Scottish Marches. The castle became the headquarters of the Council of the North and was repaired by Thomas Howard, third Duke of Norfolk, in 1527 but after the Council's relocation to York in the mid-sixteenth century it fell into decline. It was built in 1379 on the remains of an eleventh-century motte and bailey castle and consisted of a quadrangular curtain wall with four rectangular corner towers and a large gatehouse in the east wall, enclosing an inner courtyard. A middle and outer ward originally existed but these are now covered by the adjacent farm. The domestic ranges have also disappeared. The castle is privately owned and has recently undergone extensive repair.

13 Muriel was sometimes called 'Marcella'.

14 His viscountcy was of the second creation, in 1483.

15 *Close Rolls*, vol. 2, pp. 90–91, 92 and 220. Muriel Howard had a daughter by de Lisle, Elizabeth, who, in March 1504, married a cousin of the king, Henry Courtenay, later Earl of Devonshire, and afterwards Marquis of Exeter. She died c. 1516 without issue. Exeter was beheaded and attainted for treason by Henry VIII in 1539. See Brenan and Statham, fn, p. 89, and *Complete Peerage*, vol. 8, p. 61.

16 The appointment was made on 25 June at Westminster, with effect from 16 June. See *Patent Rolls*, vol. 1, p. 239. He was commissioned to collect the benevolence, or tax, granted the crown by Act of Parliament (11 Henry VII, *cap.* 10), in November 1505.

17 Traditionally, Henry VII's financial policy has been considered miserly, if not rapaciously exploitative of his subjects, but its severity has more recently been questioned. See, for example, G. R. Elton, 'Henry VII: Rapacity or Remorse?', *Historical Journal*, vol. 1 (1988), pp. 21–39.

18 Such as the Annuity to the Earl of Surrey Act (11 Henry VII, *cap.* 41) and Estates of the Earl of Surrey Act (11 Henry VII, *cap.* 40), both in 1495.

19 *Close Rolls*, vol. 2, p. 288. Pevsner and Wilson, p. 78 and p. 451.

20 *DNB2*, vol. 28, p. 421.

21 Margaret was annoyed by the attention lavished on Surrey by her bride-groom. She told her father: 'As for news, I have none to send but that my lord of Surrey is in [such] great favour with the king here that he cannot forebear the company of him no time of the day.' Ellis, *Original Letters*, first series, vol. 1, p. 41.

22 Clifford Brewer, *The Death of Kings* (London, 2000), p. 111.

23 A copy of the formal petition for an Act of Restitution, granted to Thomas Earl of Surrey, is in Arundel Castle Archives, G2/9.

24 *LPFD*, vol. 1, p. 172. The Dukes of Norfolk hold the hereditary title of Earl Marshal to this day.

25 BL Cotton MS Titus B, i, fol. 104B; reprinted in Allen, *Letters of Richard Fox*, p. 54.

26 Hall, *Chronicle*, p. 525. The Howards' ships were the merchantmen *Barbara* and *Mary of Barking*. See Geoffrey Moorhouse, *Great Harry's Navy* (London, 2005), p. 5.

27 An ocean-going sailing ship, with the aftermost mast fore-and-aft rigged and the other masts square-rigged.

28 Grafton, vol. 2, p. 242. See also Stow, *Annals*, p. 489, and Holinshed, vol. 3, p. 811. An early folk ballad records Barton's death at Sir Thomas Howard's hand: '*Lord Howard took a sword in his hand, / And off he smote Sir Andrew's head; / "I must have left England many a day, / If you were alive as you are dead." / He caused his body to be cast, / Over the hatchboard into the sea, / And about his middle, three hundred crowns; / "Where'er you land, this will bury thee."*'

29 Hall, *Chronicle*, p. 525.

30 Allen, *Letters of Richard Fox*, p. 54.

31 A large merchant ship armed for naval operations.

32 Vergil, p. 27, and Stow, p. 490.

33 Allen, *Letters of Richard Fox*, p. 58.

34 'Crayer' – a small trading vessel. Today's naval parlance would call this 'swarm attack', although history demonstrates that the success of such tactics depends on high speed and numbers.

35 Grafton also calls him Sir Alphonse Charant. He was from the *Sanchade Gana*, one of six Spanish ships that had joined Howard's fleet.

36 Short crossbow bolts or arrows.

37 A long edged and hooked weapon, used at sea to repel boarders, and on land, against attacking horsemen. The name 'morris' comes from 'Moorish', supposedly describing the origin of the weapon.

38 BL Cotton MS, Caligula D, vi, fol. 107.

39 A. Spont, 'Letters and Papers Relating to the War with France 1512–3', *Navy Records Society*, vol. 10 (1897), p. 134.

40 Alice was the widow of Sir William Parker and was twelve years older than Howard. In 1514, Surrey confirmed her holding of his manor of Barnshall, in Stoke-by-Nayland, Suffolk, for her life as part of her jointure. See: Arundel Castle MS, G1/5. When Alice made her will in December 1518, she provided money to build a tomb for her husband in Brittany. She died later that month. See *DNB2*, vol. 28, p. 337.

41 Probably the *Jenett of Purwyn* captured earlier from Andrew Barton.

42 Howard's natural sons may be those later mentioned in a licence, dated 2 July 1519, granted to 'Charles Howard, one of the gentlemen of the Privy Chamber and George Howard, one of the King's Surgeons' allowing them to import 1,000 tuns, or large barrels, of Gascon wine into England. See Brenan and Statham, fn p. 94.

43 The Howard Cup is now in the Victoria and Albert Museum in London. A 'grace cup' was traditionally used for communal drinking at the end of a meal, although this magnificent example may only have been for display. It stands 10.7 inches (27.3 cm.) high and is decorated with later, additional silver-gilt mounts, hallmarked for 1526, including Catherine of Aragon's pomegranate badge. The cover is topped by a figure of St George slaying the dragon. At its heart is an elephant ivory cup of twelfth-century date, which was believed by the Howards to be a relic of the martyred Archbishop of Canterbury, St Thomas Becket (1118–70). Catherine later returned the cup to Thomas Howard, third Duke of Norfolk, and it passed down through the Howard family before being given away by the twelfth duke early in the nineteenth century. It was sold at Christie's auctioneers, London, in 1931 and acquired by Lord Wakefield who presented it to the museum. It is illustrated in Richard Marks and Paul Williamson (eds), *Gothic Art for England 1400–1547* (London, 2003), p. 318.

44 An angel was worth 3s 4d, or 40 pence.

45 Brenan and Statham, pp. 93–4.

46 BL Cotton MS Caligula D, vi, fols 106–7. Dated 7 May 1513.

47 BL Cotton MS Caligula D, vi, fol. 104.

48 Plantagenet (?1480–1542) was the bastard son of Edward IV by Elizabeth Lucie. He became deputy of Calais in 1533 but was arrested in 1540, suspected of treason, and, despite being declared innocent, died in the Tower. His de Lisle title was of the fourth creation.

49 Allen, *Letters of Richard Fox*, pp. 64–5.

50 Later, he reorganised the royal dockyard at Deptford on the River

Thames. An agreement between him, as Great Admiral of England, and John Heron, Treasurer of the Chamber, and John Hopton, Comptroller of the King's Ships, dated 9 June 1517, was for the construction of 'pond or afloat dock for certain ships to ride in'. See BL Add. Charters, 6,289. This was planned to accommodate five of the biggest ships in Henry VIII's burgeoning navy.

51 Grafton, *Chronicle*, vol. 2, p. 269.

52 Hall, *Chronicle*, p. 555.

53 Nottinghamshire Archives, DD/P/6/1/31/10.

54 Hall, *Chronicle*, p. 545.

55 Hall, *Chronicle*, p. 557.

56 Hall, *Chronicle*, p. 557.

57 In the sixteenth century, water was rarely drunk because of the known dangers of contamination: dysentery was commonly the scourge of armies. 'Small' or weak ale and wine were drunk instead by the soldiery.

58 Barr, *Flodden*, p. 104.

59 Head, *Ebbs and Flows*, p. 35.

60 Hall, *Chronicle*, p. 560.

61 The English camp at Milfield is six miles (10 km.) from Wooler on the A697 road to Coldstream.

62 Barr, *Flodden*, pp. 133–8.

63 Grafton, *Chronicle*, vol. 2, p. 275.

64 Laing, *Flodden*, p. 150.

65 Barr, *Flodden*, pp. 167–8.

66 Brooks, *Battlefields*, p. 287. The bagpipe lament 'Flowers of the Forest', written c. 1750, to commemorate the Scottish dead at Flodden, is still played at military funerals.

67 Hall, *Chronicle*, p. 564.

68 They are now held by the College of Arms in London, although some doubt has been raised about their authenticity.

69 James's head was later buried in St Michael's church, Wood Street, London. The antiquary John Stow reported later in the sixteenth century that, after the dissolution of the Carthusian house, the king's body, still wrapped in lead, was thrown into a lumber room 'amongst the old timber and rubble. Since [such] time, workmen there, for their foolish pleasure, hewed off his head. Lancelot Young [Master Glazier to Elizabeth I] feeling a sweet savour to come from thence and seeing the same dried from all moisture, and yet the form remaining with the hair of the head and [red] beard, brought it to London to his house in Wood Street, where for a time he kept it for the sweetness. In the end [he] caused the sexton of that church to bury it amongst other bones, taken out of their

charnel house.' John Stow, *Survey of London* (two vols, Oxford, 1908), vol. 1, p. 298.

70 Margaret, Henry's sister, and wife to James IV, had given birth to a son, seventeen months before. The infant was crowned James V of Scotland on 21 September 1513 at Stirling Castle.

71 BL Cotton MS Vespasian F, iii, fol. 15. This detailed French aid to Scotland: 25,000 gold crowns, forty cartloads of gunpowder, 400 hand-guns and 6,000 spears, the same number of maces and the tactical assistance of French military advisers, led by a knight called d'Aussy. The same day Catherine wrote to Wolsey, 'a post has come with news from Lord Howard which she has sent the king'. She repeated: 'I think it is God's doing that his subjects should gain such a victory in his absence.' See BL Cotton MS, Caligula, B, vi, fol. 35.

72 BL Egerton MS 2,014, fol. 2. Reprinted in part, Byrne, *Letters, Henry VIII*, pp. 20–21.

73 BL Cotton MS Vitellius, B, ii, fol. 50.

74 The ceremony of Howard's creation as [second] Duke of Norfolk is in BL Egerton MS 985, fol. 59.

75 Copies of the Letters Patent creating Thomas Howard [second] Duke of Norfolk for his services to the crown in Scotland and granting the augmentation of arms, is in Arundel Castle archives, G1/83.

76 Head, *Ebb and Flows*, p. 41.

77 Ellis, *Original Letters*, first series, vol. 1, pp. 116–17.

Chapter 2: Guardians of England

1 Vergil, *Anglica Historia*, p. 6.

2 The blue-grey stock dove, *Columba oenas*, is similar to a pigeon.

3 See John Holmes, 'A Catalogue of French Ambassadors in England', *Gentleman's Magazine*, vol. 169 (1840), p. 484. Two letters from de la Guiche are in BL, Cotton MS Caligula E i, fol. 59 and Caligula E ii, fol. 116.

4 From the Old English *cnafa*, originally a term for a male servant but by the early sixteenth century the word had become a taunt, meaning a deceitful and unreliable scoundrel.

5 He sold second-hand clothes.

6 Formerly called the 'Priory of the Blessed Virgin without Bishopsgate'. The area of Spitalfields in London's East End is a corruption of 'hospital'. For more information on the priory, see: *Survey of London*, vol. 27, *Spitalfields and Mile End* (London, 1957), p. 22. The hospital had 180 beds for the poor. Twenty years later the priory church was in decay and the roof fell in during August 1538. (See a letter from the Lord Mayor

of London, Sir Richard Gresham, to Thomas Cromwell, in National Archives SP1/135/7.) The priory was dissolved in 1539.

7 Walter Thornbury, *Old and New London*, vol. 2, p. 149 (London, 1878). The house and the preaching cross can be seen on a copperplate map of London, engraved c. 1553–9, the relevant section of which is illustrated in Adrian Prockter and Robert Taylor, *A–Z of Elizabethan London* (London, 1979), p. 30.

8 Grafton, *Chronicle*, vol. 2, p. 290.

9 Or 'Fight for your neighbourhood'.

10 Grafton, *Chronicle*, vol. 2, p. 291.

11 For a description on how 'Bucklers' was played, see Sally Wilkins, *Sport and Games of Medieval Cultures* (Westport, 2002), p. 131.

12 Grafton, *Chronicle*, vol. 2, p. 292.

13 Vergil, p. 245.

14 Wriothesley, vol. 1, p. 11. These trials – from the French *Oyer et Terminer*, 'to hear and determine' – were presided over by justices commissioned by the crown.

15 Grafton, *Chronicle*, vol. 2, p. 293.

16 Then called 'Gracious Street'.

17 Grafton, *Chronicle*, vol. 2, p. 293.

18 Ibid.

19 Holinshed, *Chronicles*, vol. 3, p. 624.

20 Ibid., p. 625.

21 Grafton, *Chronicle*, vol. 2, p. 294. A large number of interlopers had appeared among the rioter prisoners, a group later called 'the black wagon'. Holinshed, *Chronicles*, vol. 3, p. 625, reported that 'Diverse offenders that were not taken, hearing that the king was inclined to mercy, came well [dressed] to Westminster and suddenly stripped them-[selves to] their shirts, with halters, and came in among the prisoners willingly to be partakers of the king's pardon. One John Gelson, yeoman of the crown, was the first that began to spoil [loot] and exhorted others to do the same. Because he fled and was not taken, he came in with a rope among the other prisoners and so had his pardon.'

22 She had been promised by her father to Philip, the son of Maximilian, Archduke of Austria, under a treaty of 5 August 1480.

23 This included an allowance of twenty shillings a week for food and drink and the wages of a household of two women, a young maid, a gentleman, a yeoman and three grooms. She was also allowed £15 11s 8d a year for the upkeep of seven horses.

24 Bapst, p. 153, confirms that three children were born to Howard and his first wife and names the first two as Lady Muriel and Lady Catherine

but does not provide any authority for this statement. Robinson, p. 25, says she had four sons who all died in infancy. They were buried in the Howard chapel of St Mary's church, Lambeth.

25 *Complete Peerage*, vol. 12, p. 554.

26 Monetary calculations have been derived from a model available on the Internet. See: Lawrence H. Officer's 'Comparing the Purchasing Power of British Pounds from 1264 to 2006 ...' URL: *http://www.measuringworth.com*. A jointure is the property and income settled on a wife to support her if she outlives her husband.

27 *Lords Journal*, vol. 1, pp. 18–23.

28 Pollard, *Wolsey*, p. 76.

29 Vergil, p. 285.

30 Pollard, *Wolsey*, p. 107, and Vergil, pp. 262–5.

31 Vergil, pp. 262ff. An angry Wolsey swore that Buckingham would 'sit upon [his] skirts' for this insult, and the next day Buckingham appeared at court, insolently wearing a short coat and explained to the king that this simple stratagem would foil Wolsey's plans for revenge against him.

32 Starkey, *Personalities* ..., p. 65.

33 He claimed descent from Thomas of Woodstock (1355–97), seventh and youngest son of King Edward III, Earl of Buckingham and Duke of Gloucester.

34 The roll file of the court of the Lord High Steward is in the National Archives, KB/8/5.

35 *LPFD*, vol. 3, pt i, pp. cxxxi–iii.

36 Gilbert's confession is in BL Harleian MS 283, fol. 70. It includes the allegation that Buckingham wished that God 'would not suffer the king's issue to prosper as appears by the [death o]f his son and that his daughters prosper not and that the king's [grace] has no issue male ...'

37 The chaplain, Delacourt and Knyvett were jealous of the favour shown to Hopkins in Buckingham's household. Henry Corsley, the prior of the Carthusian house, wrote a letter, signed by all eight of his community, protesting their innocence of any involvement in the prophecies and urging that Hopkins should be sent to some other Carthusian house for appropriate punishment. In the event, Hopkins is believed to have died in the Tower, broken-hearted at the fate of his patron. See *VCH: Somerset*, vol. 2 (ed. William Page), (London, 1911), pp. 118–23.

38 BL Stowe MS 164, fol. 3.

39 Hall, *Chronicle*, p. 624, and *LPFD*, vol. 3, pt i, p. cxxxiv.

40 14/15 Henry VIII, *cap.* 20. The Act talks of Buckingham's 'many treasons in the counties of Gloucester, Somerset, the City of London, the coun-

ties of Kent and Surrey . . .' A late sixteenth-century copy of the attainder is in National Archives, SP 30/28/209.

41 The countess later told Thomas Cromwell she provided Norfolk with five children.

42 While in Ireland, eighteen of his bored soldiers planned to steal a ship and engage in a little lucrative piracy in the Irish Sea. Surrey was disappointed to discover that legally he could not hang them. 'If I shall make a proclamation, upon pain of death, as it shall be needful many times to do, I have no authority to put any of them to death that shall break the same,' he complained. Eventually, this authority was granted to him but those of noble rank escaped capital punishment. See *State Papers*, vol. 2, pp. 42–5.

43 For example, between April 1523 and January 1524, he spent only twenty-three days at home. See Childs, p. 27.

44 Skelton was born c. 1460 and died on 21 June 1529 and was buried in the parish church of St Margaret's Westminster, alongside the Abbey. He was tutor to Prince Henry when he was Duke of York and later rector of Diss in Norfolk, when he enjoyed the patronage of the Norfolks, particularly that of Agnes, second wife of the second Duke of Norfolk and the countess's mother-in-law. The *Garland* poem is more than 1,600 lines long. He also wrote a poem praising the Earl of Surrey after his military raid on northern France at the end of 1522. See Greg Walker, *John Skelton and the Politics of the 1920s* (Cambridge, 1988), p. 26.

45 Surrey was rarely a happy general. At this time he wrote of being 'decayed in body as well as being worn out in purse by these four years' of continuous military service.

46 His attacks on Wolsey are contained in his somewhat sarcastic poems *Speak Parrot* (c. 1521), *Colin Clout* (1521–2) and *Why Come ye not to Court?* (1522). See H. L. P. Edwards, *Skelton: The Life and Times of an Early Tudor Poet* (London, 1949), pp. 204–8, and Melvin Tucker, 'The More–Howard Connections of John Skelton', *Moreana*, vol. 37 (1973), pp. 19–21.

47 See Walker, *John Skelton and the Politics of the 1920s* (Cambridge, 1988), pp. 29–30.

48 She would have been about twenty-six when the poem was written. She died on 18 September 1534.

49 The few remains of Bourchier's monumental brass – an inscription in Latin, six decorative elbow-cops with Bourchier knots, and four shields – are in St Edmund's chapel in Westminster Abbey. He was chief carver ('*cironomon mense*') to Elizabeth, the queen of Edward IV. The effigy, once depicted in armour, was stolen from his Purbeck tomb, probably

during the Edwardian reformation in the mid-sixteenth century.

50 See *Gentleman's Magazine*, new series, vol. 23 (1845), p. 261. Muriel is sometimes recorded as a sister to Surrey, but she died in 1513 at Lambeth and was buried at Greenwich.

51 The average male life expectancy during this period was around forty years.

52 Brenan and Statham, vol. 1, p. 109.

53 Tucker, p. 141.

54 Arundel Castle Archives, G1/4, and Tucker, pp. 141–2.

55 National Archives, PCC, PROB/11/21. A certified copy is in Arundel Castle Archives, T1.

56 Martin, *History of Thetford*, Appendix VIII, p. 38.

57 Hearses in the sixteenth century were not the modern-day funeral vehicles but temporary structures beneath which the coffin rested while Masses were said for the soul of the departed.

58 A Middle English term for a pack animal, from the Old French *sometier*.

59 Carlisle Herald was one of the earliest titles for an English herald, mentioned in Edward III's expedition to Scotland in 1327. See Wagner, p. 20 and p. 177.

60 Robinson, p. 22, and Clare Gittings, *Death, Burial and the Individual in Early Medieval England* (London, 1988), p. 177.

61 Martin, pp. 122–3, and Tucker, p. 142.

62 A monumental brass to the second duke, showing him full-face in armour and Garter robes, with four shields, was laid over the grave. It is drawn by Lilley and is in Arundel Castle MS 1638 and is illustrated by Robinson, p. 14. It is now lost. Another drawing is in BL Add. MS 45,131, fol. 85.

Chapter 3: The King's 'Great Matter'

1 Singer, pp. 68–9, and Routh, p. 205.

2 The indictment alleged that Wolsey 'being not ignorant of the premises, had obtained certain Bulls from Clement VII by which he exercised jurisdiction and authority legatine to the deprivation of the king's power established in his courts of justice'. Specifically, 'he had given away the Church of Stoke-[next]-Guildford [Surrey] to one James Gorton ... to the contempt of the king and his crown ... and had caused the last wills and testaments of many ... to be exhibited and proved in his court and their goods and chattels to be administered by such as he appointed'. Wolsey also 'made diverse visitations out of his dioceses and drawn diverse pensions from abbeys to the contempt of the king and his laws'. The court sentenced him as 'he was out of the king's protection, and his

lands, goods and chattels forfeit and that his person might be seized upon'. See Cobbett, vol. 1, pp. 370–71.

3 Catherine had at least six pregnancies over the nine years 1509–18. A daughter was still-born on 31 January 1510; Henry, Prince of Wales, who lived just fifty-two days; another son, also called Henry, who lived for just a few hours after being born in November 1513; Mary, born in 1516; a still-born boy in the autumn of 1517; and a daughter also born dead, on 10 November 1518.

4 The child was also said to have been born in a building on the north side of the churchyard, formerly called 'Jericho' – a cover name for a 'house of pleasure' owned and allegedly utilised by Henry VIII. See the Revd Alfred Suckling's *Antiquities and Architecture ... of the County of Essex* (London, 1845), p. 27. He adds: 'It is a very remarkable situation to have chosen for the purposes of debauchery as it not only abuts upon the churchyard but is actually within a stone's [throw] of the residence of the monks.'

5 See Garrett Mattingly's *Catherine of Aragon* (London, 1950), p. 173, and Scarisbrick, p. 152.

6 In 1533, Sir George Throgmorton (or Throckmorton) had a painful conversation with Henry, with Cromwell standing by. He related how he told the king, 'I feared if you did marry Queen Anne [Boleyn] you [would] have meddled both with the mother [Lady Elizabeth Boleyn] and the sister [Mary Boleyn]. And his grace said "Never with the mother." And [Cromwell] ... said: "Nor with the sister either – and therefore put that out of your mind."' See *LPFD*, vol. 12, pt ii, pp. 332–3. Mary Boleyn had married William Carey (c. 1500–28), a Gentleman of Henry's Privy Chamber, on 4 February 1520. He was the happy recipient of a number of royal grants of property from 1522, doubtless in return for his acquiescence in the affair.

7 Cavendish, p. 389.

8 There is probably no truth in the story that she had a stunted sixth finger on one hand. See N. Sanders, *Rise and Growth of the Anglican Schism* (London, 1877), p. 25.

9 The castle, complete with battlements, was made of wood, covered with green canvas. From each end tower hung a banner emblazoned with 'lovelorn hearts'. The entertainment was probably organised by William Cornish, Master of the children of the Chapel Royal, who died the following year. See Anglo, pp. 120–21.

10 *LPFD*, vol. 4, pt ii, p. 1504.

11 *State Papers*, vol. 1, p. 278.

12 Wilson, p. 245.

13 Crapelet, pp. 102–5.

14 Crapelet, pp. 124–5.

15 *LPFD*, vol. 4, pt ii, p. 1507.

16 *LPFD*, p. 2003.

17 Scarisbrick, p. 160. Did Wolsey try bribery to stave off disaster? On 4 October 1529, William Capon, Dean of one of the Cardinal's new colleges, at Ipswich, leased the Benedictine priory at Felixstowe to Norfolk and others at a rent of £20 a year. See National Archives, E 24/23/27.

18 National Archives E 30/1456. Depositions taken at Stansted and Thetford, 16 July 1528.

19 Scarisbrick, p. 247.

20 Years later, Chapuys was described by Sir William Paget, then one of Henry's secretaries of state, as 'a great practicer, with which honest term we cover tale-telling, lying, dissimulating and flattering'. See *State Papers*, vol. 10, p. 466.

21 Scarisbrick, p. 233.

22 BL Cotton MS Vitellius B, xii, fol. 171, and *State Papers*, vol. 1, pp. 343–4.

23 Cavendish, pp. 92–100ff.

24 *LPFD*, vol. 4, pt iii, p. 2675.

25 Froude, p. 121.

26 *LPFD*, vol. 4, pt iii, p. 2681.

27 *LPFD*, vol. 4, pt iii, p. 2679.

28 Singer, p. 39.

29 *LPFD*, vol. 4, pt iii, p. 2681; Chapuys to Charles V, 25 October 1529.

30 Singer, pp. 68–9.

31 BL Cotton MS Cleopatra E, iv, fol. 178, and Merriman, vol. 1, pp. 67–8.

32 'The same lord Cardinal, knowing himself to have the foul and contagious disease of the great pox, broken out upon in diverse places of his body, came daily to your grace [Henry, whispering] in your ear and blowing upon your most noble grace with his most perilous and infective breath to the marvellous danger of your highness.' See MacNalty, p. 161.

33 Hutchinson, *Thomas Cromwell*, p. 35, and Merriman, vol. 1, p. 69.

34 Oedema, once known as dropsy, is a swelling of an organ or tissue through the accumulation of fluid, sometimes caused by heart or kidney disease.

35 *CDP Spanish*, vol. 4, pt i, pp. 449–50.

36 Cawood was a manor of the Archbishopric of York.

37 The *pallium*, a mantle, normally richly embroidered with three bands in the shape of the letter 'Y'.

38 Vergil, p. 333.

39 Merriman, vol. 1, p. 327. Cromwell to Wolsey, 17 May 1530.

40 *LPFD*, vol. 4, pt iii, p. 3013.

41 Pollard, *Wolsey*, p. 288.

42 See *London Topographical Record*, vol. 10 (1916), pp. 77–8. The house, opposite the parish church of St Mary Somerset, had originally been built in the thirteenth century by the Bigod family and was held by the dukes of Norfolk until the third duke sold the property to the Lord Mayor, Sir Richard Gresham. In 1542, John Cooke bequeathed 'the Duke of Norfolk's place' to the Corporation of London. It was purchased in 1583 by Thomas Sutton, later founder of the Charterhouse charity.

43 For more on Dr Augustine and his role in Tudor espionage, see Hammond, p. 223, and pp. 225ff.

44 *LPFD*, vol. 4, pt iii, p. 3035.

45 Wriothesley, vol. 1, p. 16. Wolsey's body was placed in a wooden coffin, dressed in fine vestments, a mitre on his head and a crosier across his chest. The lid was left off and the mayor of Leicester was summoned to view the corpse 'to avoid false rumours that might happen to say that he was not dead, but still living'. He was buried in the Lady Chapel of the abbey at 4.00 a.m. the next morning amid a terrifying loud and violent thunderstorm. See Cavendish, p. 395.

46 *LPFD*, vol. 4, pt iii, p. 3057.

47 *CDP Spanish*, vol. 4, pt ii, p. 263.

48 *CDP Spanish*, vol. 4, pt i, p. 630.

49 *CDP Spanish*, vol. 4, pt i, p. 734.

50 For details of the laws providing the foundation of the break with Rome, see Hutchinson, *Thomas Cromwell*, pp. 49–51 and 53–5.

51 *State Papers*, vol. 1, pp. 392–3.

52 Ellis, *Original Letters*, third series, vol. 2, p. 276.

53 *CSP Milan*, p. 557.

54 She was led from Westminster Hall to the Abbey by a procession of monks wearing golden copes; thirteen mitred abbots, followed by the choristers of the King's Chapel Royal with two archbishops, four bishops and the lords wearing their ermined Parliament robes. Suffolk carried her crown and two earls her sceptres. The new queen walked under a rich canopy of cloth of gold, wearing a dress of crimson velvet powdered with ermine fur, beneath a purple robe, and the Dowager Duchess of Norfolk carrying her train. Afterwards there was a grand dinner in Westminster Hall, eating 'delicate meats' off gilt plates. See Wriothesley, vol. 1, pp. 19–22, and BL Egerton MS 985, fol. 48.

55 Suffolk was granted the far lesser office of wardenship of the forests south

of the River Trent in recompense. At least Suffolk had the satisfaction of presiding over the coronation as Lord High Steward.

56 *LPFD*, vol. 6, pp. 357 and 682.

57 Byrne, *Lisle Letters*, vol. 1, p. 552. The cost of Norfolk's frenetic journey was £333 6s 8d.

58 Embarrassingly, a surviving pre-written circular letter, addressed from the queen to Lord Cobham, her chamberlain, had originally announced the birth of a prince. The letter 'S' had to be squeezed in and added to the word to correctly report the sex of the child. See BL Harleian MS 283, fol. 75.

59 The other godmother was Margaret, Marchioness of Dorset. Gertrude Courtenay, Marchioness of Exeter, was her godmother at her confirmation that immediately followed. The next morning there were celebratory fires lit in the streets of London and free wine offered up at the bonfires.

60 Hall, *Chronicle*, p. 806.

61 A letter from Sir Thomas Vaux to Norfolk, on 18 April 1533, reported Catherine's vehement protests about relinquishing the title of queen. See BL Cotton MS Otho, C, x, fol. 177.

62 *CDP Spanish*, vol. 5, pt ii, pp. 60–69.

63 Elton, *Policy and Police*, p. 278.

64 National Archives, SP 1/82/151.

65 26 Henry VIII, *cap.* 1.

66 Misprision – the crime of deliberately concealing knowledge of a treasonable act, from the Anglo-Norman *mesprisioun*.

67 26 Henry VIII, *cap.* 22. See Tanner, p. 383. A 'schismatic' is someone guilty of splitting a Church in two, from the old French *scismatique*.

68 BL Arundel MS 152, fol. 294.

69 *LPFD*, vol. 8, p. 385.

70 *LPFD*, vol. 8, p. 1. Another translation is 'the big fuck', which is probably more accurate, given Norfolk's sometimes coarse speech.

71 *LFPD*, vol. 9, p. 335.

72 Stafford (?1512–56) was a distant relative of the third Duke of Buckingham.

73 *LPFD*, vol. 8, p. 251.

74 *LPFD*, vol. 9, p. 293.

75 *LPFD*, vol. 8, p. 169.

76 Froude, p. 296.

77 Before she died, Catherine wrote a typically pious last letter to Henry: 'The hour of my death now approaches and at this moment my love for you compels me to remind you a little of the salvation of your soul. This

last, you should put before all mortal considerations, abandoning ... all those concerns of the flesh on account of which you have plunged me into manifold miseries and yourself into more anxieties. Yet this, I forgive you and I both hope, and with holy prayers implore, that God will forgive you. I commend the daughter of our marriage to your care whom, I beseech you to behave towards her entirely in that fatherly fashion which I have on other occasions desired of you.' Henry's reaction is unrecorded. Vergil, p. 335.

78 *LPFD*, vol. 10, p. 51.

79 *LPFD*, vol. 10, p. 71.

80 Wriothesley, vol. 1, p. 33, said 'she took such a fright ... that it caused her to travail [labour] and so was delivered afore her full time which was a great discomfort to all this realm'. The Papal Nuncio in Paris, Ridolfo, Bishop of Faenza, doubted she was pregnant at all. He told the Papal Secretary Ambrogio in March 'that woman pretended to have miscarried of a son, not being really with child, and to keep up the deceit, would allow no one to attend her but her sister, whom the French king here in France [knew] as one of the greatest and most infamous lewd women'. See BL Add. MS 8,715, fol. 220B. In this the bishop was at least partially misinformed – Mary, of course, had already been banished from court.

81 *CDP Spanish*, vol. 5, pt ii, p. 28.

82 Ellis, *Original Letters*, first series, vol. 2, pp. 59–60, and Strype, *Ecclesiastic Memorials*, vol. 1, i, p. 434.

83 Wriothesley, vol. 1, p. 38.

84 A copy of the dispensation to marry is in Arundel Castle Archives, G1/5.

Chapter 4: A Woman Scorned

1 BL Cotton MS Titus B, i, fol. 383.

2 *Gentleman's Magazine*, new series, vol. 23 (1845), p. 262.

3 *State Papers*, vol. 2, pp. 38–9.

4 National Archives, SP 60/1/65. In September 1534, when the prospect of having again to serve in Dublin was raised (but not fulfilled), Norfolk told Cromwell, 'If the king really wishes to send me to Ireland he must first construct a bridge over the sea for me to return freely to England, whenever I like.' See *CDP Spanish*, vol. 5, pt i, p. 254.

5 The Letters Patent creating him Lieutenant General of the English army in Scotland, dated 26 February 1523, are in Arundel Castle Archives, G1/84.

6 Arundel Castle Archives, A113.

7 See Harris, *English Aristocratic Women* ... , pp. 18–19.

8 Corrie, Revd George (ed.), *Sermons of Hugh Latimer* (Parker Society,

Cambridge, 1844), p. 253. Latimer (?1485–1555) faced a number of charges of heresy during his career, before resigning his bishopric in protest at the Act of the Six Articles in 1539. He was committed to the Tower on the accession of the Catholic Mary I in 1553 and burned with another Protestant martyr, Bishop Nicholas Ridley, at Oxford on 16 October 1555.

9 BL Cotton MS Titus B, i, fol. 383. Letter to Thomas Cromwell, 26 June 1536. Holland had apartments in Norfolk's grand mansion at Kenninghall, Norfolk, and, despite Elizabeth's claims, was probably born of gentle blood.

10 Harris, *English Aristocratic Women . . .*, pp. 86–7.

11 Arundel Castle Archives, G1/5. A seventeenth-century copy of the original, now apparently lost.

12 *CDP Spanish*, vol. 4, pt i, p. 509, and pt ii, pp. 629, 720.

13 *LPFD*, vol. 4, pt iii, p. 3035.

14 Byrne, *Lisle Letters*, vol. 1, fn, p. 350.

15 Harris, 'Marriage', p. 375.

16 National Archives, SP 1/76/38.

17 National Archives, SP 1/76/39.

18 BL Cotton MS Vespasian F, xiii, fol. 79. Cromwell also received letters from Elizabeth, the estranged third wife of Sir Walter Hungerford. In 1536, she sought his protection from her husband, claiming she had been imprisoned in his house at Farleigh, Somerset, for four years and that he had tried to poison her.

19 BL Cotton MS Titus B, i, fols 383, 391–2.

20 BL Cotton MS Titus B, i, fol. 84.

21 Harris, 'Marriage', p. 375.

22 BL Cotton MS Titus B, i, fol. 383.

23 BL Cotton MS Titus B, i, fol. 383.

24 BL Cotton MS Titus B, i, fol. 386.

25 Robinson, p. 25.

26 BL Cotton MS Titus B, i, fol. 84.

27 BL Cotton MS Titus B, i, fol. 125.

28 BL Cotton MS Titus B, i, fol. 390. See also *LPFD*, vol. 12, pt ii, pp. 341–2.

29 BL Cotton MS Titus B, i, fol. 389.

30 *LPFD*, vol. 12, pt i, p. 119.

31 National Archives, SP 1/144/16.

32 BL Cotton MS Vespasian F, xiii, fol. 75.

33 National Archives, SP 1/114/56.

34 Harris, *English Aristocratic Women. . .*, pp. 179–80.

35 National Archives, SP 1/158/249.

36 BL Cotton MS Titus B, i, fol. 152, and see Wood, *Letters*, vol. 3, p. 190.

Chapter 5: 'Dreadful Execution'

1 *LPFD*, vol. 11, p. 347.

2 The dispensation is printed in full by Nott, p. xxviii. For the location of the wedding, see Brenan and Statham, p. 172.

3 Lord Thomas Howard (1512–37) was the second son of Thomas, second Duke of Norfolk, and his second wife, Agnes. The antiquary John Leland was probably one of his childhood tutors. Howard arrived at court in 1533 for the marriage of his niece Anne Boleyn to Henry.

4 First Act of Succession, 1534, 26 Henry VIII, *cap.* 13.

5 Second Act of Succession, 1536, 27 Henry VIII, *cap.* 7.

6 28 Henry VIII, *cap.* 18. See Head, 'Attainder of Lord Thomas Howard', pp. 3–16. The references to 'succession' come from section nine of the Second Act of Suppression.

7 *LPFD*, vol. 11, p. 64.

8 BL Add. MS 17,492. The volume, in its original stamped leather covers, also includes verse penned by other contemporary poets, including Henry Howard, Earl of Surrey, and Sir Thomas Wyatt.

9 BL Cotton MS Vespasian F, xiii, fol. 134B. Her household was now modest: she had only one gentleman and a groom that looked after her clothes, 'another that keeps her chamber and a chaplain that was with her in the court'.

10 Byrne, *Lisle Letters*, vol. 3, p. 458.

11 Wriothesley, vol. 1, p. 53. This seems unlikely and is probably a product of the paranoia of the period. Fitzroy had attended Anne Boleyn's execution more than six weeks before. If he had been poisoned, as part of a wider Boleyn plot against the king and his heirs (so that Anne could marry one of her alleged accomplices), it must have been a very slow-acting poison.

12 For information about Gostwick's career, see Elton, *Revolution*, pp. 192–3 and fns. Gostwick, later knighted, left detailed advice on how to run an estate to his son and heir, discussed in A. G. Dickens's 'Estate and Household Management in Bedfordshire, *c.* 1540', in *Bedfordshire Historical Record Society*, vol. 36 (1956), pp. 38–45. It is reprinted by Williams in *Historical Documents*, pp. 910–12. He later became Treasurer of Tenths and First Fruits.

13 Remarkably bad or shocking, in the mid-sixteenth-century sense.

14 Sadler (1507–87) was in Cromwell's service before becoming a gentleman of the Privy Chamber around 1536 and was appointed one of Henry's secretaries the following year. He was knighted in 1542.

15 *LPFD*, vol. II, p. 76. Gostwick asked Cromwell if he could purchase 'a little mule of the Duke of Richmond, now in my custody'.

16 *LPFD*, vol. II, p. 97.

17 Surrey rode Richmond's own horse, which together with its saddle, had been sent to him.

18 Cited by Childs, p. 122.

19 Sir Thomas Boleyn handed over the King's Privy Seal on Sunday 18 June and it was delivered to Thomas Cromwell on 29 June and he was appointed Lord Privy Seal on 1 July, with a fee of twenty shillings a day. He was also created Baron Cromwell of Oakham eight days later.

20 Then a small parish to the north of London.

21 Shooter's Hill – at 443 feet (132 m.) the highest point in south London – is near Greenwich. Its name was first recorded in 1226.

22 National Archives, SP 1/105/245. Norfolk to Cromwell, Kenninghall, 5 August 1536, and see *LPFD*, vol. II, p. 102.

23 *LPFD*, vol. II, p. 103. Norfolk to Cromwell, Kenninghall, 6 August 1536.

24 Knowles, p. 181.

25 *LPFD*, vol. II, p. 183.

26 Robinson, p. 30.

27 Swales, p. 254.

28 At this stage Henry was bluffing, as he had no ready forces to defeat the rebels. He was also furious, as he always was at any sign of opposition to his reign. He promised the insurgents that 'a great army' would invade their neighbourhoods 'as soon as they come out of them and to burn, spoil and destroy their goods, wives and children, with all extremity, to the fearful example of all lewd subjects'. See *LPFD*, vol. II, p. 226.

29 *LPFD*, vol. II, p. 246.

30 *CDP Spanish*, vol. 5, pt ii, p. 269. He took 'a quantity of ammunition' and artillery out of the Tower as well as arrows and handguns.

31 *LPFD*, vol. II, p. 252.

32 Hutchinson, *Cromwell*, p. 112. Cromwell served as a teenage mercenary soldier in the French army that was routed by Spanish forces at the Garigliano River, near Cassino, Italy, on 28 December 1503. The survivors, including Cromwell, fell back, naked and half-starving, on Rome. Ibid., p. 9.

33 *CDP Spanish*, vol. 5, pt ii, p. 268.

34 *LPFD*, vol. II, p. 230.

35 Robinson, p. 31.

36 In 1525 Norfolk was involved in suppressing a 4,000-strong protest against a new tax in East Anglia. The Duke of Suffolk cracked down hard on the rioters which triggered new disturbances. Norfolk met the

protestors' leaders at Huntingdon and told them: 'I am sorry for your case. If you depart home to your dwellings, I will be a means to your pardon.' The new tax was withdrawn and thus the duke's reputation was locally enhanced. See Chapman, p. 25. Norfolk was good at dealing with the lower classes – normally with a firm hand. At one stage, Henry appointed him, with others, to keep the peace regarding laws affecting 'hunters, workmen, artisans, servants, innkeepers, mendicants, vaga-bonds and others calling themselves travelling men'. See Cornwall Record Office, Arundel papers, AR/22/30.

37 *LPFD*, vol. ii, p. 243.
38 A falcon cannon could fire a ball weighing about two pounds (0.91 kg.) and was an anti-cavalry and infantry weapon.
39 Also called a hackbut, harquebus or arquebus. This form of light gun was used by infantry throughout the sixteenth century. Sometimes the butt was curved so that, when levelled, it rested against the chest rather than the shoulder. The Royal Armouries possess two breech-loading hackbuts once owned by Henry VIII. One, bearing the monogram 'H.R' and the date of 1537, weighs 9.5 lb (4.31 kg.) and the other, jocularly known as 'King Henry's fowling piece', a massive 18 lb (8.17 kg.). Both were originally fired by a wheel-lock mechanism.
40 *LPFD*, vol. ii, p. 250.
41 *LPFD*, vol. ii, p. 254.
42 *LPFD*, vol. ii, p. 259.
43 *LPFD*, vol. ii, p. 258.
44 *LPFD*, vol. ii, p. 282.
45 *LPFD*, vol. ii, p. 280.
46 From the translation of the Greek for 'Jesus'.
47 Meaning the common good of the people.
48 *LPFD*, vol. ii, p. 298.
49 Ibid.
50 Hoyle, p. 288. See *State Papers*, vol. i, p. 518.
51 *LPFD*, vol. ii, p. 347. Henry, in his reply from Windsor on 27 October, sought to reassure Norfolk: 'We do not only know your loyalty, wisdom and great experience to be such, as being now joined and in company with our good cousin of Shrewsbury, in what state . . . you find things, will direct them in such sort as shall be to our honour, your sureties, and the discomfiture of our rebels . . . You desire us, in case [of] any mischance should happen to you, to be a good lord to your children . . . Surely good cousin, albeit we trust certainly in God, that no such thing shall fortune. Yet, we would you should perfectly know that if God should . . . take you out of this transitory life before us, we should not fail to remember your

children, being your lively images and in such wise, to look [after] them with our princely favour, for your assured truth and service, as others ... should not be discouraged to follow your steps in that behalf.' See *State Papers*, vol. 1, pp. 493–5.

52 *State Papers*, vol. 1, pp. 495–6.

53 *LPFD*, vol. 11, p. 360–61.

54 He told Cromwell the will was 'sealed in a box, which I require you to keep unopened while I live ... If I should die at this time in my master's service, see my will performed and beg the king, whom I [would] have supervisor of it and whom I love better than myself and trust more than the rest of the world. Since I saw you, I have not been well but for a continual lax [diarrhoea]. I think such thing has grown about my heart that it would cost me my life.' His desire to serve the king 'and to anger my enemies will, I trust, make me shortly strong and lusty. If you knew the crafty drifts [plots] used here to bring me out of credit, you would say I am not well handled. But God shall send a shrewd cow short horns and, for my part, *veritas libersbit* [truthfulness is free].' See *LFPD*, vol. 12, pt i, pp. 118–19.

55 National Archives, SP 1/115/175. Partially reprinted in *LPFD*, vol. 12, pt i, p. 145. Norfolk sent a copy of the 'seditious prophecy' on to Cromwell, but kept the original 'to try out the writer by the hand'. He told the Lord Privy Seal: 'There are many seditions in these parts, yet I trust the nobles and substantial yeomen.'

56 *LPFD*, vol. 12, pt i, p. 145. The first verse of the song, hardly a catchy number, ran: 'The hunt is up, the hunt is up. / The masters of art and doctors of divinity / Have brought this realm out of a good unity / Three nobleman have take[n] this to stay: / My lord of Norfolk, Lord Surrey and my lord of Shrewsbury. / The duke of Suffolk might a made England merry.'

57 'Religious' – meaning abbots, priors and monks.

58 National Archives, SP 1/116/92, reprinted in *State Papers*, vol. 1, pp. 538–9 and Byrne, *Henry VIII Letters*, pp. 168–71.

59 National Archives, SP 1/115/244.

60 National Archives, SP 1/116/83. See also Elton, *Policy and Police*, p. 297.

61 National Archives, SP 1/116/108. Those to be executed were selected 'by the advice of the council and gentlemen of these parts'.

62 Cited by Wilson, p. 402.

63 Burial of the executed rebels was forbidden by priests in several places. At Brigham, Richard Cragge's remains were not allowed interment in the churchyard, so his widow and a cousin buried him in a ditch. Percival

Hudson's body was buried in God's Acre at Torpenhow secretly at night. See Moorhouse, p. 313.

64 Norfolk was continually looking over his shoulder, worried about Henry's opinion of him. On 24 February 1537 he wrote to an unidentified official at court, begging him to speak well – 'befriend' – of him to the king. See BL Cotton MS Vespasian F, xiii, fol. 78B.

65 Hutchinson, *Cromwell*, p. 117.

66 *LPFD*, vol. 12, pt i, p. 277.

67 Cited by Elton, *Policy and Police*, p. 297, and Pickthorn, p. 357. The reprieve for the prisoners was short-lived. On 11 and 12 April, sixteen of the accused were found guilty of treason and condemned to death. See Bush and Bownes, fn, p. 382.

68 *LPFD*, vol. 12, pt i, pp. 322–3.

69 The Privy Council wrote to Norfolk, insisting that 'the conscience of such persons as did acquit Levening should be examined . . .' and requiring that he send the jury to London to answer for their wilfulness and also to 'travail all you can to beat out the mystery thereof'. See *Hardwick State Papers*, vol. 1, pp. 46–7. Henry's anger at the acquittal was deepened by the escape from justice, earlier that month, of sixty-five Lincolnshire rebels, of whom two were acquitted and the remainder found guilty but pardoned. See Bush and Bownes, p. 382.

70 He was also Bishop of Chalcedon, now part of the city of Istanbul on the Asia Minor side of the Bosphorus. After 1623, the title of Bishop of Chalcedon was given to Catholic Bishops of England. Mackerell's confession, dated 20 October 1536, is in *LPFD*, vol. 11, pp. 311–12.

71 Cited by Robinson, p. 31.

72 National Archives, SP 1/130/24, and *LPFD*, vol. 13, pt i, pp. 177–9 and 268. For more information, see Jonathan K. van Patten, 'Magic, Prophecy and the Law of Treason in Reformation England', *American Journal of Legal History*, vol. 27 (January 1983), pp. 1–32, and Elton, *Policy and Police*, pp. 57–8.

73 Caitiff – a vile, wicked and cowardly individual.

74 National Archives, SP 1/120/6 and 14–15.

75 *State Papers*, vol. 5, p. 99, and *LPFD*, vol. 12, pt ii, p. 186.

76 Childs, pp. 123–4.

77 National Archives, SP 1/121/96.

78 BL Add. MS 6, 113, fol. 81, and Egerton MS 985, fol. 33, give contemporary accounts of the christening of Prince Edward. See also Strype's account in *Ecclesiastic Memorials*, vol. 2, pt i, pp. 3–9.

79 *LFPD*, vol. 12, pt ii, p. 339.

80 *LPFD*, vol. 12, pt ii, p. 360.

81 The right to present a priest to an ecclesiastic benefice.

82 *LPFD*, vol. 12, pt ii, p. 355.

83 *State Papers*, vol. 1, pt ii, p. 574, and BL Cotton MS Nero C, x, fol. 2. A knell was also rung in every London church tower or steeple on 12 November from noon to six that evening. See Wriothesley, vol. 1, p. 71.

84 Wriothesley, vol. 1, p. 70.

Chapter 6: 'Prostrate and Most Humble'

1 Henry Brinklow, *The Complaynt of Roderick Mors . . . unto the parliament house of Ingland*, Strasbourg, 1542, sigs D1v–2r.

2 Cromwell boasted to Sir Thomas Wyatt in July 1537: 'The realm [goes] from good quiet and peace, to better and better. The traitors have been executed . . . so that, as far as we can perceive, the cankered hearts are weeded away.' Ellis, *Original Letters*, third series, vol. 3, p. 60.

3 31 Henry VIII, *cap.* 13. A total of 376 smaller houses were affected by the First Act of Dissolution of 1536 (27 Henry VIII, *cap.* 28) and 200 larger by the second, with a further 200 friaries.

4 Decorated panels, with religious iconography, raised above the back of an altar.

5 Knowles, p. 267. Norfolk sent the prior, William Wood, to London for trial for treason on 17 May 1537. There seems little doubt that he helped the insurgents during the Pilgrimage of Grace, but would have been covered by the royal pardon. He was executed.

6 *VCH Suffolk*, vol. 2, pp. 81–3 and 111–12.

7 Norfolk paid an annual rent of £44 19s 0¾d for Castle Rising. In the 1535 *Valor ecclesiasticus* it had an income of £306 11s 4¾d, including the average 10s a year donated by pilgrims at the shrine containing the relic of the arm of St Philip, patron saint of hatters and pastry-makers. See *VCH Norfolk*, vol. 2, pp. 356–8.

8 *VCH Norfolk*, vol. 2, p. 430.

9 Rawcliffe and Wilson, *Medieval Norwich*, p. 26. The site was rented by the duke to a brewer but was purchased by the city of Norwich in 1559 and used as a public wharf. It was then broken up into a number of smallholdings.

10 National Archives, SP 1/116/8.

11 Martin, *Thetford*, appendix xvii.

12 The properties are listed in the indenture. See Norfolk Record Office MC 67/35 511X9.

13 *LPFD*, vol. 21, pt ii, p. 273.

14 Wriothesley, vol. 1, p. 27. He was prior of the house at Beauvale in Nottinghamshire.

15 Henry had declared on 17 March 1537 that the Greenwich friars were 'disciples of the bishop of Rome and sowers of sedition' and ordered that they should be arrested 'and placed in other houses as friars as prisoners, without liberty to speak to any man till we decide our pleasure concerning them'.

16 Townshend, of Rayham, Norfolk, was a member of Norfolk's household and did well out of the monastic suppressions, being granted twenty manors in that county.

17 Knowles, pp. 254–5.

18 See G. W. Bernard's 'The Making of Religious Policy 1533–36: Henry VIII and the Search for the Middle Way', in *Historical Journal*, vol. 41 (1998), pp. 321–49, which argues that the king was the dominant force in making religious policy and his efforts should be seen as a search for a middle road between reform and tradition.

19 In the next century, the polemicist Thomas Fuller claimed that Gardiner had a 'head, if not a hand in the death of every eminent Protestant, plotting, though not acting, their destruction'. The bishop, he maintained, 'managed his malice with cunning'. See Fuller, *Church History*, book 18, pp. 12 and 17.

20 Henry Brinklow, *The Lamentacyon of a Christen Agaynst the Cytye of London ...*, ed. J. M. Cowper, in the Early English Text Society's 'extra series', vol. 22 (London, 1874), pp. 79 and 82.

21 Hare was recorder of Norwich in 1536 and appointed master of requests the following year. He died in 1557.

22 Bindoff, *History of Parliament*, vol. 1, p. 733.

23 BL Cotton MS Cleopatra, E, v, fols 313–20. Elsewhere in this volume there is an exposition of the meaning of the twelve articles of the Creed. The eighth article – 'I believe in the Holy Catholic Church' – carries the most comments and amendments by the king. See Byrne, *Letters of Henry VIII*, pp. 252–4 and p. 255.

24 Tanner, pp. 97–8.

25 The staunchly Protestant John Ponet, who was Cranmer's chaplain before 1547 and therefore no friend to Gardiner, described him as 'having a swarthy colour' and 'a hanging look, frowning brows, eyes an inch within the head, a nose hooked like a buzzard, wide nostrils like a horse ... a sparrow mouth, great paws like the devil, talons on his feet like a [griffin] two inches larger than the natural toes ... and so tied ... with sinews that he could not abide to be touched'. See: Ponet, *A Short Treatise of Politike Power ...* (London, 1556), p. 178. Gardiner was one of those happy people who are always sure of themselves: 'I do not trifle with my wit to undo myself, but travail with my honesty to preserve my country,

to preserve my prince or to preserve religion' (Muller, *Gardiner Letters*, p. 422).

26 Lacey Baldwin Smith, *Mask*, p. 138.

27 31 Henry VIII, *cap.* 40.

28 Burnet, vol. 1, pt i, book iii, p. 195.

29 On France's north-east coast. The town and its immediate hinterland (the 'Pale of Calais' – hence the expression 'beyond the pale') were an English possession between 1347 and 1558 and regarded as a bridgehead on the European mainland.

30 Quoted in Muller, *Tudor Reaction*, p. 82.

31 Hutchinson, *Last Days of Henry VIII*, p. 92. Hare continued to serve the king as a soldier, and was paid a grant of 9d (almost 4p) a day in 1542, for his loyal service in Ireland.

32 A light shallow-draught rowing boat that conveyed passengers on rivers.

33 Burnet, vol. 1, pt i, book iii, p. 195, and see also Nichols, *Narratives*, p. 237.

34 The Duchy of Cleves is in modern Germany and covers today's districts of Cleves, Wesel, Duisburg, Jülich and Berg.

35 George Paulet claimed in June 1538 that the 'king [calls Cromwell a knave] twice a week and sometimes knocks well about the pate [head] and yet when he has been well pummelled . . . he would come out of the great chamber . . . with a merry countenance'. *State Papers*, vol. 2, fn, pp. 551–2.

36 Edmund Howard, commander of the right flank at Flodden and later Comptroller of Calais and its marches, died on 19 March 1539. He had borrowed money (?from Cromwell) at exorbitant rates and had to adopt various disguises to outwit his creditors. See Strickland, vol. 2, p. 337.

37 Lacey Baldwin Smith, *Tudor Tragedy*, p. 103. Ellis, *Original Letters*, first series, vol. 1, pp. 201–2.

38 Nichols, *Narratives*, p. 259.

39 For a discussion on Henry's medical problems see Hutchinson, *Last Days of Henry VIII*, chapter five, and on Cushing's syndrome, pp. 207–9.

40 Elton, 'Cromwell's Decline and Fall . . .', p. 171.

41 *State Papers*, vol. 8, pp. 265–9.

42 Wilson, p. 451.

43 *LPFD*, vol. 15, p. 206. Cuthbert Tunstall, Bishop of Durham (1474–1559), had prohibited Protestant books and took a leading role in the passing of the Act of Six Articles. John Clerk, Bishop of Bath (d. 1541), tried to obtain the papacy for Wolsey in 1523.

44 Hume, p. 98.

45 *LPFD*, vol. 8, p. 255.

46 Cromwell's wife Elizabeth had died some time before 1529, possibly from the fatal infectious fever called 'the sweating sickness' that swept England in 1528. His two daughters, Anne and 'little Grace', both died young, possibly in the same epidemic. See Hutchinson, *Thomas Cromwell*, p. 23.

47 Byrne, *Lisle Letters*, vol. 1, p. 56.

48 Act of Precedence, 1539, 31 Henry VIII, *cap.* 10.

49 *LPFD*, vol. 15, p. 377, Kaulek, p. 193, and Hume, pp. 98–9. Marillac about this time suggested, rather snidely, that Southampton, had 'long learnt to bend to all winds'. See Kaulek, p. 190.

50 Kaulek, p. 189, and *LPFD*, vol. 15, p. 363.

51 *LPFD*, vol. 15, p. 377.

52 Malversation – corrupt behaviour in an office.

53 Kaulek, p. 191.

54 *Lords Journal*, vol. 1, p. 145.

55 *Lords Journal*, vol. 1, p. 149. Act of Attainder, 32 Henry VIII, *cap.* 62. Later copies are in BL Lansdowne MS 515, fol. 44 and Cotton MS Titus B, I, fol. 503.

56 BL Add. MS 48,028, fols 160–65.

57 The original eight-page document is in Hatfield House archives, CP 1/23.

58 Hatfield House Archives, CP 1/10–11.

59 The Act dissolving the marriage is 32 Henry VIII, *cap.* 25.

60 Fox, *Acts and Monuments*, pp. 402–3.

61 Arthur Galton, *The Character and Times of Thomas Cromwell* (Birmingham, 1887), p. 156.

62 Casady, p. 80.

63 An attendant on the king's table.

64 *LPFD*, vol. 16, p. 5.

65 Kaulek, p. 363.

66 Kaulek, p 370, and Lacey Baldwin Smith, *Tudor Tragedy*, pp. 178ff.

67 BL Cotton MS Otho, C, x, fol. 250.

68 Kaulek, p. 352, and *LPFD*, vol. 16, p. 614.

69 Longleat House, MSS of Marquis of Bath, Portland Papers, PO/Vol.1/15.

70 *LPFD*, vol. 16, p. 662.

71 *LPFD*, vol. 16, pp. 617–18.

72 *LPFD*, vol. 16, pp. 618–19.

73 *LPFD*, vol. 16, p. 620.

74 *LPFD*, vol. 16, p. 628.

75 Kaulek, p. 370.
76 *State Papers*, vol. 1, pt ii, p. 721.
77 Head, *Ebbs and Flows*, p. 189.
78 33 Henry VIII, *cap.* 21. The Act was approved by Letters Patent to spare Henry the pain of condemning his own queen.
79 An Act for due Process to be had in High Treasons in cases of Lunacy or Madness, 33 Henry VIII, *cap.* 20.
80 Kaulek, p. 388.
81 *LPFD*, vol. 17, p. 45.

Chapter 7: Down but Not Out

1 *LPFD*, vol. 21, pt i, p. 33.
2 Kaulek, pp. 420–21.
3 Kaulek, p. 416.
4 Norfolk told Sir William Fitzwilliam, Earl of Southampton, that what he feared most about the campaign was 'the lack of drink'. See BL Add. MS 32,647, fol. 115.
5 A tun held around 216 imperial gallons, or 982 litres.
6 Foists were large casks.
7 BL Add. MS 32,647, fol. 121.
8 BL Add. MS 32,647, fol. 194.
9 BL Add. MS 32,647, fol. 196. Gardiner had already sent 250 tons of barley and 125 tons each of wheat and rye for bread. Another 125 tons apiece of rye and wheat, and 500 tons of malt, 259 tons of peas and a similar quantity of beans were about to be despatched. He had also ordered 1,000 'wey' of cheese – this measurement varied between regions; in Suffolk a wey was 265 pounds (116 kg.) and in Essex 336 pounds (152 kg.).
10 BL Add. MS 32,647, fol. 193.
11 BL Add. MS 32,648, fol. 46.
12 BL Add. MS 32,648, fol. 46. Norfolk, then Earl of Surrey, was Lieutenant and Dorset was Warden of the East and Middle Marches of the border. Both appointments were dated 26 February 1523.
13 BL Add. MS 32,648, fol. 65.
14 *Chronicle of John Hardyng*, edited and published by Richard Grafton, the chronicler and printer, in January 1543. He dedicated the work to the third Duke of Norfolk. See penultimate stanza, lines 6–7. Harding (1378–1465) was an earlier English chronicler.
15 Lord William Howard was paid £24 16s 4d for his service, made up of 6s 8d per day for himself and nine servants and 8d a day 'conduct money' for riding the three hundred miles from London. See BL Add. MS 5,754, fol. 12.

16 *Hamilton Papers*, vol. 1, no. 218.

17 BL Add. MS 32,348, fol. 177, and *Hamilton Papers*, vol. 1, no. 218.

18 *Hamilton Papers*, vol. 1, no. 221.

19 BL Add. MS 32,468, fol. 96.

20 BL Add. MS 32,648, fol. 108.

21 A reformed Benedictine order called colloquially 'the Grey Monks'.

22 Bath Place or Inn was located on the north side of Holborn Bars, next to Furnivals Inn, on the west side of the city. The site is now occupied by part of the Prudential offices. See *London Topographical Record*, vol. 10 (1916), pp. 133–4.

23 Exeter Place was in the Outer Temple and was occupied by the duke in 1541–2. It was granted to Sir William Paget in 1549 and was later acquired by Robert Dudley, Earl of Leicester, who passed it on to his stepson, Robert Devereux, Earl of Essex. He plotted his abortive rebellion there against Elizabeth I in 1601. Most of the old house was pulled down in 1777. See *London Topographical Record*, vol. 10 (1916), pp. 117–18. Norfolk would have regarded his mansion at Lambeth as being in the suburbs of the city.

24 BL Add. MS 32,648, fol. 112.

25 *Hamilton Papers*, vol. 1, no. 226.

26 BL Add. MS 10,110, fol. 237.

27 BL Add. MS 32,648, fol. 114.

28 BL Add. MS 32,648, fol. 120.

29 *LPFD*, vol. 17, p. 585.

30 *LPFD*, vol. 17, p. 580.

31 Norfolk may have been drinking an infusion of blackberry leaves (*Rubus fructuosis*), which was a Tudor remedy for diarrhoea.

32 *LPFD*, vol. 17, p. 585.

33 BL Add. MS 32,648, fol. 156. The Scottish king James V fell ill on 7 December and was dead a week later, because of his despair at the defeat. For a modern account of the battle, see Brooks, p. 290. The landscape has changed radically due to agricultural enclosure and draining of the alluvial flood plain of the Esk.

34 *CDP Spanish*, vol. 6, pt ii, pp. 233–4.

35 *LPFD*, vol. 19, pt i, p. 157. Their contribution was surpassed only by Lord Ferrers's 1,000 infantry and 100 cavalry. The other formations in the army were the 'Battle' – 3,159 cavalry and 9,688 infantry – and the 'Rearguard' numbering 9,017 infantry and 547 horsemen. Ibid., p. 163.

36 *LPFD*, vol. 19, pt i, pp. 410–11.

37 *LPFD*, vol. 19, pt i, p. 433. His claims were later acidly rebutted by the Privy Council. 'The king has received your letter ... [claiming] that

we have not answered your concerns, [over] the price of victuals and insufficiency of the Flemish wagons ... and noted negligence in us, albeit we are faultless. As to the wagons, we wrote more than five days ago enlarging the number and as for the prices ... the rating is thought convenient by you and others.' BL Harleian MS 6,989, fol. 191.

38 *LPFD*, vol. 19, pt i, p. 435.

39 Suffolk told Norfolk on 8 July, 'You seem to think it strange that we, knowing the way to be taken by the king, keep it secret from you. But we are as ignorant as you. As soon as we have any inkling of his majesty's determination, we will advertise [tell] you.' See BL Harleian MS 6,989, fol. 129. Suffolk also sent the duke wine from the king's provisions, possibly as a gesture of goodwill.

40 National Archives, SP 1/189/207, and BL Harleian MS 6,989, fol. 127.

41 Montreuil, in the Pas de Calais *département*, was one of the most prosperous ports in northern Europe in the thirteenth century, until the river became silted up over the next three hundred years. It later featured in Victor Hugo's novel *Les Misérables*, published in 1861, and became the site of the headquarters of the British army in France during the First World War.

42 *State Papers*, vol. 9, pp. 727–8.

43 *LPFD*, vol. 19, pt i, p. 543.

44 National Archives, SP 1/190/24.

45 Charles V had advanced to within fifty miles (84.7 km.) of Paris before a supply shortage forced a retreat. After secret negotiations with the French, the separate peace treaty was concluded at Crépy and announced on 18 September. Savoy and Milan were surrendered to the Spanish, who, in turn, dropped their claims on Burgundy.

46 Nott, p. lxviii.

47 National Archives, SP 1/193/154.

48 *APC*, vol. 1, p. 238. The Privy Council, meeting at Oatlands, in Surrey, noted that 'the king's majesty was pleased that ... the Earl of Surrey [should] go to Boulogne'.

49 Hutchinson, *Last Days of Henry VIII*, p. 122.

50 *CDP Spanish*, vol. 8, p. 251.

51 *State Papers*, vol. 1, pp. 839–40.

52 *LPFD*, vol. 19, pt ii, p. 197.

53 It had been granted to Norfolk at the dissolution in 1538.

54 National Archives, SP 1/209/128.

55 National Archives, SP 1/210/30, and Bapst, p. 319.

56 National Archives, SP 1/213/47, and Nott, p. 198.

57 *LPFD*, vol. 21, pt i, p. 16.

58 Nott, p. 224.

59 Cited by Childs, p. 261.

60 *LPFD*, vol. 21, pt i, p. 225.

61 BL Cotton MS Titus B i, fol. 100B; *State Papers*, vol. 1, pp. 576–7. See also Nott, Appendix 38. Norfolk, in conversation with Henry, had suggested two husbands for the Duchess of Richmond; one was Thomas Seymour, 'to whom his heart is most inclined'. The king could not remember the name of the other potential spouse.

62 Nott, pp. cxx–cxxi, and *LPFD*, vol. 21, pt ii, pp. 282–3.

63 See Hutchinson, *Last Days of Henry VIII*, pp. 57–8. Henry had married the twice widowed Katherine Parr on 12 July 1543 at Hampton Court.

64 Madam d'Estampes was the blonde Anne de Pisseleu d'Heilly, who became the mistress of Francis I of France in 1526 and remained in his affections until his death in 1547. In 1533, he gave her in marriage to Jean de Brosse, whom he created duc d'Estampes.

65 *LPFD*, vol. 21, pt ii, pp. 283–5.

66 Ellis, *Archaeologia*, vol. 23 (1831), p. 62.

67 The Fleet Prison was located in Farringdon Street, on the eastern banks of the River Fleet, outside the walls of the city of London. It was built in 1197, but destroyed three times: during the Peasants' Revolt of 1381, the Great Fire of London in 1666 and during the Gordon Riots of 1780. It was finally demolished in 1846.

68 BL Harleian MS 78, fol. 24, and printed in Brenan and Statham, pp. 353–6, and Nott, pp. 167ff.

69 *APC*, vol. 1, p. 19.

70 St Nicholas Shambles was a lane, northwest of St Paul's Cathedral.

71 National Archives, SP 1/176/151.

72 National Archives, SP 1/176/156.

73 *LPFD*, vol. 18, pt i, p. 204.

74 *APC*, vol. 1, pp. 104–6.

75 *LPFD*, vol. 21, pt ii, p. 136.

76 See Hutchinson, *Last Days of Henry VIII*, pp. 171–4.

77 *APC*, vol. 1, pp. 400, 408 and 411, and *LPFD*, vol. 21, pt i, pp. 366, 377, 378 and 382.

78 *LPFD*, vol. 21, pt ii, p. 173, and Pickthorn, p. 521.

79 *CDP Spanish*, vol. 8, p. 556.

80 *LPFD*, vol. 21, pt ii, p. 252, and Muller, *Gardiner Letters*, pp. 246–7.

81 Foxe, *Acts*, vol. 4, p. 138.

82 Southwell (1504–56) was a creature of Cromwell's and one of the commissioners for the suppression of monasteries in Norfolk. He took a leading role in rounding up the conspirators in the planned insurrection

at Walsingham in that county in April 1537. See Swales, pp. 256–60. For
further information on the Walsingham incident, see C. E. Morton,
'The Walsingham Conspiracy of 1537', *Historical Research*, vol. 63 (1990),
pp. 29–43.

83 Herbert, p. 562.

84 Hume, p. 144.

85 Ely Place was the London residence of the bishops of Ely and frequently
rented to members of the court.

86 He arrived in London in June 1546.

87 *LPFD*, vol. 21, pt ii, pp. 270–71.

88 Herbert, p. 562.

89 Nichols, *Greyfriars Chronicle*, p. 52.

90 See Discussion in Lacey Baldwin Smith, *Mask of Royalty*, p. 236.

91 National Archives, SP 1/227/82, and *State Papers*, vol. 1, pp. 888–90.

92 National Archives, LR 2/115/6.

93 National Archives, SP 1/227/82.

94 The Kenninghall household consisted of the steward, almoner (who was
a priest), the comptroller, Richard Wharton; sixteen gentlemen, six
chaplains; two clerks of the kitchen; twelve servants of the chapel; fifty-
two yeomen and sixty-one grooms. Surrey's household at Kenninghall
was five gentlemen, seven yeomen and six grooms – the bulk of his
servants were at his home in Norwich. See *LPFD* Addenda, vol. 1, pt
22, p. 590. Wharton had tipped off the Duke of Suffolk in May 1537
about a seditious play, performed on May Day, about how a king should
rule. See Swales, pp. 260–61.

95 National Archives, LR 2/115/18.

96 National Archives, SP 1/227/76.

97 Herbert, pp. 565–6.

Chapter 8: The Great Survivor

1 Cited by Lacey Baldwin Smith, *Treason in Tudor England*, p. 117.

2 *LPFD*, vol. 21, pt ii, p. 277.

3 Fulmerston had worked for the Howards for ten years, beginning as a
yeoman servant and then delivering letters between Kenninghall and the
court. His daughter married another Norfolk retainer, Sir Edward Clere.
A John Fulmerston, 'collector' at the manor of Framlingham, Suffolk,
mentioned in the accounts of John Goldingham, receiver to the second
duke, when he was Earl of Surrey in 1502–3, may have been his father.
(See Norfolk Record Office, Phi 606/3.) Norfolk granted Richard Fulmerston a customs post in Ipswich in 1545. He had been Surrey's steward
since 1538. He was granted the site and possessions of the Austin Friars

at Thetford, Norfolk, described during a visitation in 1538, as 'so bare that there was no earthly thing but trash and baggage' (*VCH Norfolk*, vol. 2, p. 435). He obtained substantial rents on a large number of properties in September 1546 and also former Augustinian and friary lands in Thetford and Barnham, Suffolk. In Edward VI's reign, he was assigned the market tolls of Thetford and this led to a dispute with the town's corporation in 1572 (Norfolk Record Office, T/NS 31). His will, dated 1567, set up a free grammar school, for thirty pupils, at Thetford (Norfolk Record Office, T/NS 1–16).

4 *LPFD*, vol. 21, pt ii, pp. 280–82.
5 BL Cotton MS Titus B, I, fol. 94.
6 *CDP Spanish*, vol. 8, p. 533.
7 Ibid.
8 *LPFD*, vol. 21, pt ii, p. 310.
9 He was questioning their humanity.
10 *LPFD*, vol. 21, pt ii, pp. 313–14.
11 *LPFD*, vol. 21, pt ii, p. 326.
12 National Archives, SP 1/227/97, and Herbert, p. 564. Knyvett (1508–51), was the first son of Sir Thomas Knyvett and his wife Muriel, daughter of the second duke. He had married by 1527, Anne, the daughter of Sir John Shelton of Carrow, Norfolk. Norfolk had little sympathy for his nephew. In 1539, he described Knyvett as 'young and has a great wit and trusts too much to his wit and will neither follow the advice of his father-in-law [Shelton], nor me, but is ruled by three or four light naughty knaves of Welshmen and others' and was, moreover, running into debt. 'If he comes to you before I do, be quick with him and give not too much confidence to his words' (*LPFD*, vol. 14, pt i, p. 381).

In April 1541, he struck Surrey's squire, Thomas Clere, during a row on the tennis court at Greenwich Palace, 'in which they shed blood'. He was condemned to lose his right hand – the fist that had struck the blow. A bizarre ritual followed. 'The king's master cook, ready with his knife to do the execution and the sergeant of the scullery with his mallet; the irons laid in the fire to have seared him, and the king's surgeon with the searing cloth ready. When the execution should have been done, the king sent Mr Long [Sir Richard Long, gentleman of the Privy Chamber] to stay it till after dinner, and then the officers of the household sat again and then the king pardoned him.' (Wriothesley, vol. 1, p. 125.) Knyvett had pleaded with the king to take his left hand instead, 'for if my right hand be spared, I may hereafter do such good service to his grace as shall please him to appoint.' (Cobbett, *State Trials*, vol. 1, pp. 139–40.)

Marillac described the scene more graphically. Knyvett was 'more frightened than hurt. [He] was led by the executioner on to a scaffold, his hand bound to a block and then all the other mysteries done, even pretending to deal the blow and then his pardon was sent to him' (*LPFD*, vol. 16, pt i, p. 440). In February 1542, he was in trouble again for another misdemeanour and, six years later, was bound over in the sum of £1,000 to answer charges, probably connected with his alleged adultery with the Countess of Sussex (Bindoff, vol. 2, pp. 482–3).

13 Warner (1511–65), together with Devereux, had been in trouble earlier in 1546 for their religiously reformist beliefs (*APC*, vol. 1, pp. 114–15).

14 National Archives, SP 1/227/101.

15 Blagge (1513–51) was a favourite of the king's, who referring to his rotundity, called him 'my pig'. An evangelical, he had been caught up in the roundup of reformists earlier in 1546. He was walking in St Paul's Cathedral, London, when, he claimed, he was tricked into denying the efficacy of the Mass. He was summoned before Lord Chancellor Wriothesley and tried and condemned for heresy. He was saved by an intervention by the king himself and was pardoned. When Henry next saw him, he called out: 'Ah, my pig! Are you safe again?' Blagge, bowing low, replied: 'Yes sire. And if your majesty had not been better to me than your bishops, your pig would have been roasted ere this time' (Nichols, *Narratives*, fn, p. 42). Blagge wrote bitterly of Wriothesley's character: 'By false deceit, by craft and subtle ways, cruelty had crept full high, borne up by sundry stays' (Nott, vol. 1, p. xcvii).

16 National Archives, SP 1/227/103.

17 National Archives, SP 1/227/105.

18 26 Henry VIII, *cap.* 13.

19 Herbert, pp. 563–4.

20 Gross obesity in the body's trunk is one of the symptoms of Cushing's syndrome. Bessie's evidence about the device to lift the king up and down is puzzling. There is no mention of a lift or any other contrivance in Henry's household accounts and probably there was little need of one: the king's secret apartments were always on one floor. Her testimony probably refers to the 'king's trams' – a form of sedan chair, probably on wheels – which were used to carry Henry in the latter stages of 1546. See Hutchinson, *Last Days of Henry VIII*, pp. 149–50 and pp. 207–9.

21 The 'Vernacle' or 'Veronica'. This was the legend that Saint Veronica wiped Christ's face with her veil on the road to Calvary. The veil was said to have been placed in a marble coffer on the altar of a chapel attached to St Peter in Rome but it was later moved elsewhere in the Vatican. In 1999, a distinguished scholar said the veil was now held in Manoppella, 150 miles (241 km.) from Rome. Relics had been stripped

from English and Welsh monastic shrines as superstitious hokum by Cromwell in the late 1530s.

22 Herbert, p. 563.

23 Hume, p. 143.

24 A cap of crimson velvet, lined with ermine fur, carried before the sovereign on state occasions, but also used in crests.

25 Herbert, p. 564.

26 Moore, 'Heraldic Charge', p. 562.

27 Howard, *Memorials*, p. 36, and National Archives, SP 1/227/109.

28 National Archives, SP 1/227/114.

29 Lacey Baldwin Smith, *Mask of Royalty*, p. 255, and Starkey, *Henry VIII, Personalities* ..., p. 136.

30 SP 1/227/129, and *LPFD*, vol. 21, pt ii, pp. 288–9.

31 *LPFD*, vol. 21, pt ii, p. 289. With the duke in the Tower, the Lord Chancellor was also presented with a saddler's account for more than £10, which included £1 5s 6d for a new saddle of 'Spanish leather' for Norfolk, and £1 6s 8d for a new side-saddle for Bessie Holland. Ibid.

32 One leg, if not both, was afflicted by fistulas, the result of his jousting accidents.

33 Mary, Dowager Queen of Hungary, Regent of Flanders and sister of Charles V.

34 *CDP Spanish*, vol. 8, p. 533.

35 From 1544, Henry's eyesight was failing and his accounts include the purchase of spectacles, ten pairs at a time, from Germany. See Hutchinson, *Last Days of Henry VIII*, p. 157.

36 Henry's annotations in italics.

37 National Archives, SP 1/227/123.

38 A new edition had been published in 1545 by Georg Witzel the elder.

39 First published in 1499.

40 These works by classical authors were fashionable at this time for their apparent support for the Henrician Reformation.

41 Herbert, pp. 566–7.

42 Childs, p. 299.

43 Hume, pp. 145–6.

44 National Archives, E 101/60/22.

45 The label is a heraldic device similar to a riband, with several shorter ribands hanging down, which overlays arms to indicate they belong to an eldest son.

46 BL Harleian MS 297, fol. 256, and Herbert, pp. 567–8.

47 National Archives, SP 1/227/106, and printed in *LPFD*, vol. 21, pt ii, pp. 285–6.

48 Moore, 'Heraldic Charge', pp. 568–9.

49 Moore, 'Heraldic Charge', p. 569.

50 Grafton, *Chronicle*, vol. 2, p. 498.

51 Hume, p. 146.

52 Years later, a Norfolk man, Robert Balam, wrote to a friend in London describing the disastrous floods that afflicted the county in October 1570. He recalled the three occasions when he had wept as an adult – the loss of English-held Calais in 1558, 'the loss of the old Duke of Norfolk and his son the Earl of Surrey', and the unkindness of a friend. See Surrey History Centre, LM/COR/3/329.

53 A cross decorated with fleur-de-lis at the termination of each of its arms.

54 A 'merlett' or 'merlion' is a heraldic bird. This is an old term for martlet or swallow, often shown in arms without legs or feet in the mistaken belief that the bird could not stand on the ground. Edward the Confessor's arms actually had doves. See John Brooke-Little, *Boutell's Heraldry* (London, 1970), p. 206.

55 *LPFD*, vol. 21, pt ii, p. 365. See also National Archives, KB8/14.

56 Hume, p. 146.

57 Weever, pp. 842–3, and see Moore, 'Heraldic Charge', p. 573.

58 Hume, p. 147.

59 Cited by Chapman, p. 137.

60 *CDP Spanish*, vol. 9, p. 4.

61 Herbert, p. 565.

62 BL Stowe MS 396, fols 8–9.

63 Hume, pp. 147–8.

64 The present-day Marble Arch.

65 Hume, p. 148. The merchant Ottwell Johnson was more matter of fact about the whole business on 15 January. After complaining about his servant Jasper's failure to sell cattle at Smithfield because of their poor condition, he reported: 'the Earl of Surrey was indicted, arraigned and condemned to die as a traitor at the Guildhall in London … God be merciful unto him and also unto his father, [who] by his own writing [has] submitted himself to the king his majesty . . . .' Johnson then moved quickly on to other homely topics such as the gum he was sending Sabine Johnson for perfume, and reminding the recipient to take the pills he had bought 'to amend your stomach'. See National Archives, SP 46/5/190.

66 Surrey's body was removed to the new Howard mortuary chapel at Framlingham in 1614 and reburied there. The monument to him and his wife includes his coronet, which is not worn on the effigy's head but laid separately on a cushion by his legs, as an indication of his attainder.

(See Robinson, p. 52.) The monument was erected with funds bequeathed by his younger son, Henry Howard, Earl of Northampton. It is attributed to the sculptor Maximilian Colt, of the parish of St Bartholomew the Great, London, who also carved the monument to Elizabeth I in Westminster Abbey. See Adam White, 'A Biographical Dictionary of London Tomb Sculptors', *Walpole Society*, vol. 61 (1999), p. 31.

67 Robinson, p. 243. The sketch is in BL Harleian MS 1453, fol. 69. See also William Sessions, 'Enough Survives', *History Today*, vol. 41 (June 1991), p. 53.

68 28 Henry VIII, *cap.* 1.

69 The commission to Hertford to pronounce 'in the Parliament House [Henry's] assent for the attainder' was signed by the so-called 'dry stamp', a system of creating a facsimile of Henry's signature that had been used since September 1545. This was a small carved wooden block that was impressed on a document – probably with a special handpress – to leave a dry, imprinted signature, later inked in. Henry's will was also (suspiciously) signed by dry stamp. *LPFD*, vol. 21, pt ii, p. 408.

70 The ceremony of degrading is described in BL Egerton MS 985, fol. 65.

71 National Archives, E 101/60/22.

72 Brewer, *The Death of Kings* (London, 2000), p. 121.

73 *CDP Spanish*, vol. 9, pp. 494–8.

74 *APC*, vol. 2, p. 106.

75 At Chesworth, the Privy Council authorised Sir Thomas Seymour to take charge of the house and the contents were delivered to him. Some of the tapestries, bedding and carpets belonging to the duke were requisitioned for Edward VI's use at Nonsuch Palace. See Surrey History Centre, LM/COR/22, LM/COR/2/3 and LM/1890.

76 After her death in June 1577, she was buried with the other Howards at Framlingham. Childs, p. 316.

77 Head, *Ebbs and Flows . . .*, p. 230.

78 Norfolk's holdings were summarised as 204 horses in stables; 88 oxen, 115 steers, 407 sheep and 420 hogs. In his salt store at Kenninghall were preserved more than 400 lings [a long, slim-bodied fish of the cod family], 1,617 cod, 43 mudfish [loach], 32 barrels of white herring and 11 barrels of salmon. See Howard, *Memorials*, p. 21.

79 Robinson, p. 23.

80 Fletcher and MacCulloch, p. 145.

81 Norfolk Record Office, BL 11C/14, m.10d.

82 Possibly a description as a hard worker.

83 Norfolk Record Office, WAR 55 Bressingham Court Roll 1545–60.

84 Norfolk Record Office, BL 11C/14, m.10d. For more information, see Diarmaid MacCulloch's 'Kett's Rebellion in Context', *Past and Present* (August 1979), pp. 53–7, and the same author's 'Bondmen under the Tudors', in C. Cross et al. (eds), *Law and Government under the Tudors* (Cambridge, 1988). See also National Archives, SC 2 (Court Rolls) 192/101 – a description of the courts in Norfolk of Thomas Howard, fourth Duke of Norfolk, 1558.

85 National Archives, SP 46/1/154.

86 National Archives, SP 46/2/78–80.

87 *APC*, vol. 2, p. 206.

88 *APC*, vol. 2, p. 400.

89 *APC*, vol. 3, p. 88.

90 *APC*, vol. 3, p. 254.

91 Wriothesley, *Chronicle*, vol. 2, p. 65. He reported 'there was such a fear and disturbance among the people suddenly before he suffered that some tumbled down the ditch [moat] and some ran towards the houses nearby and fell, that it was a marvel to see and hear, but [what] the cause was, God knows'.

92 Wriothesley, *Chronicle*, vol. 2, p. 95, and Stow, *Annals*, p. 613.

93 Head, *Ebbs and Flows . . .* , p. 236.

94 Warwick and Northampton escaped death.

95 Elton, *Reform and Reformation*, p. 377. Norfolk's goods passed from Somerset to Northumberland in 1550.

96 Rutland Papers, pp. 118–19.

97 'Reversal of the Supposed Attainder of Thomas Duke of Norfolk', 1 Mary, *cap.* 13, and 'Restitution in blood of Thomas Howard, Earl of Surrey', 1 Mary, *cap.* 1. A copy of Surrey's restitution is in Arundel Castle Archives, G2/10.

98 Green, *Framlingham*, p. 80.

99 Cruden, *History of Gravesend*, p. 176.

100 Nichols, *Chronicles of Queen Jane*, pp. 38–9.

101 Catholic Mary dropped this title from late in 1554.

102 The extent of his estates are given in Arundel Castle Archives, MD 490.

103 National Archives, PROB/11/37.

104 Norfolk Record Office, NRS 27260, fol. 199.

105 Childs, p. 315.

106 Bannerols were wide banners, displaying the marriages of the deceased's ancestors.

107 Small pennon flags.

108 Nichols, *Machyn's Diary*, p. 70.

109 Arundel Castle Archives, G1/7.

110 Nichols and Brill, *Wills of Eminent People* . . . , pp. 54–5.

111 *Gentleman's Magazine*, new series, vol. 23 (1845), p. 268.

112 Norfolk's effigy shows him in old age with a large beard. He had built a new Howard mausoleum at Framlingham in 1547 and the remains of Henry Fitzroy were moved there from Thetford and reburied under a monument erected in 1555. Both the dukes' French-style Renaissance tombs incorporate parts of the former monuments prepared for them at Thetford in the late 1530s and moved to Framlingham after the completion of the mortuary chapel. Portions of the third duke's original Thetford tomb were excavated in 1935. Other pieces, found in the 1860s, are in the British Museum. See Richard Marks, 'The Howard Tombs at Thetford and Framlingham', *Archaeological Journal*, vol. 141 (1984), pp. 252–68.

Chapter 9: An Equal of Kings

1 *Cal. Scot.*, vol. 9, p. 310.

2 Norfolk Record Office, NRS 27270 – 'Castles, honours, manors and other hereditaments as Thomas late Duke of Norfolk . . . was seized on the day of his death . . .' – not only lists his properties but also indicates how they came into the Howards' hands. It also details the possessions sold by the crown during the reign of Edward VI and the jointures of Elizabeth, Duchess of Norfolk, and Frances, Countess of Surrey.

3 He had served an apprenticeship under his grandfather, assisting him at Mary's coronation in October 1553 and at the banquet that followed.

4 A subdivision of a county having its own court.

5 A 'rape' was one of the six administrative districts which formerly divided Sussex. Each comprised several hundreds.

6 Robinson, p. 55.

7 Henry VIII spent part of his progress at Rycote after his marriage to Catherine Howard in 1540. The house was demolished in 1807 and only a small part of the front façade of the Tudor house remains.

8 Arundel paid over £2,000 as a dowry and a number of manors in Sussex, including the former monastic site at Michelham; Slinfold, Horsted and Rogate. See Arundel Castle Archives, G1/5.

9 2 and 3 Philip & Mary, *cap.* 1. See Arundel Castle Archives, G1/7.

10 Arundel Castle Archives, G2/10, copies of the Act for the restitution in blood, dated 24 October 1553, of Thomas Earl of Surrey.

11 Nichols, *Machyn's Diary*, p. 139.

12 The christening was in the Chapel Royal at the Palace of Westminster.

Among the other godparents was Elizabeth, Dowager Duchess of Norfolk. See Nichols, *Machyn's Diary*, p. 141.

13 Her body was later reburied at Arundel. Henry Machyn, the undertaker, recorded on 28 August the setting 'up of the hearse at St Clement's without Temple Bar for my young Duchess of Norfolk, the wife to the young Duke of Norfolk' and her funeral that followed on 1 September. 'The church and the place and the street [hanged with black] and [coats of] arms and by three of the clock, she was brought [to the church with] one hundred mourners and her [coffin] had a canopy of black velvet with three four staffs born over her and many banners. The Bishop of London [Edward Bonner] in his cope and his mitre [on his head] and all the choir of [St] Paul's ... and eight heralds of arms ... and many lords and knights and gentle ladies and gentlewomen [attended].' See Nichols, *Machyn's Diary*, pp. 149–50.

14 He had died in 1544.

15 As Earl Marshal, Norfolk organised Mary's funeral at Westminster in December 1558 and Elizabeth's coronation on 15 January 1559. As Chief Butler of England he organised the feast afterwards.

16 Norfolk Record Office, COL 13/53, where the document, a seventeenth-century copy, is misdated to 1561. See Blomefield, vol. 3, p. 280, and Dennis Rhodes, 'A Party at Norwich in 1562', *Norfolk Archaeology*, vol. 37 (1978–80), pp. 116–20, where convincing evidence for redating the party is provided.

17 Arundel Castle Archives, G1/6.

18 See, for example, his title and form of address in indentures and deeds, dated 1560 and 1570 in Arundel Castle Archives, G1/7.

19 A deed dated 1563 describes 'all my capital messuage or mansion as now newly built with all the edifices, orchards and gardens'. The Palace fronted Charing Cross. See Kent, 'The Houses of the Dukes of Norfolk in Norwich', *Norfolk Archaeology*, vol. 24 (1932), pp. 79–80. A settlement dated 31 July 1569 also refers to 'all that capital messuage lately re-edified and built by the said duke set lying and being in the parish of St John in Maddermarket'. See NRS 2292, 11 C 5.

20 This could be said to have been the only monastery that survived the Dissolution as, instead of closing it, Henry VIII exchanged it for lands owned by the Diocese of Norwich. However, the last monk left in 1545 and its buildings were soon demolished.

21 In the Norfolk Record Office there is a probate inventory for James Hills of Norwich, a 'tennis court keeper' for one of Norfolk's successors as duke in the early seventeenth century. See DN/INV 39/82.

22 Allen, *History of ... Lambeth*, p. 340.

23 Robinson, p. 56. North died on 31 December 1564 and Norfolk purchased it the following day. See David Knowles and W. G. Grimes, *Charterhouse* (London, 1954), p. 38.

24 Williams, *Tudor Tragedy*, p. 63.

25 Sadler Papers, vol. 1, p. 721.

26 HMC Hatfield, vol. 1, pp. 167–8.

27 Nichols, *Machyn's Diary*, p. 294. The duke had a mansion at this time within the parish of St Katherine Cree.

28 Longleat House, MSS of the Marquis of Bath, PO/Vol/5. Partially printed in *Third Report of Royal Commission on Historical MSS* (London, 1872), p. 195, and more fully in *Wiltshire Archaeological Magazine*, vol. 14 (1874), pp. 197–9.

29 See Guy, pp. 299–303.

30 HMC Hatfield, vol. 1, p. 371.

31 *DNB2*, vol. 28, p. 433, and HMC Hatfield, vol. 1, p. 461.

32 Fénelon, vol. 1, pp. 17–18.

33 Williams, *Tudor Tragedy*, p. 141, and Robinson, p. 60. The reference to the pillow recalls the murder of Darnley.

34 Guy, p. 461.

35 *Hardwick State Papers*, vol. 1, p. 190.

36 *Hardwick State Papers*, vol. 1, p. 191.

37 Guy, p. 462.

38 *Hardwick State Papers*, vol. 1, p. 520, and HMC Hatfield, vol. 1, p. 414.

39 Williams, *Tudor Tragedy*, p. 157.

40 Camden, *Historie of . . . Elizabeth*, p. 130.

41 HMC Hatfield, vol. 1, p. 419.

42 *DNB2*, vol. 28, p. 433.

43 Hatfield House, Cecil Papers, CP 156/60.

44 Hatfield House, Cecil Papers, CP 156/66.

45 Hatfield House, Cecil Papers, CP 156/67.

46 *Wiltshire Archaeological Magazine*, vol. 14 (1874), pp. 196–7.

47 A small wheel-less carriage with curtains on the sides, slung between two horses.

48 Hatfield House, Cecil Papers, CP 156/72.

49 Hatfield House, Cecil Papers, CP 153/51.

50 HMC Hatfield, vol. 1, p. 427.

51 Ibid.

52 It is ascribed to Walsingham in various contemporary hands on the manuscript copies in the British Library – Harleian MS 290, fol. 117 and Harleian MS 4,314, fol. 120. A printed version is in BL Cotton MS Caligula C, ii, fols 284–291. The printed version in Harleian MS 290 is

printed in Read, *Mr Secretary Walsingham*, vol. 1, pp. 68–79.

53 Her involvement in the murder of Darnley.

54 Another pamphlet, published as *An Answer to a Slanderous Book* – Walsingham's *Discourse* – and dated 15 March 1570, is in BL Cotton MS Julius F, xi, fols 391ff.

55 An analysis of Norfolk's debts in September 1571 indicated that his lordship of Clun in Shropshire was liable to be forfeited because of non-payment of £4,400 to Sir Rowland Heyward; the manor of Beeding in Sussex was mortgaged to the merchant tailor John Godd for £130; Wigborough Manor, Essex, was also mortgaged to William Watson for £125; and a number of jewels and plate were in pawn for £15. To clear these debts, Norfolk instructed the sale of a number of lands, including the manor of Tollesbury, Essex, for £2,200 to the appropriately named Mr Pawn. Alderman Jackman's executors were also owed £2,150, part of the Earl of Arundel's debt, which the duke was to discharge. See HMC Hatfield, vol. 1, p. 527.

56 Robinson, p. 55.

57 SPD – *Edward VI, Mary & Elizabeth, 1547–80*, p. 345. Ridolphi was to remain in Walsingham's home 'without conference [contact with the outside world] until he may be examined of certain matters which touch her majesty very nearly'.

58 HMC Hatfield, vol. 1, p. 458.

59 HMC Hatfield, vol. 1, p. 436.

60 Ibid., p. 346. Cited by Read, *Mr Secretary Walsingham*, vol. 1, p. 67.

61 Northumberland sought refuge in Scotland but was handed over to Elizabeth by Moray and beheaded at York in August 1572. Westmorland, attainted for treason, fled to Flanders and died in Nieuport in 1601.

62 Norfolk wrote to Cecil immediately after his release, saying it was no small comfort to him to be out of 'yonder pestilent, infectious house' and he feared the sickness would grow 'worse before it mends'. See HMC Hatfield, vol. 1, p. 479.

63 Arundel Castle Archives, G1/21.

64 BL Harleian MS 290, fol. 88.

65 Williams, *Tudor Tragedy*, pp. 199–200.

66 Ridolphi returned to Rome where Pope Pius V made him a papal senator and he lived for another four decades in Florence, fat and prosperous from lucrative financial transactions. He died there on 18 February 1612.

67 Robinson, p. 63, and Williams, *Tudor Tragedy*, pp. 200–202.

68 'A Carthusian', *Historical Account of the Charterhouse*, p. 115.

69 HMC Hatfield, vol. 1, p. 520.

70 HMC Hatfield, vol. 1, p. 522.

71 Ibid.

72 HMC Hatfield, vol. 1, pp. 522–3.

73 HMC Hatfield, vol. 1, p. 526.

74 HMC Hatfield, vol. 1, p. 523.

75 HMC Hatfield, vol. 1, p. 527.

76 Hatfield House, Cecil Papers, CP 6/114. Security was not as lax at the Tower as one might think from this. Prisoners 'who were concerned in the Duke of Norfolk's plot' were carefully watched and their conversations noted secretly. See Longleat House, MSS of Marquis of Bath, Dudley Papers, DU/Vol.2/26, the reports by Richard Farmer, one of those suspected by Elizabeth Massey of not bearing the queen goodwill.

77 A list of questions asked of Norfolk are in BL Cotton MS Julius F, vi. fol. 11.

78 Hatfield House, Cecil Papers, CP 5/62–66.

79 A royal bodyguard, formed by Thomas Cromwell, armed with poleaxes. Hatfield House Cecil Papers, CP 157/94.

80 National Archives, KB 8/42, roll and file of court of Lord High Steward, charges against Thomas Howard, fourth Duke of Norfolk, and also BL Lansdowne MS 256, fols 153–67, for the arraignment.

81 BL Add. MS 48,027, fols 83–125; Cotton MS Caligula D, vi, fol. 200; Sloane MS 1,421, fols 32–81; MS 2,172 fols 59–66; Stowe MS 396, fols 9, 13 and 24. See also Salmon, *State Trials*, vol. 1, pp. 82–116.

82 BL Add. MS 48,023, fols 151–2.

83 Nott, vol. 1, appendix 35, pp. lxxxii–lxxxviii. See Arundel Castle Archives, C212.

84 CRS, Pollen and MacMahon, *Venerable Philip Howard*, p. 6.

85 Robinson, p. 66.

86 Written on page 2 of the dedication to Edward VI. Dix kept the book, signing it 'Wyllym Dix' on the dedication page, on either side of an image of the young king, and on its last page. The book, 21.6 x 17.1 cm., is bound in red morocco with the gold stamp of the Hon. Thomas Greville. It is now in the library at Arundel Castle.

87 The note says the copy belonged to 'Mr Iadis, of Bryanston Square' [London], near Marble Arch, which was built between 1811 and 1821. The present whereabouts of the book are unknown.

88 From the old Norse *hap*, a mischance.

89 Thomas Howard, third Duke of Norfolk.

90 Hatfield House, Cecil Papers 5/102–3.

91 Arundel Castle Archives, T4.

92 Arundel Castle Archives, G1/22.

93 Brown, *Tryal of Thomas Duke of Norfolk*, preface; Edwards, *Marvellous Chance*, p. 398. The fight with the gentlemen pensioners is mentioned in BL Add. MS 48,027, fols 122–125B. This does not appear in contemporary printed accounts.

94 SPD, *Edward VI, Mary & Elizabeth, 1547–80*, p. 446.

95 HMC Hatfield, vol. 10, p. 446.

Chapter 10: Martyr Earl

1 Norfolk, p. 115. The original MS on which this account was based is dated c. 1630 and remains in the Arundel Castle Archives. Arundel House, approached by a narrow lane through the densely packed houses lining the south side of The Strand, had extensive gardens edging the Thames, with its own landing stairs. A fine view of Old St Paul's and the city could be seen over the rooftops from its leads.

2 Norfolk, p. 5. Possibly the silver gilt font used for the christening of Prince Edward on 15 October 1537.

3 Martin was not openly a member of the Catholic Church but was 'wholly Catholic in his judgement and affection'. He wrote that 'as long as his grace [Norfolk] did prosper, I lived in his house to my conscience without trouble. When he was in The Tower and other men ruled his house, I was willed to receive the communion or to depart.' After he left Norfolk's service he went to Europe and was ordained a priest.

4 CRS, Pollen and MacMahon, p. 2.

5 Norfolk, p. 11.

6 Norfolk Record Office MS, 21509/4 and 5. The payments also included sums paid to the Tudor bureaucracy of criminal justice: 5s for 'engrossing of his pardon for the privy signet'; 25s to 'Mr Dister and his clerks for drawing [writing] the pardon and for the charges of the passing of the Great Seal, £8 13s 7d'. Bannister's wife and two servants were paid £9 19s 10d for 'riding about the same at [the court] at Richmond'.

7 Norfolk Record Office MS 21509/368. Dix's accounts of money owed to him for the period Michaelmas 1571 to Michaelmas 1578 are in the same file.

8 Robinson, p. 70.

9 Holinshed, *Chronicles*, vol. 4, p. 376.

10 CRS, Pollen and MacMahon, p. 22.

11 23 Elizabeth I, *cap.* 6. The Act says 'that your said subject and his heirs be and shall be from henceforth, by the authority of this present Act, restored and enabled only in blood, as son and heir of the said Thomas, late Duke of Norfolk ... and that your said subject and his heirs may ...

hold and enjoy all and every such honours, castles, manors, lordships, lands, tenements, rents etc.'

12 Nichols, *Progresses*, vol. 2, p. 312. Another description is provided by Holinshed, *Chronicles*, vol. 4, pp. 435ff.

13 Going home to Arundel House from St Paul's Cathedral one day, he 'observed all the signs of all the houses' on the left side of Fleet Street 'which are some hundreds ... and coming into his house, he caused one of his servants to write them down on a paper as he named them'. Another was sent with the list and found it to be an accurate record. See Norfolk, pp. 127–8.

14 The earl also spent much time administering his estates. On 28 July 1584, he appointed Luke Baitman as his new tennis court keeper at Howard House, in succession to Anthony Norton, 'servant to me', who had held the post since the days of the fourth duke. See Arundel Castle Archives G1/9.

15 CRS, Pollen and MacMahon, pp. 31–2.

16 Williams, *Tudor Tragedy*, pp. 84–5.

17 The fourth duke, in his advice to his children on suitable members of the English aristocracy to befriend them after his execution, identified Edward de Vere, seventeenth Earl of Oxford, as one 'who might do you more good than any kinsman you have'. There were rumours that Oxford blamed Burghley for not stopping Norfolk's execution and had even planned to rescue the duke from the Tower. But Oxford was a fickle friend. In 1580–81 he accused Henry Howard, with others, of supporting Mary Queen of Scots and being covert Catholics. In turn, they asserted he was a drunkard, an atheist and a potential murderer.

In 1582, Sir Roger Townsend, one of the Howards' retainers, heard talk that thugs employed by Oxford were planning to attack Thomas Knyvett, a gentleman of Elizabeth's Privy Chamber, and a kinsman of the family, in revenge for a duel he fought with Oxford in which the earl was 'dangerously' wounded. Knyvett was duly assaulted at Blackfriars, but Townsend could not name the assailants 'for I was so far behind, as I could not discern [who] they were'. See CRS, Pollen and MacMahon, pp. 35–6.

18 The room survives and serves as the library.

19 Norfolk, p. 20.

20 Allen (1532–94) was the leader of the exiled English Catholics in Europe during Elizabeth's reign and in 1568 founded a college at Douai to instruct English students in the Catholic religion. The college was expelled in 1578 but re-established at Reims. Allen supported plans to enthrone Philip II of Spain in England. He is buried in the church of

the Holy Trinity, attached to the Venerable English College in Rome, where a memorial to him remains on the north wall.

21 See Hutchinson, *Elizabeth's Spy Master*, pp. 101–7.

22 Tierney, *Arundel*, p. 376.

23 Heywood, or Haywood, was arrested at sea by Walsingham's men and banished in early February 1584. He died in Naples in 1595. Arundel's interrogation is detailed in Pollen and MacMahon, pp. 46–8. One of Arundel's inquisitors was Lord Hunsdon, Chamberlain to the queen, who had been his father's page.

24 BL Add. MS 15,891, fol. 126.

25 Norfolk, pp. 52–6. Kellway applied for a warrant from Burghley in August 1587, empowering him to arrest papists fleeing England for France whom he 'might take in passing'. He was appointed sheriff of Hampshire in 1586–7.

26 27 Elizabeth 1, *cap.* 2 made it high treason to shelter a Catholic priest.

27 BL Cotton MS Titus B, ii, 201ff. Other copies are in Harleian MS 787, fols 46–9, and Sloane MS 2,172, fols 41–3, and Add. MS 33,594, fol. 216.

28 CRS, Pollen and MacMahon, pp. 114–15. Almost certainly the forgery was the work of Walsingham's master forger and decipherer, Thomas Phelippes. It was claimed to have been forged 'by some who had notice beforehand of his going, as the Secretary and some of his [Arundel's] greatest enemies had . . .'

29 BL Add. MS 15,891, fol. 154.

30 BL Add. MS 15,891, fol. 148.

31 BL Egerton MS 2,074, fols 13, 29, 30, 32, 39, 54.

32 BL Egerton MS 2,074, fols 23, 25, 72.

33 BL Egerton MS 2,074, fol. 46.

34 BL Add. MS 48,029, fols 111ff. CRS, Pollen and MacMahon, pp. 139–44; Norfolk, pp. 64–5.

35 Bodleian Library, Tanner MS, 78, fol. 1.

36 *Royal Commission on Historical Monuments*, 'London East', London, 1930, p. 84.

37 Tierney, *Arundel*, p. 385.

38 Hammond was 'an old aged woman . . . a laundress in the Tower'.

39 BL Add. MS 48,029, fol. 102.

40 CRS, Pollen and MacMahon, pp. 185–6.

41 BL Add. MS 48,029, fol. 81.

42 Hunsdon (?1524–96) was the son of Mary Boleyn and her first husband, and cousin to Elizabeth.

43 Norfolk, pp. 87–9.

44 Salmon, *State Trials*, vol.1 , p. 165.

45 BL Add. MS 48,029, fol. 107, Lansdowne MS 256, fol. 167, and Stowe MS 396, fol. 14. Another report has this version: 'Behold here a clean hand and an honest heart!'

46 Some reports erroneously say 'twenty-second' – this version comes from BL Lansdowne MS 94, fol. 167, and Harleian MS 834, no. 5, fols 59–62. It refers correctly to the Act against harbouring priests, 27 Elizabeth I, *cap.* 2.

47 Salmon, *State Trials*, vol. 1, p. 166.

48 Salmon, *State Trials*, vol. 1, p. 166. Popham's brief for the prosecution is in BL Egerton MS 2,074, fol. 81.

49 Robinson, p. 75.

50 Salmon, *State Trials*, vol. 1, p. 168.

51 BL Add. MS 48,029, fol. 74.

52 Norfolk, p. 94.

53 BL Add. MS 48,029, p. 110.

54 Derby returned to his Lancashire home deeply troubled by the trial and his role in it. He called his servants together and told them 'he had been more beholden to Queen Elizabeth than any of his predecessors ... but this one thing did grieve him more than all the favours that he received from her, that she had made him her High Steward to condemn the Earl of Arundel, who was condemned upon a letter, which, as he thought, was not sufficiently proved, but may well be counterfeited and "this lies heavy upon my conscience".' See Godfrey Goodman, *The Court of King James the First* ..., two vols (London, 1839), vol. 1, pp. 141–2.

55 Norfolk, p. 96.

56 She died, unmarried, from tuberculosis in 1598.

57 Arundel Castle Archives, G1/9. Arundel's debts at March 1585 totalled £17,977 and he was paying interest on loans of £4,666. Income from the Howard estates amounted to £4,249. See BL Lansdowne MS 45, no. 84.

58 Tierney, *Arundel*, p. 397.

59 Robinson, p. 78.

60 *DNB2*, vol. 28, p. 408.

61 *Fourth Report of the Royal Commission on Historical Manuscripts*, pt i, p. 372 (London, 1874).

62 Arundel Castle Archives, G1/23. It is unlikely the paper ever reached Arundel, as it fell into Burghley's hands.

63 Tierney, *Arundel*, p. 403.

64 CRS, Pollen and MacMahon, p. 332. See also Roger B. Manning, 'The Prosecution of Sir Michael Blount, Lieutenant of the Tower of London, 1595', *Historical Research*, vol. 57 (November 1984), p. 216.

65 Norfolk, pp. 68–71. Some believed he had some kind of foreknowledge

of his hour of death. About seven or eight days before, he laid out a calendar of prayers he intended to say on each day and when it came to the Sunday, he paused, and said: 'Hitherto and no further'.

66 BL Lansdowne MS 94, fol. 118.

67 BL Lansdowne MS 79, fol. 74.

68 *DNB2*, vol. 28, p. 408.

Chapter 11: Resurgam

1 Edward Hyde, first Earl of Clarendon, *History of the Great Rebellion*, two vols, London, 1702, vol. 1, p. 44.

2 According to the disgraced Secretary of State William Davison, he was one of those who urged Mary Queen of Scots' execution. See BL Cotton MS Titus C, vii, fol. 48.

3 Langton, vol. 1, p. 46.

4 Langton, vol. 1, p. 107.

5 National Archives, SP 12/211/50.

6 'Warping' – a laborious and repetitive method of moving sailing ships out of harbour, in the absence of wind. The anchor, attached to a cable, is rowed out ahead of the ship and dropped to the seabed. The crew then wind in the cable with a windlass and the ship is pulled in the direction of where the anchor has been dropped. The operation is repeated as necessary.

7 This type of warship was a larger version of the galley, lateen-rigged on three masts and carrying 300 slaves to man the oars. It was able to fire broadsides from guns mounted above the banks of oars. Six galleasses sailed with the Armada, but being more suited to naval operations in the calmer waters of the Mediterranean, suffered in the storms of the North Sea and English Channel.

8 SPD, *Elizabeth 1581–90*, p. 507, and Langton, vol. 1, pp. 288–9.

9 Cited by Robinson, p. 83.

10 *DNB2*, vol. 28, p. 322.

11 Robinson, p. 85.

12 G. P. V. Akrigg (ed.), *The Letters of James VI and I* (London, 1984), p. 179.

13 P. Croft, 'Libels, Popular Literacy and Public Opinion in Early Modern England', *Historical Research*, vol. 68 (1995), p. 278.

14 Akrigg, op. cit., pp. 257 and 250.

15 National Archives, PROB 11/123.

16 The accounts of Owen Shepherd, Receiver of Northampton's lands for 1609, show expenditure of £451 14s 6d to Richard Hovell junior for building the almshouses at the east end of the churchyard at Castle

Rising. The foundation, built around a square garden, had twelve rooms for poor women, another for their governess, and a spacious hall and kitchen. A 'decent' chapel projected from the east wall. The inmates qualified for admission if they had 'led an honest life and conversation' and in religion, were 'grave and discreet'. They had to be unmarried and at least fifty-sixty years of age, and 'no common beggar, harlot, scold, drunkard, haunter of taverns, inns or ale-houses'. See Blomefield, vol. 4, p. 673. They still accommodate eligible ladies today.

17 Suffolk sold Howard House, in Charterhouse Square, in 1611 to Thomas Sutton for £13,000. Sutton founded a charity there for forty male pensioners, known as Brothers.

18 Norman McClure, *Letters of John Chamberlain*, two vols (Philadelphia, 1939), vol. 2, p. 144, fn 6.

19 Arundel Castle Archives, G1/87.

Appendix 1: The Howard Homes

1 The site of the East Hall was for years called 'the Candle yard' because of its use in making candles for the palace.

2 Robinson, p. 37.

3 Williams, *Tudor Tragedy*, p. 44.

4 John Holland, 'chaplain to the right high and mighty' Thomas Howard, third duke, leased for twenty-one years the parsonage of Feltwell St Mary, Norfolk, to George Holland, gentleman in 1545. Were these relations of Bess Holland? See Norfolk Record Office, NAS 1/1/10/19.

5 National Archives, LR 2/115.

6 The seneschal was responsible for the administration of the Kenninghall estate.

7 National Archives, SP 1/245/145; Manning, 'Kenninghall', p. 296.

8 Howlett, 'Household Accounts of Kenninghall', pp. 53 and 58–9.

9 National Archives, C 54/559, and Thomas Allen, *History . . . of Lambeth*, pp. 340–41.

10 *Norfolk Archaeology*, vol. 3 (1849), p. 208. In 1849, a gravestone of fifteenth-century work, incised with angels, was found at a depth of fourteen feet (4.27 m.) below the surface on the site of the palace. On the reverse were the arms of the fourth duke. This slab probably came from St Benet's. Ibid., p. 418. Blomefield reports that 'in the palace yard at the entrance of a house near the river, lies a large grave stone with an abbot in his robes cut thereon' (vol. 4, p. 268).

11 Norfolk Record Office, MC 146/24 624X5.

12 Williams, *Tudor Tragedy*, p. 69.

13 Kent, p. 81.

14 Bray, *Diaries of John Evelyn*, vol. 2, pp. 269–70. The River Wensum in this period was clogged by discharges from innumerable 'bog-houses'. See Rawcliffe and Wilson, *Norwich since 1550*, p. 150.

15 Kent, p. 84.

16 Norfolk Record Office, MC 146/24 624X5.

BIBLIOGRAPHY

◆

PRIMARY SOURCES

Manuscripts

ARUNDEL CASTLE, WEST SUSSEX
MSS OF THE DUKES OF NORFOLK

A 113 – Papers relating to the household expenses of Thomas Howard, third Duke of Norfolk, and his son Henry Howard, Earl of Surrey (later third Duke of Norfolk), 1523.

C212 – Copy of a letter from Thomas Howard, fourth Duke of Norfolk, to his children shortly before his execution, 1572.

G1/4 – Papers relating to Thomas Howard, second Duke of Norfolk.

G1/5 – Papers relating to Thomas Howard, third Duke of Norfolk.

G1/6 – Papers relating to Henry Howard, Earl of Surrey.

G1/7 – Papers relating to Thomas Howard, fourth Duke of Norfolk.

G1/9 – Will of Philip Howard, Earl of Arundel, and a copy of the settlement on Anne [Dacre], Countess of Arundel, and her children, 1611.

G1/21 – Copies of three documents relating to the imprisonment in the Tower of Thomas Howard, fourth Duke of Norfolk, 1569–70.

G1/22 – Death warrant signed by Queen Elizabeth I, for execution of Thomas, fourth Duke of Norfolk, Palace of Westminster, dated 9 February 1572.

G1/23 – Copy of an anonymous note sent to Philip, Earl of Arundel, within the Tower, c. 1595.

G1/83 – Copies of Letters Patent, dated 1 February 1514, created Thomas Howard [second] Duke of Norfolk for services to the crown in Scotland and also granting an augmentation of arms and manors in Berkshire, Derbyshire, Hertfordshire, Kent, Nottinghamshire, Oxfordshire, Shropshire, Staffordshire, Warwickshire and Wiltshire.

G1/84 – Letters Patent appointing Thomas Howard, Earl of Surrey, as Lieutenant General of the English army in Scotland, dated 26 February 1523.

G1/87 – Letters Patent, restoring Thomas Howard, Earl of Arundel, all such titles of land in Norfolk, Suffolk, Cambridgeshire, Essex, Surrey and Sussex and precedence as Philip, Earl of Arundel, his father, had enjoyed, and as Earl of Surrey, to such dignities of Baronies as Thomas, late [fourth] Duke of Norfolk, his grandfather, lost by attainder; 22 November 1608.

G2/8 – Copy of Act of Attainder, 1485, against John Howard, [first] Duke of Norfolk, and of his son, Thomas.

G2/9 – Copy of a petition, dated 1510, for an Act of Restitution granted to Thomas, Earl of Surrey.

G2/10 – Copies of Act of Restitution in blood, dated 24 October 1553, of Thomas, Earl of Surrey, afterwards fourth Duke of Norfolk.

MD 490 – Extent of Estates of Thomas Howard, third Duke of Norfolk, 1554.

MS 1638 – *The Genealogie of the Princelie Familie of the Howards* by Henry Lily, 1637.

T1 – Certified copy of will, dated 31 August 1516, of Thomas Howard, second Duke of Norfolk, allotting a jointure to Agnes [Tylney] his wife and disposal of lands.

T4 – Original will, dated 31 May 1571, of Thomas, fourth Duke of Norfolk.

In the Library of Arundel Castle – a copy of the New Testament, printed by Richard Jugge, printer to the Queen's Majesty, London, 1566, bearing on the second page of dedication a letter from Thomas Howard, fourth Duke of Norfolk, to his auditor and retainer, William Dix; the Tower of London, 10 February 1572.

BRITISH LIBRARY, LONDON

Additional Charters

6,289 – Indenture between Thomas [Howard] Earl of Surrey, Great Admiral of England, and John Heron, Treasurer of the Chamber, and John Hopton, Comptroller of the King's Ships, for the construction of a pond at Deptford 'for certain ships to ride in'; 9 June 1517.

Additional MSS

5,754, fol. 12 – Payments to Lord William Howard for his service in the Scottish campaign of October 1542.

6,113, fol. 81 – Contemporary account of the christening of Prince Edward at Hampton Court; 15 October 1537.

8,715, fol. 220b – Letter from Ridolfo, Bishop of Faenza, to Signor Ambrogio, Papal Secretary, about Queen Anne's 'pretended' miscarriage; 10 March 1536.

10,110, fol. 237 – An account of Thomas Howard, third Duke of Norfolk's expedition on the Scottish borders; October 1542.

15,891, fol. 126 – Letter from Sir Francis Walsingham to Sir Christopher Hatton about the interrogation of the Earl of Arundel's secretary Mr John Keeper; Seething Lane, London, 30 January 1584.

> fol. 148 – Letter from Philip Howard, Earl of Arundel, to Sir Christopher Hatton; the Tower, 7 May 1585.

> fol. 154 – Letter from Sir Francis Walsingham to Sir Christopher Hatton about Philip Howard, Earl of Arundel; Barn Elms, Surrey, 1 May 1585.

17,492 – A small collection of sixteenth-century poetry in a quarto volume, including some by Lord Thomas Howard and his wife, Lady Margaret Douglas.

32,348, fol. 77 – Thomas Howard, third Duke of Norfolk's complaints about lack of horses and wagons in the Scottish campaign; 19 October 1542.

32,647, fol. 115 – Letter from Thomas Howard, third Duke of Norfolk, to Sir William Fitzwilliam, Earl of Southampton, about the lack of drink for the English army about to invade Scotland; 7 September 1542.

> fol. 121 – Letter from Thomas Howard, third Duke of Norfolk, to the Privy Council about the supply of beer to the king's army assembling for the military expedition against Scotland; Kenninghall, 11 September 1542.

> fol. 193 – Letter from Thomas Howard, third Duke of Norfolk, and Sir Anthony Browne, Master of the Horse, about the non-arrival of ships carrying victuals; York, 20 September 1542.

> fol. 194 – Letter from Sir George Lawson, Treasurer of Berwick, to Thomas Howard, third Duke of Norfolk, about shortages of equipment and victuals for the English army; Berwick, 18 September 1542.

> fol. 196 – Letter from Thomas Howard, third Duke of Norfolk, to Gardiner and Wriothesley, seeking their help in defending

him from blame for delayed military supplies; 21 September 1542.

32,648, fol. 46 – Letter from Thomas Howard, third Duke of Norfolk, to Gardiner and Wriothesley, asking them to intercede with the king, to prevent him being appointed Warden of the Marches; Newcastle, 12 October 1542.

fol. 65 – Letter from Henry VIII to Thomas Howard, third Duke of Norfolk, reassuring him that he will not be 'troubled' by the Wardenry of the Marches; 16 October 1542.

fol. 96 – Letter from the Duke of Suffolk and Bishop Cuthbert Tunstall announcing Norfolk's invasion of the Scottish borders; 28 October 1542.

fol. 108 – Thomas Howard, third Duke of Norfolk, and others to the Privy Council, announcing his withdrawal from Scotland; Kelso, 28 October 1542.

fol. 112 – Thomas Howard, third Duke of Norfolk, to Gardiner and Wriothesley, complaining of 'the lax'; Kelso, 28 October 1542.

fol. 114 – Thomas Howard, third Duke of Norfolk, to Wriothesley about the results of his military expedition to Scotland; 29 October 1542.

fol. 120 – Henry VIII to Norfolk, inquiring about the success of the military expedition to Scotland; 2 November 1542.

fol. 156 – Account of the Battle of Solway, 24 November 1542.

45,131, fol. 85 – Drawing of the tomb of Thomas Howard, second Duke of Norfolk, at the Cluniac abbey of Our Lady, Thetford, Norfolk.

46,372, fols 1–5v – Bill of Attainder against John Howard, first Duke of Norfolk, and Thomas Howard, Earl of Surrey, his son; 7 November 1485.

48,023 (Yelverton MS 26), fols 151–52 – Letter from Thomas Howard, fourth Duke of Norfolk, to Elizabeth I after his attainder, 'written by the woeful hand of a dead man'; the Tower, 21 January 1572. Another copy is in Add. MS.

48,027 (Yelverton MS 31) fols 83–125v – Papers relating to the imprisonment, trial and execution of Thomas Howard, fourth Duke of Norfolk, 1570–72, including contemporary accounts of his execution. This account by [William Fleetwood, Recorder of London] recounts, at fols 122–5v, a fight with gentlemen pensioners immediately after the beheading that does not seem to appear in contemporary printed accounts.

48,028 (Yelverton MS 32), fols 160–65 – Act of Attainder of Thomas Cromwell, Earl of Essex, 29 June 1540.

48,029 (Yelverton MS 33), fol. 73 – Order of arraignment of Philip Howard, Earl of Arundel; 14 April 1589.

> fols 74–80 – Charges against Philip Howard, Earl of Arundel.
>
> fol. 81 – Confession of Sir Thomas Gerard; 25 October 1588.
>
> fol. 102 – Confession of William Bennet, priest; 16 October 1588.
>
> fols 111ff – Star Chamber proceedings against Philip Howard, Earl of Arundel; 17 May 1586.

Arundel MS

152, fol. 294 – Account of the interrogation of Sir Thomas More by Thomas Cromwell; Tower of London, 31 April 1535.

Cotton MS

Caligula B, vi, fol. 35 – Catherine of Aragon to Cardinal Wolsey, announcing the victory at Flodden; 16 September 1513.

Caligula D, vi, fol. 104 – Letter from Lord Thomas Howard to Cardinal Wolsey on the morale of his sailors; Plymouth, May 1513.

> fols 106–7 – Letter from Lord Thomas Howard, to Henry VIII; 'written in the *Mary Rose*, Plymouth haven, 7 May [1513] at nine o'clock at night'.
>
> fol. 107 – Letter from Sir Edward Echyngham, describing the death of Sir Edward Howard; Plymouth, 6 May 1513.

Cleopatra E, iv, fol. 178 – Letter from Ralph Sadler to Thomas Cromwell reporting on his attempts to find him a seat in Parliament; November 1529.

Cleopatra E, v, fols 313–20 – Corrections and amendments in Henry VIII's own hand to proposals for the Act to Abolish Diversity in Opinion, the 'Six Articles'.

Julius F. vi, fol. 11 – Questions to be put to Thomas Howard, fourth Duke of Norfolk, during interrogation.

> fol. 200B – Arraignment, trial and confession of Thomas Howard, fourth Duke of Norfolk, with his confession at his execution, 1571.

Julius F. xi, fols 391ff – *Answer to a Slanderous Book that was published against the marriage of the Duke of Norfolk and the Scottish Queen*, dated 15 March 1570.

Nero C x, fol. 2 – Arrangements by Thomas Howard, third Duke of

Norfolk, for 1,200 masses to be said in London churches for the soul of Queen Jane Seymour; 8 November 1537.

Otho C. x, fol. 250 – Letter from the Privy Council to Sir William Paget, ambassador in France, about 'a most miserable case, lately revealed' [Catherine Howard]; Westminster, [12] November 1541.

Titus B. i, fol. 84 – Letter from Elizabeth, Duchess of Norfolk, to Thomas Cromwell, Redbourn; 30 December 1536.

fol. 94 – Letter from Thomas Howard, third Duke of Norfolk, to the Privy Council; mid-December 1546.

fol. 100b – Offer of 'cross marriage' between the Howard and Seymour families, June 1546.

fol. 104b – Letter from Wolsey to Bishop Fox, about Thomas Howard, Earl of Surrey's departure from court and Sir Edward Howard's incitement of Henry VIII against the Scots; Windsor, 30 September 1511.

fol. 125 – Letter from Thomas Howard, third duke, to Thomas Cromwell; Buntingford, Hertfordshire, undated.

fol. 152 – Letter from Elizabeth Howard, Duchess of Norfolk, to her brother Henry, Lord Stafford.

fol. 383ff – Five letters from Elizabeth, Duchess of Norfolk, to [Thomas Cromwell], 26 June, 24 October and 10 November 1537.

fol. 386 – Letter from Thomas Howard, third Duke of Norfolk, to Thomas Cromwell, denying his wife's charges against him.

fol. 389 – Letter from Elizabeth, Duchess of Norfolk, to Thomas Cromwell, Redbourn; 10 November 1537.

fol. 390 – Letter from Elizabeth, Duchess of Norfolk, to Thomas Cromwell, Redbourn; 24 October 1537.

Titus B, ii, fols 201ff – Letter from Philip Howard, Earl of Arundel, to Queen Elizabeth, explaining his decision to leave England.

Vespasian F, iii, fol. 15 – Letter from Catherine of Aragon to Henry VIII announcing the victory of Flodden; Woburn, 16 September 1513.

Vespasian F, xiii, fol. 75 – Letter from Mary Howard, widow of the Duke of Richmond, to her father, Thomas Howard, third Duke of Norfolk, seeking his assistance in a suit to Henry VIII to 'have justice done' her respecting her maintenance; Kenninghall, Norfolk, January 1537.

fol. 78b – Letter from Thomas Howard, third Duke of Norfolk, to a minister at court, desiring him to befriend him with the king; Carlisle, 24 February [1537].

fol. 79 – Letter from Elizabeth, Duchess of Norfolk, to Thomas Cromwell asking him to procure some venison for her 'as none was sent her since her Lord's displeasure'; Redbourn, Hertfordshire, 23 August [1534].

fol. 134b – Letter from Lady Margaret Douglas to Thomas Cromwell; August 1536.

Vitellius B, ii, fol. 50 – Letter from Cardinal Christopher Bainbridge to Henry VIII reporting how the Flodden victory was reported in Rome; 17 September 1513.

Vitellius B, xii, fol. 171 – Letter from Stephen Gardiner, secretary to Henry VIII, to Wolsey; Woodstock, Oxfordshire, August 1529.

Egerton MS

985, fol. 33 – Ceremony of the christening of Prince Edward, October 1537.

fol. 48 – Ceremonials of receiving, conveying and the coronation of Queen Anne [Boleyn], May and June 1533.

fol. 59 – Creation of Thomas Howard, second Duke of Norfolk, February 1514.

fol. 65 – Ceremony of the degrading of Thomas Howard, late [third] Duke of Norfolk and Henry Howard, late Earl of Surrey, his son [?1547].

2,014, fol. 2 – Letter written in Latin, from Henry VIII to Maximilian, Duke of Milan, reporting capture of Tournai and against the Scottish army [at Flodden], 16 September 1513.

2,074, fols 13, 29, 30, 32, 39, 54 – Interrogations of Philip Howard, Earl of Arundel; the Tower, 4–17 May 1585.

fols 23, 25, 72 – Interrogation of Lord Henry Howard in the Tower, May 1585.

fol. 46 – A list of Philip Howard, Earl of Arundel's household.

Harley MS

78, fol. 24 – Letter by Henry Howard, Earl of Surrey, to the Privy Council, promising to curb his 'heady will'; Fleet Prison, 15 July 1542.

283, fol. 75 – Circular letter from Queen Anne [Boleyn] addressed to Lord Cobham, announcing the birth of a child, with 'prince' amended to read 'princess'; Greenwich Palace, 7 September 1533.

290, fol. 88 – Letter from Mary Queen of Scots urging Thomas Howard, fourth Duke of Norfolk, to escape from house arrest at Howard House; 31 January 1571.

fol. 117 – Manuscript copy of *A Discourse touching the Pretended Match between the Duke of Norfolk and the Queen of Scots*. Another manuscript copy is in Harleian MS 4,314, fol. 120 and a printed version is in Cotton MS Caligula C ii, fols 284–91.

297, fol. 256 – Confession of Thomas Howard, third Duke of Norfolk, before the Privy Council, 12 January 1547.

834 no. 5, fols 59–2 – Arraignment of Philip Howard, late Earl of Arundel.

1,453, fol. 69 – 'Drawing of Arms of Howard, Earl of Surrey, for which he was attainted', by Sir William Dethick, Garter King at Arms, in 1586.

6,989, fol. 127 – Letter from the Privy Council to Thomas Howard, third Duke of Norfolk, about Henry VIII's secret plans to besiege Boulogne; London, 7 July 1544.

fol. 129 – The Duke of Suffolk and Sir Anthony Browne to Thomas Howard, third Duke of Norfolk, 8 July 1544.

fol. 191 – Letter from the Privy Council to Thomas Howard, third Duke of Norfolk, about failures in logistics; St James's Palace, 20 June 1544.

Lansdowne MS

45, no. 84 – List of Philip Howard, Earl of Arundel's debts at March 1585.

79, fol. 74 – Burial expenses for Philip Howard, Earl of Arundel, 22 October 1595.

94, fol. 118 – Burial Office for Philip Howard, Earl of Arundel; the Tower of London, 22 October 1595.

256, fols 153–67 – Arraignment of Thomas Howard, fourth Duke of Norfolk, before the Earl of Shrewsbury, Lord High Steward of England; 24 January 1574.

fol. 167*v* – Arraignment, trial and condemnation of Philip Howard, Earl of Arundel; 14 April 1589.

Sloane MS

1,427, fols 32–81 – Trial of Thomas Howard, fourth Duke of Norfolk, for high treason before his peers at Westminster, 26 January 1571.

2,172, fols 41–3 – Contemporary copy of a letter from Philip, Earl of

Arundel, to Elizabeth I, explaining the reasons for his decision 'to go beyond the seas' in voluntary banishment, 11–14 April 1585. (Other copies in Cotton MS, Julius F. vi, fols 69v–70, Titus B, ii, fols 201ff, Add. MS 33,594 fol. 216 and Harley MS 787, fols 46–9v.)
 fols 59–66 – Fragment of a report of the trial of Thomas Howard, fourth Duke of Norfolk, before the Lords at Westminster, 26 January 1571.

Stowe MSS
396 – Reports of State Trials, 1521–1666.
 fol. 3 – Edward Stafford, Duke of Buckingham, 1521.
 fols 8–9 – Henry Howard, Earl of Surrey, 1546.
 fols 9, 13, 24 – Thomas Howard, fourth Duke of Norfolk, 1571 [misdated 1657].
 fol. 14v – Philip Howard, Earl of Arundel, 1589.

CORNWALL RECORD OFFICE, TRURO
Arundel papers
AR/22/30 – Letters Patent from Henry VIII to Thomas Howard, third Duke of Norfolk, and others, appointing them to keep the peace regarding laws concerning 'hunters, workmen, artisans, servants, innkeepers, mendicants, vagabonds and others calling themselves travelling-men'.

HATFIELD HOUSE, HERTFORDSHIRE
MSS OF THE MARQUIS OF SALISBURY
Cecil Papers (CP)
CP 1/10 and 11 – Deposition of Thomas Howard, third Duke of Norfolk, and others respecting the marriage of Henry VIII and Anne of Cleves.

CP 1/23 – Deposition of Henry VIII to the commission investigating the validity of his marriage to Anne of Cleves, 1540.

CP 5/62–66 – Confession of Kenelm Berney; 13 January 1572.

CP 5/102–103 – Last confession of Thomas Howard, fourth Duke of Norfolk; 26 February 1572.

CP 6/114 – Declaration of Elizabeth Massey, wife of the parson in the Tower of London; 3 November 1571.

CP 153/51 – Letter from Cecil Thomas Howard, fourth Duke of Norfolk; 28 September 1569.

CP 156/60 – Letter from Thomas Howard, fourth Duke of Norfolk, to Cecil or the Earl of Leicester; 22 September 1569.

CP 156/66 – Letter from Thomas Howard, fourth Duke of Norfolk, to Queen Elizabeth I; 24 September 1569.

CP 156/67 – Letter from Queen Elizabeth I to Thomas Howard, fourth Duke of Norfolk; 25 September 1569.

CP 156/72 – Letter from Queen Elizabeth I to Thomas Howard, fourth Duke of Norfolk; 28 September 1569.

CP 157/94 – Rough notes in Cecil's hand on arrangements for the trial of Thomas Howard, fourth Duke of Norfolk; 26 February, 1572.

LONGLEAT HOUSE, WARMINSTER, WILTSHIRE
MSS OF THE MARQUIS OF BATH

Portland Papers (PO)

PO/Vol.1/15 – 'Confession of Q[ueen] Catherine Howard ... afore the Kings Counsell at Hampton Court; 12 November 1541. (Copy, certified by signatures of Thomas Cranmer, Archbishop of Canterbury, Thomas Howard, third Duke of Norfolk, and nine other members of the Privy Council.)

PO/Vol./95 – Letter from Thomas Howard, fourth Duke of Norfolk, to Elizabeth I on the subject of her marriage; Norwich, 15 November 1567.

Dudley Papers (DU)

DU/Vol.2/26 – Reports on speeches and activities of prisoners in the Tower who were concerned 'in the Duke of Norfolk's plot' by Richard Farmer.

NATIONAL ARCHIVES, KEW, SURREY

Court of Chancery – Six Clerks' Office

C 54/559 – Sale of Norfolk House, Lambeth, by Thomas Howard, fourth Duke of Norfolk, to Richard Garth and John Dister for £400, 1558.

Records of the Exchequer

E 24/23/27 – Lease by William Capon, dean of Cardinal's College, Ipswich, of the priory of Felixstowe, Suffolk, with appurtenances, to Thomas Howard, third Duke of Norfolk, Sir Philip Tylney and others, at a rent of £20 per year; 4 October [1529].

E 30/1456 – Notorial certificate of depositions by Mary, wife of Henry Bourchier, second Earl of Essex, and Agnes, relict of Thomas, second Duke of Norfolk, concerning the marriage of Catherine of Aragon and Prince Arthur; Stansted, Essex, and Thetford Priory, Norfolk, 16 July 1528.

E 101/60/22 – Accounts of Walter Stonor, Lieutenant of the Tower of London, for expenses incurred in boarding prisoners, including Thomas Howard, third Duke of Norfolk, and the Earl of Surrey.

Home Office
HO 45/14342 – Licence for removal and re-interment of the remains of Philip, Earl of Arundel, at Fitzalan Chapel, Arundel Castle, 1971.

Records of the Court of King's Bench
KB 8/5 – Roll and File of court of Lord High Steward: charges against Sir Edward Stafford, Duke of Buckingham, May 1520.

KB 8/14 – Special Commission of Oyer and Terminer with charges against Henry Howard, Earl of Surrey, 10 January 1547.

KB 8/42 – Roll and file of Court of Lord High Steward: charges against Thomas Howard, fourth Duke of Norfolk, for high treason; January 1572.

KB 8/49 – Roll and file of court of Lord High Steward and peers: charges against Philip, Earl of Arundel for high treason.

Land Revenues – Inventories
LR 2/115 – Inventory of goods of Thomas Howard, third Duke of Norfolk, at Kenninghall (fols 1 64) and at Castle Rising (fols 67–70), Norfolk, and of Henry Howard, Earl of Surrey, at St Leonard's by Norwich (fols 71–4); of the Duke of Norfolk's horses in Norfolk and Suffolk and elsewhere (fols 77–81); cattle (fols 83–4); sheep (fols 84d–5) and grain (fol. 86) as at December 1546 and notes to whom the goods have been delivered.

Probate Records, Prerogative Court of Canterbury (PCC)
PROB/11/21 – Will of Thomas Howard, second Duke of Norfolk, 1524.

PROB/11/37 – Will of Thomas Howard, third Duke of Norfolk, 1554.

PROB/11/123 – Will of Henry Howard, Earl of Northampton, 18 June 1614.

Special Collections (SC)

SC 2 (Court Rolls) 192/101 – Description of the courts in Gressenhall and Wending, Norfolk, of Thomas Howard, fourth Duke of Norfolk, 1558.

State Papers (SP)

SP 1/76/38 – Letter from Henry, Lord Stafford, to Thomas Howard, third Duke of Norfolk; Stafford, 13 May 1534.

SP 1/76/39 – Letter from Henry, Lord Stafford to Cromwell; Stafford, 13 May 1533.

SP 1/82/151 – Reports of seditious statements by the Colchester monk Dan John Frances, 22 January 1533.

SP 1/105/245 – Thomas Howard, third Duke of Norfolk, to Cromwell about the Duke of Richmond's funeral; Kenninghall, 5 August 1536.

SP 1/114/56 – Letter from Thomas Howard, third Duke of Norfolk, to Thomas Cromwell about his daughter's decision to consult lawyers about her maintenance; January 1537.

SP 1/115/175 – Letter from Thomas Howard, third Duke of Norfolk, to Thomas Cromwell; Doncaster, 26 February 1537.

SP 1/115/244 – Letter from Thomas Howard, third Duke of Norfolk, to Thomas Cromwell, February 1537.

SP 1/116/8 – Account of lands sold and purchased and annual receipts of Thomas Howard, third Duke of Norfolk, for 1537.

SP 1/116/83 – Letter from Thomas Howard, third Duke of Norfolk, to the Council in London; Carlisle, 19 February 1537.

SP 1/116/92 – Letter from Henry VIII to Thomas Howard, third Duke of Norfolk, ordering 'dreadful execution' on the inhabitants of 'every town, village and hamlet' in the rebellious north of England; 22 February 1537.

SP 1/116/108 – Letter to the Privy Council from Thomas Howard, third Duke of Norfolk, about the justice meted out to insurgents in Carlisle; 24 February 1537.

SP 1/120/6 and 14–5 – Thomas Howard, third Duke of Norfolk, to Henry VIII, March 1537.

SP 1/121/96 – Henry VIII to Thomas Howard, third Duke of Norfolk, about the establishment of a Council of the North; September 1537.

SP 1/130/24 – Confessions relating to the 'Black Fast' of Mabel Brigge; York, 11 March 1538.

SP 1/144/16 – Elizabeth, Duchess of Norfolk, to Cromwell; 3 March 1539.

SP 1/144/56 – Thomas Howard, third Duke of Norfolk, to Thomas Cromwell, March 1539.

SP 1/158/249 – Elizabeth, Duchess of Norfolk, to the Earl of Westmorland; 11 April 1541.

SP 1/176/151 – Examination of Alice Flaner by the Privy Council; 24 March 1543.

SP 1/176/156 – Examination of Millicent Arundel by the Privy Council; 28 March 1543.

SP 1/189/207–8 – Letter from the Privy Council to Thomas Howard, third Duke of Norfolk, about Henry VIII's plans to besiege Boulogne; London 7 July 1544. (See also BL Harley MS, 6,989 fol. 127.)

SP 1/190/23–5 – Letter from Sir William Paget, the King's Secretary, to Charles Brandon, Duke of Suffolk, about the sieges of Boulogne and Montreuil; 12 July 1544.

SP 1/193/154 – Letter from Henry VIII to the dukes of Norfolk and Suffolk and others, following the unsuccessful French attempt to recapture Boulogne; Westminster, 14 October 1544.

SP 1/209/129 – Letter from Thomas Hussey, treasurer to the third Duke of Norfolk, to the Earl of Surrey, about his debts; London, 26 October 1545.

SP 1/210/30 – Letter from Thomas Hussey, treasurer to the third Duke of Norfolk, to the Earl of Surrey, about his debts; London, 6 November 1545.

SP 1/213/47 – Letter from the Council of Boulogne to Henry VIII about the skirmish at St Etienne; Boulogne, 8 January 1546.

SP 1/227/76 – Letter from Henry Howard, Earl of Surrey, to the Privy Council; the Tower, ?13 December 1546.

SP 1/227/82 – Letter from John Gates and others to Henry VIII concerning their 'dawn raid' on Kenninghall; Kenninghall, 14 December 1546.

SP 1/227/97 – Testimony of Sir Edmund Knyvett, December 1546.

SP 1/227/101 – Deposition of Sir Edward Warner, December 1546.

SP 1/227/103 – Deposition of Edward Rogers, December 1546.

SP 1/227/105 – Deposition of Sir Gawen Carew, 'the king's servant', 1546.

SP 1/227/106 – Deposition of the spy John Torre, 1546.

SP 1/227/109 – Deposition of Hugh Ellis, secretary to the Earl of Surrey, 1546.

SP 1/227/114 – Lord Chancellor Wriothesley's list of questions to be put to the Earl of Surrey, December 1546.

SP 1/227/123ff – Summary of charges against Thomas Howard, third Duke of Norfolk, and Henry Howard, Earl of Surrey, annotated by Henry VIII, 1546.

SP 1/227/129 – Memoranda relating to the case of Henry Howard, Earl of Surrey, written by Sir Thomas Wriothesley, Lord Chancellor, 1546.

SP 1/245/145 – Chequer roll of the household of Thomas Howard, third Duke of Norfolk, at Kenninghall, Norfolk, [14 December] 1546.

SP 4 – Documents issued under Henry VIII's 'dry stamp', 1545–7.

SP 12/211/50 – Letter from Charles Howard, Lord High Admiral, to Elizabeth I; 23 June 1588.

SP 30/28/209 – Sixteenth-century copy of the Act of Attainder against the Duke of Buckingham.

SP 46/1/154 – Warrant under sign manual to Sir Ralph Sadler, Master of the Great Wardrobe, to deliver clothing and bedding to the Tower of London for the use of Thomas Howard, third Duke of Norfolk, and Edward Courtney; Westminster, 3 March 1548.

SP 46/2/78–81 – Draft warrant to the Treasurer of the Exchequer to pay Sir John Markham, Lieutenant of the Tower, an annual sum for 'the apparel' of Thomas Howard, third Duke of Norfolk, and £80 'as his spending money' so long as he remains his prisoner; 1548.

SP 46/5/190 – Ottwell Johnson reports the trial of Henry Howard, Earl of Surrey; London, 15 January 1547.

SP 60/1/65 – Letter from Thomas Howard, Earl of Surrey, begging to be recalled from Ireland; Dublin, 16 September 1521.

NORFOLK RECORD OFFICE, NORWICH, NORFOLK

BL [Bradfer Lawrence Collection] IIc/14 – Court Book for diverse manors, 1545–6 and 1554–5.

COL 13/53 – Seventeenth-century copy of an account, with list of dishes served, of William Mingay, Mayor of Norwich and Registrar to the Bishop of Norwich, for entertainment during one week, in which he entertained the [fourth] Duke of Norfolk and the lords and knights, 156[2].

DN/INV 39/82 – Probate inventory of James Hills of Norwich, tennis court keeper at the Duke of Norfolk's palace in Norwich, 1634.

HOW 152/ 342X6 – Copy from Patent Roll of a royal grant 'in consideration of good services' to Thomas, Lord Howard of Walden, and Henry Howard, brother of Thomas, late Duke of Norfolk, and son of Henry, late Earl of Surrey, 1603.

MC 67/35, 511X9 – Copy of a grant by Henry VIII to Thomas Howard, third Duke of Norfolk, of possessions in Thetford, Norfolk, including the Cluniac abbey of Our Lady of Thetford, dated 9 July 1540.

MC 146/24, 624X5 – File on the Ducal Palace, Norwich.

MS 21509/4 and 5 – Bill of Lawrence Bannister for the late [fourth] Duke of Norfolk's charges during his imprisonment in the Tower, 1570/1 and 1577/8.

– Account of money owed to William Dix, receiver to Thomas Howard, fourth Duke of Norfolk, and William Cantrell from the late duke's estate, Michaelmas 1571 to Michaelmas 1578.

MS 21509/368 – Letter from William Dix, receiver to Thomas Howard, fourth Duke of Norfolk, and William Cantrell to Robert Buxton about sureties for a flock of 2,800 sheep belonging to the duke, 30 July 1576.

NAS 1/1/10/19 – Copy of a ninety-nine-year lease by Sir John Holland, chaplain to the 'right high and mighty' Thomas Howard, third Duke of Norfolk, and parson of Feltwell St Mary, to George Holland, gentleman, of the rectory and parsonage of Feltwell St Mary, 1545.

NRS 2292 11 C 5 – Copy of Settlement of Thomas, fourth Duke of Norfolk, Earl Marshal of England, 31 July 1569.

NRS 27260 – Account of 'suche castles, honores, Mann[or]s and other hereytamentes as Thom[a]s late [Third] Duke of Norff. and Earle Marshall of Inglond was [seized] on the daie of his deathe', 30 August 1554.

Phi 606/3 – View of account of John Goldingham esquire, receiver of the Earl of Surrey [later second Duke of Norfolk] from Michaelmas 17 Henry VII to Michaelmas 18 Henry VII.

Phi 606/4 – View of account of John Goldingham esquire, Receiver of the Earl of Surrey, 1502/3.

T/NS 33 – Letters Patent of Henry VIII granting Richard Fulmerston and his wife Alice the site of the Friary at Thetford with its estate, including Foulden manor and the rectory of Holy Trinity, Thetford; 20 March 1539.

WAR 55 – Bressingham, Norfolk, court roll, 1545–60, (misdated 1587–94).

NOTTINGHAMSHIRE ARCHIVES, NOTTINGHAM

Portland of Welbeck Papers

DD/P/6/1/31/10 – Proclamation of Thomas Howard, [second] Duke of Norfolk, Lieutenant General of the King's Army, forbidding soldiers playing games such as dice or cards, but permitting noblemen and captains to 'play at their pleasures within their own tents'; [no date, but early sixteenth century].

BODLEIAN LIBRARY, OXFORD

Tanner MS 78, fol. 12 – Letter from Francis Mills, secretary to Francis Walsingham, to William Davison, Secretary of State, about communication between the outside world and the Earl of Arundel; 9 October 1586.

SURREY HISTORY CENTRE, WOKING, SURREY

Papers of Sir Thomas Cawarden, Steward of Crown manors (died 1559)

LM/COR/2/2 – Letter from John Mason and Richard Goodricke to [?Henry Foyce of Horsham] enclosing a copy of the Privy Council's letter of 2 April 1547 from Westminster authorising Sir Thomas Seymour, Lord High Admiral, to take charge of the house of Chesworth, Horsham, Sussex, belonging to the late attainted [Thomas Howard, third] Duke of Norfolk, and requesting the recipients to hand over to John Tochet, Seymour's servant, 'all the stuff' remaining in the house.

LM/COR/2/3 – Receipt addressed to Henry Foyce of Horsham by John Tochet, servant to Sir Edward Seymour, for household stuff at Chesworth, parcel of the late Duke of Norfolk's goods; 5 April 1547.

LM/1890 – Inventories of tapestries, bedding, carpets and cloth delivered into Sir Thomas Cawarden's charge by Edward Pigeon, some belonging to the attainted Duke of Norfolk, to be kept to the king's use at Nonsuch Palace, Surrey; 28 September 1547.

Papers of Sir William More (1520–1600)

LM/COR/3/239 – Letter from Robert Balam to William More in Blackfriars, London, describing the Norfolk floods of 5 October 1570 and recalling the three occasions when he wept as an adult, including the arrests 'of the old Duke of Norfolk and his son, the Earl of Surrey'; no date, but ?October 1570.

Printed

Allen, P. S., and H. M., *Letters of Richard Fox 1486–1527*, London, 1929.

APC – Acts of the Privy Council (new series).

    Vol. 1 (1542–7), ed. John Roche Dasent, London, 1890.

    Vol. 2 (1547–50), ed. John Roche Dasent, London, 1890.

    Vol. 3 (1550–52), ed. John Roche Dasent, London, 1891.

Byrne, Muriel St Clare (ed.), *Letters of Henry VIII*, London, 1936.

—— *The Lisle Letters*, six vols, Chicago, 1981.

Cal. Scot. – Calendar of Scottish Papers, vol. 9 (1586–8), ed. William K. Boyd, London, 1915.

Cavendish – *Life of Cardinal Wolsey by George Cavendish, his Gentleman Usher*, ed. Samuel Singer, London, 1827.

CDP Spanish – Calendars, Despatches and State Papers, Spanish

    Vol. 4, pt i (1529–30), and pt ii (1531–3), ed. Pascual de Gayangos, London, 1879–82.

    Vol. 5, pt i (1534–5), and pt ii (1536–8), ed. Pascual de Gayangos, London, 1886–8.

    Vol. 6, pt i (1538–42), and pt ii (1542–3), ed. Pascual de Gayangos, London, 1890–95.

    Vol. 8 (1545–6), ed. Martin A. S. Hume, London, 1904.

Close Rolls – Calendar of the Close Rolls, Henry VII, vol. II, 1500–1509, ed. R. E. Latham, London, 1963.

Crapelet, G. A., *Lettres de Henry VIII à Anne Boleyn*, Paris, 1835.

CRS – publications of the Catholic Record Society. Vol. 21, *Ven. Philip Howard, Earl of Arundel*, ed. John Hungerford Pollen SJ and William MacMahon SJ, London, 1919.

CSP Milan – Calendar of State Papers and Manuscripts in the Archives of Milan, vol. 1, ed. Allen B. Hinds, London, 1912.

Ellis, Henry, 'Transcript of an Original Manuscript Containing a Memorial from George Constantine to Thomas, Lord Cromwell', *Archaeologia*, vol. 23 (1831), pp. 50–78.

——— *Original Letters Illustrative of English History*, three series in eleven vols, London, 1825, 1827, 1846.

Fénelon, Bertrand de Salignac de la Mothe, *Correspondance Diplomatique de Bertrand de Salignac de la Mothe Fénelon, Ambassadeur de France en Angleterre, de 156–75*, ed. A. Teulet, seven vols, Paris and London, 1838–40.

Foxe, John, 'Acts' – *Acts and Monuments*, ed. J. Pratt, eight vols, London, 1874.

Grafton, Richard, *Chronicle or History of England, 1189–1558*, two vols, London, 1808.

Hall, Edward, *Hall's Chronicle Containing the History of England during the Reign of Henry IV . . . to the Reign of Henry VIII*, London, 1809.

Hamilton Papers – *Letters and Papers Illustrating the Political Relations of England and Scotland in the XVIth. Century* (ed. Joseph Bain), vol. 1 (1532–43), vol. 2 (1543–90), Edinburgh, 1890–92.

Hardwick State Papers – *Miscellaneous State Papers, 1501–1726*, two vols, London, 1778.

Hatfield – *Calendar of MSS of Marquis of Salisbury at Hatfield*, vol. 1, pt i, London, 1883; pt ii, London, 1888, vol. 10, London, 1894.

HMC – Historical Manuscripts Commission.

Holinshed, Raphael, *Chronicles of England, Scotland and Ireland*, six vols, London, 1807–8.

Hume, Martin A. (ed.), *Chronicle of Henry VIII of England . . . written in Spanish by an Unknown Hand*, London 1889.

Kaulek, J. (ed.), *Correspondance politique de MM. de Castillon et de Marillac (1537–42)*, Paris, 1885.

Lords Journal – *House of Lords Journal*, vol. 1, 1509–77, London, 1802.

LPFD – *Letters and Papers, Foreign and Domestic, Henry VIII*.

Vol. 1 (1509–14), ed. J. S. Brewer, London, 1862.

Vol. 3 (1519–23), pts i and ii, ed. J. S. Brewer, London, 1867.

Vol. 4 (1529–30), pt ii and pt iii, ed. J. S. Brewer, London, 1872–6.

Vol. 6 (1533), ed. James Gairdner, London, 1882.

Vol. 8 (1535), ed. James Gairdner, London, 1885.

Vol. 9 (1535), ed. James Gairdner, London, 1886.

Vol. 10 (1536), ed. James Gairdner, London, 1887.

Vol. 11 (1536), ed. James Gairdner, London 1888.

Vol. 12 (1537), pt i, ed. James Gairdner, London, 1890, and pt ii, London, 1891.

Vol. 13 (1538), pts i and ii, ed. James Gairdner, London, 1892–3.

Vol. 14 (1539), pt i, eds James Gairdner and R. H. Brodie, London, 1894.

Vol. 16 (1540–41), eds James Gairdner and R. H. Brodie, London, 1898.

Vol. 17 (1542), ed. James Gairdner, London, 1900.

Vol. 18 (1543), pt i, eds James Gairdner and R. H. Brodie, London, 1901.

Vol. 19 (1544), pts i and ii, eds James Gairdner and R. II. Brodie, London, 1903–5.

Vol. 20 (1545), pts i and ii, eds James Gairdner and R. H. Brodie, London, 1905–7.

Vol. 21 (1546), pts i and ii, eds James Gairdner and R. H. Brodie, London, 1908–10.

Addenda, vol. 1, pts i and ii, eds James Gairdner, R. H. Brodie and A. C. Wood, London, 1929 and 1932.

Muller, James, *Letters of Stephen Gardiner*, Cambridge, 1933.

Nicols, John, *The Progresses and Public Processions of Queen Elizabeth* ..., four vols, London, 1788–1821.

Nicols, John Gough (ed.), *Chronicles of Queen Jane and Two Years of Queen Mary* (from BL Harleian MS 94), July 1553–October 1554, London (Camden Society), 1850.

Nicols, John Gough (ed.), *Chronicles of Greyfriars of London*, London (Camden Society), 1852.

—— (with John Brill), *Wills of Eminent Persons Proved in the Prerogative Court of Canterbury, 1495–1695*, London (Camden Society), 1863.

—— *The Diary of Henry Machyn, Citizen and Merchant Taylor of London, 1550–63*, London (Camden Society), 1848.

—— *Narratives of the Days of the Reformation*, London (Camden Society), 1859.

Patent Rolls – Calendar of Patent Rolls, Henry VII; vol. 1 (1485–1494), London, 1914; vol. 2 (1494–1509), London, 1916.

Plumpton Correspondence – *The Plumpton Correspondence: A Series of Letters written in the reigns of Edward IV, Richard III, Henry VII and Henry VIII*, ed. Thomas Stapleton (Camden old series, vol. 4), London, 1839.

Rot. Parl. – Rotuli Parliamentorium, ut et Petitiones et Placito in Parliamento, six vols, London, 1771–83.

Rutland Papers – *Original Documents illustrative of the courts and times of Henry VII and Henry VIII selected from the private archives of . . . the Duke of Rutland*, ed. William Jerdan, London, 1862.

Sadler Papers – *State Papers and Letters of Sir Ralph Sadler*, ed. A. Clifford, two vols, London, 1809.

SPD – Calendar of State Papers Domestic:
> *Edward VI, Mary & Elizabeth, 1547–80*, ed. Robert Lemon, London, 1856.
> *Elizabeth 1581–90*, ed. Robert Lemon, London, 1865.

State Papers – State Papers Published under the Authority of His Majesty's Commission, King Henry VIII, eleven vols, London (Public Record Commission), 1830–52.

Stow, John, *The Annals of England collected out of the most Authentic Authors, Records and other Monuments of Antiquity*, London, 1605.

Strype, John, *Ecclesiastic Memorials Relating Chiefly to Religion . . .*, six vols, Oxford, 1832.

Tanner, J. R., *Tudor Constitutional Documents 1485–1603*, Cambridge, 1951.

Vergil, Polydore, *Anglica Historia 1485–1537*, ed. Denys Hay, London, 1950.

Williams, C. H. (ed.), *English Historical Documents 1485–1557*, London, 1967.

Wood, M. A. E. (ed.), *Letters of Royal and Illustrious Ladies of Great Britain*, three vols, London, 1846.

Wriothesley, Charles, *A Chronicle of England during the Reigns of the Tudors, 1485–1559*, ed. William Douglas Hamilton, two vols, London (Camden Society), 1875 and 1877.

SECONDARY SOURCES

Calculations of modern monetary values are derived from Lawrence H. Officer's 'Comparing the Purchasing Power of British Pounds from 1264 to 2006 . . .'
See: URL: http://www.measuringworth.com

Allen, Thomas, *History of the Parish of Lambeth*, London, 1826.

Anglo, Sydney, *Spectacle, Pageantry and Early Tudor Policy*, Oxford, 1969.

Bacon, Francis, *Historie of the Reigne of King Henry the Seventh*, London, 1629.

Bapst, Edmond, *Deux gentilshommes-poèts de la court de Henry VIII (George Boleyn, Vicomte Rochford, Henry Howard, Comte de Surrey)*, Paris, 1891.

Barr, Niall, *Flodden*, Stroud, Gloucestershire, 2003.

Bernard, G. W, 'The Making of Religious Policy 1533–46: Henry VIII and the Search for the Middle Way', *Historical Journal*, vol. 41 (1998), pp. 321–49.

Bindoff, S. T., *House of Commons, 1509–58, Members*, three vols, London, 1982.

Blomefield, Edward, *Essay Towards a Topographical History of the County of Norfolk*, eleven vols, London, 1805–10.

Bray, William (ed.), *Diary of John Evelyn*, four vols, London, 1879.

Brenan, Gerald, and Statham, Edward Phillips, *The House of Howard*, two vols, London, 1907.

Brooks, Richard, *Cassell's Battlefields of Britain and Ireland*, London, 2005.

Brown, Joseph, *Tryal of Thomas Duke of Norfolk by his Peers for High Treason*, London, 1709.

Burnet, Gilbert, *History of the Reformation of the Church of England*, two vols, London, 1841.

Bush, Michael, and Bownes, David, *The Defeat of the Pilgrimage of Grace*, Hull, 1999.

Camden, William, *The Historie of the most Renowned and Victorious Princess Elizabeth, late Queen of England ... composed by way of Annals*, London, 1630.

—— *Remains Concerning Britain*, London, 1674.

Campbell, Revd William, *Materials for the History of the Reign of Henry VII*, two vols, London, 1873 and 1877.

'Carthusian, A', *Historical Account of the Charterhouse*, London, 1808.

Casady, Edwin, *Henry Howard, Earl of Surrey*, New York, 1938.

Chapman, Hester, *Two Tudor Portraits: Henry Howard, Earl of Surrey and Lady Katherine Grey*, London, 1960.

Childs, Jessie, *Henry VIII's Last Victim: The Life and Times of Henry Howard, Earl of Surrey*, London, 2006.

Cobbett, William, *Complete Collection of State Trials*, thirty-three vols, London, 1809–26.

Complete Peerage – *The Complete Peerage*, ed. Vicary Gibbs et al., fourteen vols, London and Stroud, 1910–98.

Cruden, Robert P., *History of the Town of Gravesend ...*, London, 1843.

DNB2 – *Dictionary of National Biography*, new ed., eds H. G. G. Matthews and Brian Harrison, sixty vols, Oxford, 2004.

Edwards SJ, Francis, *The Marvellous Chance: Thomas Howard Fourth Duke of Norfolk and the Ridolphi Plot, 1570–72*, London, 1968.

Elton, G. R., 'Thomas Cromwell's Decline and Fall', *Cambridge Historical Review*, vol. 10 (1951), pp. 150ff.

—— *The Tudor Revolution in Government: Administrative Changes in the Reign of Henry VIII*, Cambridge, 1953.

—— *Policy and Police: Enforcement of the Reformation in the Age of Thomas Cromwell*, Cambridge, 1972.

—— *Reform and Reformation: England 1509–58*, London, 1977.

Fletcher, Anthony, and MacCulloch, Diarmaid, *Tudor Rebellions*, 4th edn, London, 1997.

Foss, Peter, *History of Market Bosworth*, Wymondham, 1983.

Froude, J. A., *The Divorce of Catherine of Aragon*, London, 1891.

Fuller, Thomas, *Church History of Great Britain*, London, 1655.

Gairdner, James (ed.), *The Paston Letters*, four vols, London, 1900–1901.

Green, R., *History, Topography and Antiquities of Framlingham*, London, 1834.

Guy, John, *My Heart is My Own: The Life of Mary Queen of Scots*, London, 2004.

Hammond, E. A., 'Dr Augustine, physician to Cardinal Wolsey and King Henry VIII', *Medical History*, vol. 19 (1975), pp. 215–49.

Harris, Barbara, 'Marriage Sixteenth-century Style: Elizabeth Stafford and the Third Duke of Norfolk', *Journal of Social History*, vol. 15 (1981), pp. 371–82.

—— *English Aristocratic Women, 1450–1550*, Oxford, 2002.

Head, David M., 'Beying ledde and seduced by the Dyvll': the attainder of Lord Thomas Howard and the Tudor law of Treason, *Sixteenth Century Journal*, vol. 13 (1982), pp. 3–16.

—— *The Ebbs and Flows of Fortune: The Life of Thomas Howard, Third Duke of Norfolk*, Athens, Georgia, 1995.

Herbert of Cherbury, Lord Edward, *Life and Raigne of King Henry the Eighth*, London, 1649.

Howard, Henry, *Indications of Memorials ... of the Howard Family*, Corby Castle, 1834.

Howlett, Richard, 'Household Accounts of Kenninghall Palace', *Norfolk Archaeology*, vol. 15 (1904), pp. 51–60.

Hoyle, R. W., *The Pilgrimage of Grace and the Politics of the 1530s*, Oxford, 2003.

Hudson, Revd William, and Tingey, John Cottingham (eds), *Records of the City of Norwich*, two vols, Norwich, 1910.

Hutchinson, Robert, *The Last Days of Henry VIII*, London, 2005.

—— *Elizabeth's Spymaster*, London, 2006.

—— *Thomas Cromwell*, London, 2007.

Hutton, William, *The Battle of Bosworth Field*, Birmingham, 1788.

Kent, Ernest, 'On the Houses of the Dukes of Norfolk', *Norfolk Archaeology*, vol. 24 (1932), pp. 73–87.

Knowles, David, *Bare Ruined Choirs*, Cambridge, 1976.

Laing, David (ed.), 'A Contemporary Account of the Battle of Flodden, 9 September 1513', *Proceedings of the Society of Antiquaries of Scotland*, vol. 7 (1867), pp. 147–51.

Langton, John, Sir, *Defeat of the Spanish Armada Anno 1588*, two vols, Naval Record Society, London, 1894.

MacCulloch, Diarmaid, 'Kett's Rebellion in Context', *Past and Present* (August 1979), pp. 53–7.

MacNalty, Sir Arthur, *Henry VIII: A Difficult Patient*, London, 1952.

Manning, Revd C. R., 'Kenninghall,' *Norfolk Archaeology*, vol. 7 (1872), pp. 89–99.

Marks, Richard, 'The Howard Tombs at Framlingham: New Discoveries', *Archaeological Journal*, vol. 141 (1984), pp. 252–68.

Martin, Thomas, *History of the Town of Thetford ...* , London, 1779.

Merriman, Roger, *Life and Letters of Thomas Cromwell*, two vols, Oxford, 1902.

Miller, Helen, *Henry VIII and the English Nobility*, Oxford, 1986.

Moore, Peter R., 'The Heraldic Charge Against the Earl of Surrey 1546–7', *English Historical Review*, vol. 116, no. 467 (June 2001), pp. 557–83.

Moorhouse, Geoffrey, *The Pilgrimage of Grace: The Rebellion that Shook Henry VIII's Crown*, London, 2002.

Muller, J. A., *Stephen Gardiner and the Tudor Reaction*, New York, 1926.

Norfolk, 14th Duke of, *Lives of Philip Howard, Earl of Arundel and of Anne Dacres, his wife*, 1st edn, London, 1857.

Nott, G. F. (ed.), *Works of Henry Howard, Earl of Surrey and of Sir Thomas Wyatt the Elder*, two vols, London, 1815–16.

Pevsner, Nikolas, and Wilson, Bill, *Buildings of England: Norfolk*, 2nd edn, vol. 2, *North-West and South Norfolk*, Harmondsworth, 1999.

Pickthorn, Kenneth, *Early Tudor Government, Henry VIII*, Cambridge, 1934.

Pollard, A. F., *Wolsey*, London, 1929.

Porter, Linda, *Mary Tudor: The First Queen*, London, 2007.

Rawcliffe, Carole, and Wilson, Richard (eds), *Medieval Norwich*, Hambledon and London, 2004.

—— *Norwich since 1550*, Hambledon and London, 2004.

Read, Conyers, *Mr Secretary Walsingham and the Policy of Queen Elizabeth*, three vols, Oxford, 1925.

Rhodes, Dennis E., 'A Party at Norwich in 1562', *Norfolk Archaeology*, vol. 37 (1978–80), pp. 116–20.

Robinson, John Martin, *The Dukes of Norfolk*, Chichester, 1995.

Routh, E. M. G., *Sir Thomas More and his Friends*, Oxford, 1934.

Ryrie, Alec, *The Gospel and Henry VIII: Evangelicals in the Early English Reformation*, Cambridge, 2003.

Salmon, Thomas (ed.), *A Compleat Collection of State Tryals for High Treason*, four vols, London, 1719.

Scarisbrick, J. J., *Henry VIII*, New Haven and London, 1991.

Sessions, William, *Henry Howard, the Poet Earl of Surrey: A Life*, Oxford, 1999.

Singer, S. W., *The Life of Sir Thomas More by his son-in-law William Roper*, London, 1822.

Smith, Lacey Baldwin, *A Tudor Tragedy: The Life and Times of Catherine Howard*, London, 1961.

—— *Henry VIII: The Mask of Royalty*, London, 1971.

—— *Treason in Tudor England: Politics and Paranoia*, London, 1986.

Starkey, David, *The Reign of Henry VIII: Personalities and Politics*, London, 2002.

Strickland, Agnes, *Lives of the Queens of England from the Norman Conquest*, six vols, London, 1866.

Swales, T. H., 'Opposition to the Suppression of the Norfolk Monasteries', *Norfolk Archaeology*, vol. 33 (1962–6), pp. 254–65.

Tierney, the Revd M. A., *History and Antiquities of the Castle and Town of Arundel*, London, 1834.

Tucker, Melvin J., *The Life of Thomas Howard, Earl of Surrey and Second Duke of Norfolk, 1443–1524*, The Hague, 1964.

VCH – Victoria County History of England.
  Norfolk, vol. 2, ed. William Page, London, 1906.
  Suffolk, vol. 2, ed. William Page, London, 1907.

Wagner, Sir Anthony, *Heralds of England*, London, 1967.

Weever, John, *Ancient Funerall Monuments*, London, 1631.

Williams, Neville, *A Tudor Tragedy: Thomas Howard, Fourth Duke of Norfolk*, London, 1964.

Wilson, Derek, *In the Lion's Court: Power, Ambition and Sudden Death in the Reign of Henry VIII*, London, 2002.

INDEX

◆